ADOLESCENCE

Contemporary Studies

second edition

ALVIN E. WINDER, PH.D.
University of Massachusetts

D. VAN NOSTRAND COMPANY

New York Cincinnati Toronto London
Melbourne

D. Van Nostrand Company Regional Offices:
New York   Cincinnati   Millbrae

D. Van Nostrand Company International Offices:
London   Toronto   Melbourne

Copyright © 1974 by Litton Educational Publishing, Inc.
Library of Congress Catalog Card Number: 74–1998
ISBN: 0–442–27574–9

Published by D. Van Nostrand Company
450 West 33rd Street, New York, N.Y. 10001

Published simultaneously in Canada
Van Nostrand Reinhold Ltd.   78-6457

10 9 8 7 6 5 4 3 2 1

ACKNOWLEDGMENTS

Grateful acknowledgment is made to the following publishers and individuals for permission to reprint material which is in copyright or of which they are the authorized publishers:

The American Academy of Political and Social Science: for permission to reprint "The Beige Epoch: Depolarization of Sex Roles in America" by Charles Winick, *The Annals,* March 1968; " 'The Times They Are-A-Changin' ': The Music of Protest" by Robert A. Rosenstone, *The Annals,* March 1969.

American Journal of Orthopsychiatry: for permission to reprint "Sexual Morality and the Dilemma of the Colleges" by Dana L. Farnsworth, M.D., Vol. 35, No. 4, July 1965, pp. 676–681. Copyright © the American Orthopsychiatric Association, Inc. Reproduced by permission.

Avon Books: for permission to reprint "How Old Will You Be in 1984?" edited by Diane Divoky. Copyright © 1969 by Avon Books.

The College Entrance Examination Board: for permission to reprint "The School as a Social Environment in College Admissions" by Edgar Z. Friedenberg from *The Behavioral Sciences and Education* © 1963.

Daedalus, Journal of the American Academy of Arts and Sciences, Boston, Mass.: for permission to reprint "Youth: Fidelity and Diversity" by Erik H. Erikson, Winter 1962, *Youth: Change and Challenge.* "Inner and Outer Space: Reflections on Womanhood" by Erik H. Erikson, Spring 1964, *The Woman in America.* "Sequence, Tempo, and Individual Variation in the Growth and Development of Boys and Girls Aged Twelve to Sixteen" by J. M. Tanner, Fall 1971; "Adolescence in America: From Idea to Social Fact" by David Bakan, Fall 1971; and "An Uptight Adolescence" by Phyllis La Farge, Fall 1971, *Twelve to Sixteen: Early Adolescence.*

Horizon Press: for permission to reprint "The Universe of Discourse in Which They Grow Up" by Paul Goodman from *Compul-*

sory Mis-education, copyright 1964 by Horizon Press, New York.

Indiana University Press: for permission to reprint "Youth and Social Change" by Frank Musgrove from *Youth and the Social Order.*

J. B. Lippincott Company: for permission to reprint "Religious-Psychological Conflicts of the Adolescent" by James A. Knight from *Adolescence: Care and Counseling,* ed. Gene L. Usdin.

Journal of Health, Physical Education, Recreation: for permission to reprint passages of "Drug Use and Abuse Among Youth" by Alvin E. Strack, January 1968.

The Journal Press: for permission to reprint "Parental Interaction of the Adolescent Boy" by W. W. Meissner, S.J., *Journal of Genetic Psychology,* 1965, pp. 225–233.

Kenneth Keniston: for permission to reprint his "Heads and Seekers: Drugs on Campus, Counter-Cultures, and American Society," *The American Scholar,* Winter, 1968/69.

The New York Times: for permission to reprint "Bob Dylan: Reluctant Hero of the Pop Generation," *Magazine,* May 7, 1972. © 1973 by the New York Times Company. Reprinted by permission.

Random House, Inc.: for permission to reprint "Jobs" by Paul Goodman from *Growing Up Absurd,* by Paul Goodman. Copyright © 1960 by Paul Goodman. "Notes on the New History" by Robert J. Lifton, *The Atlantic Monthly.* Copyright © 1969 by Robert J. Lifton. Reprinted from *History and Human Survival,* by Robert J. Lifton.

Saturday Review: for permission to reprint "Children of the Apocalypse" by Peter Marin. Copyright 1970 by Saturday Review Co., September 19, 1970. Used with permission.

Scientific American, Inc.: for permission to reprint "How Ideology Shapes Women's Lives" by Jean Lipman-Blumen. Copyright © 1972 by Scientific American. All rights reserved.

Sociology and Social Research: for permission to reprint "Primary and Formal Family Organization and Adolescent Socialization" by William R. Larson and Barbara G. Myerhoff, University of Southern California, 1965.

Straight Arrow Books: for permission to reprint selected passages from *Living Poor With Style* by Ernest Callenbach. © 1972 by Ernest Callenbach and published by Straight Arrow Books. All rights reserved.

Transaction, Inc.: for permission to reprint "Hallelujah the Pill?" by Ruth B. Dixon, *Society Magazine,* November 1970 and "Mainlining Jesus: The New Trip" by Robert Lynn Adams and Robert Jon Fox, *Society Magazine,* February 1972, pp. 50–56.

The University of Chicago Magazine: for permission to reprint "The Lost Dimension and the Age of Longing" by Sidney E. Mead, May 1966. Copyright 1966 by the University of Chicago.

PREFACE

Young people in America today are a focus of interest from several academic directions. Teachers, counselors and others in the educational community who work with youth are asking new questions about the present generation of students. What do they want? What is education's responsibility to them? How can they best be reached? From another vantage point, sociologists and others who watch the American cultural scene are devoting increasing attention to the role of youth in contemporary society—as both innovators and reactors. And as adolescence comes to be viewed less as a time of apprenticeship for adulthood than as a lifestage in its own right, it has become a subject of renewed interest to many contemporary psychologists as well.

Each of these disciplines is producing a growing body of articles and commentaries on adolescents and the so-called "youth culture." But to date little of this literature has been easily accessible for assigned reading on a class basis. Courses in teacher preparation and counseling, sociology, and adolescent psychology have not been materially assisted by the fact that college and university libraries offer single-copy availability of virtually all that is being written in this expanding area. Culling significant articles from the burgeoning mass of work in the field has been time-consuming, and providing multiple copies has been difficult.

This collection, the outgrowth of classes in adolescent psychology, educational sociology, foundations of education, and principles of guidance and human development, attempts to bring together in one volume the best contemporary work on the dynamics of adolescence. It has been designed to be interesting and provocative to students of contemporary problems as well as those who will work directly with adolescents in a variety of professional contexts.

The foregoing remarks prefaced also the first edition with its articles reflecting the most up-to-date concerns then being expressed by both educators and social scientists. The six years between the first edition and the present revision have witnessed the emergence of a number of patterns that reflect the interaction between young people and their society. The directions marked by adolescent behavior were in some instances already clear in 1968. Accordingly, themes such as political activism, disaffection with the schools as an agent of socialization, and a lack of enthusiasm for trying to make the system work were to be noted already in the first edition.

Among new areas of expressive behavior that have since emerged, two are especially noteworthy. The first one centers on the adolescent's search for a transcending experience through drugs, music, and a variety of spiritual experiences. The second of these new areas involves an extension of changing sexual mores into a movement to redefine the roles of women—and therefore men's roles also—in society.

It was not clear in 1968 whether the disadvantaged adolescent would develop separate modes of expression and be faced with separate life decisions. This does not seem to have been the case. The impact of the culture seems to have been that of a powerful leveler of both class and racial differences. Thus there have been no misgivings that this edition's focus on the process of growing up from ages twelve through twenty predominantly reflects the problems and behavior patterns of the white, middle-class adolescent.

Following an overall rationale that I have called "Adolescence as a Subject for Study," I have presented twenty-seven contemporary studies of adolescence. Heading the collection is Part I: *Normal Growth and Development,* whose seven essays explore fundamental physical, psychological, and anthropological factors at play during this critical stage of life.

Part II presents essays dealing with the behavioral manifestations of the coping patterns developed by adolescents to deal with the breakdown of traditional values in a society in rapid transition. Drug use, sociopolitical activism, changing of sexual values, and spiritual seeking in new cults and in music are the themes of this section.

Part III provides the reader with a number of essays concerned with the life decisions that adolescents are called upon to make in order to advance toward adulthood. These decisions are concerned with the family, the school, religion, work, and the changing roles of women.

An attempt has been made to include selections representative of the many forms in which contemporary studies of adolescence are being written today. Some clinical discussions have been included, as have several speculative articles by recognized spokesmen. The volume also contains psychoanalytically-oriented treatments of personality, several sociologically-oriented views of youth within the society as a whole, and a few firsthand documents from young people themselves. Many of these articles appeared originally in scholarly journals. Some come from the popular press, which has been concerning itself increasingly with the phenomenon of youth in modern America.

Selections have been chosen for readability as well as relevance. Each has been included for the unique contribution it makes to the total collection, which is structured so that it can readily form the basis of any exploration into the conditions of adolescence.

A short introductory essay preceding each of the four parts is designed to present the student with key themes he will encounter in each section. Care has been taken to insure that technical concepts are on a level that will be accessible to the general student reader.

CONTENTS

TO THE STUDENT

ADOLESCENCE AS A SUBJECT FOR STUDY

Youth is probably the center of more attention today than at any other period in our history. Advertising designed to capture the affluent youth market has created an image of slim, carefree, uninhibited youth that appeals not only to adolescents but to most adults as well. An "accent on youth" in fashion, entertainment, and general demeanor has provided an entire nation with a new model that says it is better to be young and beautiful than mature and responsible.

At the same time, modern communications media have zeroed in on adolescents' quarrels with the adult world and, in the process, may even have sharpened the differences between established society and its reluctant heirs. Adolescents and adults coexist uneasily today in a maelstrom of confusion about one another. Accusations and counter-accusations are traded in news media. Youth's outspoken pronouncements on social, moral, and political issues often shock their elders, many of whom feel that today's young people are "further out" than they ought to be. In spite of a popular worship of youth, today's amplified dialogue between the generations is producing a good deal of static.

Interpreters have come forward from all corners to explain youth to the adult community and to itself. Adolescents are said to doubt the capacity of the adult world to offer them an appropriate way of life. Adults are represented as defensive: pricked by guilt over the compromises they have made, for which idealistic youth now indicts them. It appears that the static is, after all, an indicator of disturbances. Indeed, the very nature of adolescence as a life stage in our society appears to be shifting.

At one time, it was enough to say that adolescence was a "difficult" period in which young people no longer quite understood the nature or limits of their physical makeup. They were said to kick over lamps, lose control of their voices, and experience all manner of physical sensations that were new and strange. We now know that much more than physical maturation takes place at this stage of life. It is also a period of psychological transformation, often called the discovery of self. As the education critic, Edgar Friedenberg, states:

> Adolescence is the period during which a young person learns who he is, and what he really feels. It is the time during which he differentiates himself from his culture, though on the culture's terms. It is the age at which by becoming a person in his own right, he becomes capable of deeply felt relationships to other individuals perceived clearly as such.[1]

Viewed in this light, adolescence is a time of transition between childhood and adulthood. If, as has been suggested, there is a reluctance on the adolescent's part to enter the adult society, then the nature of this life stage must be altered. It will no longer be a transition. It will become a stage that the individual will be reluctant to leave. It will become not a preparation for adult life but a way of life in itself. Under such conditions, adolescence as we know it could even become extinct.

Let us explore this idea further. Anthropologists have often noted that nonliterate societies have nothing that quite corresponds to adolescence as we understand it. There is instead the *rite de passage:* a ceremony of widely varying duration that symbolizes the end of the initial life stage (childhood) and the entree into the second stage (adulthood) with its commensurate privileges and responsibilities. The end of childhood may be determined by chronological age or by an event signaling the attainment of a certain capacity, such as the killing of a particular wild animal. In neither case is the attainment of what we call "maturity" requisite to the assumption of adult roles.

But growing up in a modern industrial democracy is a very different affair. The privileges of childhood begin to fade at around ten or eleven years of age, although full acceptance into adult society is still ten or more years away. What is expected to occur during the transition period is the attainment of a highly differentiated and closely secured individual identity. Unlike non-literate tribal societies, the conditions of life in a modern urbanized nation-state de-

---

1. Edgar Z. Friedenberg, *The Vanishing Adolescent* (New York: Dell, 1959), p. 29.

mand flexibility, mobility, and, above all, the capacity to engage in a lifetime of consistent choice-making. Whereas nonliterate tribesmen are assured their position in the total social scheme virtually by birth, our society demands, increasingly, that its members carve out their places through their own efforts. Their ability to do so is contingent upon their having evolved a highly differentiated personal identity.

We have seen that this kind of identity is not a human universal. It is rather an adjunct to, perhaps a requirement of, a certain mode of social life. But modes of human behavior have a way of becoming valued over and above their relation to the conditions which gave rise to them. Thus, individuality, which emerged as a by-product of our social system, has become a value in itself. The historian, Herbert Muller, has asserted that civilization's only gain, in comparison with the values and virtues of tribal and peasant cultures, has been the growth of individual self-consciousness. It seems clear that, through most of America's history at least, the ideal of the strongly motivated, autonomous individual has played a decisive role in shaping our society. Are we now about to discard that ideal? Have we created a social system in which individual identity —and hence the traditional function of the adolescent period—is no longer relevant?

It is Marshal McLuhan's thesis, in *Understanding Media,* that modern society is undergoing a "retribalization" or return to older modes of social organization. He has said that new technologies have reversed the centuries-old trend toward rationalization and fragmentation which gave rise to the ideal of individual self-consciousness and the private point of view. No less a partisan of individualism than Edgar Friedenberg has been pushed to a reexamination of his position by the strength of McLuhan's analysis. If the developments which McLuhan envisions do occur, the extinction of adolescence as we know it would seem assured.

It seems important today, therefore, that we understand more about the nature of the adolescent experience and how it is being affected by changes in American society as a whole. This collection is an attempt to foster such an understanding through selected pieces from the growing body of professional literature on adolescence. Although psychologists have long been interested in the dynamics of the transition from childhood to a fully formed adult personality, attention to the cultural and institutional setting in which the process occurs has come about only in the last two or three decades. We are now evolving what might be called a sociology of adolescence, to complement an older psychology of adolescence.

This in turn has led some psychologists to reexamine the adolescent period in the light of new insights concerning the influence of social institutions on adolescent personality formation. What has emerged is a dual view of the adolescent as at once an individual and a member of society. The articles in this collection have been selected to underscore both the individual psychological nature of adolescence and its cultural and institutional components.

Part I presents some physical and psychological foundations basic to an understanding of the adolescent experience. Part II provides review of the behavioral manifestations that reflect adolescent coping patterns in response to contemporary social forces. Part III deals with the life decisions young people have to make in the face of a society whose values are rapidly changing.

We hope that the student will find this choice and organization of the material helpful in understanding the adolescent experience in contemporary society.

A comment is necessary here to explain the exclusive use of the pronoun he when referring to both he and she in the introductory parts of the book. The use of he reflects current English usage and denotes reference to both he and she; it is not a reflection of the sexual politics of the author.

PART I

NORMAL GROWTH AND DEVELOPMENT

In this book we are especially mindful of the sociocultural conditions of contemporary adolescence. Accordingly, much of our focus will fall on adolescence in the context of American society during the present decade. But adolescence is, first and foremost, a period when the individual defines himself as an emergent personality. His first task at this time is to revise his view of himself to reflect the fact that he is no longer a child. Only after differentiating his newly maturing self from an earlier and less defined personality can he look about him and begin with some assurance to carve out a role in the ongoing adult society.

Before the reader can explore the meanings of adolescence as a period during which young people are seeking a sense of self-definition, he must first start with a working definition of the term adolescence. David Bakan, author of the first essay, has chosen to provide the reader with a definition of our contemporary use of the term by placing it within a historical perspective—the development of certain social forces within the United States in the late nineteenth and early twentieth centuries. These were compulsory education, child-labor legislation, and the development of a distinct "juvenile delinquency" penal code. The social rationale provided to gain wide popular support for these ideas and their enactment into legislation was that they would provide a framework that would give youth the most favorable background to achieve certain kinds of success and status as adults. These well-intentioned forces, however, succeeded in institutionalizing the notion of communities withholding the rights and privileges of adulthood from its members for a lengthy transitional period of the human life cycle. The period starting at the age of twelve—and terminating at sixteen, eighteen, or twenty-one (according to the particular criterion)—became known as the adolescent period.

The reader, having achieved through Dr. Bakan's essay some historical perspective on the emergence of adolescence, can now turn to an understanding of the forces operating within and upon the growing individual within this time span of his life. An initial approach to the study of these forces is to examine the effects of physical maturity in the teenager. J. M. Tanner is a specialist in the field of child health and growth. His essay, "Sequence, Tempo, and Individual Variation in the Growth and Development of Boys and Girls Aged Twelve to Sixteen," provides a very full account of what recent research can tell the reader about the physical changes occurring among boys and girls during the adolescent period of their lives.

Researchers in adolescent behavior have generally felt on safer ground when restricting themselves to the exploration of anatomic and physiological variables than when venturing into the complex and little understood relationship between physical and social-emotional development.

Musgrove's essay presents a bridge between these two areas of concern, for the biology of physical change is not in itself sufficient to account for the phenomenon known as adolescence. "Youth and Social Change" is a report of a comparative study of youth in a number of pre-literate societies. The author asks the question: What kind of a society affords youth high social status, and how is their status related to social experimentation and change? Bearing in mind Bakan's outline of the development of adolescence in the United States, the reader should note Musgrove's strongest point: youthful members of any traditional society in which there are no respected roles for teenagers form an alienated and deviant group prone to initiate experimentation and change for the whole society.

The essay, "Normal Adolescence," emphasizes the complex interaction between biological aspects, psychological factors, and the general cultural determinants of the environment. Adolescence is divided into two periods, early and late. Early adolescence is concerned with the loosening of ties to the parents, the reevaluation of attitudes and values formed in childhood, and the testing of childhood defenses and adaptive patterns against reality. Since adolescence is a period of rapid growth and major hormonal change, a major task of this period is the adapting to these changes by both boys and girls. This adaptation reinforces the acceptance of masculinity in the boys and femininity in the girl. This is followed by a testing out of sex roles in relation to members of the opposite sex.

The major task of late adolescence is identity-seeking, that is, the capacity to see oneself as having continuity and sameness. It is the consistent organization of experience. The quest for identity is the search for someone and something to be true to. The teenager asks the question: What do people stand for? Part of this seeking people and causes to which youth can commit themselves is the choosing of a future occupation. Another part involves the establishment of a sexual identity and a sense of intimacy with someone of the opposite sex. The essay concludes with the criteria that indicate a successful resolution of adolescence and the passage into adulthood.

Current psychological and sociological theories of adolescence employ the twin concepts *alienation* and *commitment* with respect to what the adolescent experiences as he attempts to carve out a new identity. In this regard *fidelity*—a sense of disciplined devotion—is seen as the strongest need, and greatest virtue, of the adolescent years by Erik Erikson in his essay "Youth: Fidelity and Diversity." At this time youth asks two questions: "Is there a place for me in the future?" and "Do I have the capacities to fit myself into this place?" The first question can be answered affirmatively only as the adolescent relates himself to the adults in his world who have found "their place." Poorly adjusted adults who attempt to convey an image of adjustment while actually unhappy and unsure of their capabilities are quickly unmasked as "finks" by today's adolescents. Indeed, the pursuit of "truth" is a distinguishing feature of this period of life when the young person is carefully assessing reality.

Phyllis La Farge's statement in "An Uptight Adolescent" differs from the other essays in this section in that it cannot be said to be scientific in the conventional sense. She neither describes an original investigation nor does she reflect on the research of others, but rather, she provides a personal reminiscence of a young woman, herself a parent, about her early adolescence. Mrs. La Farge's reminiscence is aided by a set of diaries to stimulate her memory. Her own experience was not necessarily typical or conventional even a generation ago, yet the reader may find that much of what she says confirms his own experience. Many readers, perhaps, will respond with a knowing nod of their heads to the set of signals Mrs. La Farge says were "blipped out at girls like me." As she summarizes their message: ". . . achieve if you want, but remember it will set you apart from other girls and make it harder to attract boys. If you achieve, prepare to interrupt your achievement at an appropriate (marriageable) age. Achieve but be cool about it, hide it if possible, and above all, don't claim that achievement has any prerogatives." Other psychological influences that were prevalent during Mrs. La Farge's youth, however, have changed drastically, as she notes and as we will see in subsequent readings.

One

Normal Growth

The idea of adolescence as an intermediary period of life has its origins in nineteenth-century America. The development of an urban-industrial society during the second half of the nineteenth century left young people bereft of their traditional place in American society. Three major social movements coalesced at this time to make a social fact out of adolescence: compulsory education, child-labor legislation, and special legal procedures for juveniles.

DAVID BAKAN

Adolescence in America: From Idea to Social Fact

THE IDEA OF ADOLESCENCE

Often a technical term is invented in order to create a social condition and a social fact; such has been true with respect to the term "adolescence." The idea of adolescence as an intermediary period in life starting at puberty and extending to some period in the life cycle unmarked by any conspicuous physical change but socially defined as "manhood" or "womanhood" is the product of modern times. The *Oxford English Dictionary* traces the term to the fifteenth century. Prior to that, if we follow the thought of Philip Aries,[1] the notion

1. P. Aries, *Centuries of Childhood* (New York: Knopf, 1962).

5

of childhood hardly existed, let alone the idea of the prolongation of childhood beyond puberty, as the term adolescence suggests.

Meaningful ascription of serious role characteristics for this period of life occurs, perhaps for the first time, in Rousseau's *Emile,* in which he characterized the period of adolescence as being beyond the earlier period of weakness of childhood and as a second birth. "We are born, so to speak, twice over; born into existence, and born into life; born a human being and born a man."[2] His aim was explicitly to prolong childhood, including the condition of innocence, as long as possible.

Although *Emile* has had considerable influence since its publication, the conversion of the idea of adolescence into a commonly accepted social reality was largely associated with modern urban-industrial life. Rousseau may have *invented* adolescence, as maintained by Musgrove,[3] but the notion as it is commonly understood in contemporary thought did not prevail prior to the last two decades of the nineteenth century and was "on the whole an American discovery."[4] The idea received an important stamp of reality from G. Stanley Hall in his monumental two-volume work on *Adolescence,* which he proudly presented to the reader as "essentially the author's first book" in 1904.[5] In point of fact he had introduced the idea as a special stage of development earlier.[6] In *Adolescence* he complained that we in America, because of our history, "have had neither childhood nor youth, but have lost touch with these stages of life because we lack a normal developmental history ... Our immigrants have often passed the best years of youth or leave it behind when they reach our shores, and their memories of it are in other lands. No country is so precociously old for its years."[7] The giving of social reality to adolescence would, as it were, youthen the nation.

By reviewing some of the history, I will attempt to show in this essay that the invention or discovery of adolescence in America was

2. Jean Jacques Rousseau, *Emile,* trans. Barbara Foxley (New York: Dutton, 1966; originally published 1762), pp. 128, 172.
3. F. Musgrove, *Youth and the Social Order* (Bloomington, Ind.: Indiana University Press, 1964). Musgrove titles one of his chapters "The Invention of the Adolescent" (pp. 33–57).
4. John Demos and Virginia Demos, "Adolescence in Historical Perspective," *Journal of Marriage and the Family,* 31 (1969), 632–638.
5. G. Stanley Hall, *Adolescence: Its Psychology and Its Relations to Physiology, Anthropology, Sociology, Sex, Crime, Religion, and Education* (New York: D. Appleton and Company, 1904).
6. G. Stanley Hall, "The Moral and Religious Training of Children," *Princeton Review* (January 1882), pp. 26–48.
7. Hall, *Adolescence,* p. xvi.

largely in response to the social changes that accompanied America's development in the latter half of the nineteenth and the early twentieth century, and that the principal reason was to prolong the years of childhood. Adolescence was added to childhood as a second childhood in order to fulfill the aims of the new urban-industrial society which developed so rapidly following the Civil War.

HISTORICAL BACKGROUND

From the days of the early settlement of America to the second half of the nineteenth century, America suffered a chronic labor shortage. It sought to overcome this labor shortage through slavery, the encouragament of immigration, and industrialization. The incompatibility of slavery and industrialization plagued America during much of its early history, and that incompatibility remained until the Civil War, the Emancipation Proclamation, and the Thirteenth Amendment resolved it in favor of industrialization. But with the development of urban-industrial society, the nation became possessed of new contradictions characteristic of modern technological society, most serious among them the presence of a large number of persons who were mature by historical standards but immature in the new context.

The country changed dramatically during the second half of the nineteenth century. In 1880 the railroad network was completely integrated; there was no longer a frontier; the number of cities that had populations of more than 8,000 almost doubled in the decade from 1880 to 1890. By the year 1900 more than a third of the population was living in cities and more than half the population of the North Atlantic area lived in cities of more than 8,000 persons. In 1890 more than a third of the American population were people of foreign parentage. The question of property was becoming increasingly salient, as testified to by the proliferation of criminal laws designed to protect property rights—a not unimportant fact when we consider the question of juvenile delinquency, because most juvenile crimes are crimes against property, such as burglary, larceny, robbery, and auto theft.

The low level of "morality" of the new occupants of the burgeoning cities was a matter of frequent comment. Drinking, sexual immorality, vagrancy, and crime were not only intrinsically threatening to orderliness, but were also particularly distressing influences on the young. The rapid breeding, the continuing threat of "street Arabs," evoked a strong cry that the state intercede in restraining and training the young. In an address before the American Social Science Association in 1875, the influential Mary Carpenter said that if the parents of the young fail in their duty, then the whole society suffers; it was therefore the duty of the state to intercede and "stand *in loco parentis* and do its duty to the child and to society, by seeing that he is properly brought up."[8] Not the least of the dangers was the presence of un-American ideas and ideologies brought by the new immigrants, which were considered threatening to the basic fiber of American life. Even private education, as compared with public education, was regarded as a threat, the fear being that the children would not be sufficiently socialized and "Americanized." The Ku Klux Klan, for example, took a firm stand against private education.

As a result of these conditions, three major social movements developed, all of which conspired to make a social fact out of adolescence: compulsory (and characteristically public) education, child labor legislation, and special legal procedures for "juveniles." By the explicit citation of a precise chronological age, the legislation associated with these three areas essentially removed the vagueness of all previous ideas of the time at which adolescence terminates. Thus adolescence became the period of time between pubescence, a concrete biological occurrence, and the ages specified by law for compulsory education, employment, and criminal procedure.

There is no doubt that these movements were strongly motivated, at least on the conscious level, by humanitarian considerations. The rhetoric in defense of these three types of law was always cast in terms of the benefit and the saving quality that they would have for the young. The presumption that the various child welfare laws were principally created for the benefit of youth must, however, be confronted with the fact that there has been only a small degree of legal attention to the serious problem of child abuse in our society. The so-called "battered child" was not discovered until the late 1940's and early 1950's, and to this day appropriate protective and social support legislation is still quite negligible in contrast to the magnitude of the problem and the frequency of cases of cruelty to children.[9] The confluence of humanitarian considerations with the major economic, social, and political forces in the society needs to be clearly recognized. Indeed, the recognition of these underlying

---

8. As cited in Grace Abbot, ed., *The Child and the State* (Chicago: University of Chicago Press, 1938), II, 372.
9. See M. G. Paulsen, "The Law and Abused Children," in R. E. Helfer and C. H. Kempe, *The Battered Child* (Chicago: University of Chicago Press, 1968), pp. 175–207; and D. Bakan, *Slaughter of the Innocents: A Study of the Battered Child Phenomenon* (San Francisco: Jossey-Bass, 1971; Toronto: Canadian Broadcasting Corp., 1971).

forces may help us to understand some of the failures to fulfill humanitarian aims and the disabilities which currently prevail with respect to that period of life that we call adolescence.

COMPULSORY EDUCATION

In the late nineteenth century, public compulsory education for children between six and eighteen, characteristically to age sixteen, was introduced widely in the United States. English common law had given parents virtually complete control over the education of the child, a principle prevalent in colonial America and throughout most of our early history. However, the general legal position later became that: "The primary function of the public school . . . is not to confer benefits upon the individual as such." Rather "the school exists as a state institution because the very existence of civil society demands it. The education of youth is a matter of such vital importance to the democratic state and to the public weal that the state may do much, may go very far indeed, by way of limiting the control of the parent over the education of his child."[10]

In the case of a father who had violated the compulsory attendance law, the court stated in its opinion:

> The course of study to be pursued in the public schools of our state is prescribed either by statute or by the school authorities in pursuance thereof. These schools include not only elementary schools, but high schools as well . . . A parent, therefore, is not at liberty to exercise a choice in that regard, but, where not exempt for some lawful reason, must send his child to the school where instruction is provided suitable to its attainments as the school authorities may determine.[11]

It has been held that even a competent parent may not engage in domestic education on the following grounds:

> We have no doubt many parents are capable of instructing their own children, but to permit such parents to withdraw their children from the public schools without permission from the superintendent of schools, and to instruct them at home, would be to disrupt our common school system and destroy its value to the state.[12]

---

10. Newton Edwards, *The Courts and the Public Schools: The Legal Basis of School Organization and Administration,* rev. ed. (Chicago: University of Chicago Press, 1955), p. 24.
11. *Miller* v. *State,* 77 Ind. App. 611, 134 N. E. 209, as cited by Edwards, *The Courts and the Public Schools,* p. 524.
12. *State* v. *Counort,* 69 Wash. 361, 124 Pac. 910, 41 L.R.A. (N.S.) 95, as cited by Edwards, *The Courts and the Public Schools,* p. 522.

At the same time the school authorities have been granted virtually complete discretionary powers with respect to suspension, expulsion, and punishment.[13] Such power rests in the hands of school authorities even in cases where the pupil has violated no rules. In one case, for example, a pupil was expelled for general misbehavior. In holding that the board of education had power to expel the pupil, the court said:

> In matters not whether rules have been announced by either the directors or teachers. If the conduct of the pupil is such as reasonably to satisfy such school officers that the presence of that pupil is detrimental to the interests of the school, then the power of expulsion is conferred.[14]

Thus, it has turned out that the power of the state in America is such that it can, through its officials, not only compel school attendance, but also bar a pupil access to educational resources. Certainly there have been numerous legislative acts and court actions which would qualify particular cases. However, the total thrust of the various steps that have been taken since the middle of the nineteenth century has been in the direction of increasing the power of the state rather than protecting the rights of young people and their parents.

At the same time as the legal power of school authorities over the pupils and their parents has been great, the schools have been derelict in the teaching of law—instruction which some regard as essential for people living in a democracy. In a society that is heavily dependent for its functioning on law, it is important that an appreciation of law, how it works, and its limits be taught in the public schools. One critic of this aspect of American education, in discussing the matter of education on due process, indicates that it is taught as though it applies only to criminals and that it fails to reflect itself in procedural fairness in school disciplinary matters. The idea of freedom of the press is characteristically not brought to bear in connection with school newspapers. "One of the difficult problems," he laconically comments, "is whether [proposed] law courses will be permitted to ventilate these issues, given the anxiety about them."[15]

---

13. Edwards, *The Courts and the Public Schools*, pp. 601ff.
14. *State* v. *Hamilton*, 42 Mo. App. 24, as cited by Edwards, *The Courts and the Public Schools*, p. 603.
15. Alex Elson, "General Education in Law for Non-Lawyers," in The American Assembly, Columbia University, *Law in a Changing America* (Englewood Cliffs, N.J.: Prentice-Hall, 1968), pp. 183–191, 189.

Although from time to time there have been steps to increase the knowledge of law among educators, the emphasis has been on the kind of legal knowledge that an educator might require to deal with relationships of the school to outside institutions and individuals rather than on teaching law to students. One article along these lines, for example, deals with the legal structure of education, pupil personnel policies, control of pupil conduct, staff personnel policies, curricula, and liability. Illustrations are that: physical education coordinators should be expert in the law of liability for pupil injuries; guidance teachers should be familiar with compulsory education laws and their enforcement; curriculum coordinators should understand the legal position of parents in relation to school studies and activities; business administrators should understand contract law; personnel administrators should understand the legal aspects of employing and discharging teachers; and teachers of the history or philosophy of education should be acquainted with the relevant judicial opinions.[16]

CHILD LABOR

The movement to restrict child labor in the United States also provided a definition of the termination of adolescence. Though there is a considerable amount of variation from state to state, the laws with respect to employment give specific minimum ages for definitions of maturity of different kinds: eighteen, minimum age for work in "hazardous occupations"; under eighteen, eight-hour day and forty-hour week; under eighteen, employment certificate required; under sixteen, limited hours of night work; sixteen, minimum age for factory work and employment during school hours; fourteen, minimum age for work outside of school hours. These are fairly typical laws governing age and employment.

The regulation of child labor has been one of the most controversial issues in this country since the nineteenth century. The harm to children from work in factories has been stridently declaimed. On the other hand, the virtues of work, the harm associated with idleness, and even the economic discriminatory effect of such legislation have also been consistently indicated. As an example, Senator Alexander Wiley, in questioning the representative of the American Federation of Labor before a Senate subcommittee to investigate

---

16. E. E. Reutter, Jr., "Essentials of School Law for Educators," in Harold J. Carter, ed., *Intellectual Foundations of American Education* (New York: Pitman Publishing Corporation, 1965), pp. 216–225.

juvenile delinquency said: "To me when I see the youth of this country in idleness, walking the streets of the cities, [I feel] we are meeting a challenge to our common sense because we know idleness breeds not only crime but everything else."[17] There have been repeated charges that the legal regulation of child labor is partly responsible for the widespread unemployment among young people, particularly Negroes.[18]

Adolescents in the labor force were a common occurrence throughout American history. In 1832 about 40 per cent of the factory workers in New England were children. Starting a few years after the Civil War the major historical trend of a chronic labor shortage began to reverse itself, with ever-increasing evidences of labor surplus. With the changes in the kinds of work needed in the growing cities in the second half of the nineteenth century, an increasing proportion of females sought gainful employment. Indeed, the possibility of a close relationship between the various movements in connection with "child saving" and female employment has been seriously suggested.[19] Labor began to organize. The Knights of Labor, the precursor of the American Federation of Labor, was founded in 1869. In 1885 it had a membership of 100,000; a year later it could boast a membership of 730,000. Virtually from its founding, the Knights of Labor began its campaign for the prohibition of child labor. In spite of its efforts, child labor increased. The participation rate of youth between the ages of ten and fifteen in the labor force increased until 1900 and then began to decline. Indeed, in the decade which ended in 1900, the number of child laborers in the canneries, glass industry, mines, and so forth in the South tripled. The effort to control the labor supply in the United States was evident also in legislation to restrict immigration. In 1882 the Chinese Exclusion Act, barring immigration of Chinese laborers, was passed and was followed by other laws which severely restricted immigration.

---

17. *Juvenile Delinquency: Hearings before the Subcommittee to Investigate Juvenile Delinquency,* Senate, 1955 (New York: Greenwood Press, 1968), p. 86.
18. See, for example, the effort to counter these charges by H. M. Haisch of the U.S. Department of Labor: H. M. Haisch, "Do Child Labor Laws Prevent Youth Employment?" *Journal of Negro Education,* 33 (1964), 182–185.
19. "Although child saving had important symbolic functions for preserving the prestige of middle-class women in a rapidly changing society, it also had considerable instrumental significance for legitimizing new career openings for women. The new role of social worker combined elements of an old and partly fictitious role—defender of family life—and elements of a new role—social servant. Social work and philanthropy were thus an affirmation of cherished values and an instrumentality for women's emancipation." Anthony M. Platt, *The Child Savers: The Invention of Delinquency* (Chicago: University of Chicago Press, 1969), p. 98.

Among employers there was a polarization. On the one hand there were certainly those employers who were in favor of having access to the cheap labor of young people and new immigrants; on the other hand the nature of industrial requirements was changing rapidly in favor of more skilled, and especially more reliable, workers. One of the most serious interferences with the reliability of labor was alcohol, and the prohibition movement grew simultaneously with the efforts to remove young people from the labor market and to restrict immigration. The prohibition movement gained increasing support from industrial leaders, "who were not unaware of the economic implications of the trade in intoxicants."[20]

The belief, common during the early part of the nineteenth century, that the children of the poor should work and that education of the children of the poor was filled with social danger tended to decline in the course of the century. The enlightened leaders of industry, taking ever longer views of history, recognized the dependence of industry on the existence of a reasonably educated labor force, educated not only with respect to knowledge and skill, but also with respect to bureaucratic subordination and reliable work habits.[21] At the same time, organized labor sought not only reforms in the conditions of child labor, but also education for their own children, to increase the likelihood of vertical social mobility. The continuing interest of both industry and labor in the education of the young is evidenced by the clear agreement on this on the part of both the National Association of Manufacturers and organized labor.[22]

One of the classic conflicts in connection with child labor was that between the textile manufacturers of the North and those in the South. The northern manufacturers charged that the South had a competitive advantage from its greater use of young workers.[23] Among the factors that eventually led to a resolution of the conflict was the later discovery, resulting in part from the changed nature of manufacture and experience of some restrictive legislation, that, as the *Textile World Journal* in 1918 put it: "The labor of children under fourteen years of age is not only inefficient in itself, but tends to lower the efficiency of all departments in which they are em-

20. John Allen Krout, *The Origins of Prohibition* (New York: Russell and Russell, 1967), p. 302.
21. For an analysis of relations between education and industry see John Galbraith, *The New Industrial State* (Boston: Houghton Mifflin, 1967).
22. See Charles R. Sligh, Jr., "Views on Curriculum," *Harvard Educational Review,* 4 (1957), 239–245; Walter P. Reuther, "What the Public Schools Should Teach," *Harvard Educational Review,* 4 (1957), 246–250.
23. Stephen B. Wood, *Constitutional Politics in the Progressive Era: Child Labor and the Law* (Chicago: University of Chicago Press, 1968), p. 9.

ployed; also children of fourteen to sixteen years, worked on a short time basis, are scarcely less efficient and have a disorganizing effect in the departments where they are utilized. Because of these facts, and entirely apart from humanitarian considerations, large numbers of southern mills will not re-employ children of these ages."[24]

JUVENILE DELINQUENCY

Quite analogous to the "invention of adolescence," as Musgrove put it, was the "invention of delinquency," as Anthony M. Platt puts it in his book on the history of the notion of delinquency in the United States.[25] The humane motivation associated with the development of the notion of the juvenile delinquent was the desire to remove young people from the rigidities and inexorabilities associated with criminal justice and to allow wider discretionary powers to authorities in dealing with juveniles. The new legal apparatus was intended to separate young offenders from older offenders, and to provide corrective rather than punitive treatment. The first Juvenile Court Act was passed by the Illinois legislature in 1899 and brought together for single consideration cases of dependency, neglect, and delinquency. The hearings under the act were to be informal, the records were to be confidential, the young people were to be detained separately from adults. The aims were to be investigation and prescription rather than the determination of guilt or innocence. Lawyers were to be unnecessary. The definition of the "juvenile delinquent" in the various laws which multiplied after the model legislation in Illinois now vary for the upper limit from sixteen to twenty-one. The United States Children's Bureau had recommended nineteen, and this has been followed in about two-thirds of the states.[26]

Although the juvenile acts tended to free the courts from the obligation of imposing punishments associated with the criminal codes, they also had the effect of suspending the fundamental principle of legality, that one may not be punished for an offense unless a definite law in effect at the time when the act in question was committed has been broken. Considerations of due process were not obligatory. Guilt did not have to be established beyond a reasonable doubt. Among the acts reported under the heading of juvenile delin-

24. Cited by Wood, *Constitutional Politics*, p. 172.
25. Anthony M. Platt, *The Child Savers: The Invention of Delinquency* (Chicago: University of Chicago Press, 1969).
26. Robert W. Winslow, ed., *Juvenile Delinquency in a Free Society: Selections from the President's Commission on Law Enforcement and Administration of Justice* (Belmont, Calif.: Dickenson Publishing Company, 1968), pp. 119–120.

quency may be found the following: immoral conduct around schools, association with vicious or immoral persons, patronizing public pool rooms, wandering about railroad yards, truancy, incorrigibility, absenting self from home without consent, smoking cigarettes in public places, begging or receiving alms (or in street for purposes of).[27] As Harvey Baker of the Boston juvenile court put it in 1910:

> The court does not confine its attention to just the particular offense which brought the child to its notice. For example, a boy who comes to court for such a trifle as failing to wear his badge when selling papers may be held on probation for months because of difficulties at school; and a boy who comes in for playing on the street may ... be committed to a reform school because he is found to have habits of loafing, stealing or gambling which can not be corrected outside.[28]

Questions have been raised as to whether the procedures of such courts adequately protect the rights of young offenders and whether they are consistent with constitutional rights.[29] In some states corrective legislation has been attempted by providing for legal defense of persons who come under the jurisdiction of the juvenile courts. However, the evidence is that this is not common. Indeed, treatment by officials tends to be more kindly toward young persons who admit guilt and indicate that they will mend their ways than toward those who are defensive or those whose parents are defensive.[30] The failure of the juvenile court to achieve its avowed objectives is notorious.

Suggestions that the aim of the juvenile court is to introduce a middle-class child-rearing orientation to the courtroom are apparent in the opinion of Judge Ben Lindsey of Denver, one of the pioneers in the juvenile court movement, and in the findings of Melvin L. Kohn. In an introduction to a book called *Winning the Boy* by Lilburn Merrill, Lindsey stressed the importance of "character," rather than the act itself.

> You have not really a safe citizen until there comes into the boy's heart the desire to do right because it is right ... I ask the boy why he will not steal again and he invariably replies, "Because I will get in jail." He is afraid of jail; he is not afraid to do wrong ... Conscience is the

27. Winslow, *Juvenile Delinquency,* pp. 166–167.
28. Cited in Platt, *The Child Savers,* p. 142.
29. See Lewis Mayer, *The American Legal System* (New York: Harper and Row, 1964), pp. 146–149.
30. Winslow, *Juvenile Delinquency,* pp. 140, 150.

moral director; without it character is impossible, and character is the
greatest need, for it means that the pure in heart shall see and know
and act the truth, as surely as they shall see God.[31]

Kohn has been able to show, on the basis of comparative data
which he has collected, that there are differences in corrective actions between working-class and middle-class parents. Working-
class parents tend to punish the external consequences of an action,
as contrasted with middle-class parents who tend to punish on the
basis of intention, rather than the action itself.[32] The latter mode is
clearly suggested in Judge Lindsey's comment. Thus one way of
interpreting the development of juvenile delinquency practices is as
an effort to bring middle-class child-rearing practices into play, even
when they involved the suspension of the principle of legality.

The legal disability of those who come under the juvenile laws
is not limited to a small minority of youth in our society. "Statutes
often define juvenile delinquency so broadly as to make virtually all
youngsters delinquent ... Rough estimates by the Children's Bureau, supported by independent studies, indicate that one in every
nine youths—one in every six male youths—will be referred to
juvenile court in connection with a delinquent act (excluding traffic
offenses) before his 18th birthday."[33] As soon as the young person
gains what may be called the animal sufficiency that comes with
puberty, and may enter public places without an attendant, he
becomes subject to extraordinary powers of the state until the legal
definition of his maturity comes into being. This power of the state
differs dramatically from the power of the state over adults in our
society. The great discrepancy between adult justice and juvenile
justice and the legal vulnerability of juveniles has been one of the
major factors associated with the conversion of the idea of adolescence into the social fact of adolescence.

THE STUDY OF ADOLESCENCE

Starting with the work of G. Stanley Hall, adolescence became the
subject of a considerable amount of investigation. There can be no

31. Cited in Bernard Wishy, *The Child and the Republic: The Dawn of Modern
    American Child Nurture* (Philadelphia: University of Pennsylvania Press, 1968),
    p. 134.
32. M. L. Kohn, "Social Class and Parent-Child Relationships: An Interpretation,"
    American Journal of Sociology, 68 (1963), 471–480; M. L. Kohn, "Social Class and
    the Exercise of Parental Authority," *American Sociological Review,* 24 (1959),
    352–366; M. L. Kohn, *Class and Conformity: A Study in Values* (Homewood, Ill.:
    Dorsey Press, 1969).
33. Winslow, *Juvenile Delinquency,* p. 2.

doubt about the value of such investigation—indeed, this may be attested to by the essays in this volume. Nonetheless, this body of literature articulated with the cultural forces in the society at large. Although the intention of people like Hall to draw attention to an extremely important age period significant to the history of civilization generally, and the United States in particular, and thereby to create greater concern with proper development at that stage, was meritorious, there was another effect which needs to be pointed out. By stressing, for example, the presumptive emotional instability and unformed nature of people of that age—the work of Margaret Mead and others suggests that such phenomena of adolescence may be extrinsic rather than intrinsic[34] —Hall and others tended to put a gloss of psychopathology on this age period. Since it has long been a principle in our society that persons regarded as psychologically pathological are to be relieved of rights,[35] the effect of this literature has been to serve the general disability of persons under legal ages. In this way, the workers in the field of adolescence have tended to conspire, certainly unwittingly, with some of the forces depriving adolescents of their rights.

THE PROMISE

A major factor which has sustained the social fact of adolescence in our society has been the belief, so pervasive in our success-oriented culture, in "the promise." The promise is that if a young person does all the things he is "supposed to do" during his adolescence, he will then realize success, status, income, power, and so forth, in his adulthood.

A study by Arthur L. Stinchcombe[36] may help us to understand the operation of the promise. He studied the attitudes, behavior, and perceptions of the labor market among high school students, and found a direct and dramatic relationship between the images of the future that the students have and their rebellious attitudes and behavior. His data bear out the hypothesis "that high school rebellion, and expressive alienation, are most common among students who do not see themselves as gaining an increment in future status from conformity in high school."[37] In elaborating on the dynamics of the hypothesis, he writes: "When a student realizes that he does not

34. Margaret Mead, *Coming of Age in Samoa* (New York: W. Morrow and Co., 1928).
35. See Thomas S. Szasz, *Law, Liberty and Psychiatry* (New York: Macmillan, 1963).
36. Arthur L. Stinchcombe, *Rebellion in a High School* (Chicago: Quadrangle Books, 1964).
37. *Ibid.,* p. 49; see especially chaps. 3 and 4, pp. 49–102, titled "The Labor Market and Rebellion I; II."

achieve status increment from improved current performance, current performance loses meaning. The student becomes hedonistic because he does not visualize achievement of long-run goals through current self-restraint. He reacts negatively to a conformity that offers nothing concrete. He claims autonomy from adults because their authority does not promise him a satisfactory future."[38] Stinchcombe's hypothesis is derived from considerations of the legitimacy of bureaucratic authority as developed by Max Weber. Among the interesting derivations Stinchcombe makes from the hypothesis is an explanation of the difference between the sexes in various categories of expressive alienation. Girls are less likely to be rebellious because they perceive at least the possibility of marriage as a viable "career." He points out that the relatively high delinquency rate among Negroes is associated with the perception of the employment discrimination against Negro adult males.

As the credibility of the promise declines, the willingness of young people to accept the varieties of disabilities of adolescence equally declines. The profoundly pervasive metaphor of appropriate behavior in adolescence as a form of capital investment for the realization of returns in the future necessarily falters in cogency as the likelihood of such returns declines. The problems of order in the schools, juvenile delinquency, and other forms of expressive alienation cannot readily be solved by making small changes in the schools, Stinchcombe says.[39] It would appear that the schools cannot promise much because the society cannot promise much.

A study by William Westley and Frederick Elkin[40] of young people in an upper-class suburb of Montreal in 1951 attempted to explode the notion of the adolescent period as being one of storm and stress, nonconformity, gang formation, struggle for emancipation, and the like. The data collected in that place and time indicated considerably greater harmony and positive social adjustment by conventional standards than one might expect. However, the characterization of these young people would clearly indicate that they expected that the promise would be fulfilled. The typical youth in the study "internalizes aspirations for a professional or business career; he learns the expected patterns of language and breeding; he learns to resolve disputes by peaceable means; he learns to defer many immediate gratifications for the sake of future gains."[41]

38. *Ibid.,* pp. 5–6.
39. *Ibid.,* passim.
40. William A. Westley and Frederick Elkin, "The Protective Environment and Adolescent Socialization," in Martin Gold and Elizabeth Douvan, eds., *Adolescent Development: Readings in Research and Theory* (Boston: Allyn and Bacon, 1969), pp. 158–164; reprinted from *Social Forces,* 35 (1957), 243–249.
41. *Ibid.,* p. 158.

The major question in our society today is whether, for youth of *all* social classes, the promise has continued credibility. Unemployment among manual workers is increasingly patent. The public service advertisements directed at potential drop-outs to remain in school in order to get better jobs later are met with increasing cynicism.[42] The poor acceptance rates of college students into the labor market predicted in the early sixties[43] are rapidly materializing. Even for scientists with Ph.D.'s the possibilities for employment are extremely dismal.[44] And few young people are ignorant of the fact that a career in "free enterprise" is virtually impossible without access to capital.[45] The idyllic vision of Erik Erikson that adolescence "can be viewed as a *psychosocial moratorium* during which the individual through free role experimentation may find a niche in some section of his society, a niche which is firmly defined and yet seems to be uniquely made for him,"[46] must increasingly be viewed cynically if that niche in life is contingent upon an appropriate niche in the labor force.

One of the likely consequences of these trends will be a strong move on the part of youth and their parents to dissolve the social fact of adolescence and to remove the historical disabilities which have been created by the state and sustained by the promise. Albert K. Cohen, in 1965, indicated that he thought it was sad that youth accepted their disabilities without protest.[47] The picture soon changed. Jerry Farber's critique of what he calls America's "Auschwitz" educational system, "The Student as Nigger," originally pub-

42. See, for example, the stress on the employment advantages of school in the *National Stay-in-School Campaign Handbook for Communities* (Washington, D.C.: Government Printing Office, 1957). The campaign was sponsored jointly by the Department of Labor, Department of Health, Education and Welfare, and Department of Defense.
43. J. Folger and C. Nam, "Trends in Education in Relation to the Occupational Structure," *Sociology of Education*, 38 (1964), 19–33; R. Havighurst and B. Neugarten, *Society and Education*, 2d ed. (Boston: Allyn and Bacon, 1962).
44. Allan Cartter, "Scientific Manpower for 1970–1985," *Science*, 172 (1971), 132–140.
45. Such has been the case at least since 1885 when Andrew Carnegie, the great exponent of the idea that any able and energetic young man could "rise to the top," told a group of students that "There is no doubt that it is becoming harder and harder as business gravitates more and more to immense concerns for a young man without capital to get a start for himself." Cited in H. J. Perkinson, *The Imperfect Panacea: American Faith in Education, 1865–1965* (New York: Random House, 1968), p. 120. Ironically, one of the few spheres in which "free enterprise," with relatively little capital and high returns on investment, is still possible is in the illegal merchandising of drugs.
46. Erik H. Erikson, "The Problem of Ego Identity," in Gold and Douvan, *Adolescent Development*, p. 19; reprinted from *Identity and the Life Cycle* (New York: International Universities Press, 1959).
47. In his foreword to Musgrove, *Youth and the Social Order*, p. xix: "Do they really believe that all preparation for life must, in the nature of things, take for its model the process of becoming a thirty-second degree Mason?"

lished in 1967 in the Los Angeles *Free Press,* quickly became one of the most widely distributed underground documents in history— reprinted, reduplicated, recopied many times by student groups all over America and Canada.[48] A national clearing house of anti-public school thought has been formed in Washington, D.C., which puts out a regular biweekly newsletter called *FPS* (*the letters don't stand for anything*). Ellen Lurie has written what is fast becoming a standard manual for parents seeking to reduce state control over their children's education in the public schools.[49] This book is consistent with the United Nations Universal Declaration of Human Rights, adopted in 1948, that "Parents have a prior right to choose the kind of education that shall be given to their children."[50] The crime statistics mount at an exponential rate. Demonstrations become ever more strident. The "underground revolution"[51]gets new recruits daily.

The future? My assignment was to discuss history. The future must be left to time and other occasions.[52]

---

48. Jerry Farber, *The Student as Nigger* (New York: Pocket Books, 1970).
49. Ellen Lurie, *How to Change the Schools: A Parents' Action Handbook on How to Fight the System* (New York: Vintage Books, 1970).
50. Article 26–3.
51. Naomi Feigelson, ed., *The Underground Revolution: Hippies, Yippies and Others* (New York: Funk and Wagnalls, 1970).
52. Since the time that I wrote this, the amendment reducing the voting age to eighteen has been ratified. I am of the opinion that it will have important consequences bearing on the considerations in this essay.

The onset of puberty marks both a dramatic alteration in the growth rate and the development of the reproductive system. Some changes in body size, body shape, and body composition are common to both sexes; most, however, are sex-specific. Starting with these developmental facts, a noted British physiologist discusses the relevance of chronological age as an indicator of growth, the influence of heredity and environment on the age of puperty, and the "secular trend" toward earlier maturation.

J. M. TANNER

Sequence, Tempo, and Individual Variation in the Growth and Development of Boys and Girls Aged Twelve to Sixteen

For the majority of young persons, the years from twelve to sixteen are the most eventful ones of their lives so far as their growth and development is concerned. Admittedly during fetal life and the first year or two after birth developments occurred still faster, and a sympathetic environment was probably even more crucial, but the subject himself was not the fascinated, charmed, or horrified spectator that watches the developments, or lack of developments, of adolescence. Growth is a very regular and highly regulated process, and from birth onward the growth rate of most bodily tissues decreases steadily, the fall being swift at first and slower from about three years. Body shape changes gradually since the rate of growth of some parts, such as the arms and legs, is greater than the rate of growth of others, such as the trunk. But the change is a steady one, a smoothly continuous development rather than any passage through a series of separate stages.

Then at puberty, a very considerable alteration in growth rate occurs. There is a swift increase in body size, a change in the shape and body composition, and a rapid development of the gonads, the reproductive organs, and the characters signaling sexual maturity. Some of these changes are common to both sexes, but most are sex-specific. Boys have a great increase in muscle size and strength, together with a series of physiological changes, making them more capable than girls of doing heavy physical work and running faster and longer. The changes specifically adapt the male to his primitive primate role of dominating, fighting, and foraging. Such adolescent changes occur generally in primates, but are more marked in some species than in others. Male, female, and prepubescent gibbons are hard to distinguish when they are together, let alone apart. No such problem arises with gorillas or Rhesus monkeys. Man lies at about the middle of the primate range, both in adolescent size increase and degree of sexual differentiation.

The adolescent changes are brought about by hormones, either secreted for the first time, or secreted in much higher amounts than previously. Each hormone acts on a set of targets or receptors, but these are often not concentrated in a single organ, nor in a single type of tissue. Testosterone, for example, acts on receptors in the cells of the penis, the skin of the face, the cartilages of the shoulder joints, and certain parts of the brain. Whether all these cells respond by virtue of having the same enzyme system, or whether different enzymes are involved at different sites is not yet clear. The systems have developed through natural selection, producing a functional response of obvious biological usefulness in societies of hunter gatherers, but of less certain benefit in the culture of invoice clerk and shop assistant. Evolutionary adaptations of bodily structure usually carry with them an increased proclivity for using those structures in behavior, and there is no reason to suppose this principle suddenly stops short at twentieth-century man. There is no need to take sides in the current debate on the origins of aggression to realize that a major task of any culture is the channeling of this less specifically sexual adolescent energy into creative and playful activity.

The adolescent changes have not altered in the last fifteen years, or the last fifty, or probably the last five thousand. Girls still develop two years earlier than boys; some boys still have completed their whole bodily adolescent development before other boys of the same chronological age have begun theirs. These are perhaps the two major biological facts to be borne in mind when thinking of the adolescent's view of himself in relation to his society. The sequence of the biological events remains the same. But there has been one considerable change; the events occur now at an earlier age than formerly. Forty years ago the average British girl had her first menstrual period (menarche) at about her fifteenth birthday; nowadays it is shortly before her thirteenth. Fifty years ago in Britain social class differences played a considerable part in causing the variation of age of menarche in the population, the less well-off growing up more slowly. Nowadays, age at menarche is almost the same in different classes and most of the variation is due to genetical factors.

In this essay, I shall discuss (1) the growth of the body at adolescence and its changes in size, shape, and tissue composition, (2) sex dimorphism and the development of the reproductive system, (3) the concept of developmental age and the interaction of physical and behavioral advancement, (4) the interaction of genetic and environmental influences on the age of occurrence of puberty and the secular trend toward earlier maturation.

GROWTH OF THE BODY AT ADOLESCENCE

The extent of the adolescent spurt in height is shown in *Figure 1*. For a year or more the velocity of growth approximately doubles; a boy is likely to be growing again at the rate he last experienced about age two. The peak velocity of height (PHV, a point much used in growth studies) averages about 10.5 centimeters a year (cm/yr) in boys and 9.0 cm/yr in girls (with a standard deviation of about 1.0 cm/yr) but this is the "instantaneous" peak given by a smooth curve drawn through the observations. The velocity over the whole year encompassing the six months before and after the peak is naturally somewhat less. During this year a boy usually grows between 7 and 12 cm and a girl between 6 and 11 cm. Children who have their peak early reach a somewhat higher peak than those who have it late.

The average age at which the peak is reached depends on the nature and circumstances of the group studied more, probably, than does the height of the peak. In moderately well-off British or North American children at present the peak occurs on average at about 14.0 years in boys and 12.0 years in girls. The standard deviations are about 0.9 years in each instance. Though the absolute average ages differ from series to series the two-year sex difference is invariant.

The adolescent spurt is at least partly under different hormonal control from growth in the period before. Probably as a consequence of this the amount of height added during the spurt is to a considerable degree independent of the amount attained prior to it. Most children who have grown steadily up, say, the 30th centile line on a height chart till adolescence end up at the 30th centile as adults, it is true; but a number end as high as the 50th or as low as the 10th, and a very few at the 55th or 5th. The correlation between adult height and height just before the spurt starts is about 0.8. This leaves some 30 percent of the variability in adult height as due to differences in the magnitude of the adolescent spurt. So some adolescents get a nasty and unavoidable shock; though probably the effects of early and late maturing almost totally confuse the issue of final height during the years we are considering.

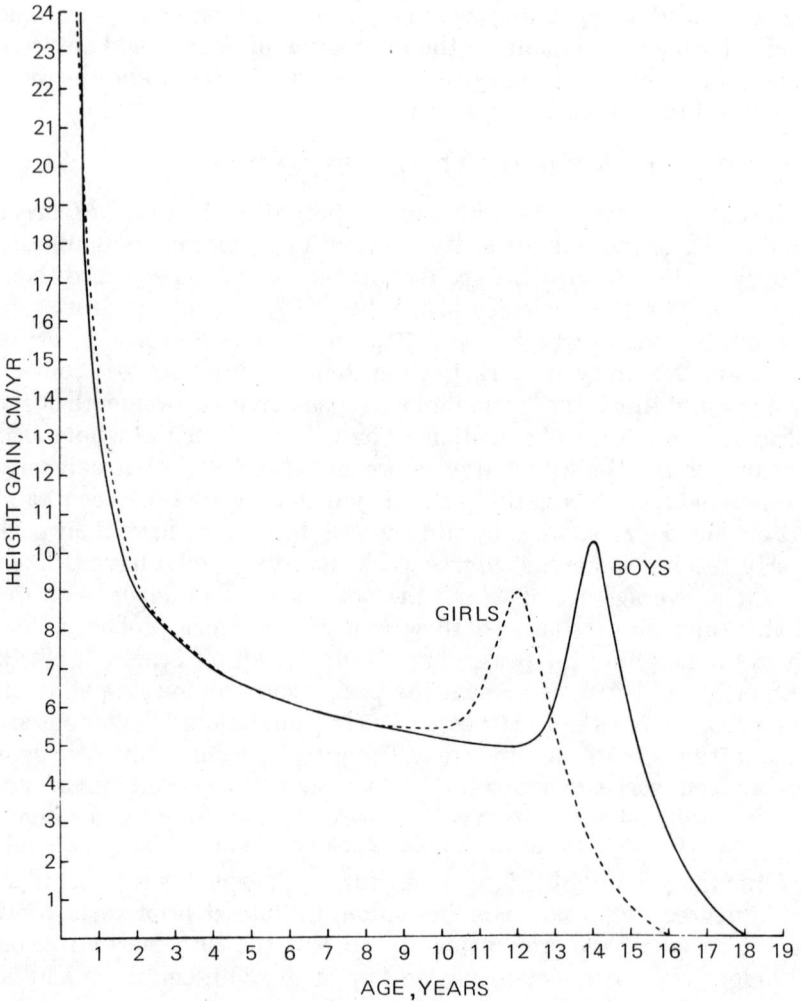

Figure 1. Typical individual velocity curves for supine length or height in boys and girls. These curves represent the velocity of the typical boy and girl at any given instant. (From J. M. Tanner, R. H. Whitehouse, and M. Takaishi, "Standards from Birth to Maturity for Height, Weight Height Velocity and Weight Velocity; British Children, 1965," *Archives of the Diseases of Childhood,* 41 [1966], 455–471.)

Practically all skeletal and muscular dimensions take part in the spurt, though not to an equal degree. Most of the spurt in height is due to acceleration of trunk length rather than length of legs. There is a fairly regular order in which the dimensions accelerate; leg length as a rule reaches its peak first, followed by the body breadths, with shoulder width last. Thus a boy stops growing out of his trousers (at least in length) a year before he stops growing out of his jackets. The earliest structures to reach their adult status are the head, hands, and feet. At adolescence, children, particularly girls, sometimes complain of having large hands and feet. They can be reassured that by the time they are fully grown their hands and feet will be a little smaller in proportion to their arms and legs, and considerably smaller in proportion to their trunk.

The spurt in muscle, both of limbs and heart, coincides with the spurt in skeletal growth, for both are caused by the same hormones. Boys' muscle widths reach a peak velocity of growth considerably greater than those reached by girls. But since girls have their spurt earlier, there is actually a period, from about twelve and a half to thirteen and a half, when girls on the average have larger muscles than boys of the same age.

Simultaneously with the spurt in muscle there is a loss of fat in boys, particularly on the limbs. Girls have a velocity curve of fat identical in shape to that of boys; that is to say, their fat accumulation (going on in both sexes from about age six) decelerates. But the decrease in velocity in girls is not sufficiently great to carry the average velocity below zero, that is to give an absolute loss. Most girls have to content themselves with a temporary go-slow in fat accumulation. As the adolescent growth spurt draws to an end, fat tends to accumulate again in both sexes.

The marked increase in muscle size in boys at adolescence leads to an increase in strength, illustrated in *Figure 2.* Before adolescence, boys and girls are similar in strength for a given body size and shape; after, boys are much stronger, probably due to developing more force per gram of muscle as well as absolutely larger muscles. They also develop larger hearts and lungs relative to their size, a higher systolic blood pressure, a lower resting heart rate, a greater capacity for carrying oxygen in the blood, and a greater power for neutralizing the chemical products of muscular exercise such as lactic acid.[1] In short, the male becomes at adolescence more adapted for the tasks of hunting, fighting, and manipulating all sorts of heavy objects, as is necessary in some forms of food-gathering.

---

1. J. M. Tanner, *Growth at Adolescence,* 2d ed. (Oxford: Blackwell Scientific Publications, 1962), p. 168.

KG.
60 ┌ STRENGTH OF ARM PULL

50 ├

40 ├   BOYS

30 ├

20 ├   GIRLS

  └─┬──┬──┬──┬──┬──┬──┬─
   11 12 13 14 15 16 17
        AGE, YEARS

KG.
60 ┌ STRENGTH OF ARM THRUST

50 ├   BOYS

40 ├

30 ├   GIRLS

20 ├

  └─┬──┬──┬──┬──┬──┬──┬─
   11 12 13 14 15 16 17
        AGE, YEARS

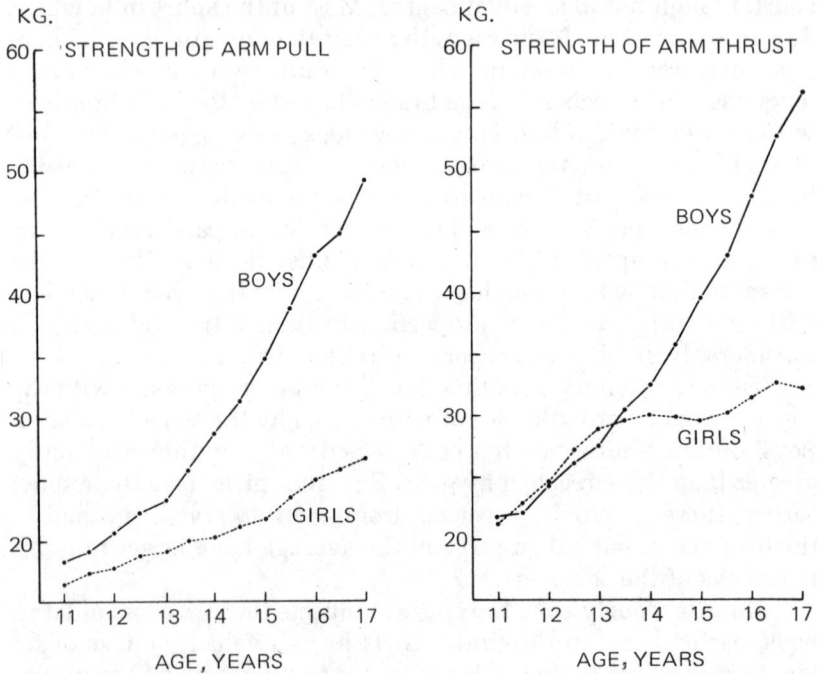

Figure 2. Strength of arm pull and arm thrust from age eleven to seventeen. Mixed longitudinal data, sixty-five to ninety-five boys and sixty-six to ninety-three girls in each age group. (From J. M. Tanner, *Growth at Adolescence*, 2d ed. [Oxford: Blackwell Scientific Publications, 1962]; data from H. E. Jones, *Motor Performance and Growth* [Berkeley: University of California Press, 1949].)

The increase in hemoglobin, associated with a parallel increase in the number of red blood cells, is illustrated in *Figure 3.*[2] The hemoglobin concentration is plotted in relation to the development of secondary sex characters instead of chronological age, to obviate the spread due to early and late maturing (see below). Girls lack the rise in red cells and hemoglobin, which is brought about by the action of testosterone.

It is as a direct result of these anatomical and physiological changes that athletic ability increases so much in boys at adolescence. The popular notion of a boy "outgrowing his strength" at this time has little scientific support. It is true that the peak velocity of

2. H. B. Young, "Ageing and Adolescence," *Developmental Medicine and Child Neurology*, 5 (1963), 451–460.

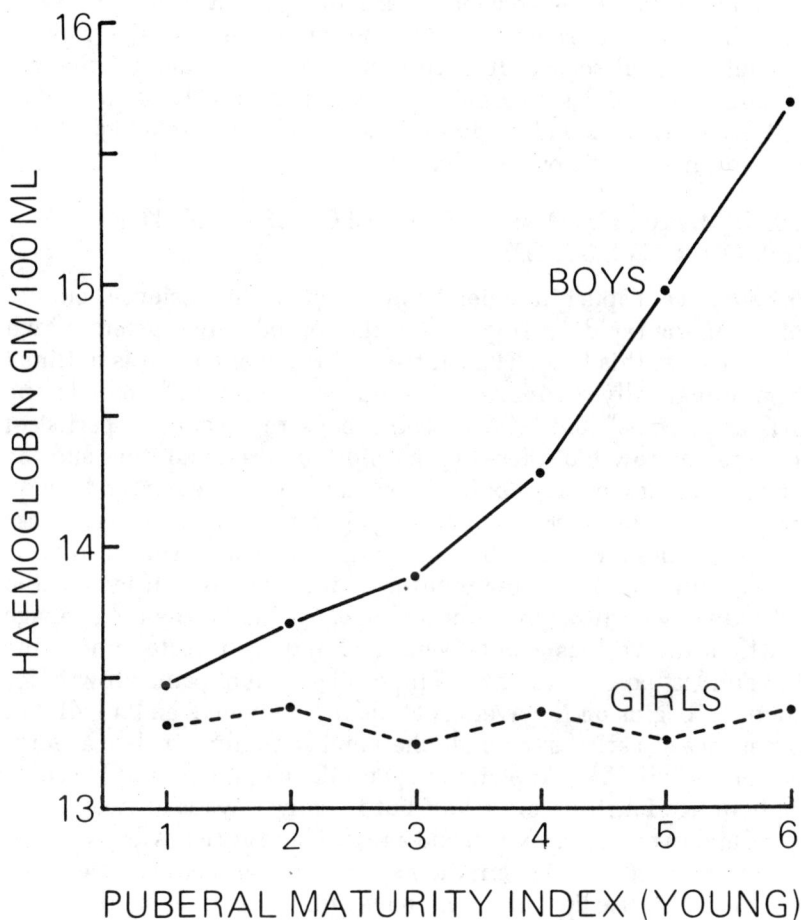

Figure 3.   Blood hemoglobin level in girls and boys according to stage of puberty; cross-sectional data. (From H. B. Young, "Ageing and Adolescence," *Developmental Medicine and Child Neurology,* 5 (1963), 451–460, cited in J. M. Tanner, "Growth and Endocrinology of the Adolescent," in L. Gardner, ed., *Endocrine and Genetic Diseases of Childhood* [Philadelphia and London: Saunders, 1969].)

strength is reached a year or so later than that of height, so that a short period may exist when the adolescent, having completed his skeletal and probably also muscular growth, still does not have the strength of a young adult of the same body size and shape. But this is a temporary phase; considered absolutely, power, athletic skill, and physical endurance all increase progressively and rapidly throughout adolescence. It is certainly not true that the changes accompanying adolescence enfeeble, even temporarily. If the adolescent becomes weak and easily exhausted it is for psychological reasons and not physiological ones.

SEX DIMORPHISM AND THE DEVELOPMENT OF THE REPRODUCTIVE SYSTEM

The adolescent spurt in skeletal and muscular dimensions is closely related to the rapid development of the reproductive system which takes place at this time. The course of this development is outlined diagrammatically in *Figure 4.* The solid areas marked "breast" in the girls and "penis" and "testis" in the boys represent the period of accelerated growth of these organs and the horizontal lines and the rating numbers marked "pubic hair" stand for its advent and development.[3] The sequences and timings given represent in each case average values for British boys and girls; the North American average is within two or three months of this. To give an idea of the individual departures from the average, figures for the range of age at which the various events begin and end are inserted under the first and last point of the bars. The acceleration of penis growth, for example, begins on the average at about age twelve and a half, but sometimes as early as ten and a half and sometimes as late as fourteen and a half. The completion of penis development usually occurs at about age fourteen and a half but in some boys is at twelve and a half and in others at sixteen and a half. There are a few boys, it will be noticed, who do not begin their spurts in height or penis development until the earliest maturers have entirely completed theirs. At age thirteen, fourteen, and fifteen there is an enormous variability among any group of boys, who range all the way from practically complete maturity to absolute preadolescence. The same is true of girls aged eleven, twelve, and thirteen.

      ... The statement that a boy is fourteen is in most contexts hopelessly vague; all depends, morphologically, physiologically, and to a considerable extent sociologically too, on whether he is preadolescent, midadolescent, or postadolescent.

---

3. Details of ratings are in Tanner, *Growth at Adolescence.*

HEIGHT SPURT
9.5-14.5

MENARCHE
10-16.5

BREAST   2   3   4   5
8-13   13-18

PUBIC HAIR   2   3   4   5

8   9   10   11   12   13   14   15   16   17
AGE, YEARS

APEX
STRENGTH
SPURT

HEIGHT SPURT
10.5-16   13.5-17.5

PENIS
10.5-14.5   12.5-16.5

TESTIS
9.5-13.5   13.5-17

G. RATING   2   3   4   5

PUBIC HAIR   2   3   4   5

8   9   10   11   12   13   14   15   16   17
AGE, YEARS

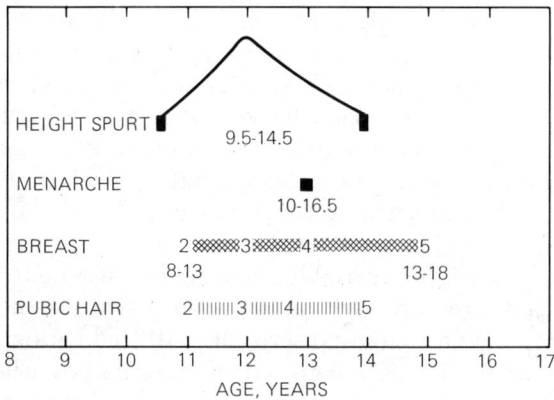

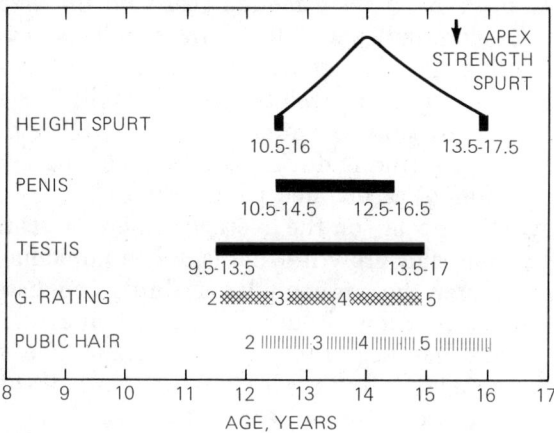

Figure 4.   Diagram of sequence of events at adolescence in boys and girls. The average boy and girl are represented. The range of ages within which each event charted may begin and end is given by the figures placed directly below its start and finish. (From W. A. Marshall and J. M. Tanner, "Variations in the Pattern of Pubertal Changes in Boys," *Archives of the Diseases of Childhood,* 45 [1970], 13.)

The psychological and social importance of this difference in the tempo of development, as it has been called, is very great, particularly in boys. Boys who are advanced in development are likely to dominate their contemporaries in athletic achievement and sexual interest alike. Conversely the late developer is the one who all too often loses out in the rough and tumble of the adolescent world; and he may begin to wonder whether he will ever develop his body properly or be as well endowed sexually as those others he has seen developing around him. A very important part of the educationist's and the doctor's task at this time is to provide information about growth and its variability to preadolescents and adolescents and to give sympathetic support and reassurance to those who need it.

The *sequence* of events, though not exactly the same for each boy or girl, is much less variable than the age at which the events occur. The first sign of puberty in the boy is usually an acceleration of the growth of the testes and scrotum with reddening and wrinkling of the scrotal skin. Slight growth of pubic hair may begin about the same time, but is usually a trifle later. The spurts in height and penis growth begin on average about a year after the first testicular acceleration. Concomitantly with the growth of the penis, and under the same stimulus, the seminal vesicles and the prostate and bulbo-urethral glands enlarge and develop. The time of the first ejaculation of seminal fluid is to some extent culturally as well as biologically determined, but as a rule is during adolescence, and about a year after the beginning of accelerated penis growth.

Axillary hair appears on the average some two years after the beginning of pubic hair growth—that is, when pubic hair is reaching stage 4. However, there is enough variability and dissociation in these events that a very few children's axillary hair actually appears first. In boys, facial hair begins to grow at about the time the axillary hair appears. There is a definite order in which the hairs of mustache and beard appear: first at the corners of the upper lip, then over all the upper lip, then at the upper part of the cheeks in the mid-line below the lower lip, and finally along the sides and lower border of the chin. The remainder of the body hair appears from about the time of first axillary hair development until a considerable time after puberty. The ultimate amount of body hair an individual develops seems to depend largely on heredity, though whether because of the kinds and amounts of hormones secreted or because of the reactivity of the end-organs is not known.

Breaking of the voice occurs relatively late in adolescence; it is often a gradual process and so not suitable as a criterion of puberty. The change in pitch accompanies enlargement of the larynx and lengthening of the vocal cords, caused by the action of testosterone on the laryngeal cartilages. During the period of breaking, the pitch is variable, and the true adult pitch associated with full growth of the larynx may not be established until late adolescence. In addition to change in pitch, there is also a change in quality or timbre which distinguishes the voice (more particularly the vowel sounds) of both male and female adults from that of children. This is dependent on the enlargement of the resonating spaces above the larynx, due to the rapid growth of the mouth, nose, and maxilla which occurs during adolescence.

In the skin the sebaceous and apocrine sweat glands, particularly of the axillae and genital and anal regions, develop rapidly during puberty and give rise to a characteristic odor; the changes occur in both sexes but are more marked in the male. Enlargement of the pores at the root of the nose and the appearance of comedones and acne, though liable to occur in either sex, are considerably commoner in adolescent boys than girls, since the underlying skin changes are the result of androgenic activity. A roughening of the skin, particularly over the outer aspects of the thighs and upper arms, may be seen in both sexes during adolescence, but again is commoner in boys than girls.

During adolescence the male breast undergoes changes, some temporary and some permanent. The diameter of the areola, which is equal in both sexes before puberty, increases considerably, though less than it does in girls. Representative figures are 12.5 millimeters before puberty, 21.5 millimeters in mature men, and 35.5 millimeters in mature women. In some boys (between a fifth and a third of most groups studied) there is a distinct enlargement of the breast (sometimes unilaterally) about midway through adolescence. This usually regresses again after about one year.

In girls the appearance of the "breast bud" is as a rule the first sign of puberty, though the appearance of pubic hair precedes it in about one in three. The uterus and vagina develop simultaneously with the breast. The labia and clitoris also enlarge. Menarche, the first menstrual period, is a late event in the sequence. It occurs almost invariably after the peak of the height spurt has been passed. Though it marks a definitive and probably mature stage of uterine development, it does not usually signify the attainment of full reproductive function. The early cycles may be more irregular than later ones and are in some girls, but by no means all, accompanied by dysmenorrhea. They are often anovulatory, that is unaccompanied by the shedding of an egg. Thus there is frequently a period of adolescent sterility lasting a year to eighteen months after menarche; but it cannot be relied on in the individual case. Similar considerations may apply to the male, but there is no reliable information about this. On the average, girls grow about 6 cm more after menarche, though gains of up to twice this amount may occur. The gain is practically independent of whether menarche occurs early or late.

NORMAL VARIATIONS IN PUBERTAL DEVELOPMENT

The diagram of *Figure 4* must not be allowed to obscure the fact that children vary a great deal both in the rapidity with which they pass through the various stages of puberty and in the closeness with which the various events are linked together. At one extreme one may find a perfectly healthy girl who has not yet menstruated though she has reached adult breast and pubic hair ratings and is already two years past her peak height velocity; at the other, a girl who has passed all the stages of puberty within the space of two years. Details of the limits of what may be considered normal can be found in the articles of Marshall and Tanner.[4]

In girls the interval from the first sign of puberty to complete maturity varies from one and a half to six years. From the moment when the breast bud first appears to menarche averages two and a half years but may be as little as six months or as much as five and a half years. The rapidity with which a child passes through puberty seems to be independent of whether puberty is occurring early or late. There is some independence between breast and pubic hair developments, as one might expect on endocrinological grounds. A few girls reach pubic hair stage 3 (see *Figure 4*) before any breast developments starts; conversely breast stage 3 may be reached before any pubic hair appears. At breast stage 5, however, pubic hair is always present in girls. Menarche usually occurs in breast stage 4 and pubic hair stage 4, but in about 10 per cent of girls occurs in stage 5 for both, and occasionally may occur in stage 2 or even 1 of pubic hair. Menarche invariably occurs after peak height velocity is passed, so the tall girl can be reassured about future growth if her periods have begun.

In boys a similar variability occurs. The genitalia may take any time between two and five years to pass from G2 to G5, and some boys complete the whole process while others have still not gone from G2 to G3. Pubic hair growth in the absence of genital develop-

---

4. W. A. Marshall and J. M. Tanner, "Variations in the Pattern of Pubertal Changes in Girls," *Archives of the Diseases of Childhood*, 44 (1969), 291, and "Variations in the Pattern of Pubertal Changes in Boys," *Archives of the Diseases of Childhood*, 45 (1970), 13.

ment is very unusual in normal boys, but in a small percentage of boys the genitalia develop as far as stage 4 before the pubic hair starts to grow.

The height spurt occurs relatively later in boys than in girls. Thus there is a difference between the average boy and girl of two years in age of peak height velocity, but of only one year in the first appearance of pubic hair. The PHV occurs in very few boys before genital stage 4, whereas 75 per cent of girls reach PHV before breast stage 4. Indeed in some girls the acceleration in height is the first sign of puberty; this is never so in boys. A small boy whose genitalia are just beginning to develop can be unequivocally reassured that an acceleration in height is soon to take place, but a girl in the corresponding situation may already have had her height spurt.

The basis of some children having loose and some tight linkages between pubertal events is not known. Probably the linkage reflects the degree of integration of various processes in the hypothalamus and the pituitary gland, for breast growth is controlled by one group of hormones, pubic hair growth by another, and the height spurt probably by a third. In rare pathological instances the events may become widely divorced.

THE DEVELOPMENT OF SEX DIMORPHISM

The differential effects on the growth of bone, muscle, and fat at puberty increase considerably the difference in body composition between the sexes. Boys have a greater increase not only in the length of bones but in the thickness of cortex, and girls have a smaller loss of fat. The most striking dimorphism, however, are the man's greater stature and breadth of shoulders and the woman's wider hips. These are produced chiefly by the changes and timing of puberty but it is important to remember that sex dimorphisms do not arise only at that time. Many appear much earlier. Some, like the external genital difference itself, develop during fetal life. Others develop continuously throughout the whole growth period by a sustained differential growth rate. An example of this is the greater relative length and breadth of the forearm in the male when compared with whole arm length or whole body length.

Part of the sex difference in pelvic shape antedates puberty. Girls at birth already have a wider pelvic outlet. Thus the adaptation for child bearing is present from a very early age. The changes at puberty are concerned more with widening the pelvic inlet and broadening the much more noticeable hips. It seems likely that these changes are more important in attracting the male's attention than in dealing with its ultimate product.

These sex-differentiated morphological characters arising at puberty—to which we can add the corresponding physiological and perhaps psychological ones as well—are secondary sex characters in the straightforward sense that they are caused by sex hormone or sex-differential hormone secretion and serve reproductive activity. The penis is directly concerned in copulation, the mammary gland in lactation. The wide shoulders and muscular power of the male, together with the canine teeth and brow ridges in man's ancestors, developed probably for driving away other males and insuring peace, an adaptation which soon becomes social.

A number of traits persist, perhaps through another mechanism known to the ethologists as ritualization. In the course of evolution a morphological character or a piece of behavior may lose its original function and, becoming further elaborated, complicated, or simplified, may serve as a sign stimulus to other members of the same species, releasing behavior that is in some ways advantageous to the spread or survival of the species. It requires little insight into human erotics to suppose that the shoulders, the hips and buttocks, and the breasts (at least in a number of widespread cultures) serve as releasers of mating behavior. The pubic hair (about whose function the textbooks have always preserved a cautious silence) probably survives as a ritualized stimulus for sexual activity, developed by simplification from the hair remaining in the inguinal and axillary regions for the infant to cling to when still transported, as in present apes and monkeys, under the mother's body. Similar considerations may apply to axillary hair, which is associated with special apocrine glands which themselves only develop at puberty and are related histologically to scent glands in other mammals. The beard, on the other hand, may still be more frightening to other males than enticing to females. At least ritual use in past communities suggests this is the case; but perhaps there are two sorts of beards.

THE INITIATION OF PUBERTY

The manner in which puberty is initiated has a general importance for the clarification of developmental mechanisms. Certain children develop all the changes of puberty, up to and including spermatogenesis and ovulation, at a very early age, either as the result of a brain lesion or as an isolated developmental, sometimes genetic defect. The youngest mother on record was such a case, and gave birth to a full-term healthy infant by Caesarian section at the age of five years, eight months. The existence of precocious puberty and the results of accidental ingestion by small children of male or female sex hormones indicate that breasts, uterus, and penis will respond to hormonal stimulation long before puberty. Evidently an increased end-organ sensitivity plays at most a minor part in pubertal events.

The signal to start the sequence of events is given by the brain, not the pituitary. Just as the brain holds the information on sex, so it holds information on maturity. The pituitary of a newborn rat successfully grafted in place of an adult pituitary begins at once to function in an adult fashion, and does not have to wait till its normal age of maturation has been reached. It is the hypothalamus, not the pituitary, which has to mature before puberty begins.

Maturation, however, does not come out of the blue and at least in rats a little more is known about this mechanism. In these animals small amounts of sex hormones circulate from the time of birth and these appear to inhibit the prepubertal hypothalamus from producing gonadotrophin releasers. At puberty it is supposed that the hypothalamic cells become less sensitive to sex hormone. The small amount of sex hormones circulating then fails to inhibit the hypothalamus and gonadotrophins are released; these stimulate the production of testosterone by the testis or estrogen by the ovary. The level of the sex hormone rises until the same feedback circuit is reestablished, but now at a higher level of gonadotrophins and sex hormones. The sex hormones are now high enough to stimulate the growth of secondary sex characters and support mating behavior.

DEVELOPMENTAL AGE AND THE INTERACTION OF PHYSICAL AND BEHAVIORAL ADVANCEMENT

Children vary greatly in their tempo of growth. The effects are most dramatically seen at adolescence ... but they are present at all ages from birth and even before. Girls, for example, do not suddenly become two years ahead of boys at adolescence; on the contrary they are born with slightly more mature skeletons and nervous systems, and gradually increase their developmental lead (in absolute terms) throughout childhood.

Clearly, the concept of *developmental* age, as opposed to *chronological* age, is a very important one. To measure developmental age we need some way of determining the percentage of the child's growth process which has been attained at any time. In retrospective research studies, the per cent of final adult height may be very effectively used; but in the clinic we need something that is immediate in its application. The difficulty about using height, for example, is that different children end up at different heights, so that a tall-for-his-age twelve-year-old may either be a tall adult in the making with average maturational tempo, or an average adult in the making with an accelerated tempo. Precisely the same applies to the child who scores above average on most tests of mental ability.

To measure developmental age we need something which ends up the same for everyone and is applicable throughout the whole period of growth. Many physiological measures meet these criteria, in whole or in part. They range from the number of erupted teeth to the percentage of water in muscle cells. The various developmental "age" scales do not necessarily coincide, and each has its particular use. By far the most generally useful, however, is skeletal maturity or *bone* age. A less important one is dental maturity.

Skeletal maturity is usually measured by taking a radiograph of the hand and wrist (using the same radiation exposure that a child inevitably gets, and to more sensitive areas, by spending a week on vacation in the mountains). The appearances of the developing bones can be rated and formed into a scale; the scale is applicable to boys and girls of all genetic backgrounds, though girls on the average reach any given score at a younger age than boys, and blacks on the average, at least in the first few years after birth, reach a given score younger than do whites. Other areas of the body may be used if required. Skeletal maturity is closely related to the age at which adolescence occurs, that is to maturity measured by secondary sex character development. Thus the range of *chronological* age within which menarche may normally fall is about ten to sixteen and a half, but the corresponding range of *skeletal* age for menarche is only twelve to fourteen and a half. Evidently the physiological processes controlling progression of skeletal development are in most instances closely linked with those which initiate the events of adolescence. Furthermore children tend to be consistently advanced or retarded during their whole growth period, or at any rate after about age three.

Dental maturity partly shares in this general skeletal and bodily maturation. At all ages from six to thirteen children who are advanced skeletally have on the average more erupted teeth than those who are skeletally retarded. Likewise those who have an early adolescence on the average erupt their teeth early. Girls usually have more erupted teeth than boys. But this relationship is not a very close one, and quantitatively speaking, it is the relative independence of teeth and general skeletal development which should be emphasized. There is some general factor of bodily maturity creating a tendency for a child to be advanced or retarded as a whole: in his skeletal ossification, in the percentage attained of his eventual size, in his permanent dentition, doubtless in his physiological reactions, and possibly in the results of his tests of ability. But not too much should be made of this general factor; and especially it should be noted how very limited is the loading, so to speak, of brain growth in it. There is little justification in the facts of physical growth and development for the concept of "organismic age" in which almost wholly disparate measures of developmental maturity are lumped together.

PHYSICAL MATURATION, MENTAL ABILITY, AND EMOTIONAL DEVELOPMENT

Clearly the occurrence of tempo differences in human growth has profound implications for educational theory and practice. This would especially be so if advancement in physical growth were linked to any significant degree with advancement in intellectual ability and in emotional maturity.

There is good evidence that in the European and North American school systems children who are physically advanced toward maturity score on the average slightly higher in most tests of mental ability than children of the same age who are physically less mature. The difference is not great, but it is consistent and it occurs at all ages that have been studied—that is, back as far as six and a half years. Similarly the intelligence test score of postmenarcheal girls is higher than the score of premenarcheal girls of the same age.[5] Thus in age-linked examinations physically fast-maturing children have a significantly better chance than slow-maturing.

It is also true that physically large children score higher than small ones, at all ages from six onward. In a random sample of all Scottish eleven-year old children, for example, comprising 6,440 pupils, the correlation between height and score in the Moray House group test was 0.25 ± 0.01 which leads to an average increase of one and a half points Terman-Merrill I.Q. per inch of stature. A similar correlation was found in London children. The effects can be very significant for individual children. In ten-year-old girls there was nine points difference in I.Q. between those whose height was above the 75th percentile and those whose height was below the 15th. This is two-thirds of the standard deviation of the test score.

It was usually thought that both the relationships between test score and height and between test score and early maturing would disappear in adulthood. If the correlations represented only the effects of co-advancement both of mental ability and physical

5. See references in Tanner, *Growth at Adolescence,* and Tanner, "Galtonian Eugenics and the Study of Growth, *The Eugenics Review,* 58 (1966), 122–135.

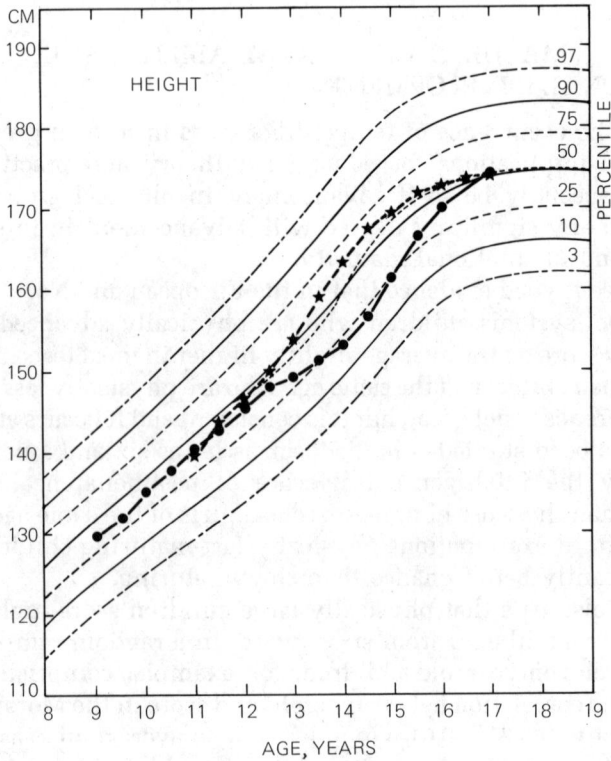

Figure 5. Height attained of two boys, one with an early and the other with a late adolescent spurt. Note how at age eleven and again at age seventeen the boys are the same height. (From J. M. Tanner, *Education and Physical Growth: Implications of the Study of Children's Growth for Educational Theory and Practice* [London: University of London Press, 1961].)

growth this might be expected to happen. There is no difference in height between early and late maturing boys when both have finished growing. But it is now clear that, curiously, at least part of the height-I.Q. correlation persists in adults.[6] It is not clear in what proportion genetic and environmental factors are responsible for this.

There is little doubt that being an early or a late maturer may have repercussions on behavior, and that in some children these repercussions may be considerable. There is little enough solid information on the relation between emotional and physiological development, but what there is supports the common sense notion that emotional attitudes are clearly related to physiological events.

The boy's world is one where physical powers bring prestige as well as success, where the body is very much an instrument of the person. Boys who are advanced in development, not only at puberty, but before as well, are more likely than others to be leaders. Indeed, this is reinforced by the fact that muscular, powerful boys on the average mature earlier than others and have an early adolescent growth spurt. The athletically-built boy not only tends to dominate his fellows before puberty, but also by getting an early start he is in a good position to continue that domination. The unathletic, lanky boy, unable, perhaps, to hold his own in the preadolescent rough and tumble, gets still further pushed to the wall at adolescence, as he sees others shoot up while he remains nearly stationary in growth. Even boys several years younger now suddenly surpass him in size, athletic skill, and perhaps, too, in social graces. *Figure 5* shows the height curves of two boys, the first an early-maturing muscular boy, the other a late-maturing lanky one. Though both boys are of average height at age eleven, and together again at average height at seventeen, the early maturer is four inches taller during the peak of adolescence.

At a much deeper level the late developer at adolescence may sometimes have doubts about whether he will ever develop his body properly and whether he will be as well endowed sexually as those others he has seen developing around him. The lack of events of adolescence may act as a trigger to reverberate fears accumulated deep in the mind during the early years of life.

It may seem as though the early maturers have things all their own way. It is indeed true that most studies of the later personalities of children whose growth history is known do show early maturers as more stable, more sociable, less neurotic, and more successful in

---

6. Tanner, "Galtonian Eugenics."

society, at least in the United States.[7] But early maturers have their difficulties also, particularly the girls in some societies. Though some glory in their new possessions, others are embarrassed by them. The early maturer, too, has a longer period of frustration of sex drive and of drive toward independence and the establishment of vocational orientation.

Little can be done to reduce the individual differences in children's tempo of growth, for they are biologically rooted and not significantly reducible by any social steps we may take. It, therefore, behooves all teachers, psychologists, and pediatricians to be fully aware of the facts and alert to the individual problems they raise.

TREND TOWARD LARGE SIZE AND EARLIER MATURATION

The rate of maturing and the age at onset of puberty are dependent, naturally, on a complex interaction of genetic and environmental factors. Where the environment is good, most of the variability in age at menarche in a population is due to genetic differences. In France in the 1950's the mean difference between identical twins was two months, while that between nonidentical twin sisters was eight months.[8] In many societies puberty occurs later in the poorly-off, and in most societies investigated children with many siblings grow less fast than children with few.

Recent investigations in Northeast England showed that social class differences are now only those associated with different sizes of family. The median age of menarche for only girls was 13.0 years, for girls with one sibling 13.2, two siblings 13.4, three siblings and over 13.7. For a given number of siblings the social class as indicated by father's occupation was unrelated to menarcheal age.[9] Environment is still clearly a factor in control of menarcheal age, but in England at least occupation is a less effective indication of poor housing, poor expenditure on food, and poor child care than is the number of children in the family.

During the last hundred years there has been a striking tendency for children to become progressively larger at all ages.[10] This is known as the "secular trend." The magnitude of the trend in

---

7. P. H. Mussen and M. C. Jones, "Self-Concepting Motivations and Interpersonal Attitudes of Late- and Early-Maturing Boys," *Child Development,* 28 (1957), 243–256.
8. M. Tisserand-Perrier, "Etude comparative de certains processus de croissance chez les jeuneaux," *Journal de genetique humaine,* 2 (1953), 87–102, as cited in Tanner, *Growth at Adolescence.*
9. D. F. Roberts, L. M. Rozner, and A. V. Swan, "Age at Menarche, Physique and Environment in Industrial North-East England," *Acta Paediatrica Scandinavica,* 60 (1971), 158–164.
10. J. M. Tanner, "Earlier Maturation in Man," *Scientific American,* 218 (1968), 21–27.

Europe and America is such that it dwarfs the differences between socioeconomic classes.

The data from Europe and America agree well: from about 1900, or a little earlier, to the present, children in average economic circumstances have increased in height at age five to seven by about 1 to 2 cm each decade, and at ten to fourteen by 2 to 3 cm each decade. Preschool data show that the trend starts directly after birth and may, indeed, be relatively greater from age two to five than subsequently. The trend started, at least in Britain, a considerable time ago, because Roberts, a factory physician, writing in 1876 said that "a factory child of the present day at the age of nine years weighs as much as one of 10 years did in 1833 ... each age has gained one year in forty years."[11] The trend in Europe is still continuing at the time of writing but there is some evidence to show that in the United States the best-off sections of the population are now growing up at something approaching the fastest possible speed.

During the same period there has been an upward trend in adult height, but to a considerably lower degree. In earlier times final height was not reached till twenty-five years or later, whereas now it is reached in men at eighteen or nineteen. Data exist, however, which enable us to compare fully grown men at different periods. They lead to the conclusion that in Western Europe men increased in adult height little if at all from 1760 to 1830, about 0.3 cm per decade from 1830 to 1880, and about 0.6 cm per decade from 1880 to 1960. The trend is apparently still continuing in Europe, though not in the best-off section of American society.

Most of the trend toward greater size in children reflects a more rapid maturation; only a minor part reflects a greater ultimate size. The trend toward earlier maturing is best shown in the statistics on age at menarche. A selection of the best data is illustrated in *Figure 6*. The trend is between three and four months per decade since 1850 in average sections of Western European populations. Well-off persons show a trend of about half this magnitude, having never been so retarded in menarche as the worse-off.[12]

Most, though not all, of the differences between populations are probably due to nutritional factors, operating during the whole of the growth period, from conception onward. The well-nourished Western populations have median menarcheal ages of about 12.8 to 13.2 years; the latest recorded ages, by contrast, are 18 years in the Highlands of New Guinea, 17 years in Central Africa, and 15.5 years in poorly-off Bantu in the South African Transkei. Well-nourished

---

11. Tanner, *Growth at Adolescence.*
12. Details on average age of menarche of various populations and the methods for collecting these statistics will be found in Tanner, "Galtonian Eugenics."

Africans have a median age of 13.4 (Kampala upper classes) or less, comparable with Europeans. Asians at the same nutritional level as Europeans probably have an earlier menarche, the figure for well-off Chinese in Hong Kong being 12.5 years.

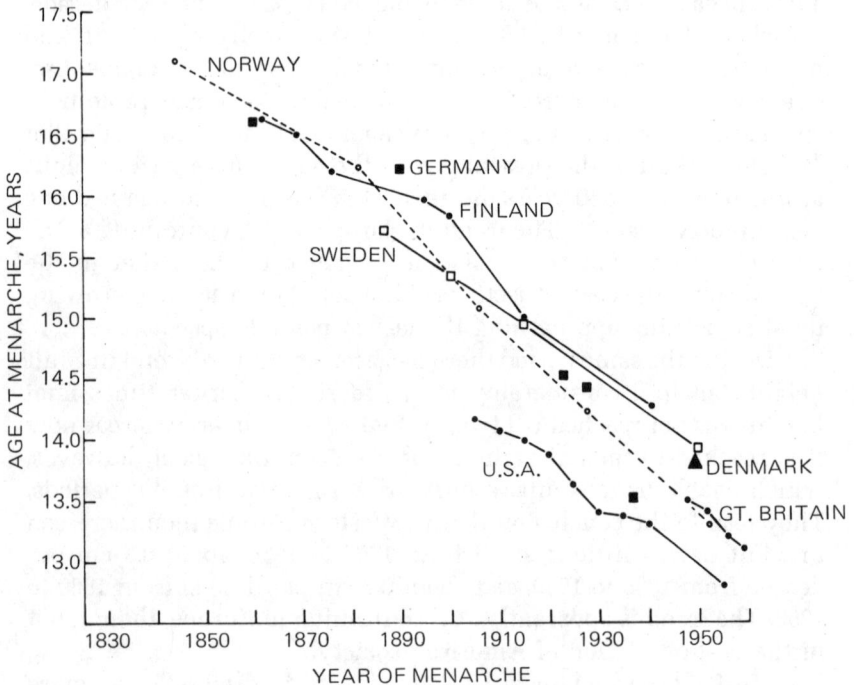

Figure 6.   Secular trend in age at menarche, 1830–1960. (Sources of data and method of plotting detailed in Tanner, *Growth at Adolescence.*)

The causes of the secular trend are probably multiple. Certainly better nutrition is a major one, and perhaps in particular more protein and calories in early infancy. A lessening of disease may also have contributed. Hot climates used to be cited as a potent cause of early menarche, but it seems now that their effect, if any, is considerably less than that of nutrition. The annual mean world temperature rose from 1850 to about 1940 (when it began to fall again); the polar ice caps have been melting and the glaciers retreating, but on present evidence it seems unlikely that this general warming up has contributed significantly to the earlier menarche of girls.

Some authors have supposed that the increased psychosexual stimulation consequent on modern urban living has contributed, but there is no positive evidence for this. Girls in single-sex schools have menarche at exactly the same age as girls in coeducational schools, but whether this is a fair test of difference in psychosexual stimulation is hard to say.

Two

Development

*This essay on the role adolescents can play in changing society suggests that
possibilities for social change in a culture derive from the status enjoyed by
its youth. Citing several non-literate societies, a noted British anthropologist
and sociologist presents a far-reaching hypothesis concerning alienated
youth and a society in transition: societies affording low status to youth
create a deviant group open to social experimentation; conversely, youth
with high status tend to perpetuate the status quo.*

FRANK MUSGROVE

Youth and Social Change

FRUSTRATION AND INNOVATION

When, in the days of World War II, Karl Mannheim looked forward
to a reconstructed postwar Britain, he emphasized the important
role that youth must play if progress and change were to be
achieved. "I believe that static societies which develop only gradually, and in which the rate of change is relatively slow, will rely
mainly on the experience of the old."[1] A dynamic society, on the
other hand, would accord youth a high status: a frustrated and stag-

---

1. Karl Mannheim, *Diagnosis of Our Time* (1943), p. 33.

nant Britain had failed to give youth "its proper place and share in public life."[2] Although Mannheim was aware that the driving force of the young originated in large measure from their "outsider" position, he saw no inconsistency in urging that they should become insiders: "the dynamic societies which want to make a new start, whatever their social or political philosophy may be, will rely mainly on the cooperation of youth. They will organize their vital resources and will use them in breaking down the established direction of social development."[3]

The truth is probably the opposite of Mannheim's thesis. It is true that high status of young people is often closely associated with a heightened tempo of social change; but it is frequently a consequence rather than a cause. Eisenstadt has pointed to great social and political movements in nineteenth-century Europe which were closely associated with the energies of young people—Mazzini's "Young Italy," the German youth movements following the rapid transformation which took place during the post-Bismarckian era, and the nationalist movements in the Near and Far East today which have relied heavily on students and young army officers.[4] But the latter have achieved importance after the social and political revolutions and not before: it was their low status in the traditional, familistic setting, in which the authority of the elders was paramount, which must be seen as an important cause of social change; their subsequent high status is a result. It is likely that revolutionary change which owes much to such circumstances will fail to maintain its forward momentum.[5] The middle- and upper-class young women of late-Victorian and Edwardian England, whose status frustrations led to the militant Suffragette movement, have been succeeded in mid-twentieth-century Britain by an enfranchised adult female population unremarkable at any social level for vigorous, let alone revolutionary, political activity.

The causes of social change are complex, and the low status of youth only one factor which merits attention. But it is a factor which has been comparatively little examined. When the modes of social

2. Ibid., p. 43.
3. Ibid., p. 36.
4. S. N. Eisenstadt, *From Generation to Generation* (1956), pp. 171–174.
5. Cf. A. J. P. Taylor's interpretation of the failure of German liberals in 1848— because they had succeeded, as students, in the movement of national liberation in 1813: "The revolution of 1848 was not the explosion of new forces, but the belated triumph of *Burschenschaft,* the students of the war of liberation who were now men in their fifties ... dependent on the princes for their salaries or pensions as civil servants." See *The Course of German History* (1945), p. 69.

change which have occurred among non-literate peoples in contact
with the West are compared, the position of the young in the indigenous societies provides at least a partial explanation of the nature of
the response. It is now many years since Fortes argued that a comparative sociology of culture contact was needed "without which we
can never hope to perceive the causes of social change."[6] In this
chapter nothing so ambitious is attempted; but a variety of circumstances in which social change has occurred—or has been resisted—
will be compared, and as far as possible the status of the young
isolated and examined for its bearing on the processes of resistance
and change.

The argument advanced in this chapter is this: that in those
societies in which the status of adolescents and young adults (particularly the males) is high, change will tend to be slow, the blandishments of an elaborate and alien civilization resisted; where their
status is low, and their seniors can effectively block their access to
adult statuses and impede their assumption of adult roles, then there
is likely to be a predisposition to change, to social innovation and
experimentation, to a ready response to the opportunities which
may be offered by an alien, intrusive culture to follow alternative
and quicker routes to power and importance. When the young are
segregated from the adult world, held in low esteem, and delayed in
their entry into adult life, they are likely to constitute a potentially
deviant population; but when they are segregated from the adult
world in a position of high status and power (for instance, in warrior
groups), a conservative society is the probable result. High status
and a sense of importance may be achieved by the young through
integration with, rather than segregation from, the adult world: they
may share their seniors' work and responsibilities, their pleasures
and pastimes; in this case, too, resistance to change is likely to be
strong.

While British anthropologists of the "functional" school have
resolutely refused to invoke psychology to account for the processes
of culture change, finding sufficient explanation in "social facts," in
the inter-relations of institutions and their capacity or incapacity to
satisfy "needs," American anthropologists have looked for light in
personality- and in learning-theory. "A well-developed learning theory," Hallowell has maintained, "is relevant to promoting further
knowledge of the whole process of cultural transmission as well as
the processes involved in acculturation and culture change."[7] The

---

6. Meyer Fortes, "Culture Contact as a Dynamic Process," *Africa* (1936), 9.
7. A. Irving Hallowell, "Culture, Personality, and Society," in A. L. Kroeber, *Anthropology Today* (1953), p. 599.

new learning which takes place when social change occurs, it is argued, is explicable only in terms of the personality organization which facilitates or impedes adjustment to new circumstances: in the process of social change, "a crucial variable may be the kind of personality structure of the people undergoing acculturation."[8]

While it is true that sociological explanations imply at least rudimentary psychological assumptions—usually somewhat crudely hedonistic views of learning and motivation—it is possible to look for the social correlates of change without venturing into the wide sea of personality-and-culture theory. The position of the young in a society's social structure can be shown to have an intimate connection with that society's stability and response to changing external circumstances. It is true that throughout the world today non-literate societies are changing whatever may be the power enjoyed by their young; but their rates and modes of change differ, and their readiness or proneness to change have varied widely at the "zero point of contact" (in Lucy Mair's phrase), even when the alien impact was similar in range, intensity, organization, and content. The standardized policy of America's Indian Affairs Department in the later nineteenth century met with a wide variety of reactions from the Indian tribes: the Makah[9] were remarkable for their degree of assimilation to American culture while remaining active and vigorous; the Sioux,[10] treated to an essentially similar program of education and Americanization, rejected the alien culture, without vigor, only with dispirited apathy. The tribes of Africa have shown a similar variety of response to the endeavors of European missionaries, labor recruiters, and government officials.

Change may be voluntary or forced,[11] but however reluctant in their first encounter, tribal societies throughout the world are undergoing change, at varying rates. The size and concentration of their populations, their proximity to or remoteness from European institutions and settlements, the administrative policies of imperial powers, are all relevant circumstances. Tribes in which the cultivation of cash crops has been successfully introduced have probably made the most important and positive changes in adapting tribal life to a new political and economic context;[12] tribes which supply mi-

---

8. Ibid., pp. 613–614.
9. See Elizabeth Colson, *The Makah Indians* (1953).
10. See G. MacGregor, *Warriors Without Weapons* (1946).
11. For a useful discussion of this distinction, see Ian Hogbin, *Social Change* (1958), pp. 98–99.
12. See A. Southall, "Social Change, Demography and Extrinsic Factors" in A. Southall (ed.), *Social Change in Modern Africa* (1961), pp. 1–13.

grant labor to distant European enterprises have often changed less; those with neither cash cropping nor migrant laborers have generally persisted in a traditional way of life. But at the zero point of impact, tribal societies showed marked differences in their proneness to change, even when the impact was similar in nature and extent.

When Her Majesty's Special Commissioner made his preliminary report on the Uganda Protectorate in 1900, he was struck by the different responses of tribes within a relatively small region of Africa. "Among the naked Nilotic negroes of the eastern half of the Protectorate missionary propaganda seems at the present time to be absolutely impossible. ... On the other hand, the Bantu-speaking natives are well inclined to religious inquiry."[13] The egalitarian Lango and Iteso, without marked distinctions of rank or political authority ("it is sometimes difficult to find a man who does not profess to be a 'somebody' "[14]), were contemptuous of alien ideas, institutions, and customs, tenacious of their own; the hierarchical, centralized states like the Baganda, among whom distinctions of rank and age were marked, and the track of seniority long, were more ready to learn alien ways. From the very first days of contact they showed themselves not only predisposed to learn a new religion,[15] but were "greedy for cloth and for almost every manufactured article up to a phonograph and a brougham."[16]

When a social system presents blockages and delays to the satisfaction of needs, particularly the urgently felt social and sexual needs of young men, the institutions of an alien civilization may be eagerly embraced. The new institutions may, indeed, create new needs,[17] but initially they offer the chance of satisfying existing needs more quickly and directly. "An individual adopts an innovation of his own free will only when he has become convinced that it offers him some kind of reward—perhaps greater efficiency, or more security, or enhanced status."[18] An established value may now

---

13. *Preliminary Report of Her Majesty's Special Commissioner on the Uganda Protectorate* (1901), cd. 671, p. 6.
14. A. L. Kitching, *On the Backwaters of the Nile* (1912), p. 160.
15. Even at the price of martyrdom at the hands of political superiors who interpreted the new learning as a threat to their authority. See R. P. Ashe, *Two Kings of Uganda* (1899), pp. 215–231, for an account of kabaka Mwanga's persecution of native Christians ("readers") in Buganda.
16. *Preliminary Report of Her Majesty's Special Commissioner on the Uganda Protectorate* (1901).
17. See the author's study, "A Uganda School as a Field of Culture Change," *Africa* (1952), 22, for an examination of an African school as an institution which meets "emergent needs" which have no strict counterpart in either the indigenous or the intrusive culture.
18. Ian Hogbin, *Social Change* (1958), p. 57.

be realized more effectively in a new way;[19] thus whereas security, land, status, and the brideprice could eventually be attained by young men throughout most of Melanesia through service to maternal uncles, Western contact offered an alternative and quicker route to independence and fully adult status: work for wages in European enterprises. The result is to undermine the authority of age: "the senior men are in a quandary. . . . The tendency is therefore towards a loosening of the ties binding the two age-groups together."[20]

New institutions may be accepted because they seem to lend support to existing social values; but their long term effect may be to undermine them. Thus European-type schools have often been supported by African parents because their immediate effect has been to discipline the young and maintain the authority of seniority. In the nineteen-thirties Lucy Mair found in the villages of Buganda that:

> The parents themselves are anxious to have their children go to school; there is no question of the children being taken from their influence against their will . . . The parents do not themselves feel that European education is likely to make their children disrespectful. Indeed I remember one father declaring that children were better kept in order at school than at home. . . .[21]

But the boys themselves may welcome school not because it supports (some of) the traditional values of the indigenous social order, but because it subverts them. As the author reported from Uganda in the nineteen-fifties: "The school appears to be most effective (with its pupils) when it is not attempting to take over the functions of tribal institutions: it is most effective not in shoring up the deficiences of tribal institutions, but when it is on wholly new ground, dealing with subjects outside the sphere of traditional instruction and pursuits."[22]

The Wilsons presented a cataclysmic view of social change under conditions of culture contact. Seeing pre-contact African societies as coherent systems ("To deny the assumption of social

---

19. Ibid., p. 94. Cf. B. Malinowski, *The Dynamics of Culture Change* (1945): "One kind of institution can be replaced by another which fulfils a similar function" (p. 52). "The ultimate reality in culture change thus hinges on the fact that corresponding institutions in two cultures satisfy analogous needs in different ways and with different techniques. . . ."
20. Ibid.
21. L. P. Mair, *An African People in the Twentieth Century* (1934), pp. 68–69.
22. F. Musgrove, "Some Refections on the Sociology of African Education," *African Studies* (1952), II. See also the author's study of African children's play: "[they] do not of their own accord bring traditional games into the school": "Education and the Culture Concept," *Africa* (1953), 23.

coherence would be to abandon all hope of analysis in history . . ."[23]), albeit with "normal opposition" which could be contained—between a boy and his mother's brother, between co-wives or a wife and her husband's people—they argued that culture contact introduced "radical opposition," fundamental and irreconcilable conflict between law and law, logic and logic, convention and convention. Social change was disequilibrium: thus Christianity and monogamy raised complex opposition within the society of the Nyakyusa: the traditional value of hospitality by the wealthy was incapable of realization with such institutions. "The opposition can only be removed by social change, economic or religious."[24]

But social change had already occurred—when some, at least, of the Nyakyusa adopted Christianity and monogamy: what the Wilsons are perhaps explaining is *further* social change. The initial acceptance of new institutions—which may have unforeseen consequences in the future—when it is voluntary, is a solution to existing tensions and frustrations. When marriage is an important sign of adult status, and when the conditions of marriage are closely controlled by the older age groups, change may be accepted because it promotes an existing value (status through marriage) while undermining another (the authority of the old). At least for the young the balance of advantage is on the side of change: they have not even necessarily learned new ideas and values, but have only found support for ideas and values which already existed, but were perhaps experimental and disreputable. Discontent with the authority of their seniors was already present. "Every real society consists of a core of orthodox norms and conforming actions round the margins of experiment that changing norms and actions emerge into sanctioned acceptance."[25]

Societies which have shown an initial proneness to change have often been characterized by the frustrations of young men whose chance of marriage is jeopardized by the power of elderly polygamists. The Mende of Sierra Leone and the Azande of the Sudan have been differently involved in contact with the West: the former have had a more sustained and intimate contact, the latter are geographically remote. Both are societies hierarchical in their social and political organization, both give power to older men, and both have been noted for their inclination to social innovation and their ready acceptance of change. Formerly among the Azande "The older men had a monopoly of wives, and in the past it was difficult for young men

---

23. G. and M. Wilson, *Analysis of Social Change* (1945), p. 23.
24. Ibid., p. 126.
25. A. W. Southall, "Norms and Status Symbols" in A. W. Southall (ed.), *Social Change in Modern Africa* (1961), p. 14.

to marry. The need of food and the hope of acquiring a sufficient number of spears with which to marry anchored a youth to his family and kin. The father of a family exercised great control over his sons who treated him with deep respect."[26] Similarly with the Mende: "Married persons constitute a definite and more senior category to those who are unmarried irrespective of the actual age of the latter." "In the old days, few men had the opportunity of obtaining a wife before they were 30, or even 35 years of age, and had proved their hardihood and diligence. Nowadays . . . a man has more opportunities to secure the amount of bridewealth through his own efforts and so achieve a wife while still in his early twenties."[27] In such circumstances the young have every reason to enter the mission school, European factory and mine.

SEGREGATION WITH HIGH STATUS

The societies which have shown themselves particularly resistant to change at least in the early phases of their contact with the culture of the West have commonly been those in which the young had a high and assured status and importance either through their close involvement in adult affairs or through segregated age-group institutions which exercised social, political, or military power. Segregated age-group organizations of this kind are to be found in tribes widely different in their political and social structures; and the precise functions of the age-groups are themselves extremely various. They are found in "segmentary tribes" without central governmental institutions—the Nuer, the Nandi, the Plains Indians, the Lango, and the Masai; they are found in centralized kingdoms like the Zulu and the Ashanti. The structure and the functions of the age-groups[28] vary: the age-range embraced, their internal subdivisions and organization, their political, educational, military or social activities and purposes. Thus the Nandi age-set[29] of young men has military significance, but the age-set system of the Nuer of the Sudan

26. E. E. Evans-Pritchard, *Witchcraft and Oracles Among the Azande* (1937), p. 16. "We shall find that social status intrudes into every phase of Azande life" (p. 14), but "it is unusually easy for the European to establish contact with them. . . . (they) are always ready to copy the behaviour of those they regard as their superiors in culture and to borrow new modes of dress, new weapons and utensils, new words, and even new ideas . . ." (p. 13).
27. K. L. Little, *The Mende of Sierra Leone* (1951), p. 140.
28. "Age-set" refers to persons who have been initiated during the successive annual ceremonies of a single initiation period; "age-group" refers more generally to any division of a population by age. Political duties may be allocated on the basis of age: the age-sets then pass through the successive age-grades of warrior and elder.
29. See G. W. B. Huntingford, *The Nandi of Kenya* (1953).

has neither a military nor a political purpose: it is a major determinant of social relationships and domestic behavior.[30] But in all cases initiation is associated with the legitimate entry into heterosexual relationships; membership of the age-group promotes status in the total community (as opposed to the family or other local group) and so functions as an integrative mechanism for the entire society. Although the anthropological evidence on change in these different tribes is often difficult to compare, and the ways of *measuring* social change so various as to make comparison particularly difficult, these societies do appear to have shown unusual persistence in their traditional ways even under considerable external pressure. Speaking of such societies Eisenstadt has observed: "The existing data fully warrant the assumption that no *structural* tendencies toward deviancy can be discerned in these age groups. . . ."[31]

The Nandi and the Nuer are both tribes whose conservatism has been fully attested and whose age-group organizations have been thoroughly and meticulously investigated and described. Nuer youths are initiated at the age of 14 to 16; they then jump "from the grade of boyhood to the grade of manhood, and the character of their social life is correspondingly transformed. . . ." "After initiation a lad takes on the full privileges and obligations of manhood in work, play, and war. Above all, he gives himself whole-heartedly to winning the favors of the maidens of the neighborhood."[32] Adult status is not dependent on marriage. Sons are married by seniority, and after one has married the family herd must reach its former strength before cattle are available for the marriage of the next. Thus a young man may not marry until his mid-twenties. In the meantime, however, he will have no problem of access to women.

Age-group membership, and particularly initiation, has been held to account more than anything else for the character and social attitudes of the Nuer: their sensitivity, pride and arrogance, their stubbornness and independence, their impatience of authority.[33] They have in the past shown no sense of inferiority in the presence of the white man, no inclination to adopt his institutions and way of life.

Similarly with the Nandi of Kenya. Proud and conservative, with a long history of resistance to British administration, they have been unwilling to change the customs, beliefs and outlook of their ancestors. Without chiefs or any form of central authority, the war-

---

30. See E. E. Evans-Pritchard, *The Nuer* (1940).
31. S. N. Eisenstadt, *From Generation to Generation* (1956), p. 280.
32. E. E. Evans-Pritchard, *Kinship and Marriage Among the Nuer* (1951), p. 51.
33. See E. E. Evans-Pritchard, *The Nuer* (1940).

rior age-set exercises great power. The age-range within an age-set might be 7 or 8 years. 10 to 15 years might elapse between the completion of one set and the opening of another. The initiates attain full adult status after a few months' seclusion; they have no need to wait until the completion of the 4-year initiation period. As warriors they can marry and make love to unmarried girls, they are responsible for military operations and enjoy wide social privileges. The younger boys' age-sets dance attendance on them, but they in their turn are assured of succession when power is formally handed over.[34]

The close connection between the power of the young and social stability is seen among the Commanche Indians when they moved from the Plateau to the Plains. In their earlier, inhospitable plateau environment they were a potentially unstable society. Dominated by the old, the young of very little account, the transformation of their culture has been described as a "striking lesson in social change."[35]

As a brigand tribe of the Plains, the young warriors on whom prosperity depended enjoyed a dominant social position; institutions evolved which promoted their cohesion and solidarity—wife-sharing, the equal distribution of spoils, the limited tenure of positions of leadership. "These men exercised no formal civil authority, but they possessed great power through prestige. In reality they managed the tribe." "Top rank in Comanche society was attained by the fine warrior. . . . When he was past the fighting age, his status declined quickly."[36]

Forcible change was eventually brought to the Comanche ("they were retired under government protection"[37]). But until this happened, they had a stability which has been attributed largely to the fact that "the individuals are not blocked in development, and the individual can contribute to the common good and participate in it according to his talents. It is a true democracy."[38]

Other societies have accorded less power to organized youth but, while they have retained the direction of affairs in the hands of the elders, they have nevertheless given to youth a sense of importance and social usefulness. Among the Nyakyusa of Tanganyika the unique institution of the age-village segregates young males from adult society from the age of 9 or 10. The original members of the age-village remain together throughout life. Although in their early

---

34. G. W. B. Huntingford, *The Nandi of Kenya* (1953).
35. Abram Kardiner, *The Psychological Frontiers of Society* (1945).
36. Ibid., pp. 55–56.
37. Ibid., p. 96.
38. Ibid., p. 423.

youth they are economically dependent on their fathers, whose fields they hoe, they have a sense of solidarity and power; they value good fellowship and cooperation; and although they are commoners, at least as they reach mature years they constitute a social and political force of which hereditary chiefs must take serious account.

The tension between the uprising and the mature generation is minimal. Inter-generation accusations of witchcraft are very rare.[39] Eisenstadt surprisingly includes the Nyakyusa among the "familistic societies" in which, "since these age groups arise as a result of strong tension between the generations, a somewhat stronger deviant potential is indicated."[40] If the Nyakyusa age-groups originated in strong inter-generation tension, they have proved a most effective social mechanism for reducing it.[41]

The Ngoni of Nyasaland also segregate their young males; and here the connection between the pride and sense of importance of young men on the one hand, and the society's conservatism on the other, is perhaps easier to see. It is true that the proud, hierarchical Ngoni, with their keen sense of social distinction and precedence, are changing: economic developments have been beyond their control, and "The economic foundations of political power and social prestige have been to a large extent undermined by the abolition of war and slavery and the exodus of men to the south for work in mines and on farms."[42] But change has for long been resisted. The initial reaction was one of "pronounced antipathy to European contact." The traditional values and customs have been overwhelmed rather than willingly surrendered. The ancient virtues of dignity, self-control and correct deportment are still valued and achieved in a changing social order.

Personal dignity and self-esteem are in large measure the outcome of life in the boys' dormitory, which young males enter at the

39. See Monica Wilson, *Good Company* (1951).
40. S. N. Eisenstadt, *From Generation to Generation* (1956), p. 249.
41. Cf. the argument that societies in which, because of child-rearing arrangements, young males are particularly hostile to their fathers and dependent on their mothers often resolve the conflict *either* through initiation ceremonies or through a change of residence for the boys at puberty. The Nuer, for example, are held to be an illustration of the former practice, the Nyakyusa of the latter: "change of residence serves the same functions that we have posited for initiation ceremonies, for example, by establishing male authority, breaking the bond with the mother, and ensuring acceptance of the male role." The absence of both initiation ceremonies and of residential change for adolescent males among the Tallensi, for example, is explained according to this theory by different methods of infant care, particularly the shorter period of exclusive mother-son sleeping arrangements. See J. W. M. Whiting, R. Kluckhohn and A. Anthony, "The Function of Male Initiation Ceremonies at Puberty," in E. E. Maccoby, T. M. Newcomb and E. L. Hartley (eds), *Readings in Social Psychology* (3rd ed. 1958).
42. Margaret Read, *Native Standards of Living and African Culture Change* (1938).

age of 6. Although the age-range in the dormitories was formerly very wide, spanning more than a dozen years, and internal distinctions of status were sharp, life in them promoted a sense of solidarity and high morale. The boys were not segregated in futile dependency: they had a valued contribution to make to the life and economy of the nation.

They were of sufficient importance to be allowed into the discussions of high affairs conducted by the senior men at the kraal gate; in caring for cattle they did a responsible job from which they gained a strong notion of their own importance. Although marriage among the Ngoni was formerly comparatively late—usually little short of 30 for men—adolescent and young adult males seem to have had no frustration or resentment against their elders. "The seeming absence of frustration and overt rebellion in the years just after puberty was due to the social recognition by relatives and by the village community of the new stage reached by boys and girls, and to the increasing responsibility required of them for carrying out allotted tasks and for preparing for their future careers."[43]

INTEGRATION WITH HIGH STATUS

Adolescents and young men may achieve a sense of high importance not from segregation in age-sets or looser age-groups associations which confer high status, power or privilege, but from close connection with the lives and affairs of adults. Eisenstadt suggests that this absence of age-group organization is a feature of those societies— often "segmentary" tribes—in which the kin group is a virtually self-sufficient social unit, in which the young can learn all the role dispositions necessary for adult life. Seniority may play an important part in the regulation of behavior, but the young have an integral role in the social order.

The Tallensi of northern Ghana, the Tikopia of Polynesia, and perhaps the Samoans, are examples of societies which are on the whole conservative and in which the young have importance through social integration. The young of Tikopia in the nineteen-twenties, although before puberty they generally went around in independent little bands, were early involved in the central concerns of the island's economy. "The child soon comes to take part in the work of the community, and so useful is it that a household without one is at a distinct loss. At first it goes out with a relative to the cultivations and intersperses its play with fetching and carrying things. Gradually most of the economic minutiae are allotted to it by its elders, including others than parents, and its performances,

---

43. Margaret Read, *Children of their Fathers* (1959), p. 170.

small in themselves, act as the emollient which allows the household machinery to run smoothly."[44] Although marriage was relatively late and the authority of elders respected, Firth found no evidence of revolt or deviation among the young, who found ample compensation in their way of life and accepted the social institutions in which they were increasingly involved—mourning obligations, affinal regulations, and duties to chiefs.

A quarter of a century later Firth found the Tikopia remarkably little changed in spite of their widening contacts with the outer world. In 1929 they had shown little inclination to go abroad to work for wages; by 1952 migrant labor was more common. But the influence of the West was incorporated into the existing social structure without appreciably changing it. "The reaction was one of incorporation—to keep the fabric of the culture intact while using in it as many foreign elements as possible. 'We, the Tikopia,' wished to remain the Tikopia."[45] Between 1929 and 1952 they had even "incorporated" the use of money, using the white man's currency for dealing with the white man, the traditional currency (bark-cloth) for transactions among themselves.

In spite of the continued efforts of Christian missionaries there was as much polygamy in 1952 as in 1929 (though the proportion of polygamous marriages was small at both dates). There was no change in the actual quantity of marriage: while there had been an increase of 33 per cent in spouses of all kinds, the population had grown by 35 per cent. Marriage was still relatively late, but the sex intrigues of young unmarrieds were still common form. The system of descent was little changed, and young men still choose their brides from a very limited geographical range: in 1952 as in 1929 one-sixth of all marriages took place between people of the same village. Although Firth senses the likelihood of imminent widespread social change, little had in fact occurred since the time of his original field-work in the twenties.

Another Polynesian people, the Samoans, accord their young a position in society similar to that in Tikopia; and while they have proved a flexible and adaptable society, like the Tikopians they incorporated Western influence without undergoing drastic social transformation. When Margaret Mead investigated their social life in the twenties, she found that the young were given tasks, according to their strength and abilities, which were functionally related to the work of the adult world. Marriage was neither a prerequisite

---

44. R. Firth, *We, the Tikopia* (1957 ed.), p. 150.
45. R. Firth, *Social Change in Tikopia* (1959), p. 46.

of fully adult status nor a necessary condition of sexual experience. Margaret Mead contrasted the Samoan condition with that often found in Pacific communities: "In many parts of the South Seas contact with white civilization has resulted in the complete degeneration of native life, the loss of native techniques and traditions, and the annihilation of the past. In Samoa this is not so."[46]

The Tallensi of Ghana provide a final example of the integration of the young and social stability and conservatism which seem to be closely associated with it. Although the Tallensi desire some of the material products of Western civilization, and are prepared, as migrant laborers, to work for them, they "still preserve the culture bequeathed to them by their forefathers and the social structure of their own, homogeneous society."[47]

The Tallensi are a "segmentary" and extremely egalitarian society, although they enjoin respect for age and seniority. But the young do not enter institutionalized age-groups with concerns distinct from those of their elders: "the social sphere of adult and child is unitary and undivided."[48] Children and adolescents share in the work of their elders as they are able; they have in consequence a sense of social purpose and importance, and of rights to which they are properly entitled. Young people learn their social and economic roles from close association with their parents or older siblings. "The child is from the beginning oriented towards the same reality as its parents. . . . The interests, motives and purposes of children are identical with those of adults, but at a simpler level of organization. Hence the children need not be coerced to take a share in economic and social activities. They are eager to do so."

The Tallensi have resisted fundamental changes in their social system. Even the returning laborer-migrants, bringing back foreign ideas and exotic information, "have made no appreciable impression on the native scheme of values and beliefs, or in their practical knowledge. . . . Though they are one of the influences modifying the strict letter of custom in minor respects, they are not a disintegrating ferment in the native social order."[49]

It is the contention of this chapter that such social resilience, conservatism and stability are directly causally related to the status and importance accorded to adolescents and young adults. There are

---

46. Margaret Mead, *Coming of Age in Samoa* (Pelican Books 1954), p. 216.
47. Meyer Fortes, *The Dynamics of Clanship among the Tallensi* (1945), p. 12.
48. Meyer Fortes, *Social and Psychological Aspects of Education in Taleland* (1938), p. 8.
49. Meyer Fortes, *The Dynamics of Clanship among the Tallensi* (1945), p. 12.

undoubtedly circumstances in which a society with "integrated" youth may succumb to, or even readily accept, profound social change. The Ovimbundu of Angola may be such a people. Childs has described how, from later childhood, boys and girls assume a definite role in the work of the adult community. A boy at this age may make his first trip with a trading caravan, and will help his father in the fields. From the period of later childhood an Ovimbundu is a responsible person: he assumes considerable, and growing, economic responsibility, and is accounted legally responsible for his actions.[50]

More recent studies have shown profound changes in Umbundu society. The position of the Ovimbundu as traders and their deep involvement in the economic life of Europeans may be important factors in "the very rapid social change"[51] that has occurred. But the change does not appear to be a vigorous and vital response to new opportunities: "The present Umbundu social system deprived of any form of public life ticks over, as a man who has been paralysed may continue to live."[52]

SEGREGATION WITH LOW STATUS

Segregated age-group institutions do not necessarily confer high status on the young or promise certain progress towards it. They may, on the contrary, signalize the rejection of the young from the central concerns of a society, underline their inferior standing, suggest their futility, and direct their attention to matters irrelevant to the major preoccupations of the adult world. Such age-groups will be potentially deviant or at least experimental in new social forms which may provide an escape from the blockages from which their members suffer.[53]

Among the Tiv of Nigeria age-mates formerly constituted a mutual aid society for (largely ineffectual) protection against their elders, particularly fathers and senior brothers. The latter possessed

---

50. See G. M. Childs, *Umbundu Kinship and Character* (1949).
51. A. C. Edwards, *The Ovimbundu under Two Sovereignties* (1962), p. 155.
52. Ibid., p. 160.
53. Eisenstadt has argued that such potentially deviant age-groups, which do not function as mechanisms of social integration, are likely to arise in "familistic societies": it is one of his major hypotheses that "Age groups tend to arise when the structure of the family or descent group blocks the younger members' opportunities for attaining social status within the family (a) because the older members block the younger ones' access to the facilities which are prerequisites of full adult roles, and/or (b) the sharpening of incest taboos and restrictions on sexual relations within the family unit postpones the younger members' attainment of sexual maturity": S. N. Eisenstadt, *From Generation to Generation* (1956), p. 248.

tsav by virtue of their age: supernatural power which ensured potency and skill, and was augmented by eating human flesh. The victim was provided by some other person, and the man who ate the flesh incurred a "flesh-debt" which could be discharged only by supplying a close relative as an exchange victim.

Elders rich in *tsav* were consequently a serious menace to their younger kin. They were also powerful through their control over their sons' possibilities of marriage. Fully adult status was impossible until a man was married; but marriage could take place only when his father (or older married brother) supplied him with one of his daughters to give in exchange for a bride. The institution of exchange marriage placed a young man's advance to adult status at the caprice of his elders.

The younger Tiv had always been noted for their willingness for social experimentation, but the possibilities for this in the traditional society were limited. In 1927 an edict of the colonial government forbade exchange marriage and at a blow opened the floodgates of social change. The edict was resisted by the old, since it undermined the very basis of their power. But the young accepted it with eagerness, "in fact these had been consulted and had been enthusiastically in its favor."[54] Change now "ramified in every aspect of the culture." Freed from the tyranny of the old, young men fortified their position by working for wages in railway developments and other European enterprises. Henceforth, "A man could get a wife through his own efforts, without waiting his turn, which depended on the priority of claims within the group, and without dependence on his father."

Still more dramatic was the social change among the Manus of New Guinea in the interval between Margaret Mead's original study of them in the nineteen-twenties and her return visit twenty-five years later. The sheer weight of the Western impact, particularly in the shape of the American Army, must be held largely responsible for the fact that the Manus are "a people who have moved faster than any people of whom we have records, a people who have moved in fifty years from darkest savagery to the twentieth century, men who have skipped over thousands of years of history in just the last twenty-five. . . ."[55]

A money economy has become established among the Manus, the clothing and calendar of the West, American-type marriage "for

---

54. See Margaret Mead (ed.), *Culture Patterns and Technical Change* (1953), pp. 114–143.
55. Margaret Mead, *New Lives for Old* (1956), p. 8.

love". Old "avoidances" (for example of mothers-in-law) have disappeared. But most significant of all, the position of the young in Manus society has changed, their importance has increased through Western education and more direct involvement in adult affairs. The sullen, aggressive, and brittle human relationships of the past seemed to have been generally superseded by easy and harmonious social intercourse.

Change had not been accepted with reluctance: "the great avidity with which they seized on new situations"[56] had been the striking feature of their response to the massive contact of the West. In their traditional society the young had constituted an outsider group: trained in physical skills, prudery and respect for property, they were otherwise left to their own devices. Manus society was characterized by the cultural non-participation of the young, marked cultural discontinuity between the generations. "There is no attempt to induct the child into this alien adult world," wrote Margaret Mead in 1928. "He is given no place in it and no responsibilities."[57] "Manus children live in a world of their own, a world from which adults are wilfully excluded, a world based on different premises from those of adult life."[58] The result was latent deviance and a marked predisposition to seek in a new way of life personal significance unattainable in the old.

REWARDS AND PENALTIES

Latent deviance is likely to become actual when the rewards of change are sufficiently attractive, when they promise a real solution to the status difficulties of the young. (If the high rewards for the new behavior continue, *further* change is likely to be impeded.) Similar educational techniques aimed specifically at fundamental culture-change will have widely different results if the social rewards of change are markedly different. It has commonly been observed that a new member of an organization, society, or nation learns the new behavior required of him more rapidly if he enjoys, or is promised, a position of high status; if his position is more lowly, although he is exposed to similar influences, he is more likely to cling to his former attitudes, values and customs. New recruits to the armed services, business institutions, neighborhoods, more readily

---

56. Ibid., p. 158.
57. Margaret Mead, *Growing up in New Guinea* (Pelican Books 1942), p. 78.
58. Ibid., p. 66.

learn the speech idioms, methods of deportment and characteristic modes of behavior, when they have success in the society's activities and are rewarded with enhanced prestige and formal standing. There is considerable evidence from American studies of immigrants that those who are rewarded with high status positions quickly become "acculturated"; those of lower occupational rank cling more tenaciously to their former style of life (and tend, where possible, to occupy the same residential areas). If social change is to be effectively promoted among immigrants, they must be offered suitable rewards in the new system. As an American sociologist has recently concluded: "If we are interested in acculturating immigrants to the United States, our social structure must be sufficiently open to offer them upward occupational mobility."[59]

One of the most striking contrasts in the history of social change is that between the response of the Dakota Indians and the Janissaries of the Ottoman Empire to essentially similar methods of (forcible) "re-education." The resounding success in the case of the latter and the dismal failure in the case of the former, are intelligible in terms of the social penalties and rewards attendant on the "new learning."

The remarkable educational institutions of the Ottoman Turks, in which Christian slaves, the "Tribute of Blood," were prepared for the work of defending, extending, and ruling the domains of their masters, are not only among the most spectacular, but the most successful, in the history of education. For at least two centuries after the Turks captured Constantinople in 1453, slaves taken from the "familistic" peasant societies of Greece, Albania, Serbia, Bosnia and Bulgaria, were successfully inducted into the Mohammedan culture which they triumphantly carried half way to Dover.

The sons of shepherds and herdsmen were taken from their Greek Orthodox homes and trained to rule an Islamic Empire. Every boy was aware that he was a potential Grand Vizier. "The Ottoman system deliberately took slaves and made them ministers of state. It took boys from the sheep-run and the plough-tail and made them courtiers and the husbands of princesses; it took young men whose

59. S. Alexander Weinstock, "Role Elements: A Link between Acculturation and Occupational Status," *British Journal of Sociology* (1963), p. 14. It is also the case that the role which goes with high occupational status spills over into wider areas of life, only marginally connected with work, than is commonly the case with a more lowly occupation. A wider area of life is necessarily changed for the immigrant corporation lawyer than for the doorman.

ancestors had borne the Christian name for centuries, and made
them rulers of the greatest Muhammedan states, and soldiers and
generals in invincible armies whose chief joy was to beat down the
Crown and elevate the Crescent."[60]

The Christians were not taken as young children but at or a little
before puberty, between the age of 10 and 14. They had learned one
way of life and must now learn another. They had every inducement
to do so. Their material needs were well cared for: the commanding
officer of a battalion was the "Soup Maker," the second-in-command
the "Head Water Carrier"; the regimental colors were the soup caul-
dron itself.

The majority were destined for a military career in which the
top command positions were open to them. A carefully selected
minority were embarked on a 14-year course of training and education, with rigorous weeding out along the route, for posts in the civil
administration. The best entered the Palace School of the Grand
Seraglio (there were usually some 300 pages, 600 during the reign of
Soleyman the Magnificent in the sixteenth century). Three auxiliary
schools (and later a fourth) each contained a similar number.

Those who passed with distinction through the first six or eight
years of the course entered upon more specialized training in the
Hall of the Expeditionary Force, the Hall of the Commissariat, the
Hall of the Treasury, or the Hall of the Bedchamber. The liberal arts,
the arts of government and of war, were the subjects studied under
notable scholars, mathematicians, and musicians who enjoyed royal
patronage. Though technically "slaves," and debarred from handing
on wealth or position to their children, they had social and political
eminence. Out of 60 Grand Viziers who have been traced in Turkish
history, 48 were trained at the Palace School (the remaining 12,
slaves also, started less promisingly in the artisan schools).[61]

Machiavelli and the Imperial Ambassador to Constantinople in
the mid-sixteenth century have left contemporary testimony to the
success of the system, to the stability and durability of a social and
political order which, in the high prestige and power which it gave

---

60. See H. H. Lybyer, *The Government of the Ottoman Empire at the Time of Soleyman the Magnificent* (1913). Cf. the sentimental and psychologically unreal version of H. A. L. Fisher, *A History of Europe* (1936), p. 402: "The Janissary was a
slave. The affections which sweeten the character, the interests which expand the
mind, the ideals which give elevation to the will, were denied him. An iron
discipline effaced the past and impoverished the future . . . he went forth to slay
the enemies of the Sultan and of Allah with the inflamed and contracted fanaticism of a monk."
61. See Barnette Miller, *The Palace School of Muhammad the Conqueror* (1941),
pp. 6–7.

to young warriors and administrators, albeit of alien origin, had a built-in safeguard against deviation. (It was only with the establishment of hereditary offices in the civil and military hierarchies that the system failed to work effectively after the seventeenth century. The revolutionary "Young Turks" of the twentieth century were the outcome of an increasingly closed and rigid social system.)

Machiavelli had offered no hope of internal support to the would-be invader of the Turkish state. He could not "expect his enterprise to be aided by the defection of those whom the sovereign has around him. ... Whosoever, therefore, attacks the Turk must reckon on finding a united people. ..." Attacks against the kingdoms of Western Europe were much more hopeful "since you will always find in them men who are discontented and desirous of change. ..."[62]

Busbecq, who was Imperial Ambassador to Constantinople intermittently between 1555 and 1562, analyzed this stability and high morale in greater detail:

> No distinction is attached to birth among the Turks; the deference to be paid to a man is measured by the position he holds in the public service ... honors, high posts and judgeships are the rewards of great ability and good service. If a man be dishonest, or lazy, or careless, he remains at the bottom of the ladder, an object of contempt, for such qualities there are no honors in Turkey. This is the reason that they are successful in their undertakings, that they lord it over others, and are daily extending the bounds of their empire. These are not our (European) ideas; with us there is no opening left for merit; birth is the standard for everything; the prestige of birth is the sole key to advancement in the public service.[63]

The Federal authorities of America attempted, in the later-nineteenth and early-twentieth centuries, to induct the youth of the Indian tribes into the culture of white America. Their methods— enforced and prolonged schooling of the young away from their parents, an "immensely thoughtful and costly experiment in federal Indian education"[64]—nowhere met with the resounding success of the remarkably similar institutions of the Ottoman Turks, and often with pathetic failure. This was not because the American soldiers, administrators, and educators lacked the thoroughness, ruthlessness, resources or pedagogical skills of the Turks in the days of Soleyman the Magnificent. The Indian children had learned one culture; they refused to learn another. Whereas the Turks offered boundless social

---

62. N. Machiavelli, *The Prince,* trans. N. H. Thomson (1913), Bk. 4, pp. 24–25.
63. Quoted C. T. Forster and F. H. B. Daniell, *The Life and Letters of Ogier Ghiselin de Busbecq* (1881), vol. 1, pp. 152–155.
64. Erik H. Erikson, *Childhood and Society* (1951), p. 98.

rewards for social change and new learning, the Americans offered not top command posts in the army, civil administration, and business corporations; but only life as marginal men and second-class citizens on the reserves.

There were some tribes for whom even this was an escape from the social blockages and frustrations of the indigenous order. Thus the Makah, formerly characterized by rigid social stratification, were more successfully assimilated than most: as fishermen they found rewards in the prosperity of wider American markets. And re-education was ruthless: "Parents who refused to send their children to school were imprisoned until they saw the uselessness of refusal."[65] But a similar technique and equal ruthlessness left the once vigorous and self-confident Dakota only apathetic, listlessly discarding the new values and customs they were taught.

The proud and virile Dakota had hunted buffalo across the prairie: an egalitarian society, "a hunter democracy, levelling every potential dictator and every potential capitalist."[66] The young male was accorded prestige and importance. "Every educational device was used (by the Dakota) to develop in the boy a maximum of self-confidence. . . . He was to become a hunter after game, woman and spirit." In his upbringing, emphasis was placed on "his right to autonomy and on his duty of initiative."[67] The federal authorities aimed to bring about change to the American way of life through systematic teaching. "Children were virtually kidnapped to force them into government schools, their hair was cut and their Indian clothes thrown away. They were forbidden to speak in their own language. . . . Parents who objected were also jailed. Where possible, children were kept in school year after year to avoid the influence of their families."[68] These measures failed. The American cowboy culture was an inadequate recompense for the best of a vanished tribal life.

THE BEST OF BOTH WORLDS

Poised between the old world and the new, the young in non-literate tribal societies have often been able to use the new world to perpetuate the old. Savings from wages earned as migrant laborers have enabled them to return to their traditional societies not to change them, but to secure with their wealth a valued status within the

65. Elizabeth Colson, *The Makah Indians* (1953), p. 20.
66. E. H. Erikson, p. 101.
67. Ibid., p. 128.
68. See G. MacGregor, *Warriors Without Weapons* (1946).

traditional framework. They have a sociological significance not un-like that of the eighteenth-century nabobs who returned from India to buy positions in English society which, in the majority of cases, could not have been theirs if they had remained at home. Far from aiming to transform the society to which they returned after exotic experiences abroad, they attained significance precisely by support-ing the social structure which gave them the chance to buy a place in the squirearchy, the exclusive clubs, and the most expensive and exclusive of them all, the House of Commons.

Inevitably the enriched tribesman changes his society to some extent when he returns. He belongs to a class of *nouveaux riches* which threatens established political and social authorities. He en-joys independence of paternal (and avuncular) authority. And yet if such men desire status in terms of the social order in which they grew up, they will seek to preserve it, to minimize the effect that they themselves have upon it. There is no gain in buying one's way into an aristocracy which has been undermined and is in a state of decay.

Young men of the Tonga tribe on the shores of Lake Nyasa regard it as normal to spend some part of their early lives working in the Rhodesias or South Africa. "Young men consider their stay in the village, before they go off to the towns, as a period of marking time."[69] But even while they are away, they maneuver for office and position within the traditional social structure. They are concerned to maintain the traditional values and social order, and "when they return from an urban life abroad they settle again in the pattern of Tonga life which is still dominated by traditional values. There are no obvious signs of social disorganization and the Tonga still hold together as a tribal unit distinct from other such units around them."

Similarly with the Tikopia and the Tallensi. The young men of Tikopia who go abroad to work retain their rights and interests in the homeland. Though clearly they are a potential threat to estab-lished authorities when they return with comparative wealth, they seek not to overthrow traditional authorities but to enter into alli-ance with them. By the late nineteen-thirties the young men of Taleland were also leaving home in large numbers to work else-where for wages. But "labor migrants remain strongly attached to their families and natal settlements, and it is always assumed that they will eventually return ... and when they do return they resume the traditional way of life."[70]

69. See J. Van Velsen, "Labour Migration as a Positive Factor in the Continuity of Tonga Tribal Society," in A. Southall, *Social Change in Modern Africa* (1961).
70. Meyer Fortes, *The Dynamics of Clanship Among the Tallensi* (1945), p. 11.

The *nouveaux riches* among the Ngoni have used the wealth they earned in European work to buy social status in traditional terms. They have converted cash into cows. If they were formerly cultivators, without cattle, the mere possession of cows will not in itself bring high social status. "But if he goes with due deference to the older men who own cattle to ask for advice and technical help about building his kraal and breeding in his herd, in course of time they will include him in their discussions about cattle when they sit in the men's talking place."[71] But what he cannot do for himself he can do for his sons. His cattle can secure them well-connected brides, and his grandchildren at least will be assured of the highest social standing through the dignity of birth on the mother's side. Social change is impeded by contact with the West.

In all these instances young men had a position of some importance or significance even in the "pre-contact" social order; they were not potential deviants looking for an escape from their frustrations in the opportunities of a new civilization. The new civilization has enabled them to become even more important in traditional terms; they are even less inclined to deviate from old standards, customs and values. It may be one of the ironies of the human condition that any society must choose between social conservatism and rigidity, or the oppression of its young.

---

71. Margaret Read, *Native Standards of Living and African Cultural Change* (1938), p. 32.

An understanding of the psychological factors in normal adolescent development requires first, a knowledge of family relationships in early childhood, and second, a grasp of the pattern developed in preadolescence to cope with a return of childhood conflicts. Adolescence itself is divided into two phases. Early adolescence is characterized by the experience of strong erotic and aggressive forces. Late adolescence is concerned with the ability to control and regulate one's behavior. Separation from parents, a capacity for love, and a commitment to work mark the resolution of this period of life.

ALVIN E. WINDER

Normal Adolescence: Psychological Factors

The study of human behavior at any developmental level involves an understanding of the complexity of interactions between the biological aspects of development, the general cultural aspects of the environment, and psychological factors. A mathematics of personality has yet to be devised that makes it possible to treat these interactions as they occur in life, that is, as parallel forces acting simultaneously on the individual. It is necessary, until such a system is devised, to deal with each aspect separately. After the appropriate studies have produced information and insights about the effects of each of these separate forces, the diverse data must be integrated so that we can then better understand the totality of forces acting upon an individual at any given time in his development.

In the present essay, the focus is on the psychological factors that influence human development in the adolescent years. The author defines these psychological factors as the dynamics of the internal (intrapsychic) functioning of the adolescent and his closer relationships with people. Parents are the people of greatest importance to the teenager at the beginning of the period; subsequently, his peers become more important. This circle of influence widens as he moves towards adulthood and becomes subject to direct and indirect influence of others—teachers, employers, and acquaintances from geographically and even culturally different areas.

The primary elements entering into the intrapsychic dynamics are: the forces and demands of the sexual and aggressive drives (the id); the mediating part of the personality that utilizes intellectual language and other human capacities in the task of both maintaining psychological equilibrium and coping with demands from the self and from the external world (the ego); the individual's own value system which embodies concepts of right and wrong, moral imperatives, and ideals (the superego). The content in adolescence of id, ego, and superego and how they function together in relation to the external world depends upon his earlier childhood development. This past history has provided the individual with certain characteristic ways of managing himself and of relating to others and with certain underlying conflicts.

The ease or difficulty with which the individual passes through the adolescent stage of development is determined by his past experience in childhood and by his underlying conflicts which will become revived in adolescence. Before discussing adolescence proper, it is therefore necessary to review those aspects of childhood —and preadolescent—development which are specifically relevant to an understanding of adolescent experience.

CHILDHOOD EXPERIENCE

The closest relationship for children of both sexes in infancy and early childhood is with their mother. The mother generally provides the early nurturing experiences, thereby setting the stage for a sense of interpersonal trust to develop in the infant. As the first experience of socialization, this prepares the ground for the earliest sense of self to develop within the child.

The nature of the nurturing experience in the first year of life is such that mother can never be present to satisfy every demand, with the result that some dissatisfaction and mistrust of the mother is an inevitable component of the infant's personality at the end of the first year of life. Socialization, the major task of the child's second year, requires that mother enforce her demands through disciplining her offspring. It is, therefore, inevitable that the child will sometimes feel frustrated by his mother in both these experiences and that he will develop mixed feelings towards her. These ambivalent feelings of love and resentment play an important role in child development since they mean that the child brings some suspicion and mistrust—and even some rebellion against authority—to all relationships.

When children are about three years old they become inquisitive about the fact that males have a penis and females do not. Both sexes, even though told otherwise, fantasize that the girl is lacking a penis for reasons having to do with injury, punishment, or not being sufficiently loved by the mother. Out of these fantasies both sexes develop what Freud has described as castration anxiety. The problem of castration anxiety is handled differently by each sex. The girl may deny she does not have a penis or, if she accepts the fact, she will for a time become preoccupied with its absence. The girl, having already experienced ambivalent feelings towards her mother, now tends to project blame on the maternal figure for denying her a penis. She then, as a consequence of this feeling of resentment, turns towards her father as the primary object of her love. She is now in the Oedipal phase of development which is characterized by strong feelings both sexual and affectionate towards her father and jealous and rivalrous towards her mother.

The boy faces an equally serious problem: the penis, though present, may be lost. A boy may respond by becoming fearful of roughhouse games and physical injury, or he may defy his fear and plunge into activities that may be daring and dangerous. By the age of four, he has entered his phase of the Oedipus conflict, with sexual and affectionate feelings directed towards his mother and feelings of rivalry directed towards his father.

Normal development results in both the boy and girl giving up the close erotic relationship to the parent of the opposite sex and replacing it with a desexualized attitude of tenderness and affection.

Both rivalrous and ambivalent attitudes and feelings towards the parent of the same sex are repressed. These repressed urges are now replaced by the child's identification with that parent, the boy with his father and the girl with her mother. This repression and identification is the crucial step leading to the attainment of an appropriate and clearly defined sexual identity. The meaning of this sexual identity for both sexes has been clearly expressed by Erikson:

> The ambulatory and infantile genital stage adds to the inventory of basic social modalities in both sexes that of "making" in the sense of "being on the make." The word suggests head-on attack enjoyment of competition, insistence on goal, pleasure of conquest. In the boy the emphasis remains on "making" by phallic-intrusive modes; in the girl it sooner or later changes to "making" by teasing and provoking or by milder forms of "snaring," i.e., by making herself attractive and endearing. The child thus develops the prerequisites for initiative, i.e., for the selection of goals and perseverance in approaching them.[1]

The resolution of the Oedipal conflict and identification with the parent of the same sex marks the beginning of the latency period.

1. Erik H. Erikson, *Childhood and Society* (New York: Norton, 1950), p. 86.

Both sexes have now subordinated their "making" behavior—the intrusiveness of the boy and the provocativeness of the girl—for the dominant social mode of initiative; that is, the child enters the world of childhood with a sense of sharing and performance. He is now ready to combine with other children for the purpose of learning and planning, and is prepared to profit from association with the community of adults outside the immediate family. This period of time extends from the youngster's entry into school at about age six until the end of the fifth grade when the child should be in his eleventh year.

PREADOLESCENCE

Adolescence begins with puberty. The onset for girls coincides with the beginning of menstruation which generally occurs between age eleven and age thirteen. The onset for boys can be marked at the start of ejaculation which takes place usually between age thirteen and age fifteen. Changes in endocrine balance take place prior to these occurrences. These changes, which have been going on since age eight or nine, result in vague bodily sensations and emotional stirrings. Preadolescents tend to be particularly interested in and conflicted about sex. Parents and society both approach the problem of puberty with ambivalence. On the one hand, society condemns sexual pleasure, while on the other there is considerable exposure of children to sexuality through magazines, movies, and television. Both parents and schools, even schools with sex-education programs, communicate this ambivalence to the children.

The preadolescent greets information with a mixture of eagerness and apprehension. Information often cannot be assimilated by the youngster as he tries to deal with the cultural double standard. He vacillates between denial of interest in the subject and exploration of it through the secrecy of the preadolescent peer group. There he speculates about the sexual experiences of adolescence and adulthood. These speculations contain an admixture of reality and distortions handed down by older teenagers, books, and jokes.

The preadolescent boy is likely to be uneasy in the company of girls. The comradeship of boys is both safe and reassuring; when on the other hand he responds to girls who are already developing interest in him, it is usually with teasing and aggressive behavior. Girls tend to be forward in their desire to gain the attention of their male agemates. This tomboy behavior, which is quite common in preadolescent girls, seems to be a return of the Oedipal envy of the male and is reflected in aggressive behavior that suggests a denial of femininity.

The revival of childhood conflicts is the single most characteristic aspect of the approach of puberty. The major conflict that threatens to surface into awareness in both sexes is the struggle between the desire to be once again dependent upon mother and the wish for independence. The revival of these conflicts announce themselves in a variety of possible behavioral manifestations. These usually take the form of behaviors designed to relieve anxiety or release tension. Some youngsters manifest vastly increased energy but experience difficulty in directing it into useful channels. Others show a great increase in appetite, which may have its roots in both anxiety and hormonal change.

A third common form of behavior is regressive and is characterized by disorderliness, dirtiness, stubbornness, unruliness, and disobedience.

Children differ in their attempts to deal with these preadolescent strivings. The coping pattern that is most fraught with danger for later adjustment is that of denial. These youngsters cling to the adaptive patterns of latency in hopes of postponing and denying the imminence of change. Some youngsters regress, exhibiting rebellious behavior characteristic of their struggle for autonomy which occurred at a much earlier age.

Many children appear ready for puberty and make the transition with a minimum of the behavioral manifestations just described. Occasionally youngsters exhibit a pseudo-maturity and a flight into heterosexuality suggesting an attempt to solve conflicts with the parents by embracing a mature independence for which they are chronologically ill prepared.

ADOLESCENCE: SOME INTRODUCTORY REMARKS

The psychological changes accompanying adolescence can be more easily understood if it is divided into two separate developmental levels. The first of these, early adolescence, is initiated by an increase in the strength of instinctual forces. The onset of puberty is accompanied by the experience of strong erotic and aggressive impulses which appear without the aim of conscious effort to call them forth and seem to demand expression, much to the chagrin of the individual. A boy may find that he has to deal with highly erotic fantasies involving his sister or his mother. In view of the fact that his ego is continually threatened and sometimes temporarily overwhelmed, it is with great difficulty that he manages to keep these fantasies from expression and even detection. In order to reestablish equilibrium and exercise control over his impulses, he must expend excessive energy. As a result of this need to reestablish a balance, the youngster may become rigid in his behavior, lack spontaneity, and even inhibit his intellectual endeavors. Junior high school teachers are well aware of the seventh- or eighth-grade slump, the inattention, disciplinary difficulties, and seeming lack of motivation in this age group.

The first level of adolescence usually ends in the middle teens. The age fifteen to sixteen represents the transitional period between early and late adolescence. It is in the second phase that the balance shifts from the instincts to the capacity to control and regulate one's behavior.

A unique characteristic of adolescence that clearly distinguishes it from adult behavior is the recurrent alternation of periods of disturbed behavior with periods of relative quiet. These disturbances, which usually involve rebellion and experimentation, frequently cause consternation among parents and the community who expect the now adult-sized teenager to act in accordance with his stature. Sometimes these disturbances represent the overwhelming of ego control by the instincts. At other times they indicate attempts to express and consolidate new controls and coping methods. During the periods of calm that follow these episodes, the adolescent has the opportunity to think over what has happened and to ponder consequences—both successes and failures. If parents and community are understanding enough to support him through this period, he will discard unsuccessful behavior and gain additional ego strength through mastery of the situation.

Although the emphasis here is that much teenage behavior should be viewed as characteristic of attempts to master adolescent conflicts, the adolescent struggle may be resolved by pathological means. A major concern is with the individual who passes through these years with a minimum of storm and stress. Such individuals are often considered by adults as ideal models of behavior. They have not, however, experienced the constructive changes of adolescence, nor have they worked through the creative handling and expression of id impulses. Later, though adult in years, they remain emotionally immature. A few turn into the psychopathic killers about whom neighbors tell the media: "He was such a nice, quiet young man!"

Some individuals experience adolescence over a longer period of time. The protraction of adolescence may extend for a few years or longer. For them adolescence has become "a way of life."

The most serious problem occurs with those teenagers for whom adolescence cannot be bridged without the emergence of serious symptoms that can successfully block the way to a successful resolution of adolescent problems. These symptoms include chronic depression and schizophrenia.

EARLY ADOLESCENCE

As has been mentioned earlier, adolescence begins with puberty and is manifested psychologically by an increase in erotic and aggressive drives. Repressed sexual interests in the parents and repressed incestuous wishes and fantasies begin to force their way into awareness. The awareness of these impulses is too painful to tolerate and necessitates the utilization of a number of ego defenses to block or transform them. Attitudes towards parents vary from being loving and childishly dependent to finding them uncongenial and dangerous. A youngster may disappear for long periods of time or erupt into churlishness and become very difficult to live with.

Sooner or later the adolescent seeks to solve this conflict by a partial withdrawal from the emotional relationship with his parents. While this step towards resolution of this conflict is a necessary stride towards adulthood, it nevertheless causes a great deal of anguish to the young teenager. Less dependence on his parents also means less acceptance of their emotional support. Movement away from his parents means a decrease in the influence on him of their current attitudes and values as well as a decrease in those attitudes and values he internalized through his childhood identification with them. The consequence is that at the time the young person is most in need of the support of his parents he can accept it least. The entire situation results in his feeling both insecure and confused.

The loosening of these old ties has, however, some salubrious effects. First, attitudes and values formed in childhood can now be reevaluated. Secondly, childhood defenses and adaptive patterns can now be tested against the reality of growing up, and when necessary, revised. Children, for example, are inclined to take their parents' judgments about whom to befriend and whom to reject, and act on these evaluations as if they were their own. Young teenagers begin to question these judgments, not only voicing critical statements about parents' selections, but also striking up relationships that parents find unsuitable for them. This courting of unacceptable relationships may create much anxious concern for parents; for the adolescent, it provides an opportunity to weigh and test out attitudes that he previously accepted without question. Another example of this weighing and testing of reality, and one for which parents seem totally unprepared, is the teenager's criticism of both their political ideology and their life style.

It is important to note here that the teenager's turning away from his parents leaves him with feelings of sadness, irritability, and lack of energy that normally constitute reactions to mourning the loss of a loved person. He is in fact mourning the loss of the internalized parental image. The parents, of course, are still present—with the result that the cause of the depression is obscure to both parents and adolescent. The parents, for want of a better word, label their child as moody.

Moody, confused, and unable to turn to his parents for support, the young adolescent sometimes reacts to this situation with fear that he is going crazy. In need of supportive relationships, he turns outside the family towards other adults who can help him decide limits on his behavior, offer him guidance, and provide identification figures. He forms transient relationships with junior high school teachers and coaches and with camp counselors. These are trial identities and are very important to the growth of the teenager. Each of these identities, as they provide new behavior patterns, further develop the uniqueness of the individual.

Some of these new modes of behavior seem acceptable to the young adolescent, are integrated into his personality, and provide for future motivations, values, and attitudes. Even though these relationships with adults are a necessary part of growing up, they are potentially too overwhelming to be lasting. The adolescent cannot yet allow his tentative and yet weak self to be overwhelmed by the stronger more firmly fixed identity of the adult. These new relationships are often as quickly forsaken as they were originally created.

Distance from parents is maintained by a constant disagreement with almost all they do and say. Obedience to parental wishes is completely at odds with the development of individuality. Some adolescents, usually with parental understanding, rebel and are able to move easily towards independence. For many the withdrawal involves great difficulty and they go through a period remaining tied and dependent—meanwhile creating the illusion of independence by behaving negativistically and frequently seeming sullen and quick to anger, although at times their behavior is pleasant and cooperative.

While transient adult relationships help cushion the adolescent's breakaway from his parents, their importance in providing for this function is greatly overshadowed by the adolescent peer group. The peer group provides him with both a sense of belonging and a feeling of strength and power. America in the 1970s with its greatly expanded means of communication and transportation has unified peer group language, customs, music, social institutions, and philosophies to the extent that peer group attitudes now reflect the traits of a broader youth culture.

Peer group acceptance requires that the young exhibit a high degree of conformity to the structures of the youth culture. Two major phenomena of the youth culture will serve as examples of the needs that they fulfill. These are music and dancing. Each provides a means of expressing sexual and aggressive urges in symbolic form. The primitive beat of hard rock music and the gyrations of the performers are sexual and stimulating. Early in the seventies, the Rolling Stones were established as the most popular group on both sides of the Atlantic. Don Heckman, rock music critic for the New York Times, describes Mick Jagger in a recent Stones concert.

> As the ball bounces away from Jagger, he looks out at the audience, purses his lips into a sneer, and starts into his patented heel-and-toe boogie step. He wears a shirt-tight white jump suit, the shirt open in a deep gash to the waist. His pants are tailored of a silk-like material that clings so tightly that his genitalia are pushed up and out—a sexual display as aggressively protuberant as a fifties teenage girl in a pointy bra.[2]

Lyrics, performance, and beat coalesce to provide the teenage audience with images of violence and sexuality. A typical and highly electric sharing of performer and audience fantasies of violence is noted in Heckman's description of the Stones' very popular "Midnight Rambler":

> Keith Richard sways through a long threateningly erotic guitar introduction as Mick slowly removes a bright gold sash. On the first line, "You've heard about the Boston Strangler" the lights suddenly dip and Jagger is outlined in a deep red floodlight. He slinks around the stage, a slim-hipped multi-sexual reincarnation of Jack the Ripper.

Although for the young teenager dancing offers an incomplete discharge of sexual tension, it provides a means of expressing more specific sexual and aggressive urges both symbolically and in action. Many current dances have an openly erotic quality. The rolling of the pelvis, the thrusting of the hips and the undulating thigh movements are openly sexual. The rules of the dance, however, offer a built-in protection for the young adolescent. These rules require that the dancers rarely touch and never embrace each other. In this way,

---

2. Don Heckman, "As Cynthia Sagittarius Says—'Feeling . . . I mean isn't this what the Rolling Stones are all about?' " *New York Times* (Magazine, July 16, 1972).

while sexual urges can be expressed and intercourse symbolically enacted, the participants are protected from closer physical contact.[3]

Early adolescence is a period of rapid growth and major hormonal changes. As a result of this the youngster must be prepared to accept both a vastly changed physical self and a new self-image. The girl must accept and integrate the changes resulting in menstruation, breast development, and the broadening of her hips. The boy must integrate voice change, hair growth, and a considerable increase in size and physical strength. These changes in both sexes provide for an acceptance of femininity in the girl and masculinity in the boy. Sexual role, however, seems to be in a state of redefinition in American culture. The unisexual dress habits of the young adolescent would seem to reflect their confusion about how to fit the biological changes accompanying puberty with a gender determined self-image consonant with the gender definitions provided by the culture.

A major task for the young adolescent is that of achieving a healthy relationship with a member of the opposite sex. Puberty brings with it a consuming interest in things sexual. Youngsters evince an intense curiosity and avid pursuit of sexual information. Conversations between adolescents may be openly sexual and long hours may be spent on the telephone disseminating peer group gossip and exploring encounters with the opposite sex. Young people are preoccupied, more frequently than adult society would care to admit, with heterosexual daydreams and masturbatory fantasies.

First approaches between the sexes are marked by apprehension. They consist of bantering and teasing which turns to hostility if the threat of closeness becomes too great. Playful roughhousing offers expression to physical sexual urges. Not all youngsters are ready for even this limited and tentative contact. Some find it less threatening to remain for a time in latency while denying sexual feelings and desires. Frequently they defend against these promptings by plunging into intellectual interests while denying the existence of their emotional responses. At the opposite extreme, some girls behave in a manner described as "boy crazy" as if they were embracing sexuality as a means of overcoming their fears and doubts.

Dating should normally occur towards the end of early adolescence between fifteen and sixteen in girls and a year or so later in

---

3. Ironically, the exact opposite was the case in much dancing during the early adolescence of the parents of today's young teenagers in the 1930s and 1940s; embraces were often so close as to become clearly sexual—"dryhumping" in the phrase of novelist James T. Farrell.

boys. Relationships between the sexes, at this time, are still more physical than emotional. This is not to say that coitus is common during this period, but rather that the participants are still learning the meaning of their sexual role and their acceptability to the opposite sex.

LATE ADOLESCENCE

Prior to the middle of the nineteenth century, children even in industrial countries moved rapidly from childhood to adulthood— assuming the responsibilities and prerogatives of adults as early as age fourteen. In the United States, the establishment of compulsory education and child-labor laws produced a lengthening of this period between childhood and adulthood. Thus adolescence as a developmental level came into being.

The twentieth century witnessed a continuation of this lengthening process. A culture relying upon increasing technological skill of its members requires a long period of educational apprenticeship for the practice of these skills. The continued development and use of automation threatens to result in a further shrinking of the labor force, and it becomes good economics to keep young people off the labor market until their early twenties. The result of these two influences has been to further extend this period between childhood and adulthood, from the middle to the late teens, and in some cases even into the early twenties. In order to comprehend present realities, it is necessary to look into the problems and concerns of the second period of adolescence.

The major task of late adolescence is identity-seeking. Erikson defines identity as: "The capacity to see one's self as having continuity and sameness. It is consistent with the organization of experience."[4]

The background for this search for a new and unique identity is prepared during the phase of early adolescence. During this time there has occurred a definite loosening of ties to the parents and an intense preoccupation with self. This loosening of ties to internalized parental values is replaced with an outwardly directed concern with cultural values and ideologies.

Parents and society are now viewed with a new objectivity; their failings and hypocrisies seem to stand out with clarity, while solutions to social problems seem clear and self-evident. Parents and other adults are measured against strict moral values, their words

---

4. Erik H. Erikson, *Childhood and Society* (New York: W. W. Norton, 1950).

are compared with their deeds, and the accusation, "you say one thing and do another," is often made. The teenager alternates moods of cynicism with ones of idealism. He is much concerned with the gulf between appearance and reality in both adult behavior and his own thinking.

The adolescent's major question in his search for new human models with whom to identify is: "What do these individuals stand for?" The selection of meaningful individuals takes place within the structure of the society he knows. He, therefore, looks for them within the school and the work situation, and in groups that provide for a religious or ideological fellowship. The representatives of the adult world that are available for selection need to represent one or more of the following values: they must have a technical competence, a mastery of a method of scientific inquiry, an ability to articulate a convincing truth, a strong sense of justice and fairness, a standard of artistic truth or a personal authenticity.

For the individual youngster the commitment both to an ideal and an ideal person helps to fill the void resulting from an increasing independence from his parents. This person is a substitute to fill the void, a substitute who is uncontaminated by the incestful wishes and guilts that were part of the child's relationship with his parents.

The relationship to this representative adult and what he stands for is easier to sustain when, as is frequently the case, it is supported by one's peers. Important for many young idealists is the fact that there are other young people who share their outlook. The group they form together around the adult and his cause is a group in which belonging is not primarily based upon mutual personal interest, but upon mutual interest in an ideal and its human representative.

Part of this search for people and causes to which youth can commit themselves is the choosing of a future occupation. Among the many determinants of occupational choice, there are: parental identifications made in childhood; capacity to appraise one's talents and abilities; the effects of residual conflicts of childhood; and the willingness of society through social and economic rewards to confirm one's preferred choice. These factors may coalesce for the young person in the personalities of several representative adults who help him to understand and develop his capacities and who through their example offer him a view of working in the world with which he can identify and, therefore, emulate.

The task of seeking and finding one's sexual identity begins at puberty. Its further exploration and development awaits the period of late adolescence. Falling in love begins now to involve a feeling of intense concern with one's beloved. Where in early adolescence the relationship between the sexes was restricted to erotic explora-tion, now a quality of tender affection between the partners makes its appearance alongside of sexual feelings. Sexual experiences which were previously self-centered now become shared.

The development of intimacy involving both tender and erotic feelings between young men and women in their late teens raises the question of sexual intercourse. Should it be acceptable for adoles-cents at an appropriate age to engage in coitus and does such an experience foster healthy psychological development? The tradi-tional morality holds that the delay of sexual experience is necessary for full social development, that sexual intercourse is an activity of adulthood and to engage in it prior to that time is not conducive to emotional stability or psychological growth. Furthermore, most youngsters have internalized society's prohibitions against pre-marital sex and they will react with guilt and internal conflicts when they defy these prohibitions.

On the other hand, the new morality stresses that the sexual mores are outdated, that medical science can prevent accidental and unwanted pregnancy and provide protection from and treatment of venereal disease. With these fears set aside, the new morality takes as its positive credo that physical sex should occur only after love and friendship have developed. A final argument is that the choice of a marital partner can be much more intelligently made if the sexual factor has been previously evaluated from the standpoint of personal experience.

Our culture seems to be moving towards a greater acceptance of some kinds of sexual experience between late adolescents. The major consideration in a period of transition involves the individual's read-iness, based upon his life history, to accept whichever view is most compatible with his individual maturity.

THE RESOLUTION OF ADOLESCENCE

American culture is moving rapidly to lower that age at which one receives adult prerogatives. The voting age was lowered to eighteen at the beginning of the 1970s, and many states are moving to estab-lish eighteen as the age at which one legally assumes adult status. The boundary, however, between adolescence and adulthood is most fluid. While the adolescent wants to assume adult prerogatives and use them responsibly and judiciously, he may feel that his indepen-dence and identity are not secure enough for him to function as an adult. He vacillates between being responsible and altruistic on the one hand, and self-centered and autonomous on the other. His expression of autonomy is characterized by parents as an aloofness which serves to defend him as much against his own dependency wishes as against the influence of adults. This defensiveness reveals that he has not yet successfully accomplished the task of separation from his parents. His status is still one of rebellion rather than of independence.

A continued narcissistic preoccupation with self suggests that the search for identity is still incomplete. In this case the adolescent is prone to use his recently received adult prerogatives as a means of self-exploration rather than in terms of their appropriate functions. Alcohol and marijuana are used not to achieve relaxation but to explore the parameters of self. Drug-induced "highs" can be used in an attempt to deal with internal conflicts. Vehicles may be used not primarily for transportation, but for the purposes of independence of parents, of defiance, and of escape and freedom from restraint. The car or motorcycle may represent the human body and the continual fixing and readjusting may symbolize the desire to improve one's self. Political independence may represent an opportunity not to participate responsibly in the political process, but rather to press for rebellion against all adult values—thereby asserting one's pseudo-independence of all parental values.

The resolution of adolescence is neatly summed up by the report of the GAP Committee on Adolescence in their paper on Normal Adolescence. They state that "the resolution of adolescence is characterized by: (1) the attainment of separation and independence from the parents; (2) the establishment of sexual identity; (3) the commitment to work; (4) the development of a personal moral value system; (5) the capacity for lasting relationships and for both tender and genital sexual love in heterosexual relationships; and (6) a return to the parents in a new relationship based upon a relative equality."[5]

---

5. Group for the Advancement of Psychiatry, Committee on Adolescence, *Normal Adolescence* (GAP Report No. 68), pp. 829–830.

Fidelity, Diversity, and Identity are the three concepts that Erik H. Erikson, the noted student of human behavior, brings to an understanding of youth. He sees the adolescent's search for identity as at bottom a search for something to which he can fully commit himself. Through analyses of the youthful tragic hero, Hamlet, and one of Sigmund Freud's case studies, Erikson develops the concept that adolescents need to explore a diversity of alternatives as preparation for the critical act of fixing their fidelity on a realistic goal.

ERIK H. ERIKSON

Youth: Fidelity and Diversity

The subject of this paper is a certain strength inherent in the age of youth. I call it the sense of and the capacity for Fidelity. To do justice to this theme, I would have to account for the strengths (I call them basic virtues, in the older sense of the word) arising in the stages of life which precede and follow youth. Only in this way could I hope to indicate the place of youth in the evolutionary scheme of the human life cycle, only in this way make plausible the fact that the virtue Fidelity could not develop earlier in life and must not, in the crises of youth, fail its time of ascendance. Obviously, however, such an accounting would demand more than space allows. I must refer the reader to a footnote,[1] which can do no more than list the virtues of which Fidelity is one, and point to publications offering a rationale of the evolutionary scheme from which they all emerge. We can take only a brief look at the stage of life which immediately precedes youth, the school age, and then turn to youth itself.

The school age, which intervenes between childhood and youth, finds the child, previously dominated by the experience of play,

---

1. Virtue once connoted "inherent strength" and "active quality." In this sense, I consider the following basic virtues (essential to, if not identical with, ego strength) to be anchored in the successive stages of life: Hope, in infancy; Will and Purpose, in the play age; Skill, in the school age; Fidelity, in youth; Love, in young adulthood; Care, in adulthood; Wisdom, in old age. For an evolutionary and genetic rationale of this concept of the life cycle, see the writer's "The Roots of Virtue," in *The Humanist Frame*, Sir Julius Huxley, ed. London: Allen and Unwin, 1961; Harper and Brothers, 1961. For a more detailed exposition, see the writer's forthcoming book, *Life Cycle and Community*, in which the other stages of development are treated in chapters analogous to the one presented here.

ready, willing, and able to apply himself to the rudimentary skills required, eventually wielding the tools and weapons, the symbols and concepts, of his culture. Also, it finds him eager to realize actual roles (previously play-acted) which promise him an eventual identity within the specializations of his culture's technology. However, the stage by stage acquisition during individual childhood of each of man's evolutionary gains leaves the mark of infantile experience on his proudest achievements. The play age bequeaths to all methodical pursuits a quality of grandiose delusion; and the school age leaves man with a naive acceptance of "what works."

As the child makes methods his own, he also permits accepted methods to make him their own. To consider as good only what works, and to feel accepted only if things work, to manage and to be managed, can become his dominant delight and value. And since technological specialization is an intrinsic part of the human horde's or tribe's or culture's system and world image, man's pride in the tools that work with materials and animals extends to the weapons which work against other humans as well as against other species. That this can awaken a cold cunning as well as an unmeasured ferocity rare in the animal world is, of course, due to a combination of developments. Among these we will be most concerned (because it comes to the fore during youth) with man's need to combine technological pride with a sense of identity: a double sense of personal self-sameness slowly accrued from infantile experiences and of shared sameness experienced in encounters with a widening part of the community.

This need too is an evolutionary necessity as yet to be understood and influenced by planning: for men—not being a natural species any more, and not a mankind as yet—need to feel that they are of some special kind (tribe or nation, class or caste, family, occupation, or type), whose insignia they will wear with vanity and conviction, and defend (along with the economic claims they have staked out for their kind) against the foreign, the inimical, the not-so-human kinds. Thus it comes about that they can use all their proud skills and methods most systematically against other men, even in the most advanced state of rationality and civilization, with the conviction that they could not morally afford not to do so.

It is not our purpose, however, to dwell on the easy perversion and corruptibility of man's morality, but to determine what those core virtues are which—at this stage of psychosocial evolution—need our concerted attention and ethical support; for antimoralists as well as moralists easily overlook the bases in human nature for a strong ethics. As indicated, Fidelity is that virtue and quality of adolescent ego strength which belongs to man's evolutionary heritage, but which—like all the basic virtues—can arise only in the interplay of a life stage with the individuals and the social forces of a true community.

The evidence in young lives of the search for something and somebody to be true to is seen in a variety of pursuits more or less sanctioned by society. It is often hidden in a bewildering combination of shifting devotion and sudden perversity, sometimes more devotedly perverse, sometimes more perversely devoted. Yet, in all youth's seeming shiftiness, a seeking after some durability in change can be detected, whether in the accuracy of scientific and technical method or in the sincerity of conviction; in the veracity of historical and fictional accounts or the fairness of the rules of the game; in the authenticity of artistic production (and the high fidelity of reproduction) or in the genuineness of personalities and the reliability of commitments. This search is easily misunderstood, and often it is only dimly perceived by the individual himself, because youth, always set to grasp both diversity in principle and principle in diversity, must often test extremes before settling on a considered course. These extremes, particularly in times of ideological confusion and widespread marginality of identity, may include not only rebellious but also deviant, delinquent, and self-destructive tendencies. However, all this can be in the nature of a moratorium, a period of delay, in which to test the rock-bottom of some truth before committing the powers of body and mind to a segment of the existing (or a coming) order. "Loyal" and "legal" have the same root, linguistically and psychologically; for legal commitment is an unsafe burden unless shouldered with a sense of sovereign choice and experienced as loyalty. To develop that sense is a joint task of the consistency of individual life history and the ethical potency of the historical process.

Let a great tragic play tell us something of the elemental nature of the crisis man encounters here. If it is a prince's crisis, let us not forget that the "leading families" of heaven and history at one time personified man's pride and tragic failure. Prince Hamlet is in his twenties, some say early, some late. We will say he is in the middle of his third decade, a youth no longer young and about to forfeit his moratorium. We find him in a tragic conflict in which he cannot make the one step demanded simultaneously by his age and his sex, his education, and his historical responsibility.

It we want to make Shakespeare's insight into one of "the ages of man" explicit, we know that such an endeavor seems reprehensible to the students of drama, if undertaken by a trained psychologist.

Everybody else (how could he do otherwise?) interprets Shakespeare in the light of some prevailing if naive psychology. I will not try to solve the riddle of Hamlet's inscrutable nature, because his inscrutability is his nature. I feel sufficiently warned by Shakespeare himself, who lets Polonius speak like the caricature of a psychiatrist:

> And I do think—or else this brain of mine
> Hunts not the trail of policy so sure
> As it has us'd to do—that I have found
> The very cause of Hamlet's lunacy.

Hamlet's decision to play insane is a secret which the audience shares with him from the start, without their ever getting rid of the feeling that he is on the verge of slipping into the state he pretends. "His madness," says T. S. Eliot, "is less than madness, and more than feigned."

If Hamlet's madness is more than feigned, it appears to be aggravated at least fivefold: by habitual melancholy, an introverted personality, Danishness, an acute state of mourning, and love. All this makes a regression to the Oedipus complex, postulated by Ernest Jones as the main theme of this as of other great tragedies, entirely plausible.[2] This would mean that Hamlet cannot forgive his mother's recent illegitimate betrayal, because he had not been able as a child to forgive her for having betrayed him quite legitimately with his father; but, at the same time, he is unable to avenge his father's recent murder, because as a child he had himself betrayed him in phantasy and wished him out of the way. Thus he forever postpones —until he ruins the innocent with the guilty—his uncle's execution, which alone would free the ghost of his beloved father from the fate of being,

> doomed for a certain term to walk the night
> and for the day confined to fast in fires.

No audience, however, can escape the feeling that he is a man of superior conscience, advanced beyond the legal concepts of his time, consumed by his own past and by that of his society.

One further suggestion is inescapable, that Hamlet displays some of the playwright's and the actor's personality: for where others lead men and change the course of history, he reflectively moves

---

2. Ernest Jones, *Hamlet and Oedipus.* New York: Doubleday, Anchor, 1949.

characters about on the stage (the play within the play); in brief, where others act, he play-acts. And indeed, Hamlet may well stand, historically speaking, for an abortive leader, a still-born rebel.

We shall return to this in another context. In the meantime, all that has been stated can only support a biographic view which concentrates on Hamlet's age and status as a young intellectual of his time: for did he not recently return from studies at Wittenberg, the hotbed of humanist corruption, his time's counterpart to Sophist Athens (and today's existentialist centers of learning)?

There are five young men in the play, all Hamlet's age mates, and all sure (or even overdefined) in their identities as dutiful sons, courtiers, and future leaders. But they are all drawn into the moral swamp of infidelity, which seeps into the fiber of all those who owe allegiance to "rotten" Denmark, drawn by the multiple intrigue which Hamlet hopes to defeat with his own intrigue: the play within the play.

Hamlet's world, then, is one of diffuse realities and fidelities. Only through the play within the play and through the madness within the insanity, does Hamlet, the actor within the play-actor, reveal the identity within the pretended identities—and the superior fidelity in the fatal pretense.

His estrangement is one of identity diffusion. His estrangement from existence itself is expressed in the famous soliloquy. He is estranged from being human and from being a man: "Man delights me not; no, nor woman either"; and estranged from love and procreation: "I say we will have no more marriage." He is estranged from the ways of his country, "though I am native here and to the manner born"; and much like our "alienated" youth, he is estranged from and describes as "alienated" the overstandardized man of his day, who "only got the tune of time and outward habit of encounter."

Yet Hamlet's single-minded and tragically doomed search for Fidelity breaks through all this. Here is the essence of the historical Hamlet, that ancient model who was a hero on the folk stage for centuries before Shakespeare modernized and eternalized him:

> He was loth to be thought prone to lying about any matter, and wished to be held a stranger to any falsehood; and accordingly he mingled craft and candor in such a wise that, though his words did not lack truth, yet there was nothing to betoken the truth and to betray how far his keenness went.[3]

3. Saxo Grammaticus, *Danish History,* translated by Elton, 1894 (quoted in Jones, *Hamlet and Oedipus.* New York: Doubleday, Anchor, 1949, pp. 163–164).

It accords with the general diffusion of truth in Hamlet that this central theme is announced in the old fool's message to his son:

> Polonius: This above all: to thine own self be true
> And it must follow, as the night the day,
> Thou canst not then be false to any man.

Yet it is also the central theme of Hamlet's most passionate pronouncements, which make his madness but an adjunct to his greatness. He abhors conventional sham, and advocates genuineness of feeling:

> Seems, madam! Nay, it is; I know not "seems."
> 'Tis not alone my inky cloak, good mother,
> Nor customary suits of solemn black,
> Nor windy suspiration of forc'd breath,
> No, nor the fruitful river in the eye,
> Nor the dejected havior of the visage,
> Together with all forms, moods, shapes of grief
> That can denote me truly. These indeed seem,
> For they are actions that a man might play:
> But I have that within which passes show;
> These but the trappings and the suits of woe.

He searches for what only an elite will really understand—"honest method":

> I heard thee speak me a speech once but it was never
> acted; or, if it was, not above once; for the play I
> remember, pleased not the million ...! it was (as I
> received it, and others, whose judgments cried in
> the top of mine) an excellent play, well digested
> and in the scenes, set down with as much modesty and
> cunning. I remember one said there were no sallets
> in the lines to make the matter savoury, nor no matter
> in the phrase that might indict the author of affectation;
> but called it an honest method.

He fanatically insists on purity of form and fidelity of reproduction:

> ... let your discretion be your tutor. Suit the
> action to the word, the word to the action, with this
> special observance, that you o'erstep not the modesty
> of nature; for anything so overdone is from the purpose
> of playing whose end, both at the first and now, was,
> and is to hold, as 'twere, the mirror up to nature,
> to show virtue her own image and the very age and
> body of time his own form and pressure.

And finally, the eager (and overeager) acknowledgment of genuine character in his friend:

> Since my dear soul was mistress of her choice
> And could men distinguish, her election
> Hath sealed thee for herself; for thou hast been
> As one in suffering all, that suffers nothing,
> A man that fortune buffets and rewards
> Hast ta'en with equal thanks; and bless'd are those
> Whose blood and judgement are so co-mingled
> That they are not a pipe for fortune's finger
> To sound what stop she please. Give me that man
> That is nor passion's slave, and I will wear him
> in my heart's core, ay in my heart of heart,
> As I do thee. Something too much of this.

This, then, is the Hamlet within Hamlet. It fits the combined play-actor, the intellectual, the youth, and the neurotic that his words are his better deeds, that he can say clearly what he cannot live, and that his fidelity must bring doom to those he loves: for what he accomplishes at the end is what he tried to avoid, even as he realizes what we would call his negative identity in becoming exactly what his own ethical sense could not tolerate: a mad revenger. Thus do inner reality and historical actuality conspire to deny tragic man the positive identity for which he seems exquisitely chosen. Of course, the audience all along has sensed in Hamlet's very sincerity an element of deadliness. At the end he gives his "dying voice" to his counterplayer on the historical stage, victorious young Fortinbras, who in turn insists on having him,

> ... born like a soldier to the stage
> For he was likely, had he been put on,
> To have prov'd most royal.

The ceremonial fanfares, blaring and hollow, announce the end of this singular youth. He is confirmed by his chosen peers, with the royal insignia of his birth. A special person, intensely human, is buried—a member of his special kind.

To be a special kind, we have said, is an important element in the human need for personal and collective identities—all, in a sense, pseudospecies. They have found a transitory fulfillment in man's greatest moments of cultural identity and civilized perfection, and each such tradition of identity and perfection has highlighted what man could be, could he be all these at one time. The utopia of our own era predicts that man will be one species in one world, with a universal identity to replace the illusory superidentities which have divided him, and with an international ethics replacing all moral systems of superstition, repression, and suppression. Whatever the political arrangement that will further this utopia, we can only point to the schedule of human strengths which potentially emerge with the stages of life and indicate their interdependence on the structure of communal life. In youth, ego strength emerges from the mutual confirmation of individual and community, in the sense that society recognizes the young individual as a bearer of fresh energy and that the individual so confirmed recognizes society as a living process which inspires loyalty as it receives it, maintains allegiance as it attracts it, honors confidence as it demands it.

Let us go back, then, to the origins of that combination of drivenness and disciplined energy, of irrationality and courageous capability which belong to the best discussed and the most puzzling phenomena of the life cycle. The puzzle, we must grant throughout, is in the essence of the phenomenon. For the unity of the personality must be unique to be united, and the functioning of each new generation unpredictable to fulfill its function.

Of the three sources of new energy, physical growth is the most easily measured and systematically exercised, although its contribution to the aggressive drives is little understood. The youthful powers of comprehension and cognition can be experimentally studied and with planning applied to apprenticeship and study, but their relation to ideological imagination is less well known. Finally, the long delayed genital maturation is a source of untold energy, but also of a drivenness accompanied by intrinsic frustration.

When maturing in his physical capacity for procreation, the human youth is as yet unable to love in that binding manner which only two identities can offer each other; nor to care consistently enough to sustain parenthood. The two sexes, of course, differ greatly in these respects, and so do individuals, while societies provide different opportunities and sanctions within which individuals must fend for their potentials—and for their potency. But what I have called a psychosocial moratorium, of some form and duration between the advent of genital maturity and the onset of responsible adulthood, seems to be built into the schedule of human development. Like all the moratoria in man's developmental schedules, the delay of adulthood can be prolonged and intensified to a forceful and a fateful degree; thus it accounts for very special human achievements and also for the very special weaknesses in such achievements. For, whatever the partial satisfactions and partial abstinences that characterize premarital sex life in various cultures—whether the pleasure and pride of forceful genital activity without commitment, or of erotic states without genital consummation, or of disciplined and devoted delay—ego development uses the psychosexual powers of adolescence for enhancing a sense of style and identity. Here, too, man is never an animal: even where a society furthers the genital closeness of the sexes, it does so in a stylized manner. On the other hand, the sex act, biologically speaking, is the procreative act, and there is an element of psychobiological dissatisfaction in any sexual situation not favorable in the long run to procreative consummation and care—a dissatisfaction which can be tolerated by otherwise healthy people, as all partial abstinences can be borne: for a certain period, under conditions otherwise favorable to the aims of identity formation. In the woman, no doubt, this dissatisfaction plays a much greater role, owing to her deeper engagement, physiologically and emotionally, in the sex act as the first step in a procreative commitment of which her monthly cycle is a regular bodily and emotive reminder.

The various hindrances to a full consummation of adolescent genital maturation have many deep consequences for man which pose an important problem for future planning. Best known is the regressive revival of that earlier stage of psychosexuality which preceded even the emotionally quiet first school years, that is, the infantile genital and locomotor stage, with its tendency toward autoerotic manipulation, grandiose phantasy, and vigorous play.[4] But in youth, autoerotism, grandiosity, and playfulness are all immensely amplified by genital potency and locomotor maturation, and are vastly complicated by what we will presently describe as the youthful mind's new historical perspective.

The most widespread expression of the discontented search of youth is the craving for locomotion, whether expressed in a general "being on the go," "tearing after something," or "running around"; or in locomotion proper, as in vigorous work, in absorbing sports, in rapt dancing, in shiftless *Wanderschaft,* and in the employment and misuse of speedy animals and machines. But it also finds expression through participation in the movements of the day (whether the riots of a local commotion or the parades and campaigns of major

4. The classical psychoanalytic works concerned with psychosexuality and the ego defenses of youth are: Sigmund Freud, *Three Essays on the Theory of Sexuality,* standard edition (London: The Hogarth Press, 1953), vol. 7; and Anna Freud, *The Ego and the Mechanisms of Defence,* New York: International Universities Press, 1946. For the writer's views, see his *Childhood and Society.* New York: W. W. Norton, 1950.

ideological forces), if they only appeal to the need for feeling "moved" and for feeling essential in moving something along toward an open future. It is clear that societies offer any number of ritual combinations of ideological perspective and vigorous movement (dance, sports, parades, demonstrations, riots) to harness youth in the service of their historical aims; and that where societies fail to do so, these patterns will seek their own combinations, in small groups occupied with serious games, good-natured foolishness, cruel prankishness, and delinquent warfare. In no other stage of the life cycle, then, are the promise of finding oneself and the threat of losing oneself so closely allied.

In connection with locomotion, we must mention two great industrial developments: the motor engine and the motion picture. The motor engine, of course, is the very heart and symbol of our technology and its mastery, the aim and aspiration of much of modern youth. In connection with immature youth, however, it must be understood that both motor car and motion pictures offer to those so inclined passive locomotion with an intoxicating delusion of being intensely active. The prevalence of car thefts and motor accidents among juveniles is much decried (although it is taking the public a long time to understand that a theft is an appropriation for the sake of gainful possession), while automobiles more often than not are stolen by the young in search of a kind of automotive intoxication, which may literally run away with car and youngster. Yet, while vastly inflating a sense of motor omnipotence, the need for active locomotion often remains unfulfilled. Motion pictures especially offer the onlooker, who sits, as it were, with the engine of his emotions racing, fast and furious motion in an artificially widened visual field, interspersed with close-ups of violence and sexual possession —and all this without making the slightest demand on intelligence, imagination, or effort. I am pointing here to a widespread imbalance in adolescent experience, because I think it explains new kinds of adolescent outbursts and points to new necessities of mastery. The danger involved is greatly balanced in that part of youth which can take active charge of technical development, manages to learn, and to identify with the ingeniousness of invention, the improvement of production and the care of machinery, and is thus offered a new and unlimited application of youthful capacities. Where youth is underprivileged in such technical experience, it must explode in riotous motion; where it is ungifted, it will feel estranged from the modern world, until technology and nontechnical intelligence have come to a certain convergence.

The cognitive gifts developing during the first half of the second decade add a powerful tool to the tasks of youth. J. Piaget calls the gains in cognition made toward the middle teens, the achievement of "formal operations."[5] This means that the youth can now operate on hypothetical propositions, can think of possible variable and potential relations, and think of them in thought alone, independent of certain concrete checks previously necessary. As Jerome S. Bruner puts it, the child now can "conjure up systematically the full range of alternative possibilities that could exist at any given time."[6] Such cognitive orientation forms not a contrast but a complement to the need of the young person to develop a sense of identity, for, from among all possible and imaginable relations, he must make a series of ever narrowing selections of personal, occupational, sexual, and ideological commitments.

Here again diversity and fidelity are polarized: they make each other significant and keep each other alive. Fidelity without a sense of diversity can become an obsession and a bore; diversity without a sense of fidelity, an empty relativism.

The sense of ego identity, then, becomes more necessary (and more problematical) wherever a wide range of possible identities is envisaged. Identity is a term used in our day with faddish ease; at this point, I can only indicate how very complicated the real article is.[7] For ego identity is partially conscious and largely unconscious. It is a psychological process reflecting social processes; but with sociological means it can be seen as a social process reflecting psychological processes; it meets its crisis in adolescence, but has grown throughout childhood and continued to re-emerge in the crises of later years. The overriding meaning of it all, then, is the creation of a sense of sameness, a unity of personality now felt by the individual and recognized by others as having consistency in time—of being, as it were, an irreversible historical fact.

The prime danger of this age, therefore, is identity confusion, which can express itself in excessively prolonged moratoria (Hamlet offers an exalted example); in repeated impulsive attempts to end the moratorium with sudden choices, that is, to play with historical

---

5. B. Inhelder and J. Piaget, *The Growth of Logical Thinking from Childhood to Adolescence.* New York: Basic Books, 1958.
6. Jerome S. Bruner, *The Process of Education.* Cambridge: Harvard University Press, 1960.
7. See the writer's "The Problem of Ego-Identity" in *Identity and the Life Cycle: Psychological Issues* (New York: International Universities Press, 1959), vol. I, no. 1.

possibilities, and then to deny that some irreversible commitment has already taken place; and sometimes also in severe regressive pathology, which we will illustrate presently. The dominant issue of this, as of any other stage, therefore, is that of the active, the selective, ego being in charge and being enabled to be in charge by a social structure which grants a given age group the place it needs —and in which it is needed.

In a letter to Oliver Wendell Holmes, William James speaks of wanting to "rebaptize himself" in their friendship—and this one word says much of what is involved in the radical direction of the social awareness and the social needs of youth. From the middle of the second decade, the capacity to think and the power to imagine reach beyond the persons and personalities in which youth can immerse itself so deeply. Youth loves and hates in people what they "stand for" and chooses them for a significant encounter involving issues that often, indeed, are bigger than you and I. We have heard Hamlet's declaration of love to his friend Horatio, a declaration quickly broken off—"something too much here." It is a new reality, then, for which the individual wishes to be reborn, with and by those whom he chooses as his new ancestors and his genuine contemporaries.

This mutual selection, while frequently associated with, and therefore, interpreted as a rebellion against or withdrawl from, the childhood environment, is an expression of a truly new perspective which I have already called "historical"—in one of those loose uses of an ancient overspecialized word which sometimes become necessary in making new meanings specific. I mean by "historical perspective" something which every human being newly develops during adolescence. It is a sense of the irreversibility of significant events and an often urgent need to understand fully and quickly what kind of happenings in reality and in thought determine others, and why. As we have seen, psychologists such as Piaget recognize in youth the capacity to appreciate that any process can be understood when it is retraced in its steps and thus reversed in thought. Yet it is no contradiction to say that he who comes to understand such a reversal also realizes that in reality, among all the events that can be thought of, a few will determine and narrow one another with historical fatality, whether (in the human instance) deservedly or undeservedly, intentionally or unintentionally.

Youth, therefore, is sensitive to any suggestion that it may be hopelessly determined by what went before in life histories or in history. Psychosocially speaking, this would mean that irreversible childhood identifications would deprive an individual of an identity of his own; historically, that invested powers should prevent a group from realizing its composite historical identity. For these reasons, youth often rejects parents and authorities and wishes to belittle them as inconsequential; it is in search of individuals and movements who claim, or seem to claim, that they can predict what is irreversible, thus getting ahead of the future—which means, reversing it. This in turn accounts for the acceptance by youth of mythologies and ideologies predicting the course of the universe or the historical trend; for even intelligent and practical youth can be glad to have the larger framework settled, so that it can devote itself to the details which it can manage, once it knows (or is convincingly told) what they stand for and where it stands. Thus, "true" ideologies are verified by history—for a time; for if they can inspire youth, youth will make the predicted history come more than true.

By pointing to what, in the mind of youth, people "stand for," I did not mean to overemphasize the ideological explicitness in the meaning of individuals to youth. The selection of meaningful individuals can take place in the framework of pointed practicalities such as schooling or job selection, as well as in religious and ideological fellowship; while the methods of selection can range from banal amenity and enmity to dangerous play with the borderlines of sanity and legality. But the occasions have in common a mutual sizing up and a mutual plea for being recognized as individuals who can be more than they seem to be, and whose potentials are needed by the order that is or will be. The representatives of the adult world thus involved may be advocates and practitioners of technical accuracy, of a method of scientific inquiry, of a convincing rendition of truth, of a code of fairness, of a standard of artistic veracity, or of a way of personal genuineness. They become representatives of an elite in the eyes of the young, quite independently of whether or not they are also viewed thus in the eyes of the family, the public, or the police. The choice can be dangerous, but to some youths the danger is a necessary ingredient of the experiment. Elemental things are dangerous; and if youth could not overcommit itself to danger, it could not commit itself to the survival of genuine values—one of the primary steering mechanism of psychosocial evolution. The elemental fact is that only when fidelity has found its field of manifestation is the human as good as, say, the nestling in nature, which is ready to rely on its own wings and to take its adult place in the ecological order.

If in human adolescence this field of manifestation is alternately one of devoted conformism and of extreme deviancy, of rededication and of rebellion, we must remember the necessity for man to react (and to react most intensively in his youth) to the diversity of conditions. In the setting of psychosocial evolution, we can ascribe a long-range meaning to the idiosyncratic individualist and to the rebel as well as to the conformist, albeit under different historical conditions. For healthy individualism and devoted deviancy contain an indignation in the service of a wholeness that is to be restored, without which psychosocial evolution would be doomed. Thus, human adaptation has its loyal deviants, its rebels, who refuse to adjust to what so often is called, with an apologetic and fatalistic misuse of a once good phrase, "the human condition."

Loyal deviancy and identity formation in extraordinary individuals are often associated with neurotic and psychotic symptoms, or at least with a prolonged moratorium of relative isolation, in which all the estrangements of adolescence are suffered. In *Young Man Luther* I have attempted to put the suffering of a great young man into the context of his greatness and his historic position.[8]

It is not our purpose, however, to discuss what to many youths is the most urgent question, and yet to us the most difficult to answer, namely, the relation of special giftedness and neurosis; rather, we must characterize the specific nature of adolescent psychopathology, or, even more narrowly, indicate the relevance of the issue of fidelity to the psychopathology of youth.

In the classical case of this age group, Freud's first published encounter with an eighteen-year-old girl suffering from *"petite hysterie* with the commonest of all ... symptoms," it is interesting to recall that at the end of treatment Freud was puzzled as to "what kind of help" the girl wanted from him. He had communicated to her his interpretation of the structure of her neurotic disorder, an interpretation which became the central theme of his classical publication on the psychosexual factors in the development of hysteria.[9] Freud's clinical reports, however, remain astonishingly fresh over the decades, and today his case history clearly reveals the psychosocial centering of the girl's story in matters of fidelity. In fact, one might say, without seriously overdoing it, that three words characterize her social history: sexual infidelity on the part of some of the most important adults in her life; the perfidy of her father's denial of his friend's sexual acts, which were in fact the precipitating cause of the girl's illness; and a strange tendency on the part of all the

---

8. *Young Man Luther.* New York: W. W. Norton, 1958; London: Faber and Faber, 1959.
9. Sigmund Freud, *Fragment of an Analysis of a Case of Hysteria,* standard edition (London: The Hogarth Press, 1953), vol. 7.

adults around the girl to make her a confidante in any number of matters, without having enough confidence in her to acknowledge the truths relevant to her illness.

Freud, of course, focused on other matters, opening up, with the concentration of a psychosurgeon, the symbolic meaning of her symptoms and their history; but, as always, he reported relevant data on the periphery of his interests. Thus, among the matters which somewhat puzzled him, he reports that the patient was "almost beside herself at the idea of it being supposed that she had merely fancied" the conditions which had made her sick; and that she was kept "anxiously trying to make sure whether I was being quite straightforward with her—or perfidious like her father." When at the end she left analyst and analysis "in order to confront the adults around her with the secrets she knew," Freud considered this an act of revenge on them, and on him; and within the outlines of his interpretation, this partial interpretation stands. Nevertheless, as we can now see, there was more to this insistence on the historical truth than the denial of an inner truth—and this especially in an adolescent. For, the question as to what confirms them irreversibly as a truthful or a cheating, a sick or a rebellious type is paramount in the minds of adolescents; and the further question, whether or not they were right in not accepting the conditions which made them sick, is as important to them as the insight into the structure of their sickness can ever be. In other words, they insist that the meaning of their sickness find recognition within a reformulation of the historical truth as revealed in their own insights and distortions, and not according to the terms of the environment which wishes them to be "brought to reason" (as Dora's father had put it, when he brought her to Freud).

No doubt, Dora by then was a hysteric, and the meaning of her symptoms was psychosexual; but the sexual nature of her disturbance and of the precipitating events should not blind us to the fact that other perfidies, familial and communal, cause adolescents to regress in a variety of ways to a variety of earlier stages.

Only when adolescence is reached does the capacity for such clear regression and symptom formation occur: only when the historical function of the mind is consolidated can significant repressions become marked enough to cause consistent symptom formation and deformation of character. The depth of regression determines the nature of the pathology and points to the therapy to be employed. However, there is a pathognomic picture which all sick youth have in common and which is clearly discernible in Freud's description of Dora's total state. This picture is characterized first of all by a denial of the historical flux of time, and by an attempt to challenge retrospectively, while retesting in the present all parental premises before new trust is invested in the (emancipated) future.

The sick adolescent thus gradually stops extending experimental feelers toward the future; his moratorium of illness becomes an end in itself and thus ceases to be a moratorium (Dora suffered from a "*taedium vitae* which was probably not entirely genuine," Freud wrote). It is for this reason that death and suicide can be at this time such a spurious preoccupation—one leading unpredictably to suicide (and to murder)—for death would conclude the life history before it joins others in inexorable commitment. (Dora's parents found "a letter in which she took leave of them because she could no longer endure life. Her father ... guessed that the girl had no serious suicidal intentions.") There is also a social isolation which excludes all sense of solidarity and can lead to a snobbish isolation which finds companions but no friends (Dora "tried to avoid social intercourse," was "distant" and "unfriendly"). The energy of repudiation which accompanies the first steps of an identity formation (and in some youngsters can lead to the sudden impulse to annihilate) is in neurotics turned against the self ("Dora was satisfied neither with herself nor with her family").

A repudiated self in turn cannot offer loyalty, and, of course, fears the fusion of love or of sexual encounters. The work inhibition often connected with this picture (Dora suffered from "fatigue and lack of concentration") is really a career inhibition, in the sense that every exertion of skill or method is suspected of binding the individual to the role and the status suggested by the activity; thus, again, any moratorium is spoiled. Where fragmentary identities are formed, they are highly self-conscious and are immediately put to a test (thus Dora obviously defeated her wish to be a woman intellectual). This identity consciousness is a strange mixture of superiority, almost a megalomania ("I am a majority of one," one of my patients said), with which the patient tries to convince himself that he is really too good for his community or his period of history, while he is equally convinced of being nobody.

We have sketched the most obvious social symptoms of adolescent psychopathology, in part to indicate that, besides the complicated structure of specific symptoms, there is in the picture presented of each stage an expression of the dominant psychosocial issue, so open that one sometimes wonders whether the patient lies by telling the simple truth or tells the truth when he seems most obviously to lie.

The sketch presented, however, also serves as a comparison of the isolated adolescent sufferer with those youths who try to solve their doubt in their elders by joining deviant cliques and gangs. Freud found that "psychoneuroses are, so to speak, the negative of perversions,"[10] which means that neurotics suffer under the repression of tendencies which perverts try to "live out." This has a counterpart in the fact that isolated sufferers try to solve by withdrawal what the joiners of deviant cliques and gangs attempt to solve by conspiracy.

If we now turn to this form of adolescent pathology, the denial of the irreversibility of historical time appears to be expressed in a clique's or a gang's delusion of being an organization with a tradition and an ethics all its own. The pseudo-historical character of such societies is expressed in such names as "The Navahos," "The Saints," or "The Edwardians"; while their provocation is countered by society (remember the Pachucos of the war years) with a mixture of impotent rage wherever murderous excess does actually occur, and with a phobic overconcern followed by vicious suppression wherever these "secret societies" are really no more than fads lacking any organized purpose. Their pseudo-societal character reveals itself in their social parasitism, and their pseudo-rebellion in the conformism actually governing their habits. Yet the seemingly unassailable inner sense of callous rightness is no doubt due to an inner realignment of motivations, which can best be understood by briefly comparing the torment of the isolated youngster with the temporary gains derived by the joiner from the mere fact that he has been taken into a pseudo-society. The time diffusion attending the isolate's inability to envisage a career is "cured" by his attention to "jobs"— theft, destruction, fights, murder, or acts of perversion or addiction, conceived on the spur of the moment and executed forthwith. This "job" orientation also takes care of the work inhibition, because the clique and the gang are always "busy," even if they just "hang around." Their lack of any readiness to wince under shaming or accusation is often considered the mark of a total personal perdition, while in fact it is a trademark, an insignia of the "species" to which the youngster (mostly marginal in economic and ethnic respects) would rather belong than to a society which is eager to confirm him as a criminal and then promises to rehabilitate him as an ex-criminal.

As to the isolate's tortured feelings of bisexuality or of an immature need for love, the young joiner in social pathology, by joining, has made a clear decision: he is male with a vengeance, she, a female without sentimentality; or they are both perverts. In either case,

---

10. Sigmund Freud, *Fragment of an Analysis of a Case of Hysteria,* standard edition (London: The Hogarth Press, 1953), vol. 7.

they can eliminate the procreative function of genitality together and can make a pseudo-culture of what is left. By the same token, they will acknowledge authority only in the form chosen in the act of joining, repudiating the rest of the social world, where the isolate repudiates existence as such and, with it, himself.

The importance of these comparative considerations, which have been stated in greater detail elsewhere, lies in the impotent craving of the isolated sufferer to be true to himself, and in that of the joiner, to be true to a group and to its insignia and codes. By this I do not mean to deny that the one is sick (as his physical and mental symptoms attest), nor that the other can be on the way to becoming a criminal, as his more and more irreversible acts and choices attest. Both theory and therapy, however, lack the proper leverage, if the need for (receiving and giving) fidelity is not understood, and especially if instead the young deviant is confirmed by every act of the correctional or therapeutic authorities as a future criminal or a lifelong patient.

In Dora's case, I have tried to indicate the phenomenology of this need. As to young delinquents, I can only quote again one of those rare newspaper reports which convey enough of a story to show the elements involved. Kai T. Erikson and I have used this example as an introduction to our article, "The Confirmation of the Delinquent."

JUDGE IMPOSES ROAD GANG TERM FOR BACK TALK

Wilmington, N.D. (UP)—A "smart alecky" youth who wore pegged trousers and a flattop haircut began six months on a road gang today for talking back to the wrong judge.

Michael A. Jones, 20, of Wilmington, was fined $25 and costs in Judge Edwin Jay Roberts Jr.'s superior court for reckless operation of an automobile. But he just didn't leave well enough alone.

"I understand how it was, with your pegged trousers and flattop haircut," Roberts said in assessing the fine. "You go on like this and I predict in five years you'll be in prison."

When Jones walked over to pay his fine, he overheard Probation Officer Gideon Smith tell the judge how much trouble the "smart alecky" young offender had been.

"I just want you to know I'm not a thief," interrupted Jones to the judge.

The judge's voice boomed to the court clerk: "Change that judgment to six months on the roads."[11]

I quote the story here to add the interpretation that the judge in this case (neither judge nor case differs from a host of others) took

11. Erik H. Erikson and Kai T. Erikson, "The Confirmation of the Delinquent," *The Chicago Review,* Winter 1957, 10:15–23.

as an affront to the dignity of authority what may have also been a desperate "historical" denial, an attempt to claim that a truly antisocial identity had not yet been formed, and that there was enough discrimination and potential fidelity left to be made something of by somebody who cared to do so. But instead, what the young man and the judge made of it was likely, of course, to seal the irreversibility and confirm the doom. I say "was likely to," because I do not know what happened in this case; we do know, however, the high recidivity of criminality in the young who, during the years of identity formation, are forced by society into intimate contact with criminals.

Finally, it cannot be overlooked that at times political undergrounds of all kinds can and do make use of the need for fidelity as well as the store of wrath in those deprived in their need by their families or their societies. Here social rejuvenation can make use of and redeem social pathology, even as in individuals special giftedness can be related to and redeem neurosis. These are matters too weighty to be discussed briefly and, at any rate, our concern has been with the fact that the psychopathology of youth suggests a consideration of the same issues which we found operative in the evolutionary and developmental aspects of this stage of life.

To summarize: Fidelity, when fully matured, is the strength of disciplined devotion. It is gained in the involvement of youth in such experiences as reveal the essence of the era they are to join— as the beneficiaries of its tradition, as the practitioners and innovators of its technology, as renewers of its ethical strength, as rebels bent on the destruction of the outlived, and as deviants with deviant commitments. This, at least, is the potential of youth in psychosocial evolution; and while this may sound like a rationalization endorsing any high-sounding self-delusion in youth, any self-indulgence masquerading as devotion, or any righteous excuse for blind destruction, it makes intelligible the tremendous waste attending this as any other mechanism of human adaptation, especially if its excesses meet with more moral condemnation than ethical guidance. On the other hand, our understanding of these processes is not furthered by the "clinical" reduction of adolescent phenomena to their infantile antecedents and to an underlying dichotomy of drive and conscience. Adolescent development comprises a new set of identification processes, both with significant persons and with ideological forces, which give importance to individual life by relating it to a living community and to ongoing history, and by counterpointing the newly won individual identity with some communal solidarity.

In youth, then, the life history intersects with history: here individuals are confirmed in their identities, societies regenerated in their life style. This process also implies a fateful survival of adolescent modes of thinking in man's historical and ideological perspectives.

Historical processes, of course, have already entered the individual's core in childhood. Both ideal and evil images and the moral prototypes guiding parental administrations originate in the past struggles of contending cultural and national "species," which also color fairytale and family lore, superstition and gossip, and the simple lessons of early verbal training. Historians on the whole make little of this; they describe the visible emergence and the contest of autonomous historical ideas, unconcerned with the fact that these ideas reach down into the lives of generations and re-emerge through the daily awakening and training of historical consciousness in young individuals.

It is youth, then, which begins to develop that sense of historical irreversibility which can lead to what we may call acute historical estrangement. This lies behind the fervent quest for a sure meaning in individual life history and in collective history, and behind the questioning of the laws of relevancy which bind datum and principle, event and movement. But it is also, alas, behind the bland carelessness of that youth which denies its own vital need to develop and cultivate a historical consciousness—and conscience.

To enter history, each generation of youth must find an identity consonant with its own childhood and consonant with an ideological promise in the perceptible historical process. But in youth the tables of childhood dependence begin slowly to turn: no longer is it merely for the old to teach the the young the meaning of life, whether individual or collective. It is the young who, by their responses and actions, tell the old whether life as represented by the old and as presented to the young has meaning; and it is the young who carry in them the power to confirm those who confirm them and, joining the issues, to renew and to regenerate, or to reform and to rebel.

I will not at this point review the institutions which participate in creating the retrospective and the prospective mythology offering historical orientation to youth: obviously, the mythmakers of religion and politics, the arts and the sciences, the stage and fiction—all contribute to the historical logic preached to youth more or less consciously, more or less responsibly. And today we must add, at least in the United States, psychiatry; and all over the world, the press, which forces leaders to make history in the open and to accept reportorial distortion as a major historical factor.

I have spoken of Hamlet as an abortive ideological leader. His drama combines all the elements of which successful ideological leaders are made: they are the postadolescents who make out of the very contradictions of adolescence the polarities of their charisma. Individuals with an uncommon depth of conflict, they also have uncanny gifts, and often uncanny luck with which they offer to the crisis of a generation the solution of their own crisis—always, as Woodrow Wilson put it, being "in love with activity on a large scale," always feeling that their one life must be made to count in the lives of all, always convinced that what they felt as adolescents was a curse, a fall, an earthquake, a thunderbolt, in short, a revelation to be shared with their generation and with many to come. Their humble claim to being chosen does not preclude a wish to universal power. "Fifty years from now," wrote Kierkegaard in the journal of his spiritual soliloquy, "the whole world will read my diary." He sensed, no doubt, that the impending dominance of mass ideologies would bring to the fore his cure for the individual soul, existential-ism. We must study the question (I have approached it in my study of young Luther) of what ideological leaders do to history—whether they first aspire to power and then face spiritual qualms, or first face spiritual perdition and then seek universal influence. Their answers often manage to subsume under the heading of a more embracing identity all that ails man, especially young man, at critical times: danger from new weapons and from natural forces aggravated by man's misuse of nature; anxiety from sources within the life-history typical for the time; and existential dread of the ego's limitations, magnified in times of disintegrating superidentities and intensified in adolescence.

But does it not take a special and, come to think of it, a strange sense of calling, to dare and to care to give such inclusive answers? Is it not probable and in fact demonstrable that among the most passionate ideologists there are unreconstructed adolescents, trans-mitting to their ideas the proud moment of their transient ego recov-ery, of their temporary victory over the forces of existence and history, but also the pathology of their deepest isolation, the defen-siveness of their forever adolescing egos—and their fear of the calm of adulthood? "To live beyond forty," says Dostoevsky's under-ground diarist, "is bad taste." It warrants study, both historical and psychological, to see how some of the most influential leaders have turned away from parenthood, only to despair in middle age of the issue of their leadership as well.

It is clear that today the ideological needs of all but intellectual youth of the humanist tradition are beginning to be taken care of by a subordination of ideology to technology: what works, on the grandest scale, is good. It is to be hoped that the worst implications of this trend have outlived themselves already in fascism. Yet, in the technological superidentity, the American dream and the Marxist revolution also meet. If their competition can be halted before mutual annihilation, it is just possible that a new mankind, seeing that it can now build and destroy anything it wishes, will focus its intelligence (feminine as well as masculine) on the ethical question concerning the workings of human generations—beyond products, powers, and ideas. Ideologies in the past have contained an ethical corrective, but ethics must eventually transcend ideology as well as technology: the great question will be and already is, what man, on ethical grounds and without moralistic self-destruction, must decide *not* to do, even though he could make it work—for a while.

Moralities sooner or later outlive themselves, ethics never: this is what the need for identity and for fidelity, reborn with each generation, seems to point to. Morality in the moralistic sense can be shown by modern means of inquiry to be predicated on superstitions and irrational inner mechanisms which ever again undermine the ethical fiber of generations; but morality is expendable only where ethics prevail. This is the wisdom that the words of many languages have tried to tell man. He has tenaciously clung to the words, even though he has understood them only vaguely, and in his actions has disregarded or perverted them completely. But there is much in ancient wisdom which can now become knowledge.

As in the near future peoples of different tribal and national pasts join what must become the identity of one mankind, they can find an initial common language only in workings of science and technology. This in turn may well help them to make transparent the superstitions of their traditional moralities and may even permit them to advance rapidly through a historical period during which they must put a vain superidentity of neonationalism in the place of their much exploited historical identity weakness. But they must also look beyond the major ideologies of the now "established" world, offered them as ceremonial masks to frighten and to attract them. The overriding issue is the creation not of a new ideology but of a universal ethics growing out of a universal technological civilization. This can be advanced only by men and women who are neither ideological youths nor moralistic old men, but who know that from generation to generation the test of what you produce is in the *care* it inspires. If there is any chance at all, it is in a world more challenging, more workable, and more venerable than all myths, retrospective or prospective: it is in historical reality, at last ethically cared for.

Serious concern for the period of life called adolescence occurs in literature for the first time in Rousseau's Emile. *He speaks of adolescence as a rebirth into existence. Phyllis La Farge, who writes sensitively about herself during this period of her life, finds that her own experiences reflect and agree with Rousseau's idea of a rebirth. She is, as a creative artist, able to recreate much of her adolescent conflict, despair, and uniqueness, providing the reader with much that is unique and yet generalizable to the experiences of others.*

PHYLLIS LA FARGE

An Uptight Adolescence

Early adolescence, perhaps more than other periods in life, feels in memory as if it were uniquely one's own. No one else could have been so tentative, so lyrical, and so despairing by turns. At the time one felt unique, too, perhaps especially in my generation. When I was an adolescent there was far less of a youth culture supporting and generalizing as well as blunting the experience of the individual. I was doubtful that anyone else felt as I did and uncertain in my attempts to interpret the self emerging in me. Enough of this still lingers so that I feel most comfortable if I do not generalize but speak of my own adolescence in specifics.

I was twelve in 1945. For me the end of World War II in Europe came during recess in a girls' private school in New York City. It was announced by the sallow hysteric whose title was Head of the Middle School. That very winter she had disbanded our French class after we had reduced the white Russian emigre teacher to tears once too often. The hysteric thought she could make us guilty enough so that we would sign up for a new French class in a more docile frame of mind. Her strategy failed. No one signed up, not even the class goody-goody, me. We knew that there was no real question of the school's discontinuing French. We waited out a week of extra study halls and sure enough we were back with Mme. T., with her black suit buttoned too tightly over her large breasts, her braids coiled over her ears, and, just in front of her braids, a neatly trimmed fringe of black sideburns.

The end of the war in the Pacific came on an island off the coast of Maine where I was visiting with my mother and my sister. The day was brilliant. My mother and I walked on a path that was a foot-worn trough in the pine mulch, looking at the headlined *Times* we had picked up at the dock. "But it is not the same for us as it is for other people," she said. She meant that the fathers and husbands of others would return, whereas my father, who had died in the war, would not. This is the only time in those years that I can remember her mentioning what she thought grief had done to us—that it had set us apart.

Set apart from my peers and from an important part of my younger life: these sensations of isolation and discontinuity were the strongest experiences of my early adolescence. While the war went on I felt a continuity, even if of an abstract sort, with my father. The newsreels at the 85th Street Translux on Madison Avenue proved that we were still living in the same piece of time in which he had died; in my consciousness the jiggly black and white images (Dresden, Salerno) were of a piece with the event of his death. But when the war was over we were in a new time he had not known.

There were other, more specific discontinuities. A year or so before the end of the war my mother had sold the house in the country where we had lived and taken an apartment in New York where she herself had been raised. We spent most of the summer in my maternal grandmother's Westchester house where my mother had lived as a child. There was continuity but it was with my mother's earlier years (we had spent no more than a few weeks there each year as small children). Continuity with my own and my sister's earlier experience was broken.

My mother's decisions gave me a latter-day Jamesian adolescence. My sister, my mother, and I became the pawns of a beautiful and powerful woman—my grandmother—who found in us an acceptable rationale for continuing to live in a house and in a style which she clung to for reasons of her own. I lived with auras and essences and intimations that I only half understood. I picked up tastes, prejudices, turns of phrase that belonged to the two or three earlier generations who had lived in my grandmother's house and in the other family houses nearby. Auras and tastes which lingered on with the same long half-life of old photographs, old records, old coats and canes in the closets of country houses, old toys in top floor playrooms. Treasures if there is enough going on and if there is not, as there was not for me, then a complex burden, not unlike the burden of foreign parentage, beloved and yet rejected because it appears an impediment to defining oneself in a new land or, as in my case, in one's own time.

I saw no one my own age except my sister all summer and no adults except family. I learned no sports, no crafts. I had a few tennis lessons and a few riding lessons with ludicrous results (it seems improbable that I could have ended up clinging upside down to the neck of a horse but this is what I recall—perhaps the whole business simply felt that way). Everything I attempted was done "cold," that is without the support of other people doing and enjoying it. Performance became synonymous with an unattainable perfection. I withdrew into what I could do—read and swim, paint watercolors. I could have gone to camp if I had wanted (yet as I write it, it seems a paltry solution) but I could least of all have dared what might have freed me. And no one prodded.

I learned to read the few people I was with minutely. Survival seemed to depend—I make it sound conscious but it wasn't—on an understanding of character and motivation. An Argus grew within me (and is with me still). On summer mornings my grandmother ate breakfast in bed and my mother until her nerves drove her out to garden sat in a chair beside the bed reading the *Times.* I, too, spent a few minutes in the room remembering the pleasure I had felt there as a small child, and feeling it no more. In the summer of 1948 I wrote in my diary:

> Ga crushes Mummy and fixes everything in her mind. Exasperating but I am still detached enough to be intrigued by the patterned carpet of Ga's bedroom. Ever since the idyllic mornings that I spent crawling on the floor of her bedroom the intricate blue and purple design has fascinated me. I am still young enough to enjoy rolling the hatstand down the paths and halls of my imagination's castle on this carpet.

(I went on to write that the news was bad in the summer of 1948 and that I always read the fashion page and Billy Rose first. The news has become so bad since that I have almost ceased to read it and Billy Rose is dead.)

It was in those years of early adolescence that I think I learned to counter pain with observation, not only of people but things—carpets, plants, language, paintings—and to think even if awkwardly, pompously about my own experience. Characteristic of those years, too, is the "betweenness," the awkward position between a child's pleasures and perceptions and a more adult mode, and the sense of change and changing suggested by the repeated word "still." The first "still" points ahead to a time when I might no longer be able to bear my family situation, in fact, almost insinuates that I expect someday not to be able to bear it. The second "still" harks back to a child's enjoyment. Early adolescence brings not only a sense of change and the changing nature of experience but, perhaps as a result of an awareness of change, an altered perception of time. Time begins to move faster, summers are not as long; the more static "timeless" world of childhood is passing. Ambitious person that I am, I think I began in the twelve to sixteen years to equate the passage of time with some sort of progress. (It took a long time to shake that notion.)

My sister and I became very close; we lived in our heads, at the same time longing for involvement, action, most of all people our own age. Twenty-five years later we are still convinced that for us friends are not what they are for others: to us they still seem benefactions not at all to be taken for granted. "I must build myself a world inside myself," I wrote in a 1947 diary entry which expresses much of what we felt, "a secret place, impenetrable to all but those I love. And yet from this seclusion I love people."

My sister was my ideal. I thought it was better to have curly hair, to be very fair. I valued what she was—absolute, intense, uncompromising—and I knew I could not attain to it; beside her I felt a trimmer. I was still a Roman Catholic (my diaries are full of prayers) but I was already aware that she was more religious than I and this gave her a kind of worthiness I had an inkling I could not hope for. My passion for the events of the day (I was an avid reader of newspapers in my teens) seemed second-rate beside her passion for poetry and the natural world. She became the model for later love. I wonder how often such models grow out of the close affections of early adolescence, taking siblings or friends for models rather than parents.

But I falsify if I suggest only the negative. The longing for the companionship of peers and the chance to do things with people my own age was so overriding that I tended to underrate what I had—and even now risk doing so in writing about those years. I have written recently about my relationship with my mother and do not want to repeat it here except to say that she cared for me so much and was (is) a person of such moral passion and honesty that she gave my life a kind of guarantee.

Important, too, was the experience every summer of a large household and of an extended family of aunts, uncles, great-aunts, all living nearby. I took it so for granted that there was always someone to turn to, family or not family, that I could be bored and confined by what I had (and, true, there was no one my own age). Only later did I value as nearly priceless the sense of a world small enough to perceive it whole, the play of people above and below stairs, with and against each other, the stuff that novels used to be made of—and to continue to feel as I did inarticulately in adolescence that it was experience that fitted me to a time earlier than my own.

It was easy to live in such a world without social consciousness even in the late forties. I thought my relatives snobbish and prejudiced, but I had no concrete alternatives to their point of view beyond a vague liberalism and I would not have known where to turn for other models.

Along with the discontinuities specific to my circumstances came the discontinuities of puberty, the changes in my own body. The changes of adolescent bodies are subject matter for Goldoni or the Marx brothers, if only adolescents could feel that way. I had hips before I had breasts; it seemed cruel mismanagement. My mother, slender, erect, and a puritan in her corseting as well as in the control of her emotions, bought me a girdle. I wore it with a Carter's knit undershirt, the kind with the little string tied about level with breast bone. Cotton knit in contact with other fabrics is bound to roll itself into a little ridge. It is this ridge circumnavigating my hips which I remember above all else from the marriage ceremony of my uncle—this and the little string bow which kept popping out of the slit neck of my dress. It seemed impossible that the entire gathering, absorbed in a high nuptial mass, was not eyeing me.

Self-consciousness about my body and appearance were overwhelming for several years. I did not put it into words, or even think it, but there was always the possibility that my body, like some not quite predictable tyrant, a sort of Ubu Roi, would betray me, that something else would bulge or sweat or all at once sprout hair and so depart from the firm, predictable body of childhood.

It still strikes me as fathomless that when it came I did not recognize the menses for what it was, although it had been explained by my mother and the headmistress at school. Perhaps its gaudiness was too removed from their restrained explanations. (I see the headmistress's earnest, thin-lipped face still as she wrote the Latin derivation on the blackboard. Somehow she got through the entire talk without a single mention of sexuality. Lord knows what she might have said, given the time, the place, and her own nature, but still it seems a feat.) Perhaps it was too abrupt a discontinuity with the body I had always known. Perhaps I had expected menstruation to be accompanied with immediate radical change in the rest of me, that the little girl spending a warm September weekend at her grandmother's would be instantly transformed into an adult woman. Transformation is another, more positive way of stating the

discontinuities of early adolescence. It is longed for and feared, signaling as it does changes in, if not the end of the self one knows.
Perhaps the fear of transformation explains something else; after my
mother's "talk" I remember weeping a great storm of emotion as I
took my before-bed shower and looked down (perhaps in fear? in
memory the feeling is one of extreme mortalness) at my still childish body.

In my generation rites of passage were inadequate if there at all.

Yet when I finally did know what had happened to me I felt
along with confusion at least a hint of the quiet and private immen-
sity that I knew years later in pregnancy and after the birth of my
children.

This is the point: years later. In my time and in my milieu
childhood was protracted and protected; the gap between readiness
and fulfillment which is characteristic of human animals was at its
widest; moreover, sex and birth were remote from those around me
(at least as far as I knew). Possibly these factors—extreme in my case
but generally present in upper-middle-class families of my generation—added to a fear of transformation and to a longing for it, forcing
the young to hold in abeyance what is vital to them, refusing to
sanction a chance to assay it. It was done in the name of education
and in the name of culture, or rather one kind of culture. Central to
this culture is a premise that a certain male bonding is necessary to
achievement whether military or intellectual. Bonding takes time—
namely the adolescent years. It leaves girls with a long wait, a
delayed promise, and all the consequences to development which
inaction brings. The current young question the premise on which
this culture is founded without entirely knowing that they do so. At
the same time that they refuse to keep the sexual in abeyance they
whittle away at the protracted childhood which I knew. It is not
clear what consequences their behavior will have for the culture
they came out of, the one that I was raised in.

Not included in the bonding of young men and denied easy
access to the achievement which is the reward for delay and sublimation, yet subjected to the same or greater restraints, upper-middle-class young women of my own and earlier generations were
condemned to the juggling act of pretending that they would
achieve (how else could one get through a school course that aped
a young man's?), acquiring a nonthreatening cultural *batterie de
cuisine* ("I have no accomplishments," one diary entry reads), and
longing for the encompassing love which attracted doubly, not only
as the thing one's heart and body were ready for but as the only
goody the culture would give with full approval.

The conflict created by this situation in someone like me was considerable, but it was largely unconscious, expressed in diary entries which now seem mutually exclusive but then did not seem the least bit contradictory. Windy talk about intellectual endeavor, worry about exams, the wish to transfer to a more stimulating school —and then passages about loneliness and the longing for love, essays on what a good mother should be, including this fine sentence which could only have been written by someone very young who had never had a child: "Develop the best in them [your children] in the best possible way and stamp out the bad without seeming aggressive about it." Only once did I record any conflict over the paths that lay open to me. I wince to quote my fifteen-year-old pomposities:

> There must be one person who works twenty-four hours a day to bring up children, even when the family has only two. This is the mother's job. If she is absolutely unfitted for it, then she must supply someone who will furnish love, culture, learning, and discipline. There are no substitutes for these, and they must be supplied one way or another. This is an awful thing for me to have to face. I will never want to surrender myself wholly to the job of home-making.

It goes without saying that the example of a relative or family friend who worked would have helped me. (The only one who did was constantly put down by my mother and grandmother for neglecting her children—and they were right about her.) Today I would feel that a woman interested in what at fifteen I airily referred to as the "life of the mind" may do better not to have children, but to judge by the passage quoted above, my character and conditioning were such that even in early adolescence this option was already closed to me.

In saying that sex was remote from my adolescent life I do not mean that I did not think about it all the time. But, inheriting a romantic (and lady-like) tradition, I would have found it impossible to admit it was sex I was thinking of. Instead I called it loneliness, or more disastrously, love (which, of course, I also wanted)—that is, the only love which would have been acceptable to me, especially with my Roman Catholic background and the example of my mother and grandmother's lives: complete, final, culminating in wedlock. This led to rampant fantasy life, designs on several unsuspecting young men, and a long involvement with the first young man who cared for me. I could think of it all as farcical if it didn't still make the palms of my hands sweat. Most of it came later than the early adolescent years. At sixteen I had been no more than kissed, hardly rumpled, although I knew myself on the basis of classmates' intimated experiences (girls in those days did not compare notes) to be backward.

It was another matter if sex was in a book and did not refer to me. I read Balzac's *Droll Stories* and Erich Remarque's *The Arch of Triumph*. There was nothing more so available. I was twenty-two before I found under the counter on the Avenue de l'Opera all the green-bound books that are now over-the-counter all over the United States—not to mention in your neighborhood theater. My grandmother told me not to read Thornton Wilder's *The Ides of March;* I protested in my diary, "What does an historical novel accomplish if it does not make us aware that though the vestal virgins were virgins the rest of Rome was perfectly normal?"

During the twelve to sixteen years I was apt to think about sex through anxiety about myopia and fat. Puberty brought nearsightedness; all at once I could not see the numbers on the sails of boats on Long Island Sound (the trickster, unpredictable body again). I can remember weeping all the way home from the optician as a new and stronger pair of glasses made the pavement look all at once like a Dubuffet. I never stated it to myself but in fact I believed that "Men seldom make passes at girls who wear glasses." I think I also believed that they never made passes at anyone who weighed over 120 pounds. (I lived, as I still do, on the dubious frontier between gourmandise and gluttony—with a cottage cheese metabolism.) The summer I turned fifteen I lost twenty pounds. It was a ritual, I see now, of sexual eligibility.

I am bitter about the way I and others of my generation were made to feel about physical appearance. There was scarcely an ad I looked at as I was growing up which did not equate the ideal body and the possibility of acceptance by others, especially one's peers. The price in self-hatred was enormous. We were without a counterculture and yet exposed in early adolescence to a post-World War II advertising style at once more blatant and suggestive than anything our parents had known. The sexual criterion was pronounced. Moreover, the ideal was a photograph, or rather a certain photographic style or styles. Mine is a generation that doubted itself in deep ways because we were not photographs. The dieting of WASPS like me was of a piece with noses altered and hair straightened, but of course paltry in comparison. In my case the situation was exacerbated by my particular background. It is the final refinement of having plenty to leave it on your place, and scorn for gratification can be a by-product of an ethic of control.

Inextricable from worry about fat and glasses was anxiety about social life, and in the upper-class New York milieu in which I was raised that consisted of subscription dances during Christmas and Easter vacations.

A few of my contemporaries knew boys at day school in New York, often through a brother, but I did not. Many of my Jewish classmates had (or appeared to have—I feel uncertain writing about any of this; I tended to see others through a glass, rosily) a better social life because they were part of a more cohesive society with a gregarious allegiance to each other ("Our Crowd") in which families saw to it that parties at home and membership in country clubs supplemented formal social life and brought young people together. Something like this existed in the summer life of latter-day Wharton or Jamesian WASPS but it was spotted around the map of New England. It seems to me that in the city the cohesiveness of an earlier age (my grandmother's youth) had been lost and with it a degree of confidence. The group was too big to know each other and to maintain a sense of scale. And it was no longer quite the same group. To a degree it had been infiltrated, not by robber barons and their offspring as at the turn of the century, but by what my grandmother referred to scornfully as "cafe society." (She herself was something of an infiltrator, but that is another story and one I had not figured out during those years.) In any case, most boys of this milieu were sent to boarding school so that for most adolescents there was no social contact at all except for the vacations. Some lucky girls knew boys they could write to—"I am writing this under the covers at night by the light of a flashlight," wrote a friend of mine in study hall. The rest relied on their luxuriant fantasy life.

Everything that has been written about the horrors of the college mixer dance could be applied to the subscription dances: the emphasis on superficial attractiveness, the encouragament of puny strategies and aggressive or defensive behavior, the fostering of feelings of inadequacy, almost inevitable at least for the awkward and shy. If anything these dances were worse than college dances because the participants were younger and generally more inept socially. Moreover, the girls had to invite the boys, thus reversing the stance which they were meanwhile learning to assume. And not only one boy but two, so that there would be a stag line.

The evenings began with dinner parties at which perhaps a dozen young people awkwardly battened into formal clothes did what they could to make conversation. One of my cousins always opened by asking girls whether or not they sat facing the drain when taking a bath. Bodies, tyrannical and unpredictable as ever, were just below the surface of the conversation. Suddenly brawny wrists which had thrust three inches in three months (it seemed) out of the sleeves of dinner jackets, Etna-like pimples monopolizing one's consciousness, and in that era of the strapless dress, breasts, too much or too little. I remember falsies, in their own antiseptic way as surreal as the *mamelles de Tiresias,* rising clear out of the bodice of a friend's dress. I admit it happened while she was dancing, but I'm sure they felt unreliable even at the dinner table.

After dinner as many as 350 young people congregated in the semi-darkness of the Plaza ballroom, there to manage as best they could for three hours. The underlying myth said that everyone knew everyone because everyone was from the same milieu. In fact, little clusters of people knew other clusters based on schools attended and summer friendships—and some knew scarcely anyone at all. (My position in relation to all this was particularly difficult since my mother's family was both of the milieu and at the same time half withdrawn from it, or in the case of my mother almost totally withdrawn from it.) There were people who had a good time but they tended to be the most aggressive of the boys and the "stars" among the girls. Myopia is one of my chief memories of those evenings; I could not possibly have considered wearing my glasses. But despite nearsightedness I remember individual dresses, faces, scenes sharply at a more than twenty year distance, so intensely was I keyed up to survive in what I had plunged myself into. I had not been forced to go (my sister refused to); I had chosen to, if one can associate choice with an unrelenting effort to succeed with peers. Conforming and succeeding were inextricable in my adolescence from the desire to overcome a feeling of isolation, half social, half sexual.

My situation, and perhaps the situation of many young adolescents, demanded the comfort of a fantasy self. Hand in hand with the plump, striving, myopic individual the world could see walked a glamorous, seductive ghost socially adept and at the same time lyrical, sensitive; a creature in love with spring rains and spring flowers. Glamor and lyricism are strange companions, but this never struck me; perhaps my unconscious model was the Cecil Beaton photos I had pored over as a child: English beauties in organdy grouped on the grass around the trunk of a stately tree and in the distance ponds, sheep, woods, sunlit mist, and plenty of sward.

It was the ghost who chose the dresses in which to brave the dances: black and green moire or net embroidered with peacock's eyes. And it was the ghost who began to read poetry, trying with words to flesh out feeling in the most traditional adolescent way.

"Up the airy mountain,/down the rushing glen,/We daren't go a-hunting/for fear of little men." This is where I was just before the twelve to sixteen years began. This was rapidly superseded by Alfred Noyes: "There's a barrel-organ carolling across a golden street/ In the City as the sun sinks low."
Or:

> Yes; as the music changes,
> Like a prismatic glass,
> It takes the light and ranges
> Through all the moods that pass;
> Dissects the common carnival
> Of passions and regrets,
> And gives the world a glimpse of all
> The colours it forgets.

Next came:

> Sabrina fair
> Listen where thou are sitting
> Under the glassy, cool, translucent wave,
> In twisted braids of lilies knitting
> The loose train of thy amber-dropping hair,
> Listen for dear honor's sake,
> Goddess of the silver Lake
> Listen and save!

Although there was still room for:

> Over the cobbles he clattered and clashed in the
> dark inn yard.
> He tapped with his whip on the shutter, but all
> was locked and barred.
>
> (Noyes again)

Then came quantities of Shelley, the songs of Shakespeare, fragments of Keats and Coleridge, and not a single thing from the modern period except:

> A brackish reach of shoal off Madaket—
> The sea was still breaking violently and night
> Had steamed into our North Atlantic Fleet.

I did not read even Yeats until I was in college (I would have loved him; the ghost self was Yeatsian; it stood at the edge of still brown waters and watched the flight of swans, but the water was Long Island Sound and the birds were gulls).

Others have said it, but my generation and my milieu of peers were slow to discover ourselves in our own time. We read Eliot, Pound, Yeats, and Rilke in college. I did not understand *Howl* when it first appeared. It is possible that the fare we were offered in elementary and high school had some influence on our tardiness. Literature, it was implied, had stopped somewhere around 1870. Traditional education has always operated with this sort of gap or lag and for centuries no one expected the present—or the relevant as it is called today—to be formally taught. Interested people picked it up, were part of it. I am not sure now that I believe that the present should be taught, at least in literature, and yet I am bothered by what I was taught in my early teens. Somehow it was not good enough to read three Scott novels and William Cullen Bryant in seventh and eighth grades. Now young people are starved on relevance but we were force-fed the past. Is this one reason we were so slow to put any stock in the validity of our own experience or to find our own way of seeing? Or did our adolescent years come at precisely the moment when everything that has become so apparent since was just beginning to show (the technological juggernaut, the overly rapid rate of change, political powerlessness, the substitution of symbiosis with a pop environment for a relationship with the natural world)? Were we slow because we were frozen, seeing a little and not knowing how to interpret? Whatever the answer, we started out believing that traditional tools would be adequate to interpret our experience. I think we were the last generation to believe so. When at the very end of the twelve-to-sixteen period it first occurred to me that I might try one day to be a writer, I did not question that I would write novels. I did not, for instance, consider films, as did those five or six years younger than I. (My five-year-old son, on the other hand, dictating his first story, asks, "Is it going to be a book or a show or T.V.?" And when he paints—on long pieces of shelf paper taped to the floor—he asks me to attach the paper to the cardboard tubes of paper towel rolls so that he can make a moving picture.)

For me the transformation of tools and understanding came slowly and is incomplete.

In a certain sense I feel I falsify speaking of early adolescence in terms of discontinuity and transformation, sex and sensibility. What I did was go to school. Whatever my inner sense of discontinuity and isolation, for eight months of the year there was the continuity of school and the daily contact with about twenty other girls.

My sister and I left the apartment at 8:15, walked two blocks to the Spence School and thereupon were enclosed until 3:00 and sometimes 4:00 or 4:30 in a self-contained world housed in a more or less

Georgian brick building on East 91st Street. The day began with prayers and announcements (some of the prayers sounded like announcements) and ended with sports. In between came a traditional curriculum traditionally and, in the case of many of the subjects, well taught. (It is easy to denigrate the education the school then offered. There were indeed endless grammar and spelling drills, a good deal of memorization, and, of course, *Ivanhoe,* the *Talisman,* and the *Heart of Midlothian.* But perhaps it is just worth mentioning that somewhere along the line I built a model of an Erie Canal lock, wrote a play about Catherine de Medici, and twice a week painted all afternoon with an excellent teacher. The strictest teacher was the French teacher—successor to the white Russian—yet it was she who would now and then stand on her desk to act out one of La Fontaine's fables.)

It was a lock-step day, hardly broken by lunch and the free time that followed it, yet it was in this free time and in the afternoons before the hours of homework set in that friendships were formed. It is claimed that, unlike men, women do not need or else are socialized to do without close friendship groups of their own sex. I think, however, that friendships between individual girls can be important and sometimes even durable. I, for instance, count among my closest friends two women whom I first knew in early adolescence and met at school. I notice that although I do not see them very often, I confide in them as I do not in others (and they in me) as if those early years had created a special trust. We seem to continue conversations we began twenty-five years ago.

It is perhaps only ten years since I had a nightmare that I had not done my French homework. I can still conjure up the queasy stomach which I had each morning during those palatable Episcopalian prayers. (There were Jews and Catholics in the school, but it was taken for granted that tone was at least part of what parents wanted from the place and tone was Episcopalian.) I have often wondered whether school meant to my classmates what it meant to me. I think for many it did not. For me it was an outlet for ambition—the only one available to me—something I could do and succeed at. At the same time there gleamed out at me from the pages of sturdy textbooks baubles of true interest which I snapped at like a bower-bird: tidbits about the Renaissance, about the structure of language and the derivation of words, English history and the structure of plants.

But there was a price for succeeding, or rather a double price. Doing well set one off as a "brain," winning respect but not the acceptance one craved. Moreover, it pressured one to compete with one's previous record. One mid-years I wrote a long criticism of the exam system in my diary, praising intellectual endeavor for its own sake, but when I got my marks a few days later I recorded that I was not pleased—at two B's and three A's. Pressuring myself thus I was tired by the end of the year and wrote:

> Everything is endless. The work pours in; it is only ended by nine o'clock. The weather is warmer. My head is fuzzier. I wonder what I shall remember from all this hodgepodge ... I can't remember this year at all. I remember Christmas vacation and the Big Snow [that blanketed New York in 1947]. I can recall that my hands sweated in English class from fear and hatred of Mrs. _____. I know even now that I didn't want to go back to school in October. The winter seemed interminable. The weekends were and are full of the family and the country but always accompanied by a deep down loneliness and lack of anyone to talk to my own age.

Perhaps this suggests not only the melodrama of adolescence and the depression which is the ever-present obverse of natures like mine but also at least one possible effect of a school such as the one I attended. The school was a copy of a copy of a copy—that is, it was a copy of a boy's college prep school and traditional boy's schools are copies in their picture of authority, their emphasis on competition and team sports of an all-male, more or less anglophile, achievement-oriented model of society. But girls were supposed *not* to do what the school prepared them to do, although they were subjected to a very similar education, minus some math and science, and an identical set of values (the Episcopalian prayers, the team sports, the scholastic honor rolls). As I said earlier only the achievement of marrying well was completely sanctioned. (In an earlier generation it would have been somewhat acceptable to achieve as long as one eschewed marriage, or at least didn't count on it, but in my adolescence, which coincided with the "feminine mystique," this course no longer had any status.) I am not sure that this situation was a source of conflict for many of my school contemporaries, but it was for me, not because I put less value on marriage—it was the only thing I was sure I wanted—but because I placed a value on school that they in many cases did not. I believed in it. In 1949 I wrote as follows (and the pomposity in this case seems in direct proportion to uncertainty):

> Next year I shall have to decide about college. Certainly my opinions are not those of five years ago. At that time I thought that I would never want to go to college. Now I most probably shall. I am not sure that I want to spend four years because as in the minds of most girls my age is the idea of marriage.

It seems at least possible that I could have contemplated four years of college more positively—and not been so blue at the end of a long winter of being a good girl—if I had had at home or at school any models to lead me to believe that what I was doing had a future for me on its own terms. I think it is quite clear that I thought it was perilous to extend this future even a full four years beyond high school.

As if this situation was not enough to contend with, there was in the air both at home and at school the very WASP and very American ethos (perhaps it has something to do with a pre-sputnik era in education, too) that urged high achievers never to thrust themselves forward. It was not simply a question of being lady-like (men are as affected by this as women): it was a question of being humble and humility was not exactly or only a Christian virtue but a civic one. What's good enough for everyman is good enough for anyone who gets A's, and you're rocking the boat in an un-American way if you don't think so. It was this group of ideas that was hardest for me to accommodate myself to at fifteen and sixteen. I fancied myself an intellectual. An arrogant prig was closer to the point. Nevertheless, the following episode with the school librarian still rankles:

> This morning I said something which I suppose is rather rude to Miss C. She asked what books we had gotten out of the library for the Renaissance project and I said I hadn't gotten any. Then afterwards she took me out of the library and told me a lot of things. She said that I was adolescent, having an adolescent's new discovery of brain power and the new feeling of the power of one's own ideas. She said that I was riding too high, not humble enough, and tending towards intellectual snobbery and introspection.

However well founded, it seems typical of my background that the repressive put-down came first rather than any attempt at offering the kind of freedom or challenge which would have forced me to test the wings I thought I had. Why didn't Miss C. show me the books I had been too hoity-toity to discover for myself?

The complete set of signals blipped at girls like me went something like this: achieve if you want to but remember it will set you apart from other girls and make it harder to attract boys. If you achieve prepare to interrupt your achievement at an appropriate (marriageable) age. Achieve but be cool about it; hide it if possible and above all don't claim that achievement has any prerogatives.

Needless to say I didn't articulate these signals to myself. I was not even aware of them; I just did my homework. Nevertheless, I responded to the code—by making rules for myself. There are more rules than there are prayers in my diary. When I first reread the entries before writing this piece the rules appeared ludicrous or pathetic, but I now think they represent a pretty accurate rendering of what it took to do well and at the same time be accepted in the time and the setting I grew up in. For instance:

1. Not to talk too much.
2. Not to be a fix-it.
3. To be sincere without being unwitty, stupid, or a goody-goody.
4. To be kind.
5. To avoid gossip.
6. To work hard.
7. To be friendly without being obnoxious.
8. To be sensitive without being hypersensitive.
9. To cultivate and work toward the right attitude.

Another set included these:

Placate everyone.

Strive for originality.

Early adolescents are assailed with the outer world as never before in their lives, or rather assailed with the sudden importance of succeeding in it, whether this means in work or love or friendship. In my uptight case this meant giving carte blanche to my superego. (I find the admission ignominious.) While others revolted I made rules. I had always wanted to please, not out of virtue, but because I was born cowardly about conflict. The desire to please became much more intense in adolescence and at the same time pleasing was all at once far more complicated.

Rule-making led me to distrust my own perceptions. This was its greatest drawback.

There is a cold and lonely feeling which I get living here this way [I wrote one summer about life at my grandmother's]. It creeps into me from every corner of the house, and I feel it shifting into me from each object that I touch. I sit all day building up hate for the place and the way of life in general.

But then I pulled the rug out from under myself:

This is bad because I suppose there is nothing wrong with it—the atmosphere, I mean. I am thoroughly biased at this point.

Reading old diaries is a particularly blatant form of narcissism. I am glad to say it is not one I had indulged in for many years until writing this piece. It is narcissistic because one is looking for oneself, trying to give one's present a psychic or emotional continuity in the past. I do not catch a clear reflection of myself from my adolescent diary; the elements are there but they do not have the same proportions they have now and the harping on loneliness, the lyricism, the prayers seem part of a self I have not known for a long time. I have a hunch that I might feel more of a piece with the self of childhood if I had a record of it; then I think I made fewer rules, was less ambitious and less bent on acceptance by my peers—and perhaps trusted my perceptions more. Yet if I do recognize myself in the early adolescent I once was it is in this conflict between rules and perception, a conflict which is still with me unresolved. What I perceive most of the time makes me not want to cope (it is probably significant that I use the word cope)—unless writing is coping—but the pattern is set, the sense of obligation is so strong that I can do otherwise only in spurts, and then feel guilty. One of the drawn-out, painful discoveries of adult life has been the discovery that rule-making is incompatible with the kind of writing I admire and that fantasy, the escapist reaction to too much rule-making, is almost equally incompatible. But the point I want to make here is that one's stance in relation to the outer world may be partly innate or created in childhood, but it is in a sense recreated in early adolescence and so strongly set and reinforced by a feeling of the vital importance of others that it is hard if not impossible to change. A lot of the time I am still doing my homework.

PART II

COPING WITH ADOLESCENCE: BEHAVIORAL EXPRESSIONS

The biological, psychological, and social stresses of adolescence are greatly intensified in the present period of deteriorating traditional values and continuing loss of support for the teenager from both family and community. How, then, does the adolescent cope with these stresses in a society in which a puritan revolution in reverse has resulted in the pursuit of pleasure, the breakdown of sexual inhibitions, the loss of the socializing power of traditional religious teachings, the depreciation of the work ethic, and finally, a revolution in weaponry that has made war obsolete and threatens mankind with the specter of annihilation?

The pervading theme of this section is that the behavioral expressions of contemporary American youth represent an attempt on their part to cope with these pressures while growing up in a world in which even their elders experience threat and confusion. To understand contemporary adolescent behavior it is necessary to inquire into the variety of coping methods they have developed as the means both to facilitate their growth and to seek new ways of relating to and advancing contemporary culture.

The first of these behavioral expressions is the use of drugs. The mass media treatment of youth who use drugs—and the continuous newspaper accounts of drug raids on college dormitories and student living quarters—have created an image of the young drug user as a "moral leper" deserving the legal treatment society usually reserves for the chronic offender and hardened criminal. Kenneth Keniston, in his essay "Heads and Seekers," is interested in exploring who the student drug user is and why he prefers this mode of behavioral expression. He finds that student drug users are seekers. Why do they search, and what do they seek? The increasing impoverishment of the quality of American life has left the attractiveness of a meaningful career in doubt. The repressions of the late 1960s and early 1970s have made political activism an act of futility. The image of the political process—from the abortive Bay of Pigs invasion of Cuba and the undeclared war in Vietnam to the misrepresentations of the nation's leaders—is seen as reflecting a system that is dishonest, immoral, and unresponsive to the ideals of America. Increasingly disillusioned, the drug users seek a relevance that will give meaning to their lives, and to the flatness, drabness, and meaninglessness of their college experience. To the seeker, salvation, if it is to be found at all, must be found by turning inward to the self rather than by turning outward to the wider community.

In the second essay, Alvin E. Strack provides the reader with some basic knowledge of the drugs currently in use. Starting with the basic concept of dependence, which itself suggests the substitution of a drug-induced psychologic state for a personal commitment to another person, Strack goes on to discuss the nature and effects of the major drugs in use. He portrays the effects of use and abuse of the opiates, the barbiturates and tranquilizers, the amphetamines, the hallucinogens, and the solvents. In contrast to Keniston's view of drug use by youth as a means for achieving salvation, Strack describes it as a symptom of a personal disorder. Loneliness and alienation become in this context an expression of an intrapsychic conflict which has its roots either in adolescent rebellion or in a deep-seated character neurosis. The two articles, therefore, present both sides of the debate. Methods of treatment, of course, differ radically depending upon which side one takes. While Strack supports good law enforcement as a means of decreasing the availability of drugs for the user, he views education as the key to prevention. The most important message for the professional educator to convey to young people is that drug taking is "one of the biggest 'cop-outs' of all time; it is a 'cop-out' on oneself."

Turning inward to the self through drug use is one form of coping behavior; turning outward toward the wider community is another. If we reflect back upon the activism of youth from 1964 through 1973, several major questions come to mind. First, what was the nature of this action-oriented behavior? Secondly, have the youth of those years left a style of action for which there will be heirs in their younger brothers and sisters? Finally, was activism a reaction to contradictions in the post-industrial society that will lead youth to a new set of values that will survive repression, such as the killings at Kent State? In "Notes on a New History: The Young and the Old," Robert Jay Lifton speaks of The New History as "a radical recreation of the forms of human culture."

The great events of the twentieth century have destroyed the traditions of the past, both the world view and the life patterns of a majority of people. The most awesome of these events, the Nazi genocide (symbolized by the word Auschwitz) and the U.S. atomic bombing (symbolized by the word Hiroshima), released upon the modern world man's capacity for evil and his capability for destruction. Youth has been confronted with the possibility of no future at all. Lifton believes that activism is more than just a means of coping with this all-important fact—it is a style of rebellion that permits youth while rebelling to remain open to all possible varieties of historical alternatives. If everything remains possible, then activism has a larger purpose than mounting demonstrations and attaining political objectives. This purpose the young activist sees as the absolute necessity to build a new future or a New History through which mankind can survive.

The sexual revolution is interpreted by Herbert Marcuse, the revolutionary theorist so often quoted by young activists, as a freedom granted by the political establishment in exchange for rigid conformity in other areas of life. Many social critics view changing sexual values as due to industrialism having eliminated the need for sex-linked roles, while others see the changes as related to the absent father of World War II, and the mark left on young people, now of age, by his absence. Whatever the causes, sexual values are rapidly undergoing a change, and adolescents must find their sexual identity within the context of this change.

In the initial essay on this topic, "The Beige Epoch: Depolarization of Sex Roles in America," Charles Winick provides much evidence that sex roles have become substantially neutered. Gender-linked colors that used to identify the infant he and the infant she are giving way to other colors not associated with sexual identification. Gender-linked names are being replaced by those that are less gender-specific, i.e., John and Mary are becoming less popular while Leslie, Robin, and Tracy are increasingly used. Several writers in the social sciences have recently been experimenting with de-sexing our vocabulary and searching for neuter nouns such as chairperson to replace the "sexist" chairman. The depolarization of sex roles that starts in early childhood reaches its nadir in late adolescence. Jeans, a loose-fitting top, heavy shoes, and shoulder-length hair—the uniform of the high school senior and the college student—make sexual identification at a distance almost impossible. Gender-related behavior also seems to be losing its distinctions. The teenage girl, whether in formal dating or informal sexual contacts, demands the right to be as sexually aggressive as her male companion. Garages, at least in campus communities, now employ coeds to pump gas, change tires, and check the oil.

The behavioral expressions of adolescents thus seem to represent an acceptance of and responsiveness to the depolarization of sex roles in America. The area of their greatest concern, however, is how to adapt to the changing sexual morality that accompanies the sexual revolution. In "Sexual Morality and the Dilemma of the Colleges," young people are seen as turning in increasing numbers to moralities better adapted to the individual who is biologically mature but still denied the possibility of "leading his own life" through the assumption of an adult social role. Hence the new morality, as described by Dana L. Farnsworth, with its criterion of mutual consent as the basis for premarital sexual relations—a denial of the traditional ethic which restricts sex to those who have already assumed adult roles.

The articles on music as a behavioral expression of contemporary adolescence were deliberately left to last because music has the power to integrate and express the needs, the conflicts, and the visions of the teenager seeking to create an identity out of the confusion of American culture. Craig McGregor's comment in his essay on Bob Dylan is to the point when he remarks:

> You grow up in America in the fifties and sixties, you need help to outface what's coming down. It's no accident that so many of the alternate life-concepts with which young Americans have experimented in the last two decades involve some variety of transcendentalism; mankind cannot bear too much reality (T. S. Eliot said that) and jumps into drugs, Zen, Meher Buba, astrology, I Ching, Jesus—even a hyped-up supernatural theory of Love.

As recently as the summer of 1973, the rock music festival at Watkins Glen had the largest attendance of any music festival directed to youth; music still seems to say it all. It is hard to choose which group or individual performer best represents the teenage audience. Jimi Hendrix, Janis Joplin, and Bob Dylan have been major candidates. The mantle of hero of the pop generation must eventually fall to Bob Dylan, for he above all others seems through his music to enact the dilemmas and crisis of the generation for which he sings. Craig McGregor's essay analyzes the major themes behind Dylan's music. He finds that his songs truly reflect the diverse problems of today's adolescent in his attempt to deal with the world. Dylan's heroic quality, however, derives from his having been able to write songs about his own struggles—struggles with which contemporary youth has been able to identify completely.

The songs of Bob Dylan may represent outstanding samples of the music of youth; however, popular music also includes folk, folk rock, acid rock, hard rock, and blues. Some groups like the Beatles, Buffalo Springfield, Strawberry Alarm Clock, and the Byrds sold millions of records. Robert Rosenstone's essay delineates the themes of the music of protest. The popular groups of the middle sixties spoke out against war, segregation, and the plight of youth as an oppressed minority. Toward the end of the decade musical themes merged with the mystic search of the drug culture for each individual's best route to the center of his mind. Rosenstone maintains that with the increasing irrelevance of traditional sources of information —parents and adults, the school and the press—the major function of music has been to offer youth information about what is happening. Telling it like it is, the lyrics offer adolescents an opportunity to develop a body of knowledge and a set of myths that help define their own subculture.

One

Drug Use

Student drug users can be divided into two categories: the "seekers" see drug use as an occasional assist in the pursuit of meaning or in overcoming a transient depression; regular drug users, the "heads," view their behavior as part of the "turned on" ideology of the hippie subculture. Seekers tend to be hardworking, idealistic, and on the threshold of alienation. The heads, a group characterized by genuine alienation, have found expression in an ideology that is profoundly hostile to the careerist, success-oriented middle-class America.

KENNETH KENISTON

Heads and Seekers: Drugs on Campus, Counter-Cultures, and American Society

Students who use drugs are usually treated by the mass media as an alien wart upon the student body of America. A spate of articles in popular magazines, specials on television, discussions in state legislatures and hearings by congressmen have helped create an image of the young drug user that equates "drug abuse" with moral leprosy and quite possibly with membership in the Mafia. Few subjects arouse feelings as intense and irrational as does the topic of student drug use; in few areas is there greater tendency to distort, to perceive facts selectively, and to view with alarm. Few topics are treated with so much heat and so little light.

Despite growing public agitation, however, we have remarkably little factual information about drugs on campus. Most colleges have not conducted surveys of drug use—or if they have, they have preferred not to publicize the results. Most students who use drugs do not volunteer themselves as psychological research subjects, for the mere possession of marihuana is a felony under federal law. As a result, what is known about the sociology and psychology of student drug users comes largely from that small minority of students who are sufficiently disturbed to seek out professional help. Surrounded with illegality and the taint of moral depravity, drug use on campus remains a largely unexplored area.

Yet enough information is now available from scattered studies to permit preliminary extrapolation to a coherent picture of the "student drug abuser." In the discussion that follows, I will not be concerned with the psychopharmacology or physical effects of drug use. Rather I will speculate about the meaning of this phenomenon in a variety of overlapping contexts—psychological, social, educational and historical.

To begin to understand youthful drug use, we must start from a series of more specific questions. Who uses drugs? How do we define "drug use"? What are some of the psychological factors involved in drug use? How can we explain the fact that drug use is very common in certain kinds of colleges, but virtually nonexistent in others? If, as widely claimed, student drug use is related in some way to the characteristics of modern American society, what is the nature of the relationship?

RATES AND PLACES

The term "drug" covers a multitude of substances that affect human physiology and functioning. Virtually every American is a routine user of prescribed and unprescribed psychoactive drugs like aspirin, alcohol, sleeping pills or stimulants whose primary intended effect is to alter mood, feeling, or psychological states. Indeed, at the present time, more than seventy percent of all prescriptions written in the United States are for psychoactive compounds—for example, tranquilizers, pain-killers and antidepressants. If we include—as we must—ethyl alcohol, caffeine and nicotine among drugs, then the American who has never "used" drugs is a statistical freak.

Although drug use itself is not novel in American society, what is novel is the student use of new types of drugs for the sole purpose of altering mood and state of consciousness. Most student drug use involves the hallucinogens—a family of nonaddictive drugs that includes not only marihuana (cannabis) but other hallucinogenic, psychedelic or psychotomimetic drugs like LSD, DMT, STP, psilocibin and mescaline (peyote). Some of these drugs have been widely used since the beginning of recorded history, others are recent discoveries; what is new, then, is their use by a growing segment of American college youth. To be sure, most definitions of "drug abuse" lump together distinct individuals for whom drug use and experimentation have very different meanings. But for a start, let us accept the prevailing definition of "drug user" as anyone who has *ever* tried any one of the hallucinogens, and examine the pattern of use that results from accepting this definition.

Student drug use, defined as use of the hallucinogens, is rapidly increasing. But the widely publicized estimates that one in seven, one in four, or one in two of the seven million college students in America can be considered a "drug abuser" are vastly exaggerated. Even at those few colleges where drug use is most prevalent, surveys arrive at estimates of between five and seventy-five percent of the student body who have "ever used" any of the hallucinogens. These studies, furthermore, tend to have been conducted at select colleges like California at Berkeley, Wisconsin at Madison, Michigan at Ann Arbor, Harvard, Stanford, Yale, Cal. Tech, Princeton, Antioch, Swarthmore, Wesleyan (Connecticut), Goddard and Reed. Approximately three percent of American college students attend these institutions. Among the remaining ninety-seven percent, it already seems clear that drug use is far rarer, and in many instances nonexistent. A recent Gallup Poll arrives at an estimate of five to six percent of college youth who have "ever tried" any hallucinogenic drug. Thus, while student drug use constitutes an important phenomenon, it probably touches directly less than one in ten of the young Americans who attend institutions of higher education.

The public impression of astronomically high rates of drug use in American college youth stems in part from the great visibility of the colleges where drug use is most common. Students of college cultures have found it useful to categorize colleges according to the relative presence or absence of what they term an "intellectual climate." The correlation between "intellectual climate" and rates of drug use is very close. That is, the highest rates are found at small, progressive, liberal arts colleges with a nonvocational orientation, a high faculty-student ratio, high student intellectual caliber as measured by College Boards, close student-faculty relationships, and a great value placed on the academic independence, intellectual interests, and personal freedom of students. At perhaps a dozen or so such colleges, it seems likely that the proportion of students who have ever tried marihuana or some other hallucinogen exceeds fifty percent. But there are more than twenty-two hundred other colleges in the country.

Farther down the list, with regard to both intellectual climate and drug use, are the private university colleges, like Harvard, Stanford, Yale and Chicago, and the major state universities, like Michigan, Wisconsin and California, with a tradition (at least within their Colleges of Arts and Sciences) of intellectual excellence and academic freedom. Included on this list, as well, should be the major technological institutions like Cal. Tech and M.I.T., notable for the extremely high ability of students they recruit. At such colleges, student drug use rates of between ten and fifty percent will be found at present.[1] Still farther down on the list are other state universities with a lesser reputation for academic excellence and intellectual or personal freedom. Here one thinks of colleges like Ohio State and the University of Oregon. At such institutions rates of drug use probably vary between five and twenty percent. At the bottom of the list in terms of both student drug use and intellectual climate are those colleges that together enroll the majority of American students— upgraded state teachers colleges, junior colleges, community colleges, normal schools, the smaller religious and denominational colleges, and most Catholic colleges and universities. On such campuses, student drug use rarely exceeds five percent. These are the colleges most notable for their vocational and practical orientation, the absence of serious student intellectual interests, and the presence of strong anti-intellectual student subcultures centered around technical training and/or social activities like sports and fraternities.

Nor are drug users randomly distributed *within* any one institution. At large universities that include a number of separate "schools," drug use is concentrated in the College of Arts and Sciences, the Graduate School, and in the Schools of Drama, Music, Art and Architecture. Rates of drug use are notably lower in such schools as Business Administration, Engineering, Agronomy and Education. Furthermore, within any school or faculty, drug users are most likely to be found in the most intellectual, humanistic and "introspective" fields (for example, music, literature, drama, the arts

---

1. Regional differences are also important: drug use is higher on the West Coast than on the East Coast. Also, proximity to a metropolitan center probably increases drug use, other things being equal.

and psychology); they are likely to be less common in practical, applied, extroverted and "harder" areas like engineering or economics. Indeed, there is evidence from one liberal arts college that students who use drugs are characterized by *higher* grades than those who do not. The demographic evidence suggests a strong relationship between intellectuality and drug use within the college population.

These inferences, however, are open to two different interpretations. On the one hand, we might conclude that colleges with an "intellectual climate" recruit students with special personal characteristics that make them more prone to experiment with drugs. The institution, according to this view, merely acts as a magnet for young men and women who are likely to smoke pot no matter where they go to college. On the other hand, it could be argued that the climate and culture of some colleges actively push students toward drug use regardless of their personal characteristics. If a student attends a college where "everyone" is using drugs, he is more likely to do so himself. Similarly, certain college pressures (for example, relentless pressure for grades) or certain administrative practices (for example, respect for student autonomy) may also increase the likelihood of student drug use. In practice, both these interpretations seem correct: some colleges attract large numbers of potential drug users and then expose them to a climate in which using drugs becomes even more probable. To understand this interaction, we must consider types of drug users, motivations for drug use, and some of the pressures on college students today.

TASTERS, SEEKERS AND HEADS

A "drug abuser" is often defined as anyone who has ever experimented with any of the hallucinogens—who has ever inhaled marihuana, ever ingested any other hallucinogenic drug, or, in some instances, ever taken a barbiturate to get to sleep or an amphetamine (Benzedrine, Dexedrine) before an examination. If we limit ourselves to the hallucinogens, however, we usually find that up to half of the students listed as "users" turn out to have "used" drugs no more than three times, and to have no plans to continue. To call such students drug "abusers" or even "users" is misleading. It is like applying the epithet "alcoholic" or "drinker" to the college girl who once tasted a sip of beer but didn't like it, or labeling as a "smoker" the adult who at the age of twelve smoked a cigarette behind the barn but was sick and never smoked again. Probably the single largest group called "drug abusers" are in reality *tasters.* Such individuals have no place in a discussion of why students use drugs, since these particular students no longer use them.

If we eliminate the tasters from the ranks of student drug users, we are left with a contingent of probably less than five percent of the college population. These students have used drugs (usually marihuana) a number of times, and they tell us that they "plan" to continue their experimentation. But even within this group of continuing users there are important distinctions to be made. The largest single group of actual drug users are students who have used drugs a relatively small number of times (for example, have smoked pot less than fifteen times) and who do not use them regularly (for example, not every weekend). Such a pattern of use generally indicates that, despite willingness to continue drug experimentation, the individual has in no way organized his life around it. For these occasional users, drug use is generally a part of a more general pattern of experimentation and search for relevance both within and without the college experience—it is one aspect of a more encompassing effort to find meaning in life. Such students can be termed *seekers,* in that they seek in drug use some way of intensifying experience, expanding awareness, breaking out of deadness and flatness, or overcoming depression.

Finally, there is a relatively small but highly visible group of students who have made drug use a central focus of college life. Such students use drugs often and "regularly"—for example, every weekend—and they often experiment with a variety of different drugs. For such young men and women, drug use is not just an intermittent assist in the pursuit of meaning, but a part of a more general "turned-on" ideology, and a membership card to one of the collegiate versions of the hippie subculture. Such students are generally called *heads* (pot-heads or acid-heads) by their contemporaries; and they are by far the most knowledgeable about the effects, side effects, interactions and meanings of the drugs available to students today.

But even among heads, drug use does not invariably constitute the deeply psychopathological and self-destructive phenomenon it is sometimes said invariably to be. Many such students have sufficient strength of character (and perhaps of physiology) to endure regular experimentation with marihuana (and even with more powerful hallucinogens or amphetamines) without suffering any enduring personal disorganization. Many students who use marihuana routinely do *not* experience the ominous personal deterioration, the "bad trips" or the loss of motivation that is sometimes thought to accompany even casual drug experimentation. To be sure, one of the intended effects of drug use is to produce a *transient* alteration of experience and consciousness; and to those who view this alteration from the outside, it may appear deplorable. Yet a majority of students who have used the hallucinogens report that the experience was enlightening, enjoyable or meaningful. Most students who use marihuana regularly, and many of those who use the more powerful hallucinogens, never appear in clinics or consulting rooms (much less psychiatric hospitals). They "recover" from the drug experience, not obviously the worse for the wear, sometimes proclaiming loudly that they have gained a profound and valuable (if usually ineffable) insight into their own natures or that of the world. Judged by such criteria of mental health as the ability to work, to love and to play, such individuals do not seem especially less "mentally healthy" than before their drug experiences.

A smaller but highly publicized group of "heads," however, suffers serious ill effects from even single experiences with the hallucinogens. Students with serious preexisting psychopathology are most vulnerable. And these same students seem most likely to experiment with drugs under conditions that even experienced drug users consider adverse—intense depression, personal isolation and unpleasant surroundings. In extremely rare instances, marihuana can produce panic states or transient psychotic reactions, and similar reactions to LSD have been reported more often. Perhaps more important than the highly dramatic but usually reversible drug psychosis is the danger of lapsing into some relatively enduring form of personal disorganization—most commonly, a life-style that involves a virtually total and apparently self-destructive immersion in a drug-using "hippie" subculture.

Yet even here, short-term changes and long-range effects need to be distinguished. There are clearly some individuals who "regress" into a drug-using subculture for a period of months and even years, but who eventually reemerge into a productive relationship with their fellow man and with society itself. "Dropping out" into the hippie world seems to be defined, for growing numbers of students, as a way of testing psychological and social limits as a preparation for returning to the world of action and commitment. To be sure, most Americans would argue that there are better ways of testing the relationship of self to society than by entering the hippie subculture for two years. But our evaluation of the "ominous" implications of student drug use must be tempered by an awareness that many of those who "drop out" into the drug-using world eventually slide back into the mainstream. One of the disadvantages of the opprobrium that attends drug use is that labeling drug users "felons" or irredeemable "addicts" may in fact make it virtually impossible for them to return to a productive role in society.

THE QUESTION OF MOTIVES

Drug use is no different from any other form of human behavior, in that a great variety of distinct motives can cooperate to produce it. The particular weight of each of these motives and the way they are combined differs in each individual. Furthermore, drug use is affected not only by motives and forces *within* the individual, but by what is happening *outside* of him in his interpersonal environment, and in the wider social and political world. Thus, any effort to delineate "types" of motivations that enter into drug use is bound to be an oversimplification. For example, there are many individuals who share common characteristics with drug users but who do not use drugs because drugs are not available on their particular campus. Similarly, there are individuals who have little in common with other drug users, but who nonetheless use drugs.

With these important qualifications, at least two of the more common patterns of motivation in student drug users can be defined. Consider first the "seekers." Occasional but continuing drug users are rarely part of the hippie subculture, but such students do tend to have certain common characteristics. They are generally better-than-average students; they are intellectual and antivocational in their approach to their educations; and they are likely to be uncertain as to their future career plans. Sociologically, they tend to come from upper-middle-class professional and business families. Psychologically, such students are usually intense, introspective and genuinely involved in their academic work, from which they hope to find "solutions" to the problems of life and society. (Often, however, they are disappointed in this hope.) As individuals, they usually have a great capacity for hard work. They are rarely "lazy" or indolent; and, when called upon, they can be orderly, regular and highly organized. They also find it relatively easy to separate ideas from feelings, a fact that helps explain their high grades. They are strongly opposed to the war in Southeast Asia, do not express anger readily, and are often extremely idealistic.

But despite considerable academic success and the prospects of a good graduate school (possibly with a Woodrow Wilson Fellowship thrown in), such students are less seekers after grades or professional expertise than seekers after truth. They are extremely open to the contradictory crosscurrents of American culture; they read widely, be it in the theater of the absurd, modern existentialist literature, or the writings of the New Left. They are not in any systematic way "alienated" from American society, but they have not really made their minds up whether it is worth joining, either. Often, their own life-styles and the exertions required to do well in a demanding college make such students feel "out of touch" with themselves. Although to an outside observer they usually appear more thoughtful and "in touch" than their classmates in the School of Engineering or Business Administration, they do not consider themselves to be sentient at all. On the contrary, they are continually struggling to experience the world more intensely, to make themselves capable of greater intimacy and love, to find some "rock bottom" from which they can sally forth to social and interpersonal commitments. Such students characteristically make enormously high demands upon themselves, upon experience and upon life; contrasted with these demands, their current experience is often barren, flat and dull.

Marihuana and the more powerful hallucinogens fit very neatly with the search for experience for such students. On the one hand, they promise a new kind of experience to a young man or woman who is highly experimental. On the other hand, they promise intensity, heightened sentience, intensified artistic perceptiveness, and perhaps even self-understanding. Self-understaing is, of course, a prime goal for such individuals; for they are far more inclined to blame themselves than others for the inadequacies of their lives, and they often deliberately seek through self-analysis to change their personalities.

In students of this type, beginning or increasing drug use is often associated with feelings of flatness, boredom, stagnation and depression. It is surprising how often drug users mention a major loss, depression, or feeling of emptiness in the period preceding intensified drug use. The loss may be a breakup with a girl friend, the realization that one's parents are even more fallible than one had previously known, the blow to intellectual self-esteem that almost invariably accompanies the first midterm grades in the freshman year at a selective college, or the growing sense of confusion and purposelessness that follows abandoning previously cherished vocational goals or religious values. Under such circumstances, if there is pot around, the likelihood of trying it (and continuing to use it) is increased.

The "head" is in many respects different from the "seeker." Drug use occupies a more central place in the head's life and is almost always accompanied by disengagement from ordinary social expectations, by intense and often morbid self-exploration, and by a "turned-on" ideology profoundly hostile to the careerist, materialistic and success-oriented goals of middle-class American society. Almost invariably, then, the head is a member of a drug-using subculture, in which he finds an identity that enables him to drop temporarily out of the Establishment America from which he comes and toward which he was headed. For most young men and women, of course, membership in the hippie subculture lasts a summer, a term, a year, or possibly longer, but is followed by a gradual reentry into the System. One student of drug-using college dropouts estimates that they stay in the hippie world an average of a year and a half. After this, most return to their families in the suburbs (average parental income: $15,000 a year) and usually to the highly academic colleges from which they dropped out. Only those with unmistakable artistic talent and those with major psychiatric problems (or both) are likely to remain longer.

Unlike most seekers, heads are genuinely alienated from American society. Their defining characteristic is their generalized rejection of prevalent American values, which they criticize largely on cultural and humanistic grounds. American society is trashy, cheap and commercial; it "dehumanizes" its members; its values of success, materialism, monetary accomplishment and achievement undercut more important spiritual values. Such students rarely stay involved for long in the political and social causes that agitate many of their activist classmates. For alienated students, the basic societal problem is not so much political as aesthetic. Rejecting middle-class values, heads repudiate as well those conventional values and rules that deem experimentation with drugs illicit. For heads, the goal is to find a way out of the "air-conditioned nightmare" of American society. What matters is the interior world, and, in the exploration of that world, drugs play a major role.

A second characteristic of many heads is a more or less intense feeling of estrangement from their own experience. Such students are highly aware of the masks, facades and defenses people erect to protect themselves; they are critical of the social "games" and "role-playing" they see around them. They object to these games not only in others, but even more strongly in themselves. As a result, they feel compelled to root out any "defense" that might prevent awareness of inner life; self-deception, lack of self-awareness or "phoniness" are cardinal sins. They have, moreover, a conscious ethic of love, expressed in a continual struggle for "meaningful relationships"—direct, honest and open encounters with others. This ethic is sincerely felt, but it is often difficult for the alienated to achieve in practice. Thus, perhaps the deepest guilts in such individuals spring from their internal impediments to genuineness, directness and open communication with others. As one student said, "For me, sin equals hang-up."

Despite their efforts to make contact with their "real selves" and to have "meaningful relationships" with others, alienated students often feel unusually separated from both self and others. They experience themselves as separated from others by a gray opaque filter, by invisible screens and curtains, by protective shells and crusts that prevent them from the fullness of experience. They recriminate themselves for their lack of expressiveness, spontaneity and contact. One such student described human relations as being like people trying to touch each other through airtight space suits. Another talked of a wax that was poured over his experience, preventing him from rapport with the world. Possessed of an unusually strong desire for intense experience, but also unusually full of feelings of estrangement, such students find drugs that promise to heighten experience a tempting way out of a shell.

A third frequent characteristic of alienated students is a fantasy of fusion and merger, which contrasts sharply with their current feelings of estrangement. Many have a semiconscious concept of almost mystical union with nature, with their own inner lives, or with other people—of communication that requires no words, of the kind of oneness with nature, people, or the world that has always characterized intense religious experience. For a student with unusual impatience with the boundaries that separate the self from the not-self, the powerful hallucinogens are especially attractive, for they can profoundly alter the boundaries of body and self. This change in boundaries is by no means always pleasant, and one of the most common sources of panic during drug experiences is the feeling of being "trapped" in an isolated, barricaded subjectivity. But at other times, the hallucinogens *do* produce feelings of being in unusually direct contact, even fusion, with others.

On several grounds, then, the alienated student is strongly attracted by drugs and by the hippie world. Arguments against drug use based on traditional American values carry little weight for him; on the contrary, he takes great pleasure in violating these "middle-class" norms. His feelings of estrangement from his own experience lead him to attempt to break through the boundaries, shells, walls, filters and barriers that separate him from the world. And his fantasy of fusion disposes him to seek out chemical instruments to increase his "oneness" with others. For a student who is young, alienated and anticonventional, drug use is primarily a way of searching for meaning via the chemical intensification of personal experience.

In a broader developmental context, too, immersion in the drug-using hippie subculture is generally a part of a phase of disengagement from American society. Confronted with a society whose rules and values he profoundly distrusts, the head seeks in the counter-culture of hippiedom a respite, a moratorium, or an escape from pressures and demands he does not want to confront. Yet merely to note the important element of withdrawal in the hippie's use of drugs may be to ignore the more important developmental meaning of drug use for the hippie. However ill-advised society may consider his choice of methods, the hippie is often unconsciously searching for a way to engage himself with himself and with others. And however "regressive" or "self-destructive" it may appear to some for a young man to "drop out" of American society, the hippie subcul-ture often proves a rest-and-recovery area, or even a staging area, from which unusually sensitive, talented and/or disturbed individ-uals take stock of themselves, explore their inner lives and their relationships with a small group of other people, and sometimes *return* to the established society. It seems likely that most hippies will follow this path.

There are, however, a few heads for whom drug use is both a symptom of and a trigger for serious psychopathology. In some cases, drug use clearly accelerates a downhill course upon which the individual is already embarked; in other cases, an overwhelmingly bad trip may topple a student whose previous equilibrium was frag-ile. Thus, drug use may really be a contributing factor to a picture of psychopathology. Indeed, some of those who are most compul-sively drawn to chronic drug use are the same people who can least tolerate it. Already confused and precarious, they are unable to bear the induced alterations of consciousness produced by the hallucino-gens, and may move steadily or suddenly downhill.

THE PRESSURE FOR ACADEMIC PERFORMANCE

Some of the association between type of college and rate of drug use clearly results from the fact that highly "intellectual" colleges selec-tively attract students with a particular outlook and psychology. This process of attraction is complex. Admission policies that prefer-entially admit applicants with "serious intellectual interests" pro-mote the process of selective recruitment. But even at colleges that admit almost all applicants, the power of the college image alone suffices to channel into a relatively few colleges a great many stu-dents with psychological characteristics that incline them to experi-ment with drugs. The image of the intellectual college acts as a magnet for students like the "seeker" and the "head"; for "intellec-tual" or "alienated" high school students, certain colleges promise an ingathering of kindred spirits. Conversely, the less intellectual, un-alienated, unintrospective and nonexperimental student is generally attracted to less "intellectual" colleges.

But psychological factors will only take us part way to under-standing student drug use. Knowing what college a student attends is often a more accurate index of whether he has used drugs than is exploring his conscious and unconscious motives. The probability of drug use is a product of an interaction of individual psychology, institutional climate and broader social setting. To understand what helps create a climate of opinion that is favorable to drug experimen-tation, we must examine the pressures that impinge upon students at intellectual colleges.

It is noteworthy that colleges where drug use is most common are usually "high pressure" colleges. Typically, a great majority of undergraduates are preparing themselves for professional careers that require advanced graduate training: usually, more than seven-ty-five percent of graduates plan to continue their educations after the B.A. Furthermore, the magnetism of the college image and the fine screen of the admissions office almost always yield entering freshmen who have extremely high test scores and records of out-standing academic achievement in secondary school. To be sure, many of the most "intellectual" colleges make systematic efforts to mitigate these pressures by down-playing grades, by work-study programs, and so on. But despite the efforts of the college, students themselves are likely to *feel* pressured, both by their own desire to excel intellectually, and by the entrance requirements of graduate schools. And the congregation within such "intellectual" colleges of large numbers of intellectually able, competitive students helps gen-erate an atmosphere that makes intense intellectual interests, out-standing academic performance, and approval by faculty, schol-arship boards, *et cetera,* an important standard of personal worth and community recognition.

As a result, the more intellectual colleges are noteworthy for their *lack* of emphasis on the traditional American college pastimes of fun, fraternities and football. "Play" and social life are generally downgraded. Students and faculty members agree that the purpose of college is to get a liberal education, not to improve one's social skills, not to make influential friends for later life, and not to enjoy oneself in a frivolous way. Intellectual commitment and cognitive talent are highly rewarded, while these colleges frown on "colle-giate" pranks and "childish" displays of adolescent high spirits. What is valued at such colleges (and they increasingly set the tone for American higher education at large) is the ability to delay, postpone and defer immediate gratification in the interest of acquiring a liberal education. "Serious" interests—be they intellectual, artistic or political—are enjoined by a united student-faculty culture.

Such "elite" colleges present relatively few countervailing pressures to become more relaxed, joyous, interpersonally skilled, feeling, courageous, or physically expressive. Throughout the "intellectual" sector of American higher education, the most intense pressures are highly cognitive, narrowly academic, and often quantitative. The tangible rewards of American higher education—scholarships, admission to "good" graduate schools, remunerative fellowships and community acclaim—go for a rather narrow kind of cognitive functioning that leads to writing good final examinations, constructing good term papers, being good at multiple choice tests, and excelling on Graduate Record Examinations. Most of the students who attend these colleges are headed toward a professional world that requires the same kind of abstractive intelligence. Thus, it is the outstanding graduates of such colleges who go on to equally outstanding graduate schools, and eventually to outstanding appointments in outstanding hospitals, scientific laboratories, business corporations, and university faculties.

Over the past two decades, the movement toward "intellectuality" in American colleges has been steady and marked. Throughout American higher education, cognitive, intellectual and preprofessional outlooks are on the rise, while such traditional American student pastimes as panty raids, popularity contests, campus politics and fraternity rushing are on a steady decline. The highly intellectual preprofessional student has less time and less motivation for the college pranks of his parents' generation. To survive and prosper in tomorrow's technological world, he must work terribly hard in college in order to be "really good in his field." He must perform well academically, and without "mistakes" that would lower his grade average. He must postpone a whole gamut of emotional satisfactions until he is older. A bad course, a bad year, or even taking a year off may mean not getting into graduate school or—worse—getting drafted.

There is much to be said for these pressures for intellectual performance, just as there is much that is admirable about those who possess academic skills. Today's college students at selective institutions are an unusually serious, well-informed, honest and morally concerned group. While they scorn the round of fun and frivolity that dominated the lives of previous college generations, they in fact care deeply about each other, and a growing number are intensely concerned with the social and political future of their world. Yet in describing the self-generated and educationally-generated pressures upon them, I have used the word "performance" advisedly. "Performance" suggests alien activity, acting on a stage in order to impress others, a role played for the benefit of the audience. And to growing numbers of such students, intellectual performance is increasingly seen as a kind of "role-playing" of the worst sort. Indeed, one source of the growing demand for "relevance" and "student power" is this widely shared feeling that much academic and intellectual activity is somehow "alien" to the "real" interests and concerns of the student.

And it is indeed true that although the systematic quest for cognitive competence and academic performance occupies most of the time and effort of the preprofessional student at today's selective colleges, this quest does little to inform students about life's purposes and joys. One of the peculiar characteristics of academic performance is that even when performance is impeccable, most of the other "really important" questions remain unanswered: What is life all about? What really matters? What do I stand for? Why do I bother? How much do I stand for? What is relevant, meaningful and important? What is meaningless, valueless and false? For many students, then, the pursuit of academic competence must be supplemented by a more private, less academic, noncurricular quest for the meaning of life. When large numbers of students perceive their academic efforts as irrelevant to the really important "existential" and "ultimate" questions, then the way is open for a more private search for meaning, significance and relevance. Together, they have begun to create an informal shared culture that counters and complements the academic professionalism of elite American colleges.

THE EXPERIENTIAL COUNTER-CULTURE

The "better" American colleges rarely attempt to provide students with neatly packaged answers to their existential questions. To be sure, the most demanding colleges make systematic efforts to provoke undergraduates to challenge previous beliefs and to abandon unexamined dogmas. But they expect students to arrive at individual solutions to the riddles of life, all the while occupying themselves with getting good grades and getting ahead in the academic world. The college's message is often highly paradoxical: "Ruthlessly discard previous convictions and values; don't look to us for answers; most of your questions are sophomoric, in any case."

To the most sophisticated undergraduates, the traditional avenues to significance seem irrelevant, exhausted, insincere or superficial. Traditional religious faith and the great political ideologies arouse relatively little interest among today's determinedly anti-ideological undergraduates. Nor does success within the "American way of life" constitute an answer to life's riddles for most students. There was a day when the quest for campus popularity seemed to many undergraduates but a reflection of a broader life philosophy of making friends, influencing people, and developing social skills. But today, "popularity" has become a dirty word. Nor does "getting ahead in the world" provide an answer for intellectual students, most of whom start out already ahead in the world—the children of well-educated and well-situated middle-class parents. For these students, the old American dream of giving one's children "a better chance" makes little sense: they find it pointless to struggle for greater affluence when they already have more than enough. They are more worried about how to live with what they already have.

As the traditional avenues to meaning have dried up, and as academic performance itself seems increasingly irrelevant to the major existential concerns of students, a new informal student subculture has begun to emerge. Although not opposed to the life of the mind, this subculture is anti-academic. Although students who participate in it are publicly headed for professional careers, they privately focus on experience in the present rather than on long-range goals. Theirs is an informal *experiential counter-culture,* which complements the formal culture of the academically-oriented college. Central to this counter-culture is a focus on the present—on today, on the here and now. At one level, intellectual college students are required to defer enjoyment for a distant future in their academic and preprofessional work. But, informally, they emphasize immediate pleasure and experience. While society at large expects from them a reverence for the traditions of the past and a respect for traditional institutions, they stress in their own subcultures activity and receptivity in the present. Such future-oriented qualities as control, planning, waiting, saving and postponing are little honored in the student subculture; nor are past-oriented qualities like revering, recalling, remembering and respecting much emphasized. In contrast, the experiential subculture stresses genuineness, adventure, spontaneity, sentience and experimentation. Since the past is seen as irrelevant (or "exhausted") and since the future seems profoundly uncertain, the real meaning of life must be found within present experience—even as one worries about the Graduate Record Examinations.

The experiential counter-culture has many variants, at least some of which are visible on almost every major American campus.

One variant is what is sometimes called "student existentialism." At the more sophisticated campuses, this outlook is manifest in an intense interest in existential writers, in the theater of the absurd, and in philosophers and psychologists who stress "existential" concepts. But even at less sophisticated colleges, a similar focus is apparent in student emphasis on simple human commitments as contrasted with absolute values, in a "situation ethic" that questions the possibility of long-range value commitments, and by a pervasively high estimation of sincerity, authenticity and directness. Student existentialism is humanist rather than religious, and its most immediate goals are love, immediacy, empathy, "encounter" with one's fellow man. Thus, in the counter-culture, what matters most is interpersonal honesty, "really being yourself" and a special kind of open and disinterested genuineness. What is most unacceptable is fraudulence, exploitation, "role-playing," artificiality, hypocrisy and "playing games."

Along with the focus on the present and on "existential" values goes a very great tolerance for experimentation. Youth is increasingly defined (by youth itself) as a time for exploration, trial and error, and deliberate efforts to enlarge, change, or expand personality. Experimentation in the interest of deliberate self-change is seen as essential to pursuit of meaning. Convinced that meaning is not found but created, members of the counter-culture consider their own personalities the prime vehicles for the creation of significance. Since significance emerges from the self, it is only by transforming the self that significance can be achieved. In a kind of deliberate, self-conscious and intentional identity-formation, apparently unconnected activities and experiences find their rationale. Self-exploration, psychotherapy, sexual experimentation, travel, "encounter groups," a reverence for nature, and "sensitivity training" are tools in the pursuit of meaning—along with drug use.

The high rates of drug use at the more intellectual and academically demanding colleges are therefore not to be explained solely by the presence at such colleges of students of the same psychological type—although this fact is important. In addition, the more intellectual colleges tend to impose upon students an unusually strong set of pressures for academic and intellectual performance: they require high cognitive ability, a preprofessional orientation, and a postponement of immediate gratifications without offering much in return by way of fun or answers to life's riddles. In such an environment, students have spontaneously created a counter-culture, which, while not explicitly opposed to academic pursuits, complements them with a focus on the present, on "existential" values, on personal experimentation, and on deliberate self-transformation as a way of creating meaning. Participation in this counter-culture provides a powerful support for efforts to explore oneself, to intensify relationships with other people, to change the quality and content of consciousness. It provides a sanctioning context for drug use as one of the pathways of changing the self so as to create meaning in the world.

DRUGS AS A COMMENTARY ON SOCIETY

It is widely feared that student drug use is a commentary upon American society; words like degeneracy, addiction, thrill-seeking and irresponsibility are eventually introduced into most popular discussions of student drug use. So, too, student drug use is said to be related to the excessive permissiveness of parents, to the laxness of adult standards, to breaches in law enforcement, to disrespect for law and order, and to an impending breakdown of our social fabric.

Although these particular interpretations of the social implications of drug use are incorrect, drug use *is* importantly influenced by social, political and historical factors. Those students who lust after significance or reject the prevalent values of American society are in fact reacting to and within societal context. The sense of being locked-off and enclosed in an impermeable shell is related not only to individual psychological states like depression, but to broader cultural phenomena. And the fact that a considerable number of the most able students have become convinced that significance and relevant experience are largely to be found within their own skulls is indirectly related to their perception of the other possibilities for fulfillment in the social and political world. In a variety of ways, then, student drug use is a commentary on American society, although a different kind of commentary than most discussions of youthful "thrill-seeking" would lead us to believe.

To single out a small number of social changes as especially relevant to understanding student drug use is to make a highly arbitrary decision. A variety of factors, including rapid social change, the unprecedented possibilities for total destruction in the modern world, the prevalence of violence both domestic and international, the high degree of specialization and bureaucratization of American life, and a host of others are relevant to creating the context of values and expectations within which drug use has become increasingly legitimate. But of all the factors that could be discussed, three seem particularly relevant: first, the effect of modern communications and transportation in producing an overwhelming inundation of experience, which I will term *stimulus flooding;* second, the effect of *automatic affluence* in changing the values and outlooks of the young; third, the importance of recent social and historical events in producing a kind of *social and political disenchantment* that leads many students to seek salvation through withdrawal and inner life rather than through engagement and societal involvement.

STIMULUS FLOODING AND PSYCHOLOGICAL NUMBING

Every society subjects its members to pressures and demands that they simply take for granted. Such pressures are woven into the fabric of social existence, are assumed to be a natural part of life, and become the object of automatic accomodation. These accomodations are rarely examined, yet they may profoundly alter the quality of human experience. Such is the case with the quantity, variety and intensity of external stimulation, imagery and excitation to which most Americans are subjected. As Robert J. Lifton has pointed out, modern man in advanced societies is subjected to a flood of unpredictable stimulation of the most varied kinds; by newspapers, television, radio and rapid travel, he continually exposes himself to novel and unanticipatable experience. This stimulus inundation, in turn, produces a self-protective reaction which, following Lifton, we can term psychic numbing.

Most individuals in most societies have at some point in their lives had the experience of being so overcome by external stimulation and internal feelings that they gradually find themselves growing numb and unfeeling. Medical students commonly report that after their first, often intense reactions to the cadaver, they simply "stop feeling anything" with regard to the object of their dissection. And we have all had the experience of listening to so much good music, seeing so many fine paintings, being so overwhelmed by excellent cooking that we find ourselves simply unable to respond further. Similarly, at moments of extreme psychic pain and anguish, most individuals "go numb," no longer perceiving the full implications of a catastrophic situation or no longer experiencing the full range of their own feelings. This lowered responsiveness, this psychological numbing, seems causally related to the variety, persistence and intensity of stimulation and emotion.

Most Americans have had the experience of returning to urban life from a calm and pastoral setting. Initially, we respond by being virtually deluged with the clamor of people, sights, sounds, images and colors that demand our attention and response. The beauty and the ugliness of the landscape continually strike us; each of the millions of faces in our great cities has written on it the tragicomic record of a unique life history; each sound evokes a resonant chord within us. Such periods, however, tend to be transient and fleeting; and they usually give way to a sense of numbness, of nonresponsiveness, and of profound inattention to the very stimuli that earlier evoked so much in us. We settle in; we do not notice any more.

This psychological numbing operates at a great variety of levels for modern man. Our experience, from childhood onward, with the constantly flickering images and sounds of television, films, radio, newspapers, paperbacks, neon signs, advertisements and sound trucks numbs us to the sights and sounds of our civilization. Our continual exposure to a vast variety of ideologies, value systems, philosophies, political creeds, superstitions, religions and faiths numbs us to the unique claims to validity and the special spiritual and intellectual values of each one: we move among values and ideologies as in a two-dimensional landscape. Similarly, the availability to us in novels, films, television, theater and opera of moments of high passion, tragedy, joy, exaltation and sadness often ends by numbing us to our own feelings and the feelings of others.

Modern men thus confront the difficult problem of keeping "stimulation" from without to a manageable level, while also protecting themselves against being overwhelmed by their own inner responses to the stimuli from the outer world. Defenses or barriers against both external and internal stimulation are, of course, essential in order for us to preserve our intactness and integrity as personalities. From earliest childhood, children develop thresholds of responsiveness and barriers against stimulation in order to protect themselves against being overwhelmed by inner or outer excitement. Similarly, in adulthood, comparable barriers, thresholds and defenses are necessary, especially when we find ourselves in situations of intense stimulation.

A problem arises, however, if the barriers we erect to protect ourselves from the clamors of the inner and outer world prove harder and less permeable than we had originally wanted. In at least a minority of Americans, the normal capacity to defend oneself against undue stimulation and inner excitation is exaggerated and automatized, so that it not only protects, but walls off the individual from inner and outer experience. In such individuals, there develops an acute sense of being trapped in their own shells, unable to break through their defenses to make "contact" with experience or with other people, a sense of being excessively armored, separated from their own activities as by an invisible screen, estranged from their own feelings and from potentially emotion-arousing experiences in the world. Most of us have had some inkling of this feeling of inner deadness and outer flatness, especially in times of great fatigue, let-down, or depression. The world seems cold and two-dimensional; food and life have lost their savor; our activities are merely "going through the motions," our experiences lack vividness, three-dimensionality, and intensity. Above all, we feel trapped or shut in our own subjectivity.

The continual flooding of stimulation to which modern men are subjected is thus related not only to the psychological conditions and institutional pressures that help create the feelings of numbness, but, indirectly, to the nature of perception and experience in an advanced technological society. One problem every modern American faces is how to avoid becoming entrapped in the protective shell he must construct to defend himself against being overwhelmed by stimulation. And the use of drugs, especially in the context of the experiential counter-culture, becomes more attractive to youth precisely because the drugs preferred by students often have the effect of dissipating, blurring, or breaking down the boundaries of individual selfhood and personality.

AUTOMATIC AFFLUENCE

No society in world history has ever provided its citizens with the automatic abundance that our society provides to a majority of Americans. In over ten years of interviewing students from middle-class and upper-middle-class backgrounds, I have yet to find one who has worried about finding a job, and have met relatively few who were worried about finding a *good* job. Whatever their levels of aspiration, today's advantaged youth rarely think in terms of getting ahead in the world, acquiring increasing status, or struggling to "succeed." These goals, both relevant and important to their parents (products of the 1920's and the Great Depression), are largely irrelevant to today's youth. Like youth in every era, they turn from the successes of the past to the problems of the present and future. Thus, paradoxically, although they live in a society more affluent than any before it, they are far more outraged at poverty, injustice, inequality, exploitation and cruelty than were their parents, who lived in a more impoverished society. Indeed, one of the central demands of today's politically active youth is that everyone have the benefits which they themselves have always taken for granted.

One of the undeniable benefits of affluence is that it brings increased opportunities for enjoyment and leisure, and destroys the need to devote oneself to a life of unrelenting toil in order to prosper. Affluence permits a de-emphasis of hard work, self-control and renunciation, and makes possible the development of new cultures of leisure. As work, success and achievement decline in relative importance, new values are beginning to replace them, and new patterns of consumption are beginning already to reflect these new values. As "getting ahead in the world" no longer suffices to define the meaning of life, today's advantaged students turn increasingly to explore *other* meanings of life.

Two rather different alternatives have so far been tried. The first is the solution of the political activist, who remains primarily concerned with the fact that his own affluence and freedom have not been extended to all. Within America, his concern is with the poor, the deprived, the excluded and the disadvantaged. Abroad, he focuses on the many failures of American foreign policy, failures that in his eyes involve a catastrophic gap between the values of a democratic society and the foreign policies that purportedly implement them. The activist would have us support rather than oppose movements of national liberation, and use our affluence not in military engagements but in programs of assistance to the developing nations. The activist is most likely to accept the traditional values of American society, especially those emphasizing justice, equality, opportunity and freedom, and to insist that these values be more thoroughly practiced.

The second response to the question, "What lies beyond affluence?," while not incompatible with the first, looks in a different area for an answer. This second response turns to a more fundamental critique of the premises and assumptions upon which technological America has been based. Instead of equality, it champions diversity; instead of pressing for the extension of affluence, it questions the meaning of affluence. Associated with a long tradition of romantic criticism of industrial and postindustrial society, this response points to the price of affluence—dehumanization, professionalization, bureaucracy, a loss of power over society, the absence of a sense of small scale, and the erosion of traditional community. For the romantic critic of American society, fulfillment and personal wholeness are more important than abundance and achievement. The life of the affluent middle class in America is seen as empty, spiritually impoverished, driven and neurotic; the vaguely defined alternative involves expressiveness, self-knowledge, involvement with the small group of others, the fulfillment of nonmaterial artistic, spiritual and psychological needs. "Self-actualization" is the goal; "let each man do his thing" is the motto.

Automatic affluence, then, inevitably means that many of those who experience abundance as routine, attempt to create goals beyond affluence. These goals may involve a reform of the world so as to extend affluence to all, or a critique of the technological assumptions upon which affluence itself was based. Insofar as the individual's main effort is to extend affluence, he is relatively immune to the appeals of the experiential, drug-using world, for his energies are oriented toward changing the world rather than himself. But insofar as his primary focus is antitechnological—upon self-fulfillment, personal change, and spiritual or humanistic fulfillment—this focus is highly consistent with the use of drugs. For drug use among college students is closely related to the effort to change oneself, to become more creative, to be more expressive, more emotionally open and more genuinely in contact with the world. And the use of drugs is associated with a questioning or rejection of the traditional success ethic of American life, and with a search for new styles of living more oriented to leisure, to intimate personal relationships, and to spiritual expression. Thus, affluence indirectly produces a mood among some of its recipients that makes them receptive to drug use and other forms of personal experimentation.

SOCIO-POLITICAL DISENCHANTMENT

In juxtaposing two answers to the quest for meaning beyond abundance, I have implied a certain tension between them. It is not accidental that full-time and committed political activists are rarely intensive drug users; it is also important that the full-time denizens of the drug-using hippie subculture are rarely capable of sustained political activity. Sustained engagement in an effort to change the world is rarely compatible with the kind of self-absorption and inwardness that results from intensive and regular drug use; conversely, however strongly the committed drug user may feel about the inequities of American society, his primary efforts are usually directed toward self-change, rather than changing the world around him. Although some individuals alternate at different times in their lives between activism and alienation, it is very difficult to be an active social reformer and a "head" at the same time.

This argument suggests that disenchantment with the possibilities of meaningful social action is related to the development of an outlook conducive to drug use. To trace student drug use directly to such factors as racial injustices or the war in Vietnam would, of course, be a major oversimplification. But disenchantment with meaningful and honorable political activity creates a general climate of opinion that *is,* in turn, favorable to drug use. Specifically, the change in student attitudes toward political life and social reform since the assassination of President Kennedy seems importantly connected to the rise of drug use.

The influence of Kennedy upon the attitudes of youth is often exaggerated or stated in an oversimplified way. Many of the young, of course, disliked Kennedy, as did many of their parents. Furthermore, most of those who admired Kennedy personally had no intention whatsoever of entering public life. Kennedy's impact on the attitudes of youth was indirect: he and the group around him symbolized the conviction that it was possible for young, idealistic and intelligent men and women to enter the political world and to "make a difference." Such Kennedy ventures as the Peace Corps further provided an outlet—and more importantly a symbol—for the idealistic energies of activist youth. Although Kennedy himself in fact rarely listened to the advice of students, such symbolic Kennedy acts as pots of coffee for peace marchers in front of the White House indicated at least an awareness of the opinion of the dedicated young.

The image of political life conveyed by the Johnson Administration, especially from 1966 to late 1968, was vastly different. Not only have older views of politics as a form of horse trading, "compromising," and "wheeling and dealing" been reinstated, but large numbers of American college students have come to associate political involvement with gross immorality and even with genocide. In this context, such revelations as that of covert C.I.A. funding of liberal student organizations like the National Students Association have the effect of convincing many intelligent and idealistic youth that politics—and, by extension, efforts to work to change the System from within—are dishonorable or pointless occupations.

The demise of the Civil Rights Movement and the collapse of the War on Poverty have also helped change the climate of opinion about political reform. In the early 1960's, the Civil Rights Movement was the chief catalyst for the rising tide of student political involvement. Sit-ins, Freedom Rides, the work of S.N.C.C. and other groups in the Deep South helped convince students that their efforts at social change would be honored, recognized and responded to by the society at large. Students in the early 1960's saw themselves not so much in opposition to the policies of the nation as in the vanguard of these policies; and the passage of major Civil Rights legislation in 1964, followed by the promise of a major "War on Poverty," gave support to this conviction. Thus there arose a hope that "American society would crash through" in remedying its own inequities. This hope had a widespread impact, not only upon that small minority of students who were actively involved in civil rights work, but upon others who were indirectly encouraged to plan careers of responsible social involvement.

But the events of subsequent years have altered this initial hope. The "white backlash" has made legislators extremely reluctant to assist the Negro revolution. The war in Vietnam drained funds away from domestic programs just when federal assistance was needed most. The student Civil Rights Movement for its part discovered that legal reforms exposed more clearly the depths of the problem of black Americans, and pointed toward more far-reaching psychological, social and economic changes that were more difficult to legislate from Washington. The War on Poverty collapsed into a small skirmish. Equally important, the rising militancy of black radicals has pushed white students out of organizations like S.N.C.C. and CORE with the demand, "Go home and organize your own people." Lacking national support, and "rejected" by their former black allies, white activists have increasingly despaired of working within the System, have become more radical, and are talking more militantly about "changing the System."

The changing image of political involvement has had two effects. On the one hand, it has contributed to the "radicalization" of those individuals who have remained activists: especially now among such students, disaffection with the established system is at a high that has not been reached in this country since the 1930's. But equally important, the revitalized image of the political process as dishonest, reprehensible, immoral and unresponsive to both the ideals of America and the rights of the deprived has created a climate in which it is more and more possible to argue that salvation—if it can be found at all—must be found within the self or the counter-community, rather than within the wider society. Given this belief, the individual in search of meaningful engagement with the world must either create new political institutions (as stressed by the rhetoric of the New Left), or else abandon political struggle altogether in a search for meaning within small groups of other disaffected people. It is in these latter groups that drug use is most common. If the world outside is corrupt, dehumanized, violent and immoral, the world within—the almost infinitely malleable world of perception, sensation, communication and consciousness—seems more controllable, more immediate, less corrupting, and ofttimes more pleasant. To be sure, there is a price to be paid for exclusive involvement in the interior world, but, for many young Americans, there simply seems to be no alternative.

Political and historical events do not have a direct, one-to-one relationship with drug use: the war in Vietnam does not *cause* students to smoke marihuana or experiment with LSD. But the political climate of the past few years has created a negative view of the possibility of meaningful involvement within the established institutions of the society, at the same time that it has convinced many students that society is in desperate need of reform. This climate of opinion in turn contributes to the assumption that if meaning, excitement and dignity are to be found in the world, they must be found within one's own cranium. Drug use can indeed be a kind of cop-out, not from perversity or laziness, but simply because there seems to be no other alternative. Student drug use is indeed a commentary upon American society, but it is above all an indirect criticism of our society's inability to offer the young exciting, honorable and effective ways of using their intelligence and idealism to reform our society.

This essay presents an overview of all drugs currently in use by adolescents. The discussion includes opiates, depressants, stimulants, hallucinogens, and solvents. The physical and psychological effects of each drug are described, as well as the methods of treatment, prevention, and drug education.

ALVIN E. STRACK
Drug Use and Abuse Among Youth

To start, let us consider the following proposition: Any substance capable of altering man's mood has abuse capability. What is implied in this statement, of course, is that the specific substance abused is of less direct importance to the user than the end result, and indeed, this is frequently the case. With this as a general premise, let me cite some specific drugs and substances frequently abused in our society.

We need to define three terms about which there is considerable confusion: addiction, habituation, and dependence. Through the years "addiction" and "habituation" have been used interchangeably to describe forms or results of drug use and abuse. The resulting confusion has led to decisions by the World Health Organization to replace these terms with the more general one of "dependence." Dependence is described as "a state arising from repeated administration of a drug on a periodic or continuous basis." The use of the term dependence necessitates delineating the *exact* drug which one is discussing. Therefore, we have drug dependence of the barbiturate type, drug dependence of the opiate type, etc.

OPIATES

The opiates are among the oldest drugs known to man. They have no equal, to this day, in relieving pain. They are medically irreplaceable at the present time. When properly used in medical practice, there is little or no danger of development of dependence. When abused, they produce very serious physical and psychological dependence. Drugs in this class include morphine, codeine, and other natural opium derivatives, and also heroin, which is synthetically produced from morphine. It is heroin, of course, which is the drug of choice among opiate addicts. Given intravenously, it produces a "kick" or "high" of an almost orgasmic nature, followed by the "nod" or period of oblivion which the addict also prizes. It is perhaps this double effect which makes the opiates so attractive to individuals seeking the escape from reality.

The manufacture, distribution, possession, and use of the opiates or narcotics are subject to stringent international, federal, and state regulation and control. Penalties for illicit sale are severe, and rightly so. Opiate addiction, per se, is not a crime, and yet opiate addicts have constructed a surer prison for themselves and their minds than any jailer could hope to build.

Narcotic withdrawal makes a familiar tale. Usually somewhat overdramatized, it has been portrayed on many occasions in movies, television, and other media. Withdrawal from a heavy heroin habit is indeed a painful and agonizing process. In practice today, however, and thanks to vigilant police efforts, there are few so-called "heavy" habits around, because heroin is too scarce and because the heroin bought by most addicts has been highly diluted by the seller. Hence, "cold turkey" withdrawal for most narcotic addicts is today much less formidable than it is often described.

The most prevalent form of narcotic use among young people limits itself to exempt narcotics marketed in cough syrups. The practice seems to be confined to localized areas, and the exact extent of the problem is extremely difficult to determine.

The effects of narcotic use include drowsiness and sleep; the side effects are nausea, vomiting, constipation, itching, flushing, constriction of pupils, and respiratory depression.

DEPRESSANTS: BARBITURATES AND TRANQUILIZERS

The barbiturate drugs have been used in medicine for half a century. They are used as sedatives, sleep producers, for epilepsy, high blood pressure, gastrointestinal disorders, and many other disease states. Used as directed, and in the doses prescribed, they are quite safe. Abused at high doses for long periods of time, they produce severe psychological dependence and a type of physical dependence which in at least one respect is more severe than that seen with narcotics. To be specific, abrupt withdrawal of barbiturates from a dependent individual can cause convulsions which can be fatal if untreated. It is this fact which has caused some investigators to say that the barbiturates are more toxic when abused than narcotics. Symptoms of barbiturate abuse include slurred speech, staggering gait, and sluggish reactions. The user is erratic and may easily be moved to tears or to laughter. Perhaps the best description of the barbiturate intoxicated individual is a reeling drunk who does not smell of alcohol.

Certain tranquilizers, notably those usually designated as minor tranquilizers and employed for the less severe mental and emotional disorders, have occasionally been abused, with the development of psychological and physical dependence. Symptoms in dependent individuals during withdrawal of these drugs closely resemble those seen with barbiturates.

STIMULANTS: COCAINE AND AMPHETAMINES

Cocaine is derived from the leaves of the coca tree. Although a stimulant, and not a narcotic, it is treated as a narcotic for legal control purposes. Once widely used as a local anesthetic, cocaine has disappeared from the medical scene. It is a very potent stimulant. It produces excitability, talkativeness, and a reduction in the feeling of fatigue. Cocaine may produce a sense of euphoria, increased muscular strength, and hallucinations. Its use has been associated with violent behavior.

The amphetamine derivatives have been used in medicine for about 35 years. They are very useful in the treatment of obesity, depression, hyperactivity, behavior disorders in children, and narcolepsy (a disorder characterized by excessive and sudden periods of sleep). Amphetamines increase alertness, dispel depression, mask fatigue, elevate mood, and produce a feeling of well-being. It is generally agreed that amphetamines do not produce physical dependence with abuse, but psychological dependence is common with excessive use. With abuse of amphetamines the body becomes tolerant to it, and abusers frequently use doses many times those usually employed for medical purposes. Symptoms of abuse include talkativeness, excitability, and restlessness. The abuser will suffer from insomnia, perspire profusely, have increased urinary frequency, and often exhibit tremor. Acute psychotic episodes may occur with intravenous use, or may develop with the chronic use of large doses.

Manufacture, distribution, and sale of the depressants and stimulants (except cocaine as previously mentioned) are controlled by a variety of federal and state laws, most notable of which is the recently enacted federal legislation which requires manufacturers and distributors of these drugs to register with the government and to maintain for inspection complete inventory and sales records. These laws restrict the number of times a prescription may be refilled, and place a six-month time limit on refills.

HALLUCINOGENS

The hallucinogens, which include LSD, DMT, peyote, psilocybin, mescaline, and also marijuana, have received an inordinate amount of publicity through the news media. Only one of these agents is currently considered to have any possible medical use, and that one is LSD. When used under very carefully controlled conditions, LSD has been found to be of some value in the treatment of alcoholism and certain psychosexual disorders.

If one can judge from the publicity generated by certain enthusiastic proponents of the hallucinogens, their use is increasing by leaps and bounds. A somewhat less biased view would be that abuse of these substances has increased to worrisome proportions, especially among young people of college age.

As their name suggests, the hallucinogens produce a variety of hallucinatory effects, primarily in visual perception. When abused, these substances produce a psychological dependence which, in some individuals, amounts to an almost religious fervor. The drugs do not produce physical dependence and no physical symptoms occur on withdrawal.

LSD was synthesized in the late 1930's, but its hallucinogenic effect was not discovered for several years. Abuse of this substance has become a problem only in recent years, in part because of the articulate and persuasive devotees of "expansion of consciousness." The LSD experience is certainly memorable. It involves visual, auditory, and tactile hallucinations, changes in perception, thought, mood and activity, time sense, and comprehension. All too frequently, the LSD "trip" is a shattering psychic experience which leaves the user disoriented, in panic, or even frankly psychotic. Psychosis has developed after use of LSD in individuals who previously exhibited no signs of emotional instability. Moreover, this psychotic state may persist or recur for weeks after the drug was taken. Mescaline, psilocybin, and DMT all produce effects similar to those of LSD, differing only quantitatively in their effects and duration of action. DMT is interestingly enough called the "businessman's trip," since its effect lasts only about as long as the ordinary business lunch. Manufacture, distribution, and sale of LSD is now restricted under the same federal laws governing stimulants and depressants.

The popular weed marijuana is also known as cannabis, pot, ghang, hashish, charas, and a variety of other names. Marijuana is an irregular stimulant of the central nervous system, and is a hallucinogen. It has no established medical use. It is used—usually smoked or eaten—for its ability to produce euphoria, a feeling of exaltation and dreaming, and hallucinations. Use of marijuana is associated with a distorted sense of time and distance. Panic and fear sometimes result, but the user is usually talkative and in good humor, or conversely sometimes drowsy and quiet.

Marijuana does not cause physical dependence or an abstinence syndrome. Tolerance does not appear to develop; in short, it causes little physical damage in the user. However, reports from areas of the world where the more potent forms of cannabis and marijuana are used indicate an association between continued intake of this substance and the development of psychosis. Psychological dependence, which is moderate to strong, can develop readily, especially in susceptible individuals.

The most serious problem associated with marijuana is pointed out in the *Bulletin of the World Health Organization:*

Abuse of cannabis (marijuana) facilitates the association with social groups and subcultures involved with more dangerous drugs, such as opiates and barbiturates. Transition to the use of such drugs would be a consequence of this association rather than an inherent effect of cannabis. The harm to society derived from abuse of cannabis rests in the economic consequences of the impairment of the individual's social functions and his enhanced proneness to asocial and antisocial behavior (Eddy et al., 1965).

SOLVENTS

The abuse of solvents is commonly but somewhat inaccurately labeled "glue sniffing." Inhalation of solvents contained in glues, gasoline, paint thinners, lighter fluids, and the like produces a state of excitation, exhilaration, and excitement resembling alcohol intoxication. Eventually blurred vision, slurred speech, loss of balance, and hallucinations result. Tolerance develops, but physical dependence does not occur. A strong psychological dependence develops. Reports of actual physical damage resulting from solvent abuse are rare, although the toxicity of these solvents for man is widely recognized in industry. One of the very real dangers is that of suffocation in habitues who use plastic bags to hold the glue or solvents up to the face. It is an unfortunate fact that abuse of these substances occurs to the largest extent in young adolescents.

METHODS OF TREATMENT

We are really just beginning to realize and act on the idea that abuse of drugs and other substances will require as many different methods of treatment as it has causes. Certainly, habilitation and rehabilitation will not be easy, but we must try. The comprehensive programs of California, Maryland, and New York, and the coordinated program in New York City headed by Efren Ramirez, must be given the opportunity to function effectively in this problem area. Such organizations as Daytop and Synanon must also have their chance to show what can be done. We have too few answers to turn aside any reasonable approach to cure and rehabilitation.

Legal facets of drug and substance abuse have been mentioned briefly before. I would like here to defend the role of law enforcement in preventing drug abuse. Law enforcement is primarily charged with removing one of the proximate causes of drug and substance abuse, namely, availability. There is a social need to stamp out the illicit trade in drugs and substances, and for this we are dependent in large measure on good law enforcement. They have done very well. No greater testimonial to this fact exists than the real scarcity of heroin in this country.

I would like to emphasize that it is *not* the province of law enforcement officers to be philosophical about drug addiction and abuse. They are sworn to enforce the law. It is our business to assist them whenever possible.

There are many social aspects of drug and substance abuse, but I wish to offer only a few for consideration. First, society must accept the existence of, and differentiate between, the spree or occasional drug abuser and the chronic abuser for whom abuse has become a way of life. Second, the chronic abuser is a sick individual, and however society chooses to provide care and custody for him, he should be treated as a sick man. Third, drug abuse is a symptom of some deeper, underlying disorder. It may range on the one hand from adolescent rebellion to deep-seated character disorders on the other. In all of these, loneliness and alienation play a large role.

We are left with what might be called the morality of the situation, but perhaps more precisely, the realities of the situation. One hears these days a refrain that goes something like this: "I have the right and should have the freedom to use drugs if I wish to, especially if they don't physically harm me. And even if they do harm me, they hurt only me and nobody else." This argument is frequently put forth by those who, for one reason or another, claim the right to use drugs occasionally for other than their intended medical purposes.

It is interesting that, lacking an adequate logical reason for drug abuse, these people fall back on the argument for rights and freedoms. No one, of course, wants to restrict rights or freedoms or to have to argue against them. We must recognize, though, that the "right" that these drug abusers claim is the right to be immature and uncaring about themselves and society to the point of stupidity. Society, any society, has always had the privilege of limiting individual rights and freedoms to the extent necessary to preserve the common good. This function of society extends even to protecting the individual from himself if this is necessary.

From the earliest times, man and his societies have restricted the distribution and the use of certain substances. Many early recognized the medical usefulness of certain plants and chemicals—but also their antisocial potential in terms of poisonous or intoxicant effects. Social and legal control of such substances has been accepted as a necessary limitation on individual freedom for centuries. Even the primitive societies of today have such controls in the form of a witch doctor or medicine man.

Legal controls of these substances then is not really an unnecessary, and certainly not a recent, intrusion on man's inalienable rights. They are a very real social necessity.

The delicate balance between the individual's rights, duties, and responsibilities in a society certainly enters into this picture.

Another aspect is the physical harm, or the lack of it, caused by the abuse of drugs and other substances. In this sense, physical harm means physical dependence and a withdrawal syndrome, or the toxic effect of long-term use. There is little doubt that there are substances that do *not* cause such physical harm when abused. As has already been pointed out, the real harm in these substances is their asocial or antisocial effect; their leading the abuser to association with substances which are harmful and dangerous; and the general economic impairment which they produce.

The suggestion that if drugs do harm me but no one else, then there is no reason why I should not use them, is patently ridiculous. Has the young adult gone psychotic after taking LSD harmed only himself? Who must care for him, keep him from further harming himself or others? Who has to try to put his shattered mind back together?

If you inquire of a drug abuser what he expects to get from drugs, you can expect a variety of answers:

> I want to get high.
> I want to get away.
> I want to stay awake.
> I want to go to sleep.
> I want a new thrill.
> I want to expand my consciousness.
> I want a mystic experience.
> I want to enhance my creativity.

Many users have no real reason except that "everyone was doing it," or the seldom expressed but often present need to rebel, somehow.

Many, of course, are very serious about using drugs for insight, for a mystic experience, or to enhance creativity. In the latter group one finds many of the hippies of Haight-Ashbury or Greenwich Village. They regard ingestion of drugs and other substances for these purposes as *use,* not abuse. They regard drugs as functional in this respect. They are optimistic to the point of being naive about the ability of drugs to enhance creativity or promote insights into life, love, and the things which really matter to them. They do not see abuse of drugs as dysfunctional in their lives.

Like many rebel and avant-garde groups before them, these young people have a real message to and about our society and our way of life. It is sad that most of their message is blurred and confused by being bound up with the problem of drug abuse.

Prevention is the real answer to drug abuse; the key to prevention is education. But who should educate, and what should be told about drug abuse?

The family remains of primary importance in influencing child development, and it is within the family and the home that most can be accomplished in preventing the abuse of drugs and other substances. A caring, loving, and directing home atmosphere is, and will remain, the best means of guiding youth through the difficult adolescent years. The alienation and loneliness which characterize so many abusers are much less likely to develop in a good home atmosphere. A willing ear, a kind word when needed, gentle direction, and a loving heart may be the only way to explain that most young people who are exposed to drugs do *not* abuse drugs. Most young people have no need for this kind of crutch or escape. But too many, unfortunately, must look for crutches and escapes.

To professional educators, however, will fall the role of telling young people about drugs and drug abuse. In doing this they must provide factual, clear-cut information—no horror stories, no finger-wagging. In short, they must "tell it like it is." Today's youth is quite knowledgeable concerning drugs and other substances and will quickly turn off anyone who doesn't tell a straight story about the problem. The educator, too, will often find himself in a strategic position to influence youth, either as an example setter or even in a surrogate parent role.

So what do we do for our young people? First, we listen to them as hard as we have ever listened in our lives. This shows them we care. Then tell all the facts, and in the manual for educators, *Drug Abuse: Escape to Nowhere,* I think we have the facts. It is a good starting point. But the most important message to convey to our young people is that abuse of drugs and other substances is one of the biggest "cop-outs" of all time. It is a "cop-out" on oneself.

Today's young people stress physical, material, intellectual, psychological, and spiritual self-fulfillment. I can think of very few actions that an individual can take that are more damaging to this self-fulfillment than drug abuse. Society has nothing to do with it, morality has nothing to do with it, rights and freedoms have nothing to do with it. Young people must be told: This is you—emphasis *you.* At almost any level of function you, emphasis *you,* will find yourself hung-up if you abuse drugs or substances. You will have "copped-out" on yourself. It matters little what you use—alcohol, marijuana, LSD, opiates, or whatever—it is still your "cop-out."

The total answer to the drug abuse problem lies in a judicious blend of education, legal control, more research on drugs and other substances now available, and, most important, the establishment of a dialogue across the generation gap. The latter, of course, has meaning for many social problems other than drug abuse.

Two

Activism

How does one understand the political activism of the young? Robert Jay Lifton calls them the shapers of a new history. Auschwitz and Hiroshima terminated the old history. The young, as opposed to their elders, are anti-ideological—in constant flux in contrast to being fixed in their beliefs. Relevance to the young means the raising up of a new history—a future that will be free of both the deification of nuclear weapons and the fear of destructive overpopulation. To achieve the New History youth must come to terms with three myths: the experiential myth of eliminating time and death, the transformation myth of making everything new, and the myth of generational totalism in which youth equals immortality and age is equated with historical exhaustion and death.

ROBERT JAY LIFTON

Notes on a New History: The Young and the Old

What is a New History? And why do the young seek one? I raise these questions to introduce the idea of a particular New History—ours—and to suggest certain ways in which we can begin to understand it.

We may speak of a New History as a period of radical re-creation of the forms of human culture—biological, institutional, technological, experiential, aesthetic, and interpretive. New cultural forms are not produced by spontaneous generation; they are extensions and transformations of what already exists. That which is most genuinely revolutionary makes psychological use of the past for its plunge into the future. Of special importance is the extent to which the new forms can contribute to the symbolic sense of immortality man requires as he struggles to perpetuate himself through family, race, and community, through his works, in his tie to nature, and via transcendent forms of psychic experience.

The shapers of a New History—political revolutionaries, revolutionary thinkers, extreme holocausts, and technological breakthroughs—also express the death of the old. This has been true of the American, French, Russian, and Chinese revolutions; the ideas of Copernicus, Darwin, and Freud; the mutilations of the two world wars; and, most pertinent to us, the technological revolution which produced Auschwitz and Hiroshima as well as the postmodern automated and electronic society. Each of these has been associated with "the end of an era," with the devitalization, or symbolic death, of forms and images defining the world view and life patterns of large numbers of people over long periods of time.

Great events and new ideas can thus, in different ways, cause, reflect, or symbolize historical shifts. The combination of Nazi genocide and the American atomic bombing of two Japanese cities terminated man's sense of limits concerning his self-destructive potential, and thereby inaugurated an era in which he is devoid of assurance of living on eternally as a species. It has taken almost twenty-five years for formulations of the significance of these events to begin to emerge, formulations which cannot be separated from the technological developments of this same quarter century, or from the increasing sense of a universal world society that has accompanied them.

The New History, then, is built upon the ultimate paradox of two competing and closely related images: that of the extinction of history by technology, and that of man's evolving awareness of himself as a single species. It may be more correct to speak of just one image, extraordinarily divided. And whatever the difficulties in evaluating the human consequences of this image, psychologists and historians who ignore it cease to relate themselves to contemporary experience.

The celebrated 1962 "Port Huron Statement" of the Students for a Democratic Society, which is still something of a manifesto for the American New Left, contains the assertion: "Our work is guided by the sense that we may be the last generation in the experiment with living." I think we should take this seriously, just as many of us took seriously Albert Camus's declaration that, in contrast with every generation's tendency to see itself as "charged with remaking the world," his own had a task "perhaps even greater, for it consists in keeping the world from destroying itself." What I wish to stress is the overriding significance for each generation after Hiroshima (and the SDS leaders, though twenty-five years younger than Camus, made their statement just five years after he made his) of precisely this threat of historical extinction. In seeking new beginnings, men are now haunted by an image of the end of everything.

Do the young feel this most strongly? They often say just the opposite. When I discuss Hiroshima with students, they are likely to point to a disparity between my (and Camus's) specific concern about nuclear weapons and their generation's feeling that these weapons are just another among the horrors of the world bequeathed to them. Our two "histories" contrast significantly: my (over forty) generation's shocked "survival" of Hiroshima and continuing need to differentiate the pre-Hiroshima world we knew from the world of nuclear weapons in which we now live; their (under twenty-five) generation's experience of growing up in a world in which nuclear weapons have always been part of the landscape. This gradual adaptation, as opposed to original shock, is of great importance. Man is psychologically flexible enough to come to terms with almost anything, so long as it is presented to him as an ordained element of his environment.

But such adaptation is achieved at a price, and only partially at that. The inner knowledge on the part of the young that their world has always been capable of exterminating itself creates an undercurrent of anxiety against which they must constantly defend themselves, anxiety related not so much to death itself as to a fundamental terror of premature death and unfulfilled life, and to high uncertainty about all forms of human continuity. Their frequent insistence that nuclear weapons are "nothing special" is their particular form of emotional desensitization, or what I call psychic numbing. But the young must do a great deal of continuous psychological work to maintain their nuclear "cool." And this in turn may make them unusually responsive to possibilities of breaking out of such numbing, and of altering the world which has imposed it upon them.

All perceptions of threatening historical developments must occur through what Ernst Cassirer called the "symbolic net"—that special area of psychic re-creation characteristic of man, the only creature who "instead of dealing with ... things themselves ... constantly converses ... with himself." In these internal (and often unconscious) dialogues, anxieties about technological annihilation merge with various perceptions of more symbolic forms of death. That is, Hiroshima and Auschwitz become inwardly associated with the worldwide sense of profound historical dislocation: with the disintegration of formerly vital and nourishing symbols revolving around family, religion, principles of community, and the life cycle in general; and with the inability of the massive and impersonal postmodern institutions (of government, education, and finance) to replace psychologically that which has been lost. They become associated also with the confusions of the knowledge revolution, and the unprecedented dissemination of half-knowledge through media whose psychological impact has barely begun to be discerned. There is a very real sense in which the world itself has become a "total environment"—a closed psychic chamber with continuous reverberations, bouncing about chaotically and dangerously. The symbolic death perceived, then, is this combination of formlessness and totality, of the inadequacy of existing forms and imprisonment within them. And the young are exquisitely sensitive to such "historical death," whatever their capacity for resisting an awareness of the biological kind.

The young are struck by the fact that most of mankind simply goes about its business as if these extreme dislocations did not exist, as if there were no such thing as ultimate technological violence or existence rendered absurd. The war in Vietnam did not create these murderous incongruities, but it does epitomize them, and it consumes American youth in them. No wonder, then, that so many of the young seem to be asking, How can we bring the world—and ourselves—back to life?

In referring to thể young and their quests, my examples are drawn mostly from the more radical among them; and what I say refers more to those who are white, educated, and of middle-class origin than to blacks, uneducated youth, or those of working-class backgrounds. The same is true concerning my references to my own generation. In neither case can the people I describe be anything more than a very small minority within their age group, their country, or for that matter, their university. But in both cases they seem to me to exemplify certain shared themes, psychological and historical, that in one way or another effect all people in our era and are likely to take on increasing importance over the next few decades and beyond.

Students of revolution and rebellion have recognized the close relationship of both to death symbolism, and to visions of transcending death by achieving an external historical imprint. Hannah Arendt speaks of revolution as containing an "all-pervasive preoccupation with permanence, with a 'perpetual state ... for ... posterity.'" And Albert Camus describes insurrection, "in its exalted and tragic forms," as "a prolonged protest against death, a violent accusation against the universal death penalty," and as "the desire for immortality and for clarity." But Camus also stresses the rebel's "appeal to the essence of being," his quest "not ... for life, but for reasons for living." And this brings us to an all-important question concerning mental participation in revolution: what is the place of ideology, and of images and ideas, and of the self in relationship to all three?

Men have always pursued immortalizing visions. But most of the revolutionary ideologies of the past two centuries have provided elaborate blueprints for individual and collective immortality—specifications of ultimate cause and ultimate effect, theological in tone and scientific in claim. When present-day revolutionaries reject these Cartesian litanies, they are taking seriously some of the important psychological and historical insights of the last few decades. For they are rejecting an oppressive ideological totalism, with its demand for control of all communication within a milieu, its imposed guilt and cult of purity and confession, its loading of the language, and its principles of doctrine over person and even of the dispensing of existence (in the sense that sharp lines are drawn between those whose right to exist can be recognized and those who possess no such right). This rejection represents, at its best, a quest by the young for a new kind of revolution—one perhaps no less enduring in historical impact, but devoid of the claim to omniscience, and of the catastrophic chain of human manipulations stemming from that claim.

It is, of course, quite possible that the anti-ideological stance of today's young will turn out to be a transitory phenomenon, a version of the euphoric denial of dogma that so frequently appears during the early moments of revolution, only to be overwhelmed by absolutist doctrine and suffocating organization in the name of revolutionary discipline. Yet there is reason to believe that the present antipathy to ideology is something more, that it is an expression of a powerful and highly appropriate contemporary style. The shift we are witnessing from fixed, all-encompassing forms of ideology to more fluid *ideological fragments* approaches Camus's inspiring vision of continuously decongealing rebellion, as opposed to dogmatically congealed, all-or-none revolution. I would also see it as an expression of contemporary, or what I call "protean," psychological style—post-Freudian and postmodern, characterized by interminable exploration and flux, and by relatively easy shifts in identification and belief. Protean man as rebel, then, seeks to remain open, while in the midst of rebellion, to the extraordinarily rich, confusing, liberating, and threatening array of contemporary historical possibilities.

His specific talent for fluidity greatly enhances his tactical leverage. For instance, Daniel Cohn-Bendit, a leader of the French student uprising of May, 1968, in an interesting dialogue with Jean-Paul Sartre, insisted that the classical Marxist-Leninist principle of the omniscient revolutionary vanguard (the working class, as represented by the Communist Party) be replaced with "a much simpler and more honorable one: the theory of an active minority acting, you might say, as a permanent ferment, pushing forward without trying to control events." Cohn-Bendit went on to characterize this process as "uncontrollable spontaneity" and as "disorder which allows people to speak freely and will later result in some form of 'self-organization.'" He rejected as "the wrong solution" an alternate approach (urged upon him by many among the Old Left) of formulating an attainable program and drawing up realizable demands. While this was "bound to happen at some point," he was convinced it would "have a crippling effect." In the same spirit are the warnings of Tom Hayden, a key figure in the American New Left, to his SDS colleagues and followers, against "fixed leaders"; and his insistence upon "participatory democracy," as well as upon ideology of a kind that is secondary to, and largely achieved through, revolutionary action. So widespread has this approach been that the American New Left has been characterized as more a process than a program.

I would suggest that the general principle of "uncontrollable spontaneity" represents a meeting ground between tactic and deeper psychological inclination. The underlying inclination consists precisely of the protean style of multiple identifications, shifting beliefs, and constant search for new combinations. Whatever its pitfalls, this style of revolutionary behavior is an attempt on the part of the young to mobilize the fluidity of the twentieth century as a weapon against what they perceive to be two kinds of stagnation: the old, unresponsive institutions (universities, governments, families) and newly emerging but fixed technological visions (people "programmed" by computers in a "technetronic society"). A central feature of this attempt is the stress upon the communal spirit and the creation of actual new communities. And here too we observe an alternation between conservative images of stable and intimate group ties, and images of transforming society in order to make such ties more possible than is now the case.

The process, and the underlying psychological tendencies, moreover, seem to be universal. Observing the nearly simultaneous student uprisings in America, France, Japan, Brazil, Germany, Italy, Mexico, South Africa, Czechoslovakia, Chile, Yugoslavia, and Spain, one can view them all as parts of a large single tendency, occurring within a single worldwide human and technical system. Here the planet's instant communications network is of enormous importance, as is the process of psychological contagion. To recognize the striking congruence in these rebellions, one need not deny the great differences in, say, Czech students rebelling against Stalinism, Spanish students against Falangism, and American, French, and Italian students against the Vietnam War, the consumer society, and academic injustices. In every case the young seek active involvement in the institutional decisions governing their lives, new alternatives to consuming and being consumed, and liberated styles of individual and community existence. Unspecific and ephemeral as these goals may seem, they are early expressions of a quest for historical rebirth, for reattachment to the Great Chain of Being, for reassertion of symbolic immortality.

The French example is again revealing (though not unique), especially in its extraordinary flowering of graffiti. Here one must take note of the prominence of the genre—of the informal slogan-on-the-wall virtually replacing formal revolutionary doctrine, no less than the content. But one is struck by the stress of many of the slogans, sometimes to the point of intentional absurdity, upon enlarging the individual life space, on saying "yes" to more and "no" to less. Characteristic were "Think of your desires as realities," "Prohibiting is forbidden," and, of course, the two most famous: "Imagination is power" and "Imagination is revolution." Sartre was referring to the overall spirit of these graffiti, but perhaps most to the revolutionary acts themselves, when he commented: "I would like to describe what you have done as extending the field of possibilities."

Precisely such "extending [of] the field of possibilities" is at the heart of the worldwide youth rebellion—for hippies no less than political radicals—and at the heart of the protean insistence upon continuous psychic re-creation of the self. Around this image of unlimited extension and perpetual recreation, as projected into a dimly imagined future, the young seek to create a new mode of revolutionary immortality.

Of enormous importance for these rebellions is another basic component of the protean style, the spirit of mockery. While young rebels are by no means immune from the most pedantic and humorless discourse, they come alive to others and themselves only when giving way to, or seizing upon, their very strong inclination toward mockery. The mocking political rebel merges with the hippie and with a variety of exponents of pop culture to "put on"—that is, mislead or deceive by means of some form of mockery or absurdity—his uncomprehending cohorts, his elders, or anyone in authority. (Despite important differences, there has always been a fundamental unity in the rebellions of hippies and young radicals which is perhaps just now becoming fully manifest.) In dress, hair, and general social and sexual style, the mocking rebel is not only "extending the field of possibilities," but making telling commentary—teasing, ironic, contemptuous—on the absurd folkways of "the others."

A classic example of the mocking put-on was Yippie leader Jerry Rubin's appearance at the House Un-American Activities Committee hearing on possible Communist involvement in the Chicago street demonstrations during the Democratic National Convention. The New York *Times* reporter, noting that Rubin wore a "bandolier of live cartridges," painted a vivid scene: "Bearded, beaded, barefooted and barechested, Mr. Rubin waved aloft what he called 'an M-16 rifle.' It turned out to be a toy. Later, stripped of his bullets, but still carrying his toy weapon, he was allowed into the hearing room where he spent much of the day jingling bells attached to his wrists, popping bubble gum and burning tiny sticks of incense." Here the put-on includes a dramatization of the most lurid fantasies of the adversary, together with little rituals so radically "out of place" in the particular setting that either they or the setting itself must be viewed as absurd. In contrast, the testimony of a staff investigator for the subcommittee that (again as reported by the *Times*) "the demonstrations were in line with 'the policies of Hanoi, Peking and Moscow,'" was a straight form of accusation and not, at least by intention, a put-on.

The mockery can be gentle and even loving, or it can be bitter and provocative in the extreme. Here the Columbia rebellion is illuminating. What it lacked in graffiti it more than made up for in its already classic slogan, "Up against the wall, motherfucker!" I make no claim to full understanding of the complete psychological and cultural journey this phrase has undergone. But let me at least sketch in a few steps along the way:

1. The emergence of the word "motherfucker" to designate a form of extreme transgression. The word might well have originated

with the black American subculture, and certainly has been given fullest expression there and used with great nuance to express not only contempt but also awe or even admiration (though an equivalent can probably be found in virtually every culture).

2. The use of the word in contemptuous command by white policemen when ordering black (and perhaps other) suspects to take their place in the police lineup, thereby creating the full phrase, "Up against the wall, motherfucker!" The mockery here was that of dehumanization, and use of the phrase was at times accompanied by beatings and other forms of humiliation.

3. LeRoi Jones's reclaiming of the phrase for black victims—and, in the process, achieving a classic victimizer-victim turnabout—by means of the simple expedient of adding to it, in a poem, the line, "This is a stick-up."

4. The appearance of an East Village Yippie (Youth International Party)-style group (now becoming national) which embraced Jones's reversal to the point of naming themselves the "Up-Against-The-Wall-Motherfuckers."

5. The attraction of Columbia SDS leaders to this East Village group ("Mostly because we liked their style," Mark Rudd said on one occasion); and the use of part of the phrase ("Up against the wall") for the title of a pre-uprising one-issue newspaper, and all of the phrase, including Jones's addition, to express contempt for Grayson Kirk in Mark Rudd's open letter to him published in that same newspaper. (The threatening chant "To the wall!" or "Up against the wall!" borrowed by young American radicals from the Cuban Revolution might also have figured in this sequence.)

6. The slogan's full flowering during the course of the Columbia strike, both in abbreviated and complete form, in shouted student chorus, for confronting just about all representatives of what was considered negative authority—police, city officials, administrators, and faculty. Rudd has claimed that his group adopted the slogan "in order to demonstrate our solidarity with the blacks and our understanding of the oppression they have been subjected to." But other student-strikers told me this was "a public explanation." They attributed the slogan's popularity to the students' general mood and feelings about their adversaries; and also to the presence of a few members of the East Village group. One, known as John Motherfucker, was constantly in view, wearing his "club jacket" with the organization's name lettered on it, and advocating even greater militancy. He became an object of both humor (other students thought his ideas "crazy") and affection.

7. The arrested students' renewed encounter with the police version of the shorter phrase ("Up against the wall!") when *they* were called to the police lineup.

8. Finally, Lionel Trilling's pun, in characterizing the striking students (not without affection) as "Alma-Mater-fuckers," a witty example of an important principle: the mocking of mockery.

In evaluating the significance of the phrase and its vicissitudes, the classical psychoanalytic approach would, immediately and definitively, stress the Oedipus complex. After all, who but *fathers* are motherfuckers? And who but sons yearn to replace them in this activity? Moreover, the authorities at whom the Columbia students aimed the phrase could certainly qualify, in one way or another, as father-substitutes. And there was much additional evidence throughout the student rebellions of a totem-and-taboo-like attack upon the father—as exemplified, mockingly and playfully, by another bit of French graffiti, "Daddy stinks" (*Papa pue*); and, mockingly and nastily, by Columbia students reported to have shouted at their faculty elders, "Why don't you go and die!"

But one does well to move beyond this kind of psychoanalytic explanation, to take it as at most a beginning of, rather than an end to, understanding. For if we assume that the mother in question is, so to speak, the fucker's own, we are dealing with an image of the ultimate violation of the ultimate incest taboo. Now, it has been said that this taboo is society's last inviolate principle—the only psycho-moral barricade which contemporary rebels have not yet stormed. Whether or not this is true, the bandying about of the phrase "Up against the wall, motherfuckers!" is a way of playing with an image of ultimate violation, and of retribution for that violation. The tone could be menacing and hateful, but on the whole (at least among the students) less one of irreconcilable rage than of taunting ridicule and mimicry. And the continuous reversals characterizing the whole sequence—the switches between victimizer and victim, accuser and accused—ultimately mock not only the whole social order and its linguistic and sexual taboos; like Trilling's pun, they mock the mocking phrase itself.

The tone of mockery can be a source of great unifying power. One could argue, for instance, that mockery provided the necessary continuity in the evolution, metaphorically speaking, from hippie (socially withdrawn experiments in feeling) to Yippie (activist assaults upon social institutions); as well as the psychological style around which elements of student-radical and hippie cultures could come to coexist within individual minds. In the Columbia rebellion the spirit of mockery was able to unite, if not in political action, at least in a measure of shared feeling, such disparate groups as hippies, Yippies, white student radicals, moderates, and some blacks (the police could also be included, but from across the barricades). And one can add to the list the distinguished professor whose pun I quoted, many of his faculty colleagues, a large number of Columbia students not involved in the strike, the writer of this essay, and probably most of its readers. For mockery is central to the contemporary style, confronting as it does the sense of absurd incongruity in the relationship of self to society, and ultimately of death to life, which we all share. There are moments when this incongruity can be dealt with only by the combinations of humor, taunt, mimicry, derision, and ridicule contained within the style of mockery. For when historical dislocation is sufficiently profound, mockery can become the only inwardly authentic tone for expressing what people feel about their relationships to the institutions of their world. And in this sense young rebels express what a great many other people—from conservative Wall Street broker to liberal college professor to black militant to anti-black Wallaceite—inwardly experience.

On the border of mockery are such slogans of the French students as "We are all undesirables!" and the much more powerful "We are all German Jews!" The slogans refer directly to the origins of Cohn-Bendit, the student leader, but their significance extends much further. They mock not only anti-Semitism and national-racial chauvinism, but the overall process of victimization, and the "old history" for harboring such victimization. The method by which this was done is worth noting: a vast open-air charade with thousands of students who, by shouting in unison "We are all German Jews!", momentarily became classical European victims, thereby rendering ridiculous the very categories of victim and victimizer. At this affirmative border of mockery, then, and at the far reaches of the protean style, is a call for man to cease his folly in dividing himself into what Erik Erikson has called pseudo-species, and to see himself as the single species he is.

One can observe a related if much more confusing impulse toward inclusiveness in the diversity of ideological fragments young rebels embrace. Thus hippies, for their experiments with the self, draw upon Eastern and Western mysticism, chemically induced ecstasy, and various traditions, new and old, of polymorphous sexuality. Young radicals may incorporate any of these aspects of hippie culture, and combine them with ideas and images drawn from many different revolutionary experiences (pre-Marxist utopians, anarchists, Marx, Trotsky, Lenin, Rosa Luxemburg, Mao, Castro, Guevara, Debray, Ho, Gandhi, Fanon, Malcolm X, Martin Luther King, Stokely Carmichael, and H. Rap Brown); from recent psychological and social theorists (Sartre, Camus, C. Wright Mills, Herbert Marcuse, Norman O. Brown, Erik Erikson, Abraham Maslow, and Paul Goodman); and from just about any kind of evolving cultural style (derived from jazz or black power or "soul," from the small-group movement and the Esalen-types stress upon Joy, or from camp mockery of Victorian or other retrospectively amusing periods).

Moreover, the emphasis upon the experiential—upon the way a man and his ideas *feel* to one right now, rather than upon precise theory—encourages inclusiveness and fits in with the focus upon images and fragments. Details of intellectual history may be neglected, and even revered figures are often greatly misunderstood. But the overall process can be seen as a revolutionary equivalent to the artist's inclination to borrow freely, selectively, impressionistically, and distortingly from predecessors and contemporaries as a means of finding his own way.

Of enormous importance as models are heroic images of men whose lives can be viewed as continuously revolutionary. The extraordinary lives of Mao, Castro, and especially Guevara can combine with romantic mythology of many kinds, including that of perpetual revolution. In a sense Castro and Guevara are transitional figures between the total ideologies of the past and the more fragmentary and experiential ones of the New History. But heroes and models tend to be easily discarded and replaced, or else retained with a looseness and flexibility that permit the strangest of revolutionary bedfellows. In lives as in ideologies, the young seek not the entire package but those fragments which contribute to their own struggle to formulate and change their world, to their own sense of wholeness. Their constant search for new forms becomes a form in itself.

To dismiss all this as a "style revolution" is to miss the point—unless one is aware of the sense in which style is everything. One does better to speak of a *revolution of forms*, of a quest for images of rebirth which reassert feelings of connection and re-establish the sense of immortality; and of a *process revolution*, consistent with the principles of action painting and kinetic sculpture, in which active rebelling both expresses and creates the basic images of rebellion. The novelist Donald Barthelme's statement that "fragments are the only form I trust" has ramifications far beyond the literary. However severe the problems posed by such a principle for social and especially political revolution, we deceive ourselves unless we learn to focus upon these shifting forms—to recognize new styles of life and new relations to institutions and to ideas. Indeed, we require a little revolutionizing of our psychological assumptions, so that both the young and the old can be understood, not as bound by static behavioral categories, but as in continuous historical motion.

Let us, for instance, turn to the extremely important symbolism surrounding fathers and sons. Here the theme of fatherlessness is prominent, but it does not necessarily include a search for a "substitute father."

In addition to his biological and familial relationship to his children, we may speak of the father as one who mediates between prevailing social images on the one hand and the developmental thrusts of his children (biological or symbolic) on the other. Because the father is clearly not a simple conduit, and imposes a strong personal imprint (his "personality") upon the child, we tend to fall into the lazy psychoanalytic habit of seeing every authoritative man or group coming into subsequent contact with the child from the larger society as a "substitute" for the father, as a "father figure." Yet considering the enormous part played by general historical forces in shaping what the father transmits (or fails to transmit), one might just as well say that he is a "substitute" for history, a "history figure." The analogy is admittedly a bit farfetched—a flesh-and-blood father, and not "history," conceives the child, teaches him things, and tells him off—but so is the tendency toward indiscriminate labeling of one person as a "substitute" for another. We do better, especially during periods of rapid change, to see fathers and sons as bound up in a shifting psychological equilibrium, each influencing the other, both enmeshed in forms specific to their family and their historical epoch. (Mothers and daughters are, of course, very much part of all this. But the mother's "mediation," for biological and cultural reasons, tends to be more heavily infused with nurturing; her way of representing forms of social authority tends to be more indirect, complex, and organically rooted. And revolutionary daughters, like their mothers, deserve an evaluation of their own, quite beyond the scope of this essay.) A son's developing image of the world should not be attributed to a single cause, nor considered a replacement for an earlier imprint.

Nor is the father by any means a pure representative of the past. Rather he is a molder of compromise between the history he has known and the newer one, in which the life of his family is immersed. During periods like the present he is, psychologically speaking, by no means a clear spokesman for stability and "order." He is more a troubled negotiator, caught between the relatively orderly images he can retain (or reach back for) from his own experience and the relatively disorderly ones anticipating the new shape of things. While likely to be more on the side of the former than the latter, in the midst of a revolution of forms his allegiances may not be too clear. He finds himself suspended in time, weakened by the diminishing power of old forms, and by his inability to relate himself significantly to (or even comprehend) the new.

During earlier revolutions (the French Revolution or the social revolution of the Renaissance) the old history under attack, however vulnerable, was still part of a coherent formulation of the world—theological, political, and social. One suspects that this formulation provided the fathers of the time with psychic ammunition sufficient to confront their rebellious sons. But the old history now being attacked, reflecting as it does more than two hundred years of erosion of traditional forms of every kind, permits fathers no such symbolic strength, no such capacity for confrontation. Instead we find a characteristic father-son pattern emerging in families in various parts of the world—among young American radicals (as reported by Kenneth Keniston), Japanese *Zengakuren* student-activists (whom I interviewed), and, very likely, many young French student rebels. The pattern is this: the son, fortified and recurrently exhilarated by his radical convictions, and by his sense of being ethically and historically *right,* pities rather than hates his father for the latter's "sellout" to evil social forces. He views his father as one who has erred and been misled, as a man in need of patient reeducation rather than total denunciation. And the father himself, inwardly, cannot help sharing many of these judgments, however he may try to attribute them to his son's immaturity and youthful excess. This is the sense in which fathers no longer exercise ethical, or formative, authority over their sons. They have lost their capacity to guide their offspring through the shifting forms of their common world. They can be fathers but not mentors.

This loss of mentorship is what we generally call "the absence of male authority." Its large-scale occurrence reflects the *historical* absence of a meaningful set of inner images of what one should value, how one should live. But it is experienced by the individual as a profound sense of fatherlessness. Sons feel abandoned by their fathers and perceive the world as devoid of strong men who know how things are and how they should be.

But precisely this kind of symbolic fatherlessness makes possible every variety of experiment and innovation. Just as the young lack the nurturing comfort of fixed social forms, so are they free of the restricting demands of these forms. Since nothing is psychologically certain, everything is possible. And there emerges what might be called an "unencumbered generation," in politics as well as in everyday life.

Unencumbered rebellion can include every variety of tactical and ideological foray into present-day existence—as expressed in this country's "new politics" (the young radicals' politics of confrontation, the Yippies "politics of ecstasy," and the more staid but still politically unconventional and youth-influenced campaigns of Eugene McCarthy and Robert Kennedy), and especially in contemporary novels (such as the nightmare version depicted by Sol Yurick in *The Bag*). This potential for innovation is perhaps the least understood dimension of the new rebels. It particularly confuses members of the Old Left, and provokes them either to reassert older judgments about how radicals should behave, or to attempt (often with considerable sympathy) to subsume the new rebellion under a traditional ideological label. "Anarchism" is the most tempting, because of its stress upon human relations in autonomous communities and opposition to centralized power, and because of what George Woodcock has referred to as "its cult of the spontaneous ... [and] striking protean fluidity in adapting its approach and methods to special historical circumstances." But even Woodcock speaks of "a new manifestation of the idea"; and the young themselves tend to alternate between accepting the anarchist label as one of their ideological fragments, and expressing wariness toward it as still another potential ideological trap. Perhaps Sartre was wiser in his characterization of the phenomenon to Cohn-Bendit: "You have many more ideas than your fathers had. ... Your imagination is far richer."

The formative fathers of the young rebels are the middle-aged members of the intellectual left. (I recently heard one articulate young rebel say as much to an audience made up mostly of university professors: "We are your children. You taught us what American society is like.") And the encounter between formative fathers and sons takes on special importance. On the one hand the young rebels seize upon their innovative freedom and seek to live out both the classical revolutionary myth of making all things new, and the contemporary protean myth of infinite shape-shifting to the point of rendering the past totally "irrelevant." They may thus view their formative fathers as no more than rickety impediments. But on the other hand, they give the impression of constantly seeking *something* from this group of their elders: confirmation in radicalism, adult-dispensed legitimation (psychological and ethical), authoritative support, and at times even guidance (but never direction), concerning theory and tactics. (One must keep in mind the origins of many of the ideological fragments of the young rebels in older-generation thought, such as that of Herbert Marcuse and C. Wright Mills, without viewing these origins as determining everything.) The young, then, do seek connection, but a connection that does not suffocate or even restrict. The connection may be essentially negative—the young may contrast their own activism, flexibility, and moral intensity with their elders' passivity, fixity, and shameful compromise—but even this can be a form of connection.

The "fathers" involved also crave connection. As long-standing advocates of liberal or radical programs, now puzzled or even terrified by their intellectual offspring, they too ask themselves where they can link up with what is happening. But nothing for these formative fathers is clear-cut. They do not live in a time (Confusian or biblical) in which sons are expected to honor, and seek to become like, their fathers. Nor do the young bring to them the kind of total negation expressed in a three-sentence commentary by a member of Hell's Angels: "I don't like nothin'. I don't like nobody. Fuck everything." Instead, the middle-aged left-intellectual finds the encounter to be replete with ambiguity. He is likely to be alternately attracted, repulsed, impressed, bedazzled, jarred, and bemused by young rebels and their behavior—his historical sense and paternal impulse combining to tell him he should *do* something, but what?

He at times responds by reviving his own radicalism, which can in turn take the form of either a serious re-examination of his world or of an uncritical psychological identification with the young. Or he may have the opposite response of angry and unyielding dissociation from the young, sometimes with searching criticism of their programs, but all too often with a petulant and willfully uncomprehending declaration of generational warfare. A third response, a favorite of postmodern intellectuals in times of crisis, is that of escape into technical and professionalized preoccupations—though the allergy of the young to this stance is making it more and more difficult to maintain. There are, of course, other kinds of responses, but here I want to stress the very real psychological, actually psychohistorical, problems faced by these members of the "older generation."

For instance, they experience severe feelings of guilt over reminders of never-quite-abandoned ideals and never-quite-comfortable accommodations; over not doing more to embrace the young and their movement, or if they do embrace them, over the possibility of repeating their own past political mistakes in response to a new call to revolution. They feel rage toward the young because of the severe threat they represent (sometimes accompanied by envy of the strength and conviction behind that threat), as well as rage toward themselves because of their own sense of impotence. Most of all, they perceive a fundamental threat to overall integrity, to whatever degree of wholeness they have been able to achieve in their own blend of individual and historical forms, in their decent liberalism, ordered radicalism, professional autonomy, and personal privacy— that is, a threat to the entire structure of their lives. And even those who, like Sartre, wish to acknowledge the superior imagination of their "sons" must sense that, as older models, they are likely to be rather quickly "used up," and either discarded or retained condescendingly in order to make way for new imaginative forays. It could be argued that the young have bypassed fathers for formative grandfathers, such as the seventy-year-old Marcuse and the seventy-five-year-old Mao, a pattern frequently resorted to when rapid historical change weakens the former and renders the latter in various ways more heroic. But I would see this as only one among many patterns, and point to younger models such as Guevara and Castro, as well as to such "old" young radicals as Tom Hayden. In any case, formative fathers risk inner agreement with the young's accusatory chant of "irrelevance" until they can discover their own relationship to unprecedented events.

There has been much discussion about young rebels' selection of the university as a primary target for recent upheavals. Many distinguished commentators (David Riesman, Christopher Lasch, Stephen Spender, Herbert Marcuse, Lionel Trilling, and Noam Chomsky, among others) have cautioned students about the dangers of confusing the vulnerable centers of learning they attack, and for periods of time "bring down," with society at large. Spender put the matter eloquently when he said that "however much the university needs a revolution, and the society needs a revolution, it would be disastrous ... not to keep the two revolutions apart." He went on to point out, as have others, that the university is "an arsenal from which [student-rebels] can draw the arms from which they can change society"; and that "to say 'I won't have a university until society has a revolution' is as though Karl Marx were to say, 'I won't go to the reading room of the British Museum until it has a revolution.' " Yet wise as these cautionary thoughts undoubtedly are, one also has to consider the ways in which the university's special symbolic significance makes it all too logical (if unfortunate) a target for would-be revolutionaries.

What makes universities unique is the extent to which, within them, the prevailing concepts of a society are at the same time presented, imposed, examined, and criticized. The university is indeed a training ground for available occupational slots in society, as young rebels are quick to point out; it can at its worst approach a technical instrument in the hands of the military-industrial complex. But it can also be precisely the opposite, a training ground for undermining social institutions, as Spender suggests, and as the young rebels themselves attest by the extent to which they are campus products. In most cases the university is a great many things in between. It provides for students four years of crucial personal transition—from relatively unformed adolescence to a relatively formed adulthood. And the fact that many are likely to move through continuing protean explorations during the post-university years renders especially important whatever initial adult "formation" the university makes possible. For these reasons, and because both groups are there, the university is the logical place for the rebellious young to confront their ostensible mentors, and thereby both define themselves and make a statement about society at large.

The statement they make has to do not only with social inequities and outmoded institutions, but with the general historical dislocations of everyone. And in this sense the target of the young is not so much the university, or the older generation, as the continuing commitment of both to the discredited past. But the university provides unique opportunities for the young to reverse the father-son mentorship—and, moreover, to do so *in action.* The reversal may be confused and temporary, with student and teacher moving back and forth between leadership and followership, but in the process the young can assert their advanced position in the shaping of what is to come. Though the "generation gap" seems at times to be increasing beyond redemption, there is also a sense in which the gap narrows as the young engage their elders as they never have before, and the university becomes a place of unprecedented intellectual emotional contact between the generations. And what happens at one university can be repeated, with many variations, at any other university throughout the world. Universities everywhere share a central position in the susceptibility to new currents, and tend also to present students with very real grievances; the global communications network provides not only the necessary contagion but instant instruction in the art of university rebellion. Specific actions and reactions then give way to a general historical process.

We learn more about the university in the midst of militant

social disorder by turning to the greatest of recent national upheavals, the Chinese Cultural Revolution. More than is generally realized, universities were the focus of much that took place during that
extraordinary movement. Not only were they a major source of Red
Guard activists, but within them a series of public denunciations of
senior professors and administrators by students and young faculty
members preceded, and in a sense set off, the Cultural Revolution as
a whole. These denunciations originated at Peking University,
which was the scene of many such upheavals, both before the Communist victory in China and during the subsequent campaigns of
"thought reform" that are a trademark of the Chinese Communist
regime.

The Cultural Revolution, the most extreme of these campaigns,
contrasted with more recent student rebellions elsewhere in one
very important respect: the young were called forth by their elders
(Mao and the Maoists) to fight the latter's old revolutionary battles,
and to combat the newly threatening impurities associated with
revisionism. But from the beginning there was probably a considerable amount of self-assertion and spontaneity among Red Guard
leaders and followers. And over the course of the Cultural Revolution, overzealous Red Guard groups became more and more difficult
for anyone to control, especially as they split into contending fac-
tions, each claiming to be the most authentically revolutionary and
Maoist. And during the summer of 1968 reports of jousts, fights, and
pitched battles among them, also taking place at Peking University,
revealed how within two years that institution had shifted in its
function from provider of the spark of the Cultural Revolution to
receptacle for its ashes. Significantly, members of the Red Guard
were then demoted to the status of "intellectuals" who required the
tutelage of workers and especially peasants (and the control of the
army). But Peking and other universities continued to preoccupy the
regime as places in need of fundamental reform.

Indeed, the remolding of educational institutions has been
greatly stressed over the course of the Cultural Revolution. And the
extraordinary step of closing all schools throughout China for more
than a year was both a means of mobilizing students for militant
political struggles beyond the campuses, and revamping (however
chaotically) the nation's educational process. In my book *Revolutionary Immortality* (1968), I described the Cultural Revolution as a
quest for a symbolic form of immortality, a means of eternalizing
Mao's revolutionary works in the face of his anticipated biological
death and the feared "death of the revolution." The university was
perceived throughout as both an arena of fearful dangers (revisionist
ideas) and as what might be called an immortalizing agent (for the

promulgation at the highest cultural levels of the complete Maoist thought).

In its own fashion, the Cultural Revolution was a response to the New History, which in China's case includes not only Russian and Eastern European revisionism but early manifestations of protean-ism. Chinese universities, however, have been forced to flee from contemporary confusions into what is most simple and pure in that country's Old Revolutionary History; this is in contrast to the more open-ended plunge into a threatening but multifaceted future being taken by universities throughout the rest of the world. Yet those issues are far from decided. Universities everywhere, China in-cluded, are likely to experience powerful pressures from the young for "restructuring." While this hardly guarantees equivalent re-structuring of national governments, it may well be a prelude to fundamental changes in almost every aspect of human experience.

One can hardly speak of definitive conclusions about something just beginning. Nor would I claim a position of omniscient detach-ment from the events of the New History. But having earlier affirmed its significance, I wish now to suggest some of its pitfalls, and then some potentialities for avoiding them. From the standpoint of the young, those pitfalls are related to what is best called romantic totalism. I refer to a post-Cartesian absolutism, to a new quest for old feelings. Its controlling image, at whatever level of consciousness, is that of *replacing history with experience.*

This is, to a considerable extent, the romanticism of the "youth movement." I have heard a number of thoughtful European-born intellectuals tell, with some anxiety, how the tone and atmosphere now emanating from young American rebels is reminiscent of that of the German youth movement of the late Weimar Republic (and the Hitler Youth, into which it was so readily converted). What they find common to both is a cult of feeling and a disdain for restraint and reason. While I would emphasize the differences between the two groups much more than the similarities, there is a current in contemporary youth movements that is more Nietzschean than Marxist-Leninist: It consists of a stress upon what I call experiential transcendence, upon the cultivation of states of feeling so intense and so absorbing that time and death cease to exist. (Drugs are of great importance here but as part of a general quest.) The pattern becomes totalistic when it begins to tamper with history to the extent of victimizing opponents in order to reinforce these feelings; and a danger signal is the absolute denial of the principle of histori-cal continuity.

The replacement of history with experience—with totally liberated feeling—is by no means a new idea, and has long found expression in classical forms of mysticism and ecstasy. But it has reappeared with considerable force in the present-day drug revolution, and in the writings of a number of articulate spokesmen, notably Norman O. Brown. This general focus upon the transcendent psychic experience would seem to be related to impairments in other modes of symbolic immortality. That is, the modern decline of theological concepts of immortality, on the one hand, and the threat posed by present weapons (nuclear, bacterial, and chemical) to man's biological and cultural continuity, on the other, have radically undermined symbolism of death and transcendence. In the absence of intact images of biological and cultural immortality, man's anxiety about both his death and his manner of life is profoundly intensified. One response to this anxiety—and simultaneous quest for new forms—is the unique contemporary blending of experiential transcendence with social and political revolution.

We have already noted that political revolution has its own transformationist myth of making all things new. When this combines with the experiential myth (of eliminating time and death), two extreme positions can result. One of these is the condemnation and negation of an entire historical tradition: the attempt by some of the young to sever totally their relationship to the West by means of an impossibly absolute identity replacement, whether the new identity is that of the Oriental mystic or that of the Asian or African victim of colonialism or slavery. And a second consequence of this dismissal of history can be the emergence of a single criterion of judgment: what feels revolutionary is good, what does not is counterrevolutionary.

A related, equally romantic pitfall might be called "generational totalism." The problem is not so much the slogan "Don't trust anyone over thirty" as the unconscious assumption that can be behind it: that "youth power" knows no limits because youth equals immortality. To be sure, it is part of being young to believe that one will never die, that such things happen only to other people, old people. But this conviction ordinarily lives side by side with a realization—at first preconscious, but over the years increasingly a matter of awareness—that life is, after all, finite. And a more symbolic sense of immortality, through works and connections outlasting one's lifespan, takes hold and permits one to depend a little less upon the fantasy that one will live forever.

Under extreme historical conditions, however, certain groups—in this case, youth groups—feel the need to cling to the omnipotence provided by a more literal image of immortality, which they in turn contrast with the death-tainted lives of others. When this happens, we encounter a version of the victimizing process: the young "victimize" the old (or older) by equating age with individual or historical "exhaustion" and death; and the "victim," under duress, may indeed feel himself to be "as if dead," and collude in his victimization. Conversely, the older generation has its need to victimize, sometimes (but not always) in the form of counterattack, and may feel compelled to view every innovative action of the young as destructive or "deadly." Indeed, the larger significance and greatest potential danger of what we call the "generation gap" reside in these questions of broken historical connection and impaired sense of immortality.

The recent slogan of French students "The young make love, the old make obscene gestures" is patronizing rather than totalistic, and its mocking blend of truth and absurdity permits a chuckle all around. But when the same students refer to older critics as "people who do not exist," or when young American radicals label everyone and everything either "relevant" ("revolutionary") or "irrelevant" ("counterrevolutionary") on the basis of whether or not the person, idea, or event is consistent with their own point of view, we are dealing with something potentially more malignant, with the drawing of sharp lines between people and nonpeople.

Perhaps the ultimate expression of generational totalism was that of an early group of Russian revolutionaries who advocated the suppression and even annihilation of everyone over the age of twenty-five because they were felt to be too contaminated with that era's Old History to be able to absorb the correct principles of the New. I have heard no recent political suggestions of this kind; but there have certainly been indications (aside from the Hollywood version of youth suppressing age in the film *Wild in the Streets*) that young radicals at times have felt a similar impulse; and that some of their antagonists in the older generations have felt a related urge to eliminate or incarcerate everyone *under* twenty-five.

I have stressed the promiscuous use of the word "relevant." Beyond its dictionary meanings, its Latin origin, *relevare,* "to raise up," is suggestive of its current meaning. What is considered relevant is that which "raises up" a particular version of the New History, whether that of the young rebels or of the slightly older technocrats (such as Zbigniew Brzezinski) who are also fond of the word. Correspondingly, everything else must be "put down"—not only defeated but denied existence.

Such existential negation is, of course, an old story: one need only recall Trotsky's famous reference to the "dustbin of history."

But the young, paradoxically, call it forth in relationship to the very images and fragments we spoke of before as protean alternatives to totalism. An example is the all-encompassing image of the "Establishment": taken over from British rebels, it has come to mean everything from American (or Russian, or just about any other) political and bureaucratic leadership, to American businessmen (from influential tycoons to salaried executives to storekeepers), to university administrators (whether reactionary or liberal presidents or simple organization men), and even to many of the student and youth leaders who are themselves very much at odds with people in these and other categories. And just as Establishment becomes a devil-image, so do other terms, such as (in different ways) "confrontation" and "youth," become god-images. It is true that these god- and devil-images can illuminate many situations, as did such analogous Old Left expressions as "the proletarian standpoint," "the exploiting classes," and "bourgeois remnants," the last three in association with a more structured ideology. What is at issue, however, is the degree to which a particular image is given a transcendent status and is then uncritically applied to the most complex situations in a way that makes it the start and finish of any ethical judgment or conceptual analysis.

This image-focused totalism enters into the ultimate romanticization, that of death and immortality. While the *sense* of immortality, of unending historical continuity, is central to ordinary psychological experience, *romantic totalism tends to confuse death with immortality, and even to equate them.* Here one recalls Robespierre's famous dictum, "Death is the beginning of immortality," which Hannah Arendt has called "the briefest and most grandiose definition . . . [of] the specifically modern emphasis on politics, evidenced in the revolutions." Robespierre's phrase still resonates for us, partly because it captures an elusive truth about individual death as a *rite de passage* for the community, a transition between a man's biological life and the continuing life of his works. But within the phrase there also lurks the romantic temptation to court death in the service of immortality—to view dying, and in some cases even killing, as the only true avenues to immortality.

The great majority of today's radical young embrace no such imagery; they are, in fact, intent upon exploring the fullest possibilities of life. But some can at times be prone to a glorification of life-and-death gestures, and to all-or-none "revolutionary tactics," even in petty disputes hardly worthy of these cosmic images. In such situations their sense of mockery, and especially self-mockery, deserts them. For these and the related sense of absurdity can, at least at their most creative, deflate claims to omniscience and provide a contemporary equivalent to the classical mode of tragedy. Like tragedy, mockery conveys man's sense of limitation before death and before the natural universe, but it does so now in a world divested of more "straight" ways to cope with mortality. Those young rebels who reject this dimension, and insist instead upon unwavering militant rectitude, move toward romanticized death and the more destructive quests for immortality.

The theme of militant rectitude brings us back once more to the Chinese experience—and to Maoism at the quintessential expression of romantic totalism. For we may see in Mao a paradigm of the pitfalls of a noble vision, a paradigm which has great bearing on the struggles of youth throughout the world quite apart from whatever attraction they may feel toward this extraordinary leader. Mao's unparalleled accomplishments make him perhaps the greatest of all revolutionaries. If one studies his writings, one is impressed by his tone of transcendence, his continuous insistence upon all-or-none confrontation with death in the service of revitalizing the Chinese people, so much so that I have described him as "a death-conquering hero who became the embodiment of Chinese immortality." Young rebels throughout the world can perceive something in this aura, however limited their knowledge of the concrete details of Mao's life. They can, moreover, make psychological use of his Chineseness to reinforce their condemnation of Western cultural tradition, while also viewing him as the leader of "the external proletariat" (a new term for the people of the Third World, seen as possessing a vanguard revolutionary role).

Futher, young rebels respond to Mao's militant opposition not only to Russia and America but to the "world establishment" dominated by these two great powers. And even more to his deep distrust of bureaucracies which culminated in his remarkable assault during the Cultural Revolution upon the organizational structure of his own party and regime. (Several student-radicals I asked about Mao gave as their first reason for admiring him: "He's against institutions." Though it should be added that many others find fault with him, and sometimes mock both Mao's celebrated Thought and what they regard as equally stereotyped American attitudes toward the man and his ideas.) Add to this Mao's achievements in guerrilla warfare, his affinity for the great Chinese outlaws, and his sentimental but often moving poetry with its stress upon immortality through revolution, and one can understand why even Chinese Communist spokesmen themselves have referred to him as a "romantic revolutionary."

Yet Mao's very romanticism—his glorification of the revolutionary spirit and urge to inundate all minds with that spirit—has given rise to what is perhaps the most extensive program of human manipulation known to history. And during the Cultural Revolution he has become the center of an equally unprecedented immortalization of words and personal deification that has offended even admirers of long standing. Young rebels who embrace from afar Mao's version of "permanent revolution" may too easily overlook the consequences of the recent campaign on behalf of that principle: irreparable national dissension, convoluted and meaningless forms of violence, and extreme confusion and disillusionment among Chinese youth (as well as their elders), perhaps especially among those who initially responded most enthusiastically to the call for national transformation. Nor are young rebels in the West aware of the extent to which the Maoist vision has had to be modified and in some ways abandoned in response to the deep-seated opposition it encountered throughout China.

Intrinsic in Mao's romantic-totalistic conduct of the Cultural Revolution is a pattern I call "psychism," a confusion between mind and its material products, an attempt to control the external world and achieve strongly desired technological goals by means of mental exercises and assertions of revolutionary will. Now the radical young in more affluent societies have a very different relationship to technology; rather than desperately seeking it, they feel trapped and suffocated by it (though they also feel its attraction). But they too can succumb to a similar kind of confusion, which in their case takes the form of mistaking a rewarding inner sense of group solidarity with mastery of the larger human and technological world "outside." The recent Maoist experience can find its counterpart in a sequence of experiences of young rebels in the West: deep inner satisfaction accompanying bold collective action, disillusionment at the limited effects achieved, and more reckless and ineffective action with even greater group solidarity. This is not to say that all or most behavior of young rebels falls into this category; to the contrary, their political confrontations have achieved a number of striking successes largely because they were *not* merely assertions of will but could also mobilize a wide radius of opposition to outmoded and destructive academic and national policies. Yet the enormous impact of high technology in the postmodern world, and the universal tendency to surround it with vast impersonal organizations, present an ever increasing temptation to transcend the whole system (or "bag") by means of romantic worship of the will as such, and especially the revolutionary will.

Whatever their admiration of Mao, many young rebels find themselves in tactical conflict with pure Maoists who view Mao's sayings as transcendent truths, and insist upon apocalyptic violence as the only form of authentic revolutionary action. Such pure Maoists were depicted, one might say caricatured, by Godard in his film *La Chinoise*, and have had their counterparts in the American student movement. As advocates of Maoism from a distance who lack their mentor's pragmatism and flexibility, they are somewhat reminiscent of the non-Russian Stalinists of the 1930s. But for most young rebels, Mao and Maoism are perceived less as demarcated historical person and program than as a constellation of heroic, and above all antibureaucratic, revolutionary images. The problem for these young rebels is to recover the historical Mao in all of his complexity, which means understanding his tragic transition from great revolutionary leader to despot. To come to terms with their own Maoism, they must sort out the various elements of the original—on the one hand its call for continuous militant action on behalf of the deprived, and its opposition to stagnant institutions; on the other, is apocalyptic totalism and desperate rearguard assault upon the openness of contemporary man.

Yet precisely the openness of the young may help them to avoid definitive commitments to these self-defeating patterns. They need not be bound by the excesses of either Cartesian rationalism or the contemporary cult of experience which feeds romantic totalism. Indeed, though the latter is a response to and ostensibly a replacement for the former, there is a sense in which each is a one-dimensional mirror-image of the other. Today's young have available for their formulations of self and world the great twentieth-century insights which liberate man from the senseless exclusions of the opposition between emphasis on "experience" and on the "rational." I refer to the principles of symbolic thought, as expressed in the work of such people as Cassirer and Langer, and of Freud and Erikson. One can never know the exact effect of great insights upon the historical process, but it is quite possible that, with the decline of the total ideologies of the old history, ideas as such will become more important than ever in the shaping of the new. Having available an unprecedented variety of ideas and images, the young are likely to attempt more than did previous generations and perhaps make more mistakes, but also to show greater capacity to extricate themselves from a particular course and revise tactics, beliefs, and styles—all in the service of contributing to embryonic social forms.

These forms are likely to be highly fluid, but need not by any means consist exclusively of shape-shifting. Rather, they can come to combine flux with elements of connectedness and consistency, and to do so in new ways and with new kinds of equilibria. Any New History worthy of that name not only pits itself against, but draws actively upon, the old. Only through such continuity can the young bring a measure of surefootedness to their continuous movement. And to draw upon the old history means to look both ways: to deepen the collective awareness of Auschwitz and Hiroshima and what they signify, and at the same time to carve out a future that remains open rather than bound by absolute assumptions about a "technetronic society" or by equally absolute polarities of "revolution" and "counterrevolution."

It is possible that man's two most desperately pressing problems— nuclear weapons and world population—may contribute to the overcoming of totalism and psychism. I have written elsewhere of the pattern of nuclearism, the deification of nuclear weapons and of a false dependency upon them for the attainment of political and social goals. This nuclearism tends to go hand in hand with a specific form of psychism, the calling forth of various psychological and political constructs in order to deny the technological destructiveness of these weapons. Nuclear illusions have been rampant in both America and China. There are impressive parallels between certain Pentagon nuclear policies (grotesquely expressed in the John Foster Dulles doctrine of "massive retaliation") on the one hand, and the joyous Chinese embrace of nuclear weapons as further confirmation of the Maoist view of world revolution on the other. Similarly, Pentagon (and early Herman Kahn) projections of the ease of recovery from nuclear attack bear some resemblance to the Maoist view of the weapons not only as "paper tigers" but even as a potential source of a more beautiful socialist order rising from the ashes.

Now, I think that young rebels, with their frequent combination of flexibility and inclusiveness, are capable of understanding these matters. They have yet to confront the issues fully, but have begun to show inclinations toward denouncing nuclearism and nuclear psychism as they occur not only in this country but among the other Great Powers. Insights about nuclear weapons are of the utmost importance to the younger generation—for preventing nuclear war, and for creating social forms which take into account man's radically changed relationship to his world because of the potentially terminal revolution associated with these weapons.

To the problem of world population young rebels are capable of bringing a pragmatism which recognizes both the imperative of technical programs on behalf of control and the bankruptcy of an exclusively technical approach. Looking once more at China, we find that a country with one of the world's greatest population problems has approached the matter of control ambivalently and insufficiently, mainly because of a Maoist form of psychism which insisted that there could never be too many workers in a truly socialist-revolutionary state. Yet this position has been modified, and there is much to suggest that the inevitable Chinese confrontation with the actualities of population has in itself been a factor in undermining more general (and widely disastrous) patterns of psychism. Young radicals elsewhere are capable of the same lessons—about population, about Maoist contradictions and post-Maoist possibilities, and about psychism *per se.*

Are these not formidable problems for youngsters somewhere between their late teens and mid-twenties? They are indeed. As the young approach the ultimate dilemmas that so baffle their elders, they seem to be poised between the ignorance of inexperience, and the wisdom of a direct relationship to the New History. Similarly, in terms of the life-cycle, they bring both the dangers of zealous youthful self-surrender to forms they do not understand, and the invigorating energy of those just discovering both self and history, energy so desperately needed for a historical foray into the unknown.

As for the "older generation"—the middle-aged left-intellectuals—the problem is a little different. For them (us) one of the great struggles is to retain (or achieve) protean openness to the possibilities latent in the New History, and to respond to that noble slogan of the French students, "Imagination is power." But at the same time this generation does well to be its age, to call upon the experience specific to the lives of those who make it up. It must tread the tenuous path of neither feeding upon its formative sons nor rejecting their capacity for innovative historical imagination. This is much more difficult than it may seem, because it requires that those now in their forties and fifties come to terms with the extremely painful history they have known, neither to deny it nor to be blindly bound by it. Yet however they may feel shunted aside by the young, there is special need for their own more seasoned, if now historically vulnerable, imaginations.

For both the intellectual young and old, together with society at large, are threatened by a violent counterreaction to the New History, by a restorationist impulse often centered in the lower middle classes but not confined to any class or country. This impulse includes an urge to eliminate troublesome young rebels along with their liberal-radical "fathers'" and to return to a mythical past in which all was harmonious and no such disturbers of the historical peace existed. What is too often forgotten by the educated of all ages, preoccupied as they are with their own historical dislocations, is the extent to which such dislocations in others produce the very opposite kind of ideological inclination; in this case a compensatory, strongly antiprotean embrace of the simple purities of the old history—personal rectitude, law and order, rampant militarism, and narrow nationalism.

If man is successful in creating the New History he must create if he is to have any history at all, then the formative fathers and sons must pool their resources and succeed together. Should this not happen, the failure too will be shared, whether in the form of stagnation and suffering or of shared annihilation. Like most other things in our world, the issue remains open. There is nothing absolute or inevitable about the New History, except perhaps the need to bring it into being.

Three

Changing Sexual Values

One of the most pervasive features of our cultural landscape is the depolarization of sex roles and a concomitant blurring of many other differences. The appearance, given names, and play of boys and girls have become less gender-specific. Young girls seem to demonstrate the sexual prococity and aggressiveness formerly associated with boys. Clothing and appearance are becoming increasingly ambisexual along with recreational activities, work, and family roles. Neutering of sex roles may have ominous implications for the future of society.

CHARLES WINICK

The Beige Epoch: Depolarization of Sex Roles in America

Perhaps the most significant and visible aspect of the contemporary American sexual scene is the tremendous decline, since World War II, in sexual dimorphism. Sex roles have become substantially neutered and environmental differences, increasingly blurred.

Our Age of the Neuter begins to leave its mark on young people in their very tender years. Gender-linked colors like pink and blue for children's clothing are yielding to green, yellow, and other colors which can be used for either Dick or Jane. Such names, however, are less likely nowadays. A study of a large sample of given names reported in birth announcements in the *New York Times* from 1948 to 1963 concluded that almost one-fifth of them were not gender-specific, for example, Leslie, Robin, Tracy, Dana, Lynn, although the 1923–1938 period had few such names.[1] Since the name helps to position a person in his culture, many young people are starting out with an ambisexual given name.

The hair of little girls is shorter and that of little boys is longer, and such blurring is given fashionable designations, that is, the Oliver or Beatle haircut. Other kinds of his-hers appearances are chic for young people. Boys and girls may have similar toys, and the last few years have witnessed the popularity of dolls for boys (G.I. Joe and his many imitators).

Reading habits of young people are less related to gender than they were a generation ago. Both sexes are likely to enjoy the same books, for example, *The Moon Spinners* and *Island of the Blue Dolphins,* and there is less interest in books which are clearly sex-linked, like the *Nancy Drew* series for girls or the *Hardy Boys* for boys. School curricula are offering fewer subjects which are unique to each sex, and both sexes learn some subjects, for example, typing.

THE TEENAGER

Dating behavior of teenagers reflects the crossing over of sex roles which pervades so much of the preadolescent years. The teenage girl increasingly is looking for her own satisfaction and may want to be even more equal than her date. Such tendencies have become more important since the 1950's, which experienced the first movie about a sexually aggressive teenager (*Susan Slept Here,* 1954), an extraordinarily successful novel about a sexually sophisticated girl (*Lolita,* 1958), and, perhaps most important, a series of very popular mannequin dolls, beginning with Betsy McCall in 1954 and culminating in Barbie in 1959. Barbie is a sexy teenager, and playing with her involves changing costumes and thereby preparing for dates. During the last decade, an average of more than 6,000,000 mannequin dolls was sold each year.

The rehearsal for dating provided by Barbie and her imitators may even further accelerate the social development of their owners. By the time an owner is ready to engage in actual dating, she could be much more forward than her male companion. Studies of teen

---

1. Charles Winick, *The New People: Desexualization in American Life* (New York: Pegasus, 1968), chap. vi.

dating suggest that, not too long ago, the aggressiveness displayed by many contemporary teenage girls was once found primarily in young men.[2]

So much time separated the nine-year-old with an old-fashioned baby doll from her role as mother that she could enjoy fantasies about motherhood and not be concerned about doing something about them. But the distance in years that separates a Barbie fan from a socially active ten- or eleven-year-old girl is slight, and she can easily translate doll-play fantasies into real social life. Barbie owners may be more ready than any previous generation to take the traditional male role in teenage courtship behavior.

CLOTHING AND APPEARANCE

The most conspicuous example of sexual crisscrossing is provided by clothing and appearance, which are important, because the costume we wear reflects the customs by which we live. When World War II provided an urgent occasion for a re-evaluation of social roles, Rosie the Riveter, in slacks, became a national heroine. At the same time, many of the 14,000,000 men in uniform, who had a limited number of outlets for their money, began to buy fragrance-containing colognes, hair preparations, and after-shave lotion. Wearing the uniform probably helped to allay any fears that the products' users might be unmanly or were indulging themselves.

The most recent postwar impetus for men's fragrance products was the great success of Canoe in 1959. College men traveling abroad began to bring back the sweet and citrus-scented French cologne, used it for themselves—and gave it to their girl friends. The appetite of college students and teenagers for strongly scented products in turn influenced their fathers, uncles, and older brothers.

Scent is a method of adornment by which a man of any age can unbutton his emotional self and attract attention, in frank recognition of women's growing freedom to pick and choose.[3] Very strong fragrances may have special appeal to men who are suffering from feelings of depersonalization. Just as anointing and incense helped to extend the body's boundaries and reach toward God, a man using a strong fragrance transcends his body's boundaries and creates a unified atmosphere that projects him toward people. Other men who are confused about their body-image may use zesty essences as one

---

2. Ira L. Reiss, "Sexual Codes in Teen-Age Culture," THE ANNALS, *American Academy of Political and Social Science*, Vol. 338 (November 1961), pp. 53–62.
3. Charles Winick, "Dear Sir or Madam, As the Case May Be," *Antioch Review*, Vol. 23 (Spring 1963), pp. 35–49.

way of reassuring themselves, in our deodorized age, that their body is recognizable and has exudations. For these and other reasons, men in the Scented Sixties spend three times as much money on fragrance-containing preparations as women do.

With men smelling so sweet, it is small wonder that the constitutionality of the New York State statute prohibiting a man from wearing a woman's clothes was challenged in 1964 for the first time. Apparel may oft proclaim the man, but many bells are jangling out of tune in the current proclamation. Men are wearing colorful and rakishly epauleted sports jackets, iridescent fabrics, dickies, and bibbed and pleated shirts of fabrics like batiste and voile.

Men's trousers are slimmer and in many instances are worn over girdles of rubber and nylon. Ties are slender and often feminine. The old reliable gray fedora has given way to softer shapes and shades, sometimes topped by gay feathers. Sweaters are less likely to have the traditional V-neck than a boat neck adopted from women's fashions. Padded shoulders on a suit are as out of date as wide lapels and a tucked-in waist. The new look is the soft, slender, straight-line silhouette that also characterizes the shift, which has been the major woman's dress style of the 1960's. Men accessorize their clothes with cuff links, tie bars and tacks, bracelets, rings, and watch bands.

Loss of gender is especially conspicuous in shoes, with women wearing boots or low-heeled, squat, square-toed, and heavy shoes at the same time that men's footwear has become more pointed, slender, colorful, and high-heeled. Men have adopted low-cut and laceless models from women's styles.

A modishly dressed couple might be walking along with the woman in hip-length boots, "basic black" leather coat, a helmet, and a pants suit or straight-line dress of heavy fabric. Her male companion might be wearing a soft pastel sack suit, mauve hat, and a frilled and cuff-linked pink shirt. He could sport a delicate tie and jewelry, exude fragrance, and wear tapered shoes with stacked heels. Both could have shoulder-length hair, and their silhouettes would be quite indistinguishable.

RECREATION AND LEISURE

The couple might be on the way to visit a family billiard center or bowling alley, now that both recreations have become somewhat feminized and have abandoned their connotations of the spittoon. Women are participating in many other previously male recreational activities, especially outdoor sports and competitive athletics. They accounted for 30 per cent of our tennis players in 1946 but today represent 45 per cent. The proportion of women golfers has risen from one-tenth to more than one-third in the same period. The pre-World War II golf club, which did not permit women, has become the family-centered country club. Men's city clubs have also substantially abandoned their formerly exclusionist attitudes toward women.

Social dancing has become almost a misnomer for the self-centered, nonrelational dances which have succeeded the Twist since 1961 and have largely replaced traditional steps like the waltz and fox trot, in which the man led and the woman followed. In the Frug and Boogaloo and other current favorites, there is no leading or following. The man and woman do not even have to look at each other or start or finish together.

WORK AND THE HOME

We are so familiar with decreased resistance to the employment of women and their continually improving preparation for work that we may sometimes forget some implications of the trend. Well over one-third of our workers are women, and, every year, proportionately more married women enter the labor market. Over 2,300,000 women earn more than their husbands. Now that the United States is the first country in which the majority of jobs are in service industries, it has also become the first country where men may soon be competing for what were previously women's jobs.

Men are less and less likely to require physical strength on the job. They are also hardly likely to assume a traditional male role in the home. The husband must often take over household tasks that were once assigned to the wife. Over three-fifths assist in cooking. In many ways, the husband has become a part-time wife. As one result of this trend, initiative and aggressiveness may become less common in boys, who may have less opportunity to see their fathers functioning in either a traditional or masterful manner.

FOOD AND DRINK

As Talcott Parsons has so eloquently reminded us, the social structure constitutes a subtly interrelated and almost homeostatic series of interrelationships. At a time when the most basic difference in a society—between men and women—is dwindling, we might expect to find other differences becoming less significant. Extremes of taste sensation in food and drink have diminished as part of our culture's larger homogeneization.

Blended whiskey's comparative lack of bouquet and flavor is probably the chief reason for its now accounting for over two-thirds of all domestic whiskey production. The most successful Scotches of the last fifteen years have all been brands which are light amber in color and possess a minimum of maltiness, smokiness, and body.

The dilution of distinguishing characteristics that is represented by "soft" whiskey and Scotch can be seen most dramatically in vodka, which jumped from one per cent of the 1952 domestic liquor market to 10 per cent in 1967. United States government regulations specify that it must be "without distinctive character, aroma or taste," so that its major appeal is a lack of the very qualities that traditionally make liquor attractive. Beer is also becoming "lighter" every year.

It would be logical to expect our great technological proficiency to have produced foods with an enormous range of taste, texture, and aroma. Yet our marriage of technology and convenience has led to wide acceptance of many foods with a blander and less explicit taste than in previous generations. Although access to more than 7,000 quick-preparation convenience items has exposed Americans to many new foods, the taste, aroma, and texture of such products tend to be more homogenized and less sharp than the fresh foods of earlier decades, as nonchemically treated fruits, home- or bakery-made bread, ethnic cooking, and many other contributors to strong taste experiences become less common.

INNER AND OUTER SPACE

In the Beige Epoch, color extremes are less welcome than they used to be. Even cosmetics stress paleness. The muted appearance of no-color color makes an ideal of "the suddenly, startlingly candid new beauties" whose makeup "turns on the immensely touching *au courant* look of the untouched, nude complexion."[4]

Beige has become the single most popular color for home interiors, carpeting, telephones, draperies. At the same time, interiors are less likely to have the heavy furniture, dark colors, and coarsely grained dark woods generally linked with men or the delicate furniture, light colors, and finely grained light woods that are associated with women.

Rooms with gender may soon be subjects for archaeologists, as a result of the continuing displacement of rooms by areas that merge into one another. And with the near-disappearance of masculine (for

---

4. *Harper's Bazaar*, No. 3041 (April 1965), p. 214.

example, the leather club model) or feminine (for example, the chaise longue) chairs, foam rubber has become the Space Age's upholstering of choice. It is neutral and has no "give," in contrast to traditional upholstering's indentations after someone has been sitting on it.

Our manipulation of outer space, via architecture, reflects the blurring of gender which also characterizes how we use furniture in the organization of inner space. Few clearly feminine (for example, the Taj Mahal) or masculine (for example, the Empire State Building) structures have been built during the last generation. When men and women wear the same straight-line silhouette and are surrounded by furniture which avoids protuberances or padding, it is hardly surprising that their buildings so literally resemble "filing cases for people," although Frank Lloyd Wright intended his famous description to be only a metaphor.

Function is almost as difficult to identify as gender in many new buildings. Hotel, bank, air terminal, lobby, store, office, and restaurant may look alike and play the same monotonous canned music, which provides a seamless wallpaper of sound.

THE PERFORMING ARTS

Men began to lose their dominant chairs at the head of the formerly rectangular dinner table at just about the time that they were yielding the center spotlight in each of the major performing arts to women. Caruso was the dominant figure of the Golden Age of Opera, but Birgit Nilsson, Joan Sutherland, Renata Tebaldi, Leontyne Price, and Maria Callas are typical of the divas who completely overshadow the male singers opposite whom they appear.

When Actors Equity celebrated its fiftieth birthday in 1963 by enacting some representative episodes from the recent past, not one actor did a major scene.[5] Lillian Gish, Helen Hayes, and Beatrice Lillie were the stars of the evening, performing excerpts from *Our Town, Victoria Regina,* and *Charlot's Review,* respectively. The male matinee idol (E. H. Southern, John Barrymore, Richard Mansfield, John Drew, Joseph Schildkraut) took his final bow some decades ago. It would be nearly impossible to make up a list of "first men" of the contemporary theatre, but women have dominated our stage for about forty years. Anne Bancroft, Geraldine Page, Kim Stanley, and Julie Harris are only a few younger current Broadway actresses who project characters with valid juices. Aggressive performers like

5. Paul Gardner, "3 of Stage's First Ladies Salute Actors Equity on 50th Birthday," *New York Times,* May 6, 1963.

Ethel Merman, Mary Martin, Barbra Streisand, Carol Channing, and Julie Andrews star in musicals which feature male leads who are either innocuous or nonsingers and are puny successors to the male singers, dancers, and comedians who made the American musical our happiest export.

The interrelationships and mutual reinforcement among the mass media are so pronounced that we might expect women to have assumed much greater importance in movie roles since World War II. Death or retirement claimed Humphrey Bogart, Clark Gable, Spencer Tracy, William Powell, and other actors who shouldered through the "movie movies" of the 1930's. Actresses are now more important than ever before, and Doris Day has played more consecutive starring roles than any performer since talkies began forty years ago. Marilyn Monroe became an unforgettable symbol of the child-woman, and Elizabeth Taylor is not only the highest paid performer in history ($2 million plus for *Cleopatra*) but also the prototype of the devouring Medusa in her private life. As in the earlier case of Ingrid Bergman, Miss Taylor made the key decision to leave one man for another, and both men acquiesced.

One of the most significant changes in the post-World War II performing arts was the emergence in the 1950's of the pianist Liberace as television's first and only superstar who had the qualities of a matinee idol. Liberace was not a particularly distinguished pianist, and much of his appeal seems to lie in his ability to communicate many characteristics of a five- or six-year-old child, of either gender.[6] His extraordinary rise to fame as America's biggest single concert attraction, barely thirty years after the disappearance of the virile stage idol in form-fitting doublet and dashing skin-tight breeches, is a striking commentary on changes in American fantasy needs.

WHY DEPOLARIZATION?

It would be possible to identify many other areas in which our society is manifesting a depolarization and bleaching of differences. Such neutering and role-blurring represent only one dimension in the dynamics of social change. It is possible that these trends necessarily develop in any society which becomes as highly industrialized as ours. There is reason to suspect that our acceptance of androgyny is, to some extent, one outcome of World War II. Studies of children from homes in which the father was absent during the

---

6. Charles Winick, "Fan Mail to Liberace," *Journal of Broadcasting*, Vol. 6 (Spring 1962), pp. 129–142.

war have suggested that many such children later exhibited considerable sex-role confusion.[7] Large numbers of such children could have been so affected by their fathers' absence and might be significantly represented in the ranks of today's young adults.

A fuller consideration of the conditions and factors producing neutering would include political, economic, technological, cultural, and demographic dimensions as well as rates of invention, acculturation, cultural diffusion, and resistance to change. Our no-war, no-peace situation also contributes to the situation, along with the blurring of categories in other fields.

The unique capacities of each sex are especially significant these days, when at least some quantitative aspects of a Great Society seem within reach. The emancipation of women and their greater equality and participation in the affairs of society were long overdue. But equality does not mean equivalence, and a difference is not a deficiency.

Multivalent, amorphous, and depolarized roles might theoretically lead to increased flexibility and options in behavior, but in actuality may tend to invoke uncertainty. Some tolerance of ambiguity is desirable for a healthy personality, but today's environment and culture are ambiguous enough to tax the adaptability of even the healthiest personalities.[8] The other extreme is represented by the completely polarized sex roles that we associate with the reactionary ideology of totalitarianism.

There is no evidence that any one kind of family structure is inherently healthier than any other, and history seems to suggest that almost any male-female role structure is viable, so long as there is clear division of labor and responsibilities. An equally important lesson of the past is that overly explicit roles can be pathogenic, because they do not permit the expression of individual differences or of a personal style. It is most disquieting to contemplate the possibility that the ambiguity of sex roles in our open society might ultimately prove to be almost as hazardous as the rigidities of authoritarianism.

---

7. Lois M. Stolz, *Father Relations of War-born Children* (Palo Alto: Stanford University Press, 1951).
8. T. W. Adorno, E. Frenkel-Brunswik, D. J. Levinson, and R. Nevitt Sanford, *The Authoritarian Personality* (New York: Harper, 1950), pp. 480–481.

New forms of peer relationships are springing up in the typical college experience according to the physician writing here. As a result, he notes, three sexual moralities are being intensely debated on college campuses today: the "new morality," amorality, and traditional morality. The dilemma of college officials who have no consistent mandate from parents, students, faculty, or alumni for policy in this area is here presented. Understanding of issues rather than proliferation of rules is stressed.

DANA L. FARNSWORTH

Sexual Morality and the Dilemma of the Colleges

During the last few years much interest has been focused on sexual practices in the colleges, an interest stimulated in part by the demands of students for greater freedom in this area together with confusion on the part of parents and college officials as to what should be the proper standards of behavior. It is quite difficult for parents and children to talk together frankly about sexual matters because of the great gulf in experience between the two generations. The background of our present college generation is very different from that of their parents. Social change was quite rapid during the time the parents of today were maturing but is even more so at present.

Communication between older and younger members of the college communities also is hampered by many influences, including lack of a consensus as to what the central issues are, criticism of those who become interested in the subject and lack of persons competent to hold discussion groups.

The sexual behavior of college students may be changing in the direction of practices formerly attributed to members of lower socioeconomic groups.[1] Reliable data on which to base such an opinion is not yet conclusive, but all general observations suggest this to be true. Not only is there thought to be a qualitative change in sexual practices but also an acceleration in such behavior. What was thought to be characteristic behavior at 18 or 20 years of age may now be observed in persons 16 to 18 or even younger.

--------- .

1. A. C. Kinsey, W. B. Pomeroy, C. E. Martin, and P. H. Gebhard, *Sexual Behavior in the Human Female,* (Philadelphia: W. B. Saunders Co., 1953), pp. 293–296.

There appear to be three general points of view regarding sexual behavior which can be characterized as: (1) the traditional morality, (2) the new morality, and (3) amorality. In the first of these, the traditional morality, the following principles are considered important:

——Renunciation or control of instinctual gratification permits a reasonable degree of civilization (Freud).
——Restraint tends to aid in developing a capacity for thoughtfulness concerning the welfare of others, particularly in a parental sense. Restraint also is thought to aid in the sublimation of sexual energies.
——Marriage becomes one of life's most cherished institutions when sexual restraint is practiced.
——The total moral fiber of a society is strengthened if sexual standards are maintained and weakened when sexual standards are ignored.
——Young people need help in controlling their strong impulses during their formative years.

In the new morality:

——Fidelity and consideration of others occupy a very high place.
——Physical sex is supposed to occur only after the establishment of friendship and love.
——Exploitation of the sexual partner is very much opposed.
——A high ethical component is apparent in the thinking of those who adhere to this general view even though it may not be in accordance with views traditionally held, nor with the views of many religious groups.

In the third general viewpoint, which is in effect a somewhat amoral one, the central belief is that no restrictions are needed. If sexual impulses are allowed free rein, tension, anxiety, and frustration will be lowered, and happiness, satisfaction in living and effectiveness increased. The main problem for those who hold this point of view is that of persuading other persons to accept this way of behaving.

Obviously, no one of these three viewpoints can be portrayed explicitly without some qualification. Any individual may move from one viewpoint to another, or he may adhere to one and act as if he upheld another. It is this discrepancy between outer appearance and private behavior that is confusing to many persons, young and old alike.

In the past sexual behavior has been regulated in varying degrees by religious teachings and customs based on them and by fear of disaster if something goes wrong, such as detection, disease, or pregnancy. These deterrents to free sexual behavior have become somewhat weakened, especially during the last few decades for reasons familiar to everyone. At the same time there does not appear to have been any major moral breakdown. This suggests that the present generation of young people is fully as moral as any in the past although for different reasons.

College officials are very much concerned about certain key issues with respect to sexual behavior. For example, pressures toward experience which the young person does not wish and for which he is not yet ready may be unduly effective. A certain "bandwagon" effect occurs when peer group pressures push young people into such behavior. Frequently these pressures become so strong that a young person subject to them may feel guilty for *not* indulging in behavior currently popular, just as he may feel guilty *for* doing so if his training has been conventional or idealistic.

Illegitimate pregnancies pose problems which are virtually insoluble in terms of the social, cultural, and legal framework within which colleges must operate. It is probable that those persons who become pregnant are more disturbed emotionally than those who manage their lives without this complication. A recent study at a British university confirmed this thesis clearly.[2] The loss of any student because of the failure to manage sexual life successfully is always keenly felt by college officials as well as by the student's family.

Parental attitudes in general are not consistent enough for any guidelines or policy. Although opinions regarding sexual behavior are usually very firmly held, they are sometimes favorable and at other times unfavorable toward free sexual expression. Furthermore, when college administrators are called upon to take definite action in a given situation, there is a considerable tendency to blame such officials for their attempts at restoring order rather than looking at the original source of difficulty.

Freedom of choice is desired for all students, but when peer

2. C. B. Kidd, R. Giel, and J. B. Brown, "The Antecedent Mental Health of Pregnant Unmarried Women." *Proceedings of the British Student Health Association* (Oxford: For private circulation, 1964), pp. 51–59.

group pressures and the bandwagon effect become too strong, the individual may be deprived of this freedom.

I believe it is correct to assert that most college administrators do not wish to have a series of complicated and specific rules regarding behavior in this area; they realize that attempts at enforcement create many new problems. They do not wish to develop a spy system since the main purpose of the college experience is to enable students to develop the ability to make their own decisions—hopefully wise decisions. Most administrators are averse to impose on others their personal views, varying as these do from person to person, institution to institution, and section to section in the country. Administrators also cannot and do not wish to ignore public sentiment in the communities surrounding the colleges.

The excessive emphasis on all aspects of sex and obscenity which is now prevalent in novels, plays, and the mass media of communication may enable parents, teachers, and others to become more honest about sexual education than has been possible up to now.

At the present time it seems to me that the following problems that are well nigh insoluble prevent the promotion of a satisfactory kind of sexual education. Religious views vary among sects as well as in different parts of the country. Contraception is not completely reliable no matter what assurances some people may give. For college students this reliability may be impaired by conscious maneuvering on the part of one partner to produce pregnancy. The strong views of parents either in the direction of freedom of sexual behavior or of control are not expressed in such a way as to be of much help. Those who have a vested interest in pornography are very ingenious in developing excellent arguments to prevent interference in their moneymaking activities. College administrators value freedom and dislike censorship. Drawing the line between these attitudes and the desire to be helpful in guiding the development of young people into channels which will not be destructive to their future is a very delicate matter. There is no consensus as to appropriate means of furthering sex education not only at the college level but at all stages of development. Variations in attitudes toward sexual education in different sections of the country make it almost impossible for any widespread program to be adopted. Not the least of the difficulties is that anyone working seriously for improved sexual adaptation almost invariably becomes the object of ridicule from his associates and others in the community.

Once a program is agreed upon, the question then arises as to who will carry it out. Should it be done by parents, physicians, members of the clergy, marital counselors, faculty members, or some other group? If persons in any of these groups are willing to undertake this task, then how shall they be trained? How is it possible to separate the giving of factual information from moralizing?

College officials may be reticent about imposing their views on others, but they do wish to make it crystal clear that they uphold high standards of personal behavior just as they uphold intellectual integrity. They want to encourage as much thoughtfulness in this area of behavior as in any other. They wish to develop the kind of behavior which will not bring unnecessary unhappiness or disaster to young people as they fashion a way of life which will strengthen rather than weaken family life.

In my opinion, no particular viewpoint can be forced on young people, but there should be full and frank discussion in families, in groups, between couples and between older and younger colleagues in the colleges. If students are given answers without any real awareness of the issues, they will not be helped very much. If, however, a program is developed which will enable them to get a keen awareness of the issues that are involved, I believe that they will come up with better answers than our generation has been able to evolve.

After all, the problem is of more significance to young people than to those of the older generation. It is up to them to determine what kind of a world they want their children to live in. As they discuss sexual issues, it is desirable that they recall the nature of the training they experienced and the embarrassing situations they encountered in their childhood and to relate these experiences to their present problems. Finally, they should project their thoughts into the future in terms of developing attitudes toward sex which will be helpful as they begin to raise their own children. This three-dimensional approach to the problem helps bring some objectivity in place of the rather intense urgency with which most young adolescents and early adults view such problems.

Unfortunately, those who guide the policies of institutions get little help from parents, as I have already stated, because of the confusion and variety of their views, but I fear that they get even less help from the faculty. There is a tendency to leave all such matters to the dean's office and to give inadequate support to the idea that integrity confined to intellectual matters is quite insufficient and should be extended to all facets of behavior.

Even though the colleges are not *in loco parentis* to their students in the literal sense, they do have a responsibility to encourage them to adopt reasonable standards of behavior. There is no compelling reason for college administrators to be intimidated by the accusation that they are "upholding middle-class morals." The standards of morality and how they are determined and transmitted from one generation to another are proper and necessary subjects for continuing discussion between students and faculty members.

For parents, religious leaders, college officials, and all others who have a responsibility for late adolescents and young adults in secondary schools and colleges, some standards or ideals of behavior are desirable. Let us first examine the principle, "All premarital sexual intercourse is undesirable." Deviations from that code of behavior have every imaginable variety, ranging from rape or the production of a child with illegitimate parents (at the most regrettable end of the spectrum of undesirable activities) to intercourse between engaged couples who expect to marry soon and who can marry at once if pregnancy occurs (at the least undesirable end). In each instance of departure from the ideal the individual knows of its undesirability and is aware of possible consequences. If unpleasant developments follow, he is in a position to learn from his experience; there is no one on whom he can reasonably project blame.

Let us assume another principle: "Premarital sexual relations are undesirable for those who are immature or cannot undertake the responsibility for a possible child, but for those who are mature and responsible, they are enriching and ennobling." Immediately a couple considering such relations must classify themselves, just at the time when it is only logical that they should be optimistic. It is easy to guess what the decision will be. If tragedy ensues, as it occasionally does, who can wonder that they are confused about society's inconsistent attitudes toward them.

Until we resolve our own confusions, we will not be in a favorable position to help our younger colleagues thread their way through the devious paths to development of sexual maturity. The experiences in our college psychiatric and counseling services lead us to believe that those who ignore the conventional standards are no more happy or effective than those who observe them. In fact, I believe that they have more depression, anxiety, agitation, and other inhibiting emotional conflict than those who manage to adhere to their ideals.

A large proportion of the younger students who come from families with reasonable ideals feel more comfortable if limits are set, if some guidelines are evident, and if someone is present who cares enough about them to help them avoid disaster.

As college officials, we are more concerned with the quality of future marriages and the family life they make possible than with any particular physical act in which either partner may have been involved. Of course, this does not imply that the nature and extent of sexual activities before marriage is irrelevant to the success of that marriage.

If we are to progress in making sense out of this important area of personal development, we will need sympathetic understanding and support of parents, faculty members, and the students themselves. There should then follow innumerable personal discussions, seminars, and other procedures for transmitting accurate information. At the same time the complex issues associated with choice or behavior should be explored. Opinions concerning sexual behavior should be expressed, but not put forth as scientific facts.

Sexual education and the formation of standards of sexual morality are not separable from other aspects of personal maturation, nor should they be unduly circumscribed as they are pursued in the colleges. The goal should be that of aiding each student to develop a healthy personality in which sexuality plays a constructive and satisfying part rather than being considered undignified and regrettable.

Four

Music

Bob Dylan speaks for youth. In his art he acts out indirectly youth's search for alternatives in politics, transcendentalism, community, and love. Three main strands run through his songs: his journey into belief, his questioning of contemporary sex roles, and his transcendentalism. What he has experienced and expressed in his art is what most young people have gone through in recent years, and Dylan does it superlatively well.

CRAIG McGREGOR

Dylan: Reluctant Hero of the Pop Generation

I suppose Bob Dylan is the closest thing to a culture hero this generation has. He's no prophet; apart from the fact that he's disclaimed the role, you'd have to be desperate for discipleship to follow Dylan anywhere. He has never been a profound thinker; he is, if anything, both anti-political and anti-intellectual. But he *is* a hero, in the John P. Marquand sense of someone who does something superlatively well.

Dylan writes good songs. Wilfrid Mellers, the English musicologist, thinks Dylan is the one 20th-century pop artist who may have the folk-like capacity to go on creating ("The Beatles have disbanded,

Gershwin died young, Irving Berlin, Crosby and Sinatra remained permanently adolescent, Cole Porter survived by becoming exclusively deflatory. ...."). We admire him for that.

But Dylan's role as hero has been less to lead anyone anywhere or point out new directions ("I'm not trying to lead any causes for anyone else") than to somehow enact the dilemmas and crises of the generation which he represents. Mostly he's done that through his songs—though they, of course, are part of a more personal and autobiographical process. If you look closely at Dylan's progress from adolescent self-hater ("Listen, Echo, don't ever ask Bob about being Jewish again. He doesn't like to talk about it"), to folk protest singer, to the hard drug visions of "Blonde on Blonde," to a crack-up of F. Scott Fitzgerald proportions (if Dylan hadn't fallen off his motorbike he'd have fallen off the Empire State building), to the redemptive spirituality of "John Wesley Harding," to the family-and-love ethic of "Self-Portrait" and "New Morning," a symbolic pattern emerges. Dylan has managed to act out in his art the blind-man's-buff search of young Americans for an alternate order in politics, drugs, transcendentalism, communes, love ...

At exactly the time hip kids in California were turning from acid to Jesus for transcendental kicks, Dylan was displaying an arm free of trackmarks to self-appointed Dylanologist A. J. Weberman and recording lines like "Father of minutes, Father of days, Father whom we most solemnly praise." Even that smart sideways step to the Right when the going got heavy ("Sure gonna be wet tonight on Main Street"), which seemed like a betrayal to so many radicals, was characteristically "cool": No modern hero has been less set on martyrdom than Dylan. Which is as it should be. Frail, fallible, fame-contorted, he's the sort of hero we deserve. Which is why we should look a bit closer at what he's been putting down.

One of the consistent stands to Dylan's work is its Jewishness. No one can come from his sort of background without being profoundly influenced by it, whether the process is one of rejection, compromise or acceptance (Dylan has worked his way through all three, and currently seems to be rediscovering his Jewishness all over again). You don't need to know much about his change of name from Zimmerman or his contradictory, carefully disguised relationship with his parents to realize how crucial his being Jewish is to him.

The important thing, of course, is what it means for his music. It explains, I think, a certain sensitivity which slops over into sentimentality in some of his songs ("Bob has never written anything sentimental in his whole life!" manager Albert Grossman once told me, real anger showing through that pudgy bland facade. As usual, he was wrong). Except for his very early work and one or two more recent songs, Dylan has always reserved most of his compassion for himself.

Its most obvious effect, however, has been to make religion one of the major themes—perhaps _the_ major theme—in Dylan's music. Not only does he make use of Biblical symbolism and allusions throughout his work; the central problem of what one is to believe, of man's relationship to God, recurs in song after song. In early ballads like "With God on Our Side," Dylan's personal dilemma is clear enough: God is either omnipotent and Evil, or not omnipotent and therefore not God. In middle-period songs like "Gates of Eden" and "Tombstone Blues" Dylan is still struggling for some sort of resolution, and the prolonged wrestle of one man's soul for faith is the source of the apocalyptic note in much of his writing at this time.

"John Wesley Harding" is the breakthrough: it is a penitent's album, ridden with shame, guilt and desire for atonement—Dylan's "Ash Wednesday" as surely as "Desolation Row" was his "Waste Land." In many ways, in fact, Dylan's metaphysical pilgrimage from rebellion to spiritual confusion to acceptance is very similar to that of a poet whom he has read and sometimes derided—T. S. Eliot. As an album it's a failure, rescued by two songs: "All Along the Watchtower" and "I'll Be Your Baby Tonight." As a religious statement it is confused and, to me, unconvincing; but as a testament to one man's purgation of the soul, it is unique in modern pop music.

But the logical summation of Dylan's religious impulse had to wait two more albums, till "New Morning." "Three Angels" is a quietly affirmative statement of belief, peace, contemplation; the spoken monologue, the calm low-key background, are almost perfect. "Father of Night" is nothing more or less than a psalm (A. J. Weberman: "You don't believe in God!" Dylan: "I sure do"). When the album was released, Greil Marcus dismissed "Three Angels" as a joke; other critics thought "Father of Night" was a typical Dylan put-on. A cliche it may be, a put-on it isn't. If anything, it's predictable: a long day's journey into belief.

A second strand to Dylan's music which has been largely undiscussed is its "gay" component. It's almost as though the critics have maintained a conspiracy of silence about this, though Robert Shelton, Steven Goldberg and (lately) John Gordon have referred to it briefly; most of the others have restricted themselves to veiled references to Dylan's strangely androgynous image, or to discussing whether or not the woman on the jacket of "Bringing It All Back Home" is really Dylan in drag.

Who cares? What matters, again, are the songs. There is a camp bitchiness, a penchant for the cheap put-down, which limits the effectiveness of too many of his songs, from "Positively Fourth Street" to some of the tracks on "Blonde on Blonde." Yet one of the best love songs Dylan has ever written, "It Ain't Me, Babe," expresses a rejection of a loved one without indulging in such a spiteful cutting edge. A few songs, such as "Ballad of a Thin Man," deal openly with the homosexual experience; when I saw Dylan in Australia, I criticized it to him as an "in-group" song, and he quickly defended it as dealing with something else altogether. In others the gay references are more covert, more deliberately camouflaged.

Dylan is a master of masks. If any proof were needed, his skillful manipulation of the mass media and his deliberate choice of public images provide it. More important: Dylan uses masks in his songs as well. In many of them he seems to be writing about himself in the second or third person, so that the "you," "he" or "she" is really "I"; and the alternative person Dylan creates for himself is sometimes a woman. He once told an interviewer that "Queen Jane Approximately," which he regarded as one of his best songs, was about a man. The chorus of "Just Like a Woman" ("You make love just like a woman") can only be rescued from banality if it's really addressed to ... a man? Yourself? Myself?

Dylan's songs characteristically work at different levels; it's one of the things that gives them richness, setting up reverberations in our minds that we only half comprehend. Often it's impossible to separate the man from the mask. And, anyhow, it's the music that counts.

Another theme in Dylan's music is a yearning transcendentalism which has been present from those early disks through to the latest. Dylan's religiosity is one aspect of this. Another has been his involvement in the drug culture. Like many of his contemporaries, Dylan progressed "from Burgundy to the harder stuff"; you can trace the change through songs like "Mr. Tambourine Man," with its gentle smoky images, to the extended trance-like visions in "Blonde on Blonde" ("I was on the road for almost five years. It wore me down. I was on drugs, a lot of things ..."—Dylan in the Rolling Stone interview). By the time of his last world tour, just before his crack-up, Dylan was a man on a razor—stoned, under terrible pressure, protected and babied by The Band. Hendrix, Joplin, just before they died ...

You grow up in America in the fifties and sixties, you need help to outface what's coming down. It's no accident that so many of the alternate life-concepts with which young Americans have experimented in the last two decades involve some variety of transcendentalism; mankind cannot bear too much reality (T. S. Eliot said that) and jumps into drugs, Zen, Meher Buba, astrology, I Ching, Jesus— even a hyped-up, supernatural theory of Love. One of the things that bothers me somewhat about Dylan's current "family-man" ethic, as it does about John and Yoko's overexposed arc-lit love match, is that if you put too excessive and too overt a strain upon such a fragile entity as a personal relationship, it may blow up in your face. But the way Dylan protects his own privacy, and that of his wife and five children, should help.

Finally, it's worth emphasizing again the personal nature of Dylan's music. That he's a hero is sort of accidental; he's always insisted that he writes only for himself. He's no Spokesman, because he has more sense than to think anyone can be. Throughout his career he's shrugged off old roles and adopted new ones like (strait) jackets; those who hunger after his old declamatory songs of dissent, or the apocalyptic visions of the mid-sixties, are demanding from him a consistency which he has never claimed.

This capacity for growth is one of Dylan's strengths as an artist, yet it's one which critics and admirers alike have found difficult to accept. Thus the sourness of Richard Meltzer and others about Dylan's recent work; the kernel of their complaint is that *it ain't like it used to be.* They're right. But they're as guilty as the critics who attacked Dylan for deserting folk music; they're asking him to stand still, and he never has.

In the last few years Dylan's music has lost some of its earlier intensity and power, but it's gained other virtues. "All Along the Watchtower" is one of the best songs he's ever written, a brooding, philosophic reflection upon life which is the work of a mature artist; "Lay Lady Lay" is the distillation of a mood which has persisted in his work from "Corrina" onwards; and "New Morning," though it contains more than its fair share of dross, includes two fine songs: "Sign in the Window" and "Three Angels."

As well as being a truly great artist, one of the few of our time whom one can justly call a "genius," Dylan is also, simply, someone who has been through many of the changes we have been through ourselves. He is still going through them. The difference is that he has been able to write songs about what has been happening to him along the way.

Which is what, finally, makes him a hero. Like Achilles, he does something better than anyone else. I don't like heroes. Or leaders. Or prophets. We should be all these to ourselves. And yet for the strictly limited, transient duration of each of his best songs I am prepared to vouchsafe Dylan his culture-role, simply because he has enriched my life, as he has enriched so many others. He is a Three-Minute-Twelve-track-Superacrylic-Longplay-Hero with an automatic cutoff at the song's end. No more, no less. What the hell else have we the right to ask for him?

This article was adapted from Craig McGregor's critical anthology, "Bob Dylan: A Retrospective," (New York: Morrow, 1972).

Once a medium of vapid love lyrics, popular music in the 1960s took on a new seriousness. In the words of popular songs, young musicians have expressed their alienation from and disdain for American institutions and mores. In their music, youth has worried about such things as the impact of technology on man, the confused state of American sexual practices, and the repressive nature of democratic institutions. For youth, music has both come to serve the function of helping them define and codify the standards of their own subculture.

ROBERT A. ROSENSTONE

"The Times They Are A-Changin' ": The Music of Protest

At the beginning of the 1960's, nobody took popular music very seriously. Adults only knew that rock n' roll, which had flooded the airwaves in the 1950's, had a strong beat and was terribly loud; it was generally believed that teen-agers alone had thick enough eardrums, or insensitive enough souls, to enjoy it. Certainly, no critics thought of a popular star like the writhing Elvis Presley as being in any way a serious artist. Such a teen-age idol was simply considered a manifestation of a sub-culture that the young happily and inevitably outgrew—and, any parent would have added, the sooner the better.

   Today, the view of popular music has drastically changed. Some parents may still wonder about the "noise" that their children listen to, but important segments of American society have come to recognize popular musicians as real artists saying serious things.[1] An indication of this change can be seen in magazine attitudes. In 1964, the *Saturday Evening Post* derided the Beatles—recognized giants of modern popular music—as "corny," and *Reporter* claimed: "They have debased Rock 'n Roll to its ultimate absurdity." Three years later the *Saturday Review* solemnly discussed a new Beatles record as a "highly ironic declaration of disaffection" with modern society, while in 1968, *Life* devoted a whole, laudatory section to "The New Rock," calling it music "that challenges the joys and ills of the . . . world."[2] Even in the intellectual community, popular music has found warm friends. Such sober journals as *The Listener, Columbia University Forum, New American Review,* and *Commentary* have sympathetically surveyed aspects of the "pop" scene, while in *The New York Review of Books*—a kind of house organ for the American academia—composer Ned Rorem has declared that, at their best, the Beatles "compare with those composers from great eras of song: Monteverdi, Schumann, Poulenc."[3]

The reasons for such changes in attitude are not difficult to find: there is no doubt that popular music has become more complex, and at the same time more serious, than it ever was before. Musically, it has broken down some of the old forms in which it was for a long time straight-jacketed. With a wide-ranging eclecticism, popular music has adapted to itself a bewildering variety of musical tradi-

1. The definition of "popular music" being used in this article is a broad one. It encompasses a multitude of styles, including folk, folk-rock, acid-rock, hard-rock, and blues, to give just a few names being used in the musical world today. It does so because the old musical classifications have been totally smashed and the forms now overlap in a way that makes meaningful distinction between them impossible. Though not every group or song referred to will have been popular in the sense of selling a million records, all of them are part of a broad, variegated scene termed "pop." Some of the groups, like Buffalo Springfield, Strawberry Alarm Clock, or the Byrds, have sold millions of records. Others, like the Fugs or Mothers of Invention, have never had a real hit, though they are played on radio stations allied to the "underground." Still, such groups do sell respectable numbers of records and do perform regularly at teen-age concerts, and thus must be considered part of the "pop" scene.
2. *Saturday Evening Post,* Vol. 237, March 21, 1964, p. 30; *Reporter,* Vol. 30, Feb. 27, 1964, p. 18; *Saturday Review,* Vol. 50, August 19, 1967, p. 18; *Life,* Vol. 64, June 28, 1968, p. 51.
3. "The Music of the Beatles," *New York Review of Books,* Jan. 15, 1968, pp. 23–27. See also "The New Music," *The Listener,* Vol. 78, August 3, 1967, pp. 129–130; *Columbia University Forum* (Fall 1967), pp. 16–22; *New American Review,* Vol. 1 (April 1968), pp. 118–139; Ellen Willis, "The Sound of Bob Dylan," *Commentary,* Vol. 44 (November 1967), pp. 71–80. Many of these articles deal with English as well as American popular groups, and, in fact, the music of the two countries cannot, in any meaningful sense, be separated. This article will only survey American musical groups, though a look at English music would reveal the prevalence of most of the themes explored here.

tions and instruments, from the classic Indian sitar to the most recent electronic synthesizers favored by composers of "serious" concert music.

As the music has been revolutionized, so has the subject matter of the songs. In preceding decades, popular music was almost exclusively about love, and, in the words of poet Thomas Gunn, "a very limited kind [of love], constituting a sort of fag-end of the Petrarchan tradition."[4] The stories told in song were largely about lovers yearning for one another in some vaguely unreal world where nobody ever seemed to work or get married. All this changed in the 1960's. Suddenly, popular music began to deal with civil rights demonstrations and drug experiences, with interracial dating and war and explicit sexual encounters, with, in short, the real world in which people live. For perhaps the first time, popular songs became relevant to the lives of the teen-age audience that largely constitutes the record-buying public. The success of some of these works prompted others to be written, and the second half of the decade saw a full efflorescence of such topical songs, written by young people for their peers. It is these works which should be grouped under the label of "protest" songs of the 1960's, for, taken together, they provide a wide-ranging critique of American life. Listening to them, one can get a full-blown picture of the antipathy that the young song writers have toward many American institutions.

Serious concerns entered popular music early in the 1960's, when a great revival of folk singing spread out from college campuses, engulfed the mass media, and created a wave of new "pop" stars, the best known of whom was Joan Baez. Yet, though the concerns of these folk songs were often serious, they were hardly contemporary. Popular were numbers about organizing unions, which might date from the 1930's or the late nineteenth century, or about the trials of escaping Negro slaves, or celebrating the cause of the defeated Republicans in the Spanish Civil War. Occasionally, there was something like "Talking A-Bomb Blues," but this was the rare exception rather than the rule.[5]

A change of focus came when performers began to write their own songs, rather than relying on the traditional folk repertoire. Chief among them, and destined to become the best known, was Bob Dylan. Consciously modeling himself on that wandering minstrel of the 1930's, Woody Guthrie, Dylan began by writing songs that often had little to do with the contemporary environment. Rather, his

4. "The New Music," *loc. cit.,* p. 129.
5. *Time,* Vol. 80 Nov. 23, 1962, pp. 54–60, gives a brief survey of the folk revival.

early ballads like "Masters of War" echoed the leftist concerns and rhetoric of an earlier era. Yet, simultaneously, Dylan was beginning to write songs like "Blowin' In the Wind," "A Hard Rain's A-Gonna Fall," and "The Times They Are A-Changin'," which dealt with civil rights, nuclear war, and the changing world of youth that parents and educators were not prepared to understand. Acclaimed as the best of protest-song-writers, Dylan in mid-decade shifted gears, and in the song "My Back Pages," he denounced his former moral fervor. In an ironic chorus claiming that he was much younger than he had been, Dylan specifically made social problems the worry of sober, serious, older men; presumably, youths had more important things than injustice to think about. After that, any social comment by Dylan came encapsulated in a series of surrealistic images; for the most part, he escaped into worlds of aestheticism, psychedelic drugs, and personal love relationships. Apparently attempting to come to grips in art with his own personality, Dylan was content to forget about the problems of other men.[6]

The development of Dylan is important not only because he is the leading song writer, but also because it parallels the concerns of popular music in the 1960's. Starting out with traditional liberal positions on war, discrimination, segregation, and exploitation, song writers of the decade turned increasingly to descriptions of the private worlds of drugs, sexual experience, and personal freedom. Though social concerns have never entirely faded, the private realm has been increasingly seen as the only one in which people can lead meaningful lives. Now, at the end of the decade, the realms of social protest and private indulgence exist side by side in the popular music, with the latter perceived as the only viable alternative to the world described in the former songs.[7]

THE NEGRO IN SONG

In turning to the protest songs of the 1960's, one finds many of the traditional characters and concerns of such music missing. Gone are exploited, impoverished people, labor leaders, "finks," and company spies. This seems natural in the affluent 1960's, with youths from middle-class backgrounds writing songs. Of course, there has been

---

6. Wills, *op. cit.,* gives a good analysis of his work. Though he is very quotable, there will, unfortunately, be no quotations from Dylan in this article because the author cannot afford the enormous fees required by Dylan's publisher for even the briefest of quotations.

7. It must be pointed out that, in spite of the large amount of social criticism, most songs today are still about love, even those by groups such as Country Joe and the Fish, best known for their social satire.

one increasingly visible victim of exploitation in this decade, the Negro; and the songsters have not been blind to his plight. But, egalitarian as they are, the white musicians have not been able to describe the reality of the black man's situation.[8] Rather, they have chonicled Northern liberal attitudes towards the problem. Thus, composer-performer Phil Ochs penned works criticizing Southern attitudes towards Negroes, and containing stock portraits of corrupt politicans, law officials, and churchmen trembling before the Ku Klux Klan, while Paul Simon wrote a lament for a freedom rider killed by an angry Southern mob.[9] Similarly white-oriented was Janis Ian's very popular "Society's Child," concerned with the problem of interracial dating. Here a white girl capitulates to society's bigotry and breaks off a relationship with a Negro boy with the vague hope, "When we're older things may change/But for now this is the way they must remain."[10]

Increasingly central to white-Negro relationships have been the ghetto and urban riots, and a taste of this entered the popular music. Phil Ochs, always on top of current events, produced "In the Heat of the Summer" shortly after the first major riot in Harlem in 1964. Partially sympathetic to the ghetto-dwellers' actions, he still misjudged their attitudes by ascribing to them feelings of shame— rather than satisfaction—in the aftermath of the destruction.[11] A later attempt, by Country Joe and the Fish, to describe Harlem ironically as a colorful vacation spot, verged on patronizing blacks, even while it poked fun at white stereotypes. Only the closing lines, "But if you can't go to Harlem . . ./Maybe you'll be lucky and Harlem will come to you," followed by sounds of explosion, thrust home what indifference to the ghetto is doing to America.[12] The most successful song depicting the situation of the Negro was "Trouble Coming Everyday," written by Frank Zappa during the Watts uprising in 1965. Though the song does not go so far as to approve of rioting, it paints a brutal picture of exploitation by merchants, bad schooling, misera-

---

8. This article is concerned almost exclusively with music written and performed by white musicians. While popular music by Negroes does contain social criticism, the current forms—loosely termed "soul music"—make comments about oppression similar to those which Negroes have always made. The real change in content has come largely in white music in the 1960's.
9. Phil Ochs, "Talking Birmingham Jam" and "Here's to the State of Mississippi," *I Ain't Marching Any More* (Elektra, 7237); Simon and Garfunkel, "He Was My Brother," *Wednesday Morning 3 A.M.* (Columbia, CS 9049). (Songs from records will be noted by performer, song title in quotation marks, and album title in italics, followed by record company and number in parentheses.)
10. Copyright 1966 by Dialogue Music, Inc. Used by permission.
11. Ochs, *I Ain't Marching Any More.*
12. "The Harlem Song," *Together* (Vanguard, VSD 79277). Copyright by Joyful Wisdom Music, Inc.

ble housing, and police brutality—all of which affect ghetto-dwellers. Its most significant lines are Zappa's cry, "You know something people, I ain't black, but there's a whole lots of times I wish I could say I'm not white." No song writer showed more empathy with the black struggle for liberation than that.[13]

POLITICIANS

While the downtrodden are heroes of many traditional protest songs, the villains are often politicians. Yet, politics rarely enters the songs of the 1960's. Ochs, an unreconstructed voice from the 1930's, depicts vacillating politicians in some works, and Dylan mentions corrupt ones early in the decade. But the typical attitude is to ignore politics, or, perhaps, to describe it in passing as "A yardstick for lunatics, one point of view."[14] It is true that the death of President Kennedy inspired more than one song, but these were tributes to a martyr, not a politician.[15] If Kennedy in death could inspire music, Lyndon Johnson in life has seemed incapable of inspiring anything, except perhaps contempt. In a portrait of him, Country Joe and the Fish pictured the, then, President as flying through the sky like Superman ("It's a bird, it's a plane, it's a man insane/It's my President L. B. J."). Then they fantasized a Western setting:

> Come out Lyndon with your hands held high
> Drop your guns, baby, and reach for the sky
> I've got you surrounded and you ain't got a chance
> Send you back to Texas, make you work on your ranch.[16]

One traditional area, antiwar protest, does figure significantly in the music of the 1960's. With America's involvement in Vietnam and mounting draft-calls, this seems natural enough. Unlike many songs of this genre, however, the current ones rarely assess the causes of war, but dwell almost exclusively with the effect which war has on the individual. Thus, both Love and the Byrds sing about what nuclear war does to children, while the Peanut Butter Conspiracy

---

13. Mothers of Invention, *Freak Out* (Verve, 65005). Copyright 1968 by Frank Zappa Music, Inc. All rights reserved.
14. Strawberry Alarm Clock, "Incense and Peppermints," written by John Carter and Tim Gilbert, *Strawberry Alarm Clock* (Uni., 73014). Copyright by Claridge Music, Inc.
15. Phil Ochs, "That Was the President," "*I Ain't Marching Any More;* the Byrds, "He Was A Friend of Mine," *Turn! Turn!* (Columbia, CS 9254).
16. "Superbird," *Electric Music for the Mind and Body* (Vanguard, 79244). Copyright by Tradition Music Company.

pictures the effect of nuclear testing on everyone: "Firecracker sky filled with roots of fusion . . . /We're so far ahead we're losing."[17] Most popular of the antiwar songs was P. E. Sloan's "Eve of Destruction," which, for a time in 1965, was the best-selling record in the country (and which was banned by some patriotic radio-station directors). The title obviously gives the author's view of the world situation; the content deals mostly with its relationship to young men like himself: "You don't believe in war, but what's that gun you're totin'?"[18] There are alternatives to carrying a gun, and defiance of the draft enters some songs, subtly in Buffy St. Marie's "Universal Soldier" and stridently in Ochs' "I Ain't Marching Any More."[19] Perhaps more realistic in its reflection of youthful moods is the Byrds' "Draft Morning," a haunting portrait of a young man reluctantly leaving a warm bed to take up arms and kill "unknown faces." It ends with the poignant and unanswerable question, "Why should it happen?"[20]

If many songs criticize war in general, some have referred to Vietnam in particular. The Fugs give gory details of death and destruction being wreaked on the North by American bombers, which unleash napalm "rotisseries" upon the world.[21] In a similar song, Country Joe and the Fish describe children crying helplessly beneath the bombs, and then comment ironically, "Super heroes fill the skies, tally sheets in hand/Yes, keeping score in times of war takes a superman."[22] No doubt, it is difficult to make music out of the horrors of war, and a kind of black humor is a common response. In a rollicking number, the Fugs, with irony, worry that people may come to "love the Russians" and scream out a method often advocated for avoiding this: "Kill, kill, kill for peace."[23] And one of Country Joe's most popular numbers contains the following:

> Well come on generals let's move fast
> Your big chance has come at last
> We gotta go out and get those reds
> The only good Commie is one that's dead

---

17. Love, "Mushroom Clouds," *Love* (Elektra, EKL 4001); the Byrds, "I Come and Stand at Every Door," *Fifth Dimension* (Columbia, CS 9349); Peanut Butter Conspiracy, "Wonderment," written by John Merrill, *Great Conspiracy* (Columbia, CS 9590). Copyright by 4-Star Music Company, Inc.
18. Copyright 1965 by Trousdale Music Publishers, Inc.
19. Buffy St. Marie, "Universal Soldier," Southern Publishing, ASCAP; Ochs, *I Ain't Marching Any More.*
20. *The Notorious Byrd Brothers* (Columbia, CS 9575).
21. "War Song," *Tenderness Junction* (Reprise, S 6280).
22. "An Untitled Protest," *Together.* Copyright by Joyful Wisdom music.
23. "Kill for Peace," *The Fugs* (Esp. 1028).

And you know that peace can only be won
When we blow 'em all to kingdom come.[24]

The injustice and absurdity of America's Asian ventures, perceived by the song writers, does not surprise them, for they feel that
life at home is much the same. The songs of the 1960's show the
United States as a repressive society, where people who deviate from
the norm are forced into conformity—sometimes at gunpoint; where
those who do fit in lead empty, frustrated lives; and where meaningful human experience is ignored in a search for artificial pleasures.
Such a picture is hardly attractive, and one might argue that it is not
fair. But it is so pervasive in popular music that it must be examined
at some length. Indeed, it is the most important part of the protest
music of the decade. Here are criticisms, not of exploitation, but of
the quality of life in an affluent society: not only of physical oppression, but also of the far more subtle mental oppression that a mass
society can produce.

YOUTH AS VICTIM

Throughout the decade, young people have often been at odds with
established authority, and, repeatedly, songs picture youth in the
role of victim. Sometimes the victimization is mental, as when the
Mothers of Invention complain of outworn thought patterns and say
"All your children are poor/Unfortunate victims of lies/You believe."[25] On a much simpler level, Sonny Bono voices his annoyance
that older people laugh at the clothes he wears, and he wonders why
they enjoy "makin' fun" of him.[26] Now, Bono could musically shrug
off the laughs as the price of freedom, but other songs document
occasions when Establishment disapproval turned into physical oppression. Thus, Canned Heat tells of being arrested in Denver because the police did not want any "long hairs around."[27] The Buffalo
Springfield, in a hit record, describe gun-bearing police rounding up
teen-agers on the Sunset Strip, and draw the moral, "Step out of line
the men come and take you away."[28] On the same theme, Dylan

---

24. "I Feel Like I'm Fixin' to Die," *I Feel Like I'm Fixin' to Die* (Vanguard, 9266).
   Copyright by Tradition Music Company.
25. *We're Only in It for the Money* (Verve, 65045). Copyright by Frank Zappa Music,
   Inc. All rights reserved.
26. "Laugh at Me," *Five West Cotillion*, BMI.
27. "My Crime," *Boogie* (Liberty, 7541).
28. "For What It's Worth." Copyright 1966 by Cotillion Music, Inc.—Ten East Music
   —Springaloo Toones. Reprinted by permission.

ironically shows that adults arbitrarily oppose just about all activities of youths, saying that they should "look out" no matter what they are doing.[29] More bitter is the Mother's description of police killing large numbers of hippies, which is then justified on the grounds "They looked too weird . . . it served them right."[30] Though the incident is fictional, the Mothers clearly believe Americans capable of shooting down those who engaged in deviant behavior.

Though the songs echo the oppression that youngsters have felt, they do not ignore the problems that all humans face in a mass society. Writer Tom Paxton knows that it is not easy to keep one's life from being forced into a predetermined mold. In "Mr. Blue" he has a Big-Brother-like narrator telling the title character, a kind of Everyman, that he is always under surveillance, and that he will never be able to indulge himself in his precious dreams of freedom from society. This is because society needs him to fill a slot, no matter what his personal desires. Of that slot, the narrator says, "You'll learn to love it/Or we'll break you." And then comes the chilling chorus:

> What will it take to whip you into line
> A broken heart?
> A broken head?
> It can be arranged.[31]

Though no other writer made the message so explicit, a similar fear of being forced into an unwelcome slot underlies many songs of the period.

The society of slotted people is an empty one, partly described as "TV dinner by the pool,/I'm so glad I finished school."[32] It is one in which people have been robbed of their humanity, receiving in return the "transient treasures" of wealth and the useless gadgets of a technological age. One of these is television, referred to simply as "that rotten box," or, in a more sinister image, as an "electronic shrine." This image of men worshipping gadgets recurs. In the nightmare vision of a McLuhanesque world—where the medium is the message—Simon and Garfunkle sing of men so busy bowing and

---

29. "Subterranean Homesick Blues," *Bob Dylan's Greatest Hits* (Columbia, KCS 9463).
30. *We're Only in It for the Money.* Copyright 1968 by Frank Zappa Music, Inc. All rights reserved.
31. "Mr. Blue," written by Tom Paxton, *Clear Light* (Elektra, 74011). Copyright 1966 by Deep Fork Music, Inc. All rights reserved. Used with permission.
32. Mothers of Invention, "Brown Shoes Don't Make It," *Absolutely Free* (Verve, 65013). Copyright 1968 by Frank Zappa Music, Inc. All rights reserved.

praying to a "neon god" that they cannot understand or touch one another. Indeed, here electronics seem to hinder the process of communication rather than facilitate it. People talk and hear but never understand, as the "sounds of silence" fill the world.[33] Such lack of communication contributes to the indifference with which men can view the life and death of a neighbor, as in Simon's "A Most Peculiar Man."[34] It also creates the climate of fear which causes people to kill a stranger for no reason other than his unknown origins in Strawberry Alarm Clock's "They Saw the Fat One Coming."[35]

Alienated from his fellows, fearful and alone, modern man has also despoiled the natural world in which he lives. With anguish in his voice, Jim Morrison of the Doors asks:

> What have they done to the earth?
> What have they done to our fair sister?
> Ravished and plundered and ripped her and bit her
> Stuck her with knives in the side of the dawn
> And tied her with fences and dragged her down.[36]

In a lighter tone but with no less serious an intent, the Lewis and Clark Expedition describe the way man has cut himself off from nature.

> There's a chain around the flower
> There's a fence around the trees
> This is freedom's country
> Do anything you please.

With a final thrust they add, "You don't need to touch the flowers/ They're plastic anyway."[37]

This brings up a fear that haunts a number of recent songs, the worry that the technological age has created so many artificial things that nothing natural remains. Concerned with authenticity, the songsters are afraid that man himself is becoming an artifact, or,

33. "Sounds of Silence," *Sounds of Silence* (Columbia, CS 9269).
34. *Sounds of Silence.*
35. *Wake Up ... It's Tomorrow* (Uni., 73025).
36. "When the Music's Over," *Strange Days* (Elektra, 74014). Copyright 1967 by Nipper Music, Inc. All rights reserved.
37. "Chain Around the Flowers," *The Lewis and Clark Expedition* (Colgems, COS 105). Words and music by John Vandiver. Copyright 1967 by Screen Gems—Columbia Music, Inc. Used by permission. Reproduction prohibited.

in their favorite word, "plastic." Thus, the Jefferson Airplane sing about a "Plastic Fantastic Lover," while the Iron Butterfly warn a girl to stay away from people "made of plastic."[38] The image recurs most frequently in the works of the Mothers of Invention. In one song, they depict the country as being run by a plastic Congress and President.[39] Then, in "Plastic People," they start with complaints about a girlfriend who uses "plastic goo" on her face, go on to a picture of teen-agers on the Sunset Strip—who are probably their fans—as being "plastic," too, and finally turn on their listeners and say "Go home and check yourself/You think we're talking about someone else."[40] Such a vision is frightening, for if the audience is plastic, perhaps the Mothers, themselves, are made of the same phony material. And if the whole world is plastic, who can be sure of his own authenticity?

LOVE RELATIONSHIPS

Toward the end of "Plastic People," the Mothers say, "I know true love can never be/A product of plasticity."[41] This brings up the greatest horror, that in a "plastic" society like the United States, love relationships are impossible. For the young song writers, American love is viewed as warped and twisted. Nothing about Establishment society frightens them more than its attitudes towards sex. Tim Buckley is typical in singing that older Americans are "Afraid to trust in their bodies," and in describing them as "Faking love on a bed made of knives."[42] Others give graphic portraits of deviant behavior. The Fugs tell of a "Dirty Old Man" hanging around high school playgrounds; the Velvet Underground portray a masochist; and the Mothers depict a middle-aged man lusting after his own thirteen-year-old daughter.[43] The fullest indictment of modern love is made by the United States of America, who devote almost an entire album to the subject. Here, in a twisted portrait of "pleasure and pain," is a world of loveless marriages, homosexual relationships in men's rooms, venomous attractions, and overt sadism—all masked by a middle-class, suburban world in which people consider "moral-

38. *Surrealistic Pillow* (Victor, LSP 3766); "Stamped Ideas," *Heavy* (Atco, S 33-227).
39. Uncle Bernie's Farm, *Absolutely Free.*
40. "Plastic People," *Absolutely Free.* Copyright 1968 by Frank Zappa Music, Inc. All rights reserved.
41. *Ibid.*
42. "Goodbye and Hello," written by Tim Buckley, *Goodbye and Hello* (Elektra, 7318). Copyright 1968 by Third Story Music, Inc. All rights reserved.
43. *The Fugs;* "Venus in Furs," *The Velvet Underground and Nico* (Verve, V6-5008); "Brown Shoes Don't Make It," *Absolutely Free.*

ity" important. To show that natural relationships are possible elsewhere, the group sings one tender love lyric; interestingly, it is the
lament of a Cuban girl for the dead Che Guevara.[44]

The fact that bourgeois America has warped attitudes towards
sex and love is bad enough; the songsters are more worried that such
attitudes will infect their own generation. Thus, the Collectors decry
the fact that man-woman relationships are too often seen as some
kind of contest, with a victor and vanquished, and in which violence
is more acceptable than tenderness.[45] Perhaps because most of the
singers are men, criticisms of female sexual attitudes abound. The
Mothers say disgustedly to the American woman, "You lie in bed
and grit your teeth," while the Sopwith Camel object to the traditional kind of purity by singing, "I don't want no woman wrapped
up in cellophane."[46] This is because such a woman "will do you
in/Bending your mind with her talking about sin."[47] All the musicians would prefer the girl about whom Moby Grape sings who is
"super-powered, deflowered," and over eighteen.[48]

Living in a "plastic" world where honest human relationships
are impossible, the song writers might be expected to wrap themselves in a mood of musical despair. But they are young—and often
making plenty of money—and such an attitude is foreign to them.
Musically, they are hopeful because, as the title of the Dylan song
indicates, "The Times They Are A-Changin.'" Without describing
the changes, Dylan clearly threatens the older generation, as he tells
critics, parents, and presumably anyone over thirty, to start swim-
ming or they will drown in the rising floodwaters of social change.[49]

In another work, Dylan exploits the same theme. Here is a portrait of a presumably normal, educated man, faced with a series of
bizarre situations, who is made to feel like a freak because he does
not understand what is going on. The chorus is the young generation's comment to all adults, as it mocks "Mr. Jones" for not understanding what is happening all around him.[50]

The changes going on are, not surprisingly, associated with the
carefree, joyful experiences of youth. As Jefferson Airplane sings,

44. *The United States of America* (Columbia, CS 9614).
45. "What Love," *The Collectors* (Warner Bros.-Seven Arts, WS 1746).
46. *We're Only in It for the Money;* "Cellophane Woman," *The Sopwith Camel* (Kama Sutra, KLPS 8060). Copyright by Great Honesty Music, Inc.
47. "Cellophane Woman." Copyright by Great Honesty Music, Inc.
48. "Motorcycle Irene," *Wow* (Columbia, CS 9613).
49. *Bob Dylan's Greatest Hits.*
50. "Ballad of a Thin Man/Mr. Jones," *Highway 61 Revisited* (Columbia, CS 9189). Though this song has obvious homosexual overtones, it also stands as youth's criticism of the older generation.

"It's a wild time/I see people all around me changing faces/It's a wild time/I'm doing things that haven't got a name yet."[51] The most full-blown description of the changing world is Tim Buckley's "Goodbye and Hello," a lengthy and explicit portrait of what the youth hope is happening. Throughout the song the author contrasts two kinds of people and their environments. On the one hand are the "antique people"—godless and sexless—of an industrial civilization, living in dark dungeons, working hard, worshipping technology and money, sacrificing their sons to placate "vaudeville" generals, and blinding themselves to the fact that their "masquerade towers" are "riddled by widening cracks." Opposed to them are the "new children," interested in flowers, streams, and the beauty of the sky, who wish to take off their clothes to dance and sing and love one another. What's more, the "antique people are fading away"; in fact, they are already wearing "death masks." As the song says, "The new children will live because their elders have died."[52]

Buckley's vision of the new world that is coming is obviously that of a kind of idyllic Eden before the fall, a world in which men will be free to romp and play and indulge their natural desires for love. It is a pagan world, that antithesis of the Christian ideal that would postpone fulfillment to some afterlife. Elsewhere, Buckley explicitly condemns Christianity, saying "I can't hesitate and I can't wait for pleasant street."[53] Similarly, the Doors' Jim Morrison states, "Cancel my subscription to the resurrection," and in the same song literally shrieks, "We want the world and want it now."[54] Here is the impatient demand of youth that all problems be swept aside and the world be made into paradise without delay.

HOW TO LIVE

Though the times may be changing, the songsters are well aware that—despite their brave words and demands—there is plenty of strength left in the old social order. Obviously, they can see the war continuing, Negro demands not being met, and the continuing hostility of society toward their long hair, music, sexual behavior, and experimentation with drugs. Faced with these facts, the musicians

51. "Wild Tyme (H)," *After Bathing at Baxter's* (Victor, LSO-1511). Copyright by Ice Bag Corporation.
52. "Goodbye and Hello," written by Tim Buckley, *Goodbye and Hello.* Copyright 1968 by Third Story Music, Inc. All rights reserved.
53. "Pleasant Street," written by Tim Buckley. Copyright 1968 by Third Story Music, Inc. All rights reserved.
54. "When the Music's Over," *Strange Days.* Copyright 1967 by Nipper Music Company, Inc. All rights reserved.

must deal with the problem of how to live decently within the framework of the old society. Here they tend toward the world of private experience mentioned earlier in this article in connection with Dylan. Many of their songs are almost programs for youth's behavior in a world perceived as being unlivable.

The first element is to forget about the repressive society out there. As Sopwith Camel says, "Stamp out reality . . ./Before reality stamps out you."[55] Then it is imperative to forget about trying to understand the outside world rationally. In a typical anti-intellectual stance, the Byrds describe such attempts as "scientific delirium madness."[56] Others combine a similar attitude with a strong measure of *carpe diem.* Spirit deride people who are "always asking" for "the reason" when they should be enjoying life, while H. P. Lovecraft admits that the bird is on the wing and states, "You need not know why."[57] What is important is that the moment be seized and life lived to the fullest. As Simon and Garfunkel say, one has to make the "moment last," and this is done best by those who open themselves fully to the pleasures of the world."[58]

The most frequent theme of the song writers is the call to freedom, the total freedom of the individual to "do his own thing." Peanut Butter Conspiracy carry this so far as to hope for a life that can be lived "free of time."[59] Circus Maximus and the Byrds—despite the fact that they are young men—long to recapture some lost freedom that they knew as children.[60] Such freedom can be almost solipsistic; Jimi Hendrix claims that even if the sun did not rise and the mountains fell into the sea, he would not care because he has his "own world to live through."[61] But for others, it can lead to brotherhood. As H. P. Lovecraft says, "C'mon people now, let's get together/Smile on your brother,/Try and love one another right now."[62]

A desire for freedom is certainly nothing new. What is different in the songs of the 1960's is the conviction that this freedom should be used by the individual in an extensive exploration of his own

55. "Saga of the Low Down Let Down," *The Sopwith Camel.* Copyright by Great Honesty Music, Inc.
56. "Fifth Dimension," *Fifth Dimension.*
57. "Topanga Window," *Spirit* (Ode, 21244004); "Let's Get Together," *H. P. Lovecraft* (Phillips, 600–252).
58. "Feeling Groovy," *Sounds of Silence.*
59. "Time Is After You," *West Coast Love-In* (Vault, LP 113).
60. "Lost Sea Shanty," *Circus Maximus* (Vanguard, 79260); "Going Back," *The Notorious Byrd Brothers.*
61. "If 6 Was 9," *Axis* (Reprise, S 6281).
62. H. P. Lovecraft, "Let's Get Together," written by Chester Powers, *H. P. Lovecraft.* Copyright by Irving Music, Inc.

internal world. Central to the vision of the song writers is the idea that the mind must be opened and expanded if the truths of life are to be perceived. Thus, the importance of external reality is subordinated to that of a psychological, even a metaphysical, realm. The most extensive treatment of this subject is by the Amboy Dukes, who devote half of a long-playing record to it. Their theme is stated quite simply: "How happy life would be/If all mankind/Would take the time to journey to the center of the mind."[63] Like any mystical trip, what happens when one reaches the center of the mind is not easy to describe. Perhaps the best attempt is by the Iron Butterfly, who claim that an unconscious power will be released, flooding the individual with sensations and fusing him with a freedom of thought that will allow him to "see every thing." At this point, man will be blessed with the almost supernatural power of knowing "all."[64]

Such a journey is, of course, difficult to make. But youth has discovered a short cut to the mind's center, through the use of hallucinogenic drugs. Indeed, such journeys are almost inconceivable without hallucinogens, and the so-called "head songs" about drug experiences are the most prevalent of works that can be classified as "protest."[65] In this area, the songs carefully distinguish between "mind-expanding," nonaddictive marijuana and LSD, and hard, addictive drugs which destroy the body. Thus, the Velvet Underground and Love both tell of the dangers of heroin, while Canned Heat warn of methedrine use and the Fugs describe the problems of cocaine.[66] But none of the groups hesitate to recommend "grass" and "acid" trips as a prime way of opening oneself to the pleasures and beauties of the universe. As the Byrds claim in a typical "head song," drugs can free the individual from the narrow boundaries of the mundane world, allowing him to open his heart to the quiet joy and eternal love which pervade the whole universe.[67] Others find the reality of the drug experience more real than the day-to-day world,

---

63. "Journey to the Center of the Mind," *Journey to the Center of the Mind* (Mainstream, S 6112). Copyright 1968 by Brent Music Corporation.
64. "Unconscious Power," *Heavy.*
65. There are so many "head songs" that listing them would be an impossibly long task. Some of the most popular protest songs of the decade have been such works. They include Jefferson Airplane, "White Rabbit," *Surrealistic Pillow;* the Doors, "Light My Fire," *The Doors* (Elektra EKS 74007); Strawberry Alarm Clock, "Incense and Peppermints," *Incense and Peppermints;* and the Byrds, "Eight Miles High," *Fifth Dimension.*
66. "Heroin," *Velvet Underground;* "Signed D. C.," *Love* (Elektra, 74001); "Amphetamine Annie," *Boogie;* "Coming Down," *The Fugs.*
67. "Fifth Dimension," *Fifth Dimension.*

and some even hope for the possibility of staying "high" permanently. More frequent is the claim that "trips" are of lasting benefit because they improve the quality of life of an individual even after he "comes down."[68] The Peanut Butter Conspiracy, claiming that "everyone has a bomb" in his mind, even dream of some day turning the whole world on with drugs, thus solving mankind's plaguing problems by making the earth a loving place.[69] An extreme desire, perhaps, but one that would find much support among other musicians.

A REPRESSIVE SOCIETY

This, then is the portrait of America that emerges in the popular songs of the 1960's which can be labeled as "protest." It is, in the eyes of the song writers, a society which makes war on peoples abroad and acts repressively toward helpless minorities like Negroes, youth, and hippies at home. It is a land of people whose lives are devoid of feeling, love, and sexual pleasure. It is a country whose institutions are crumbling away, one which can presumably only be saved by a sort of cultural and spiritual revolution which the young themselves will lead.

Whether one agrees wholly, partly, or not at all with such a picture of the United States, the major elements of such a critical portrait are familiar enough. It is only in realizing that all this is being said in popular music, on records that sometimes sell a million copies to teen-agers, in songs that youngsters often dance to, that one comes to feel that something strange is happening today. Indeed, if parents fully understand what the youth are saying musically to one another, they must long for the simpler days of Elvis Presley and his blue suede shoes.

If the lyrics of the songs would disturb older people, the musical sound would do so even more. In fact, a good case could be made that the music itself expresses as much protest against the status quo as do the words. Performed in concert with electronic amplification on all instruments—or listened to at home at top volume—the music drowns the individual in waves of sound; sometimes it seems to be pulsating inside the listener. When coupled with a typical light show, where colors flash and swirl on huge screens, the music helps to provide an assault on the senses, creating an overwhelming personal experience of the kind that the songs advise people to seek.

---

68. See Country Joe and the Fish, "Bass Strings," *Electric Music for the Mind and Body;* or United States of America, "Coming Down," *United States of America.*
69. "Living, Loving Life," *Great Conspiracy.*

This sort of total experience is certainly a protest against the tepid, partial pleasures which other songs describe as the lot of bourgeois America.

Another aspect of the music which might be considered a kind of protest is the attempt of many groups to capture in sound the quality of a drug "trip," to try through melody, rhythm, and volume to—in the vernacular—"blow the mind" of the audience. Of course, youngsters often listen to such music while under the influence of hallucinogens. In such a state, the perceptive experience supposedly can have the quality of putting one in touch with regions of the mind and manifestations of the universe that can be felt in no other way. Such mysticism, such transcendental attitudes, are certainly a protest against a society in which reality is always pragmatic and truth instrumental.

To try to explain why the jingles and vapid love lyrics of popular music in the 1950's evolved into the social criticism and mystical vision of the 1960's is certainly not easy. Part of it is the fact that performers, who have always been young, started writing their own songs, out of their own life experiences, rather than accepting the commercial output of older members of tin pan alley. But this does not explain the popularity of the new songs. Here one must look to the youthful audience, which decided it preferred buying works of the newer kind. For it was the commercial success of some of the new groups which opened the doors of the record companies to the many that flourish today.

THE FUNCTION OF MUSIC

Though one cannot make definitive judgments about this record-buying audience, some things seem clear. Certainly, it is true that with increasingly rapid social change, parents—and adults in general—have less and less that they can tell their children about the ways of the world, for adult life experiences are not very relevant to current social conditions. Similarly, institutions like the school and the press suffer from a kind of cultural lag that makes their viewpoints valueless for youth. Into the place of these traditional sources of information have stepped the youth themselves, and through such things as the "underground" press and popular music they are telling each other exactly what is happening. In this way, the music has achieved popularity—at least in part—because it telegraphs important messages to young people and helps to define and codify the mores and standards of their own subculture. A youngster may personally feel that there is no difference between his parents' drinking and his use of marijuana. Certainly, it is comforting to him when his friends feel the same way, and when popular songs selling millions of copies deliver the same message, there are even stronger sanctions for his "turning on." Thus, the lyrics of the music serve a functional role in the world of youth.

It is interesting to note that the popular music also puts youth in touch with serious, intellectual critiques of American life. Perhaps it starts only as a gut reaction in the song writers, but they have put into music the ideas of many American social critics. Without reading Paul Goodman, David Riesman, C. Wright Mills, or Mary McCarthy, youngsters will know that life is a "rat race," that Americans are a "lonely crowd," that "white-collar" lives contain much frustration, and that the war in Vietnam is far from just. And they will have learned this from popular music, as well as from their own observation.

The other side of the coin from criticism of contemporary life is the search for personal experience, primarily of the "mind-expanding" sort. As is obvious by now, such expansion has nothing to do with the intellect, but is a spiritual phenomenon. Here a final critique is definitely implicit. Throughout the music—as in youth culture—there is the search for a kind of mystical unity, an ability to feel a oneness with the universe. This is what drugs are used for; this is what the total environment of the light and music shows is about; and this is what is sought in the sexual experience—often explicitly evident in the orgasmic grunts and moans of performers. Through the search for this unity, the music is implicitly condemning the fragmentation of the individual's life which is endemic in the modern world. The songsters are saying that it is wrong to compartmentalize work and play, wrong to cut men off from the natural rhythms of nature, wrong to stifle sex and love and play in favor of greater productivity, wrong to say man's spiritual needs can be filled by providing him with more material possessions.

This is obviously a criticism that can only be made by an affluent people, but these youth do represent the most affluent of all countries. And rather than wallow in their affluence, they have sensed and expressed much of the malaise that plagues our technological society. The charge may be made against them that they are really utopians, but the feeling increases today that we are in need of more utopian thinking and feeling. And while one might not wish to follow their prescriptions for the good life, they have caught something of the desire for freedom that all men feel. What could be more utopian and yet more inviting in its freedom than the hopeful picture which the Mothers of Invention paint of the future:

There will come a time when everybody
Who is lonely will be free . . .
TO SING AND DANCE AND LOVE
There will come a time when every evil
That we know will be an evil
WE CAN RISE ABOVE
Who cares if hair is long or short
Or sprayed or partly grayed . . .
WE KNOW THAT HAIR
AINT WHERE IT'S AT
(There will come a time when you
won't even be ashamed if you are fat!)

Who cares if you're so poor
You can't afford to buy a pair
Of mod a-go go stretch elastic pants
THERE WILL COME A TIME
WHEN YOU CAN EVEN
TAKE YOUR CLOTHES OFF WHEN
YOU DANCE[70]

---

70. "Take Your Clothes Off When You Dance," *We're Only in It for the Money.*
Copyright 1968 by Frank Zappa Music, Inc. All rights reserved.

Courtesy of New York University

PART III

LIFE DECISIONS

The adolescent must resolve some central issues if he is to move from identity crisis to adulthood. Resolution of these issues requires that he define them and make some significant decisions that will narrow his choices and give purpose to his adult activities. He faces such major issues as: (1) his relationship to family life; (2) his adaption to an adult sexual role; (3) his mastery of appropriate education that provides both understanding of the world and tools for his participation in the economic life of his society; (4) his perception of the work ethic; and finally, (5) his determination of valid religious faith.

From cocktail party to talk show to the annual meeting of the American Sociological Association, the future of the family may be the most fashionable topic of the moment. Can the family survive? Will it survive the onslaughts on the old values that threaten the social, political, economic, ecological, and sexual order? Has the nuclear family failed to provide young people growing up within its confines with the positive beliefs and values that will lead them to provide the same set of experiences for the next generation? The consensus is that these are times of existential crisis. The old values, religion, tradition, and morality have disappeared, while nothing new has been created.

What are the changes that teenagers have been exposed to that did not confront their parents? First, the economic supremacy of the

231

male has been challenged. The promise of equal opportunity in job preparation and occupation has come closer to realization. The time is rapidly approaching when women will enjoy equal privileges with men in the job market. Secondly, parental authority has been seriously challenged. Decisions about a child's future in terms of his education and social status are falling more and more to the province of the state. Thirdly, increased female economic equality has led to a rapid decline of sexual inequality. Women, in the past, had to marry in order to be provided for; men had to marry because single women were supposed to be sexually inaccessible. A change in sexual morality—toward sexual equality—accompanied the proliferation in the 1960s of use of "the pill." This combination of factors has reduced the impetus of sexual urgency for marriage, allowing for other options.

It is within this context of changing attitudes that the reader can approach the first essay in this section which deals with formal family organization and adolescent socialization. Larson and Myerhoff have found—somewhat accidentally, as they apologetically state—a high degree of organization in the family. Authority is seen as the key variable in understanding this organization. They have investigated its source, types of goals, and techniques of influence in the family socialization process. The family appears to succeed because of the sharp divisions within its socialization process between the roles of mother and father. An interesting question is, can the organization of the family that they describe survive the blurring of these roles?

Parental interaction is a major factor in adolescent socialization. Father Meissner reports on 1278 normal high-school boys in the eastern part of the United States. His survey asked questions relating to the boys' perceptions of their parents and of their level of interaction. Most significant for the continued health of the family is his finding that 74 percent of the boys sampled felt proud of their parents and said that they would like their friends to meet them. This study also supports the findings of Myerhoff and Larson in that the boys made a sharp distinction between fathers as being cooler, less understanding, and more traditional, and mothers as being more friendly and more nervous than fathers. Meissner found further that while younger boys felt they had adequate social opportunity and freedom and accepted parental authority, the older adolescents expressed an increasing dissatisfaction with home life, the imposition of parental ideas, and the level of parental understanding of their problems and behaviors.

The single most pervasive revolutionary trend in contemporary society is the changing role of women. Complementary to the shift in the way women view themselves and their role, are the adaptions that men are required to make to relate to these changes. The whole question of sexual identity, so significant for the middle teens, is dependent upon an understanding of this revolutionary trend. Erik Erikson's essay, the first for this topic, asks if we understand sufficiently what is implied by the term "womanhood." He states that at this moment in world history it is crucial that we redefine the identity of the sexes in a way that will be consonant with our current image of men. The significant question, according to Erikson, is whether women's specific creativity has been employed "in those fateful human affairs which so far have been left entirely in the hands of gifted and driven men, and often men whose genius of leadership eventually has yielded to ruthless self-aggrandizement." Erikson leaves us with the warning that woman is never not-woman, and that any new definition of a woman's role should seek equivalence rather than equality with men, for women bring a unique perception and creativity when they take their position alongside of men in the affairs of the world, large or small.

Erikson has modified Freud's dictum "anatomy is destiny" as a way of viewing the passive role of woman in contemporary society, yet his account of feminine behavior remains tied to the biological distinction between the sexes. Jean Lipman-Blumen, as she indicates in her essay, finds that the destinies of women are shaped by powerful systems of belief that are culturally determined and transmitted implicitly. Her data is based upon the analysis of a set of questionnaires of 1,012 wives who attended college and who live in the Boston area. She finds that the life goals, satisfactions, and educational and occupational aspirations of these women were based upon either of two possible sex-role ideologies. The first, the traditional sex-role ideology, was shared by women who view the ideal life as the devoting of energies to family and volunteer social activities. The second, the contemporary sex-role ideology, was shared by women with high educational aspirations whose view of the ideal life was a combination of both family and full or part-time employment. Women with the contemporary sex-role ideology were, in adolescence, less satisfied with the lives of both of their parents and sought alternative modes of behavior. They were somewhat more withdrawn from their peers and can be said to have experienced more of an adolescence than their sisters. Those who followed the traditional sex-role ideology were, in adolescence, satisfied with their parents' life styles and unconflicted about the traditional values and behaviors assigned to women by society and their peers.

The final essay in this group asks some hard questions about the family size desires of modern women. Are we a contracepting society? Has contraception effectively reduced the ideal family size desires of young married women? Is there any indication that young women in their teens are more sensitive to the question of demographic diversity? Ruth Dixon finds the outlook at present both depressing and hopeful. We are a contracepting society, but this fact has not, however, affected family size. Young women still wish to be married, do not wish to be left out when at 19 or 20 their peers are marrying, and they want the security of the nuclear family with the standard 3.2 children. She feels that only if women's needs can be satisfied in a variety of ways will the universal pattern of early marriage and several children become an option for them rather than a compulsion. She states "only when control over reproduction can be used to choose freely a life style uniquely suited to individual qualities, will women be able to say fully and truthfully, 'Hallelujah the Pill!' "

We have already observed that one of the more curious aspects of American culture is the way in which a love, if not a worship, of youth is conjoined with fear and distrust of the young. This value confusion is evident when we look at the school system as well. On the one hand, the pressure on young people to accept adult "responsibility" earlier and more fully in certain circumscribed areas is increasing today, especially in an academic rat race that begins in the junior high school and continues, for many, through the Ph.D. Yet the basis on which success most depends is, paradoxically, the willingness to defer gratification. But what is the "payoff" for submitting to the academic pressure? The answer is well known: occupational success. What, in turn, are Americans encouraged to expect from occupational success? Two things: hardware and fun. Thus we come full circle. Young people are pressured to become responsible miniature adults so that they can afford to be children when they are older.

Submission to the academic rat race involves participation in a schooling process which can be called the development of "competence"—the acquisition of both technical and personal skills. Friedenberg has defined competence, in the lingo of middle-class youth, as: "Smile, don't get hung up, and, above all, win." It follows that the most visible pathologies should arise in those who reject, defer, cannot attain, or exceed the prescribed levels of competence. Youth from the dominant social strata appear to view their school experience as training not in understanding but in techniques for survival in the upcoming professional rat race. Eager to learn those behaviors that will bring greatest tangible success, they use the school to learn standard approved responses. Disapproval and condemnation by teachers as "smart-alecks" is the fate of youths whose creative minds produce original responses.

For those thoroughly alienated by their failure to acquire a meaningful identity in adolescence, there are other avenues of behavior. They may opt for various forms of bohemianism and head for a subculture like that described by Paul Goodman, in which disc jockeys, liquor, or drugs become a central interest and hip-talk is the semi-articulate speech.

Some have refused to be satisfied with either preparation for the rat race or withdrawal into a hip subculture and have come out into open revolt against their schools, their parents, and their communities. Since the schools have provided no vehicle for the student voice, no forum for his outrage, students have created their own medium: the underground newspaper. The reader can sample some representative selections from Diane Divoky's collection of prose and verse published in underground newspapers by high-school students throughout the country. These articles deal mainly with subjects that the students can talk about as insiders: the routines that establish the American high school as a prison and the school administration as an insensitive machine—and how television portrays the teenager.

If one is interested in youth first and education secondarily and then only in the service of youth, one must ask the question how can the young *learn* to be alive or free? There has been a response to the voice from the underground press. In some schools, the classes have opened to some degree: students use teachers' first names, there is less grading, and students can choose their own text. At the same time, educators develop modules, micro-modules, learning contracts; they innovate and reinnovate; and yet, as Peter Marin asks us, "What has it all got to do with the needs of the young?" He demands that we rehumanize the educational process. What is needed? Not skills, "but qualities of the soul; daring, warmth, wit, imagination, honesty, loyalty, grace, and resilience. But one cannot be taught these things; they cannot be programed into a machine. They seem to be learned, instead, in activity and communion—*in the adventurous presence of other real persons.*"

A decisive *rite de passage* from adolescence to adulthood is the selection of a vocation. The adolescent choice of a career involves two important questions. First he must ask, is there a meaningful job out there for him, and secondly, does he have the qualities and education to successfully perform the work he has selected? The essay by Paul Goodman addresses itself to the first question. Man's work, Goodman says, should be meaningful work, and the most unquestionably meaningful work he defines as that producing food and shelter. Alternatively, man needs to do something worthwhile, and the author feels that only one-twentieth of the American economy is devoted to these goals. Teenagers are aware of this, and Goodman quotes one adolescent as saying, "During my productive years I will spend eight hours a day doing what is no good."

Ernest Callenbach has come to feel, along with Paul Goodman, that America's system of production for profit rather than for use has succeeded in making its jobs and products profitable but useless. He asks youth to drop out of the covetous society. To be poor is "in." There is still meaningful work to be done if one is willing to accept do-it-yourself subsistance farming, communes, or odd jobs. Callenbach asserts "Coveting is a bum trip" and that the rewards of meaningless work will not satisfy human needs and restore human dignity.

Settling on a mature religious faith is also one of the life decisions adolescents have to make in coming to terms with adulthood. James Knight defines religious faith as an individual's having some feeling that there is a power in the universe greater than the individual and that life acquires a new meaning through the experiencing of this faith. Adolescent rebellion against religion involves a questioning of all religious values, for these are secondhand until a young person can modify them to fit his experiences or claim them for his own. Rebellion also serves to create distance between the youth and both parental and societal values. With the emergence of adulthood, alienation should be followed by reconciliation with these values—in a form that is distinctly personal rather than parental.

In the past few years not all young people have been content to seek religious faith in either personal introspection or through the guidance of established religious institutions. Many have sought spiritual release through ways that emphasize illumination, revelation, and intuition. Some have sought the Divine Truth proclaimed by the gurus, representative of Eastern religious cults. Others, in more typical American fashion, have found faith through the Jesus movement.

In "Mainlining Jesus: The New Trip," Adams and Fox state: "The Jesus Trip is The Great Awakening of 1740 (Jonathan Edwards) Revisited; it is American frontier religion revisited with Volkswagons and amplifiers supplanting the horses, wagons, and saddleback of Cane Ridge, Kentucky, 1801." The Jesus movement has two groups of adherents, a minority of young adults (youths) who have left the drug culture and for whom the movement acts as a point of readmittance into traditional society, and the larger group, the "Jesus-boppers" who are teenagers. The movement helps the adolescent deny his feelings and it inhibits his attempt to seek solutions to his identity conflict. The Jesus movement—in its affirmation of childhood morality, its rituals of creeds and programs, and its political conservatism—appeals to adolescents characterized by lack of rebellion against their parents and opposition to changing the system.

The settling on some sort of religious faith is also the subject of Sidney Mead, whose brief but eloquent historical survey of the subject provides our closing essay. If contemporary man believes that God is dead—and this professor of religion feels that such is the case —what can fill the spiritual void thus created? At one time, it might have been possible to replace discarded deistic concepts with a belief in man's ability to dominate nature and assist her in yielding an earthly paradise. But this faith was itself shattered by the nuclear explosion at Hiroshima, with the result that twentieth-century man is echoing the elemental question of primitive man: Do we live in a world ruled by beneficence or by an indifferent or even malevolent force? For youth coming of age today, Mead suggests, the most viable faith may well be a faith in man himself: man as a social being, needing the support of other men.

One

Family

This study identifies and discusses several major variables related to the structure and organization of the family. These include authority sources, goals, and modes of family interaction. The roles of both parents are emphasized in the adolescent's socialization process. The mother is viewed as the more personal expressive and emotional parent while the father is seen as the source of authority whose interactions are more formal and rational.

WILLIAM R. LARSON & BARBARA G. MYERHOFF

Primary and Formal Family Organization and Adolescent Socialization

Human collectivities are frequently characterized on the basis of the intimacy or impersonality of the members' interactions with one another. Groups whose members have strong emotional bonds, extensive face-to-face contacts and share a sense of similarity and identity have been called primary, and described in detail by Cooley, G. H. Mead and E. Faris to name but a few. The nuclear family has often been designated as the prototype of the primary group, for it offers the possibility of interactions as intimate and intense as people are ever likely to have. Status-differentiated, goal-oriented formal orga-

238

nizations are thought to exemplify an *opposite* kind of group, in which member's interactions are more impersonal, rational, and emotionally neutral. A bureaucratically-organized, economically-oriented collectivity such as the factory may be conceived of as a prototype of the formal group. Primary and formal groups are usually thought of as offering the members qualitatively different experiences and, indeed, are often treated as mutually exclusive. This means, for example, that the bases for interactions which take place in the family on the one hand and the factory on the other are considered to be diametrically opposed.

In the course of a study of family organization and adolescent behavior presently being conducted by the authors, it became apparent that the formal characteristics of family life were often as salient as the primary attributes, and, in fact, the dichotomy between these two kinds of groups began to appear as an over-simplification which masked similarities between them. The question raised by this observation is the subject of the present paper: What kinds of status-based, rational and unemotional interactions can be found in families? Or put another way: To what extent is the family in our society a formal organization as well as a primary group?

These questions do not originate with us. Several authors have been cognizant of the presence of formal attributes in primary groups and primary attributes in formal groups. Parsons (Parsons & Bales, 1955), in passing, has referred to the family as a kind of factory, whose product is the human personality, but he did not elaborate on this point. Blau (Blau & Scott, 1962) has indicated that in every formal organization, there arise informal, primary groups; however, he did not consider the converse, that primary groups may likewise manifest characteristics of formal organizations. Our paper is intended to explore the implications of these suggestions and to elaborate on what has thus far only been adumbrated.

This paper is, in actuality, a child of serendipity, for in the course of our research on the family, we observed what appeared to be an unexpectedly high degree of consensus on the goals held by families for their adolescent sons. Agreement on these goals seemed unrelated to the social-environmental influences exerted by class, race, and religion. Though specifically looking for manifestations of family disorganization and disruption, instead we were struck by the prevalence of organization, as indicated by high agreement on goals. If we were surprised to find this instance of formality of family organization on one dimension (agreement on goals), what other formal attributes in families might we be inclined to overlook? It occurred to us that a theoretical comparison of the family and the factory would perhaps sensitize us to the presence, in varying degrees, of features which might be found in both these kinds of groups. By focusing on the similarities between family and factory and discarding the summary and reductionist labels of "primary" and "formal," which emphasize contradictions between them, we felt we would be able to identify organizational dimensions usually neglected in family research.

In making this comparison we have concentrated on the family's influential function, that is, the family's ability to induce and sustain conformity by the child, who, in our present research is the adolescent boy.

Our comparison of ways in which families and factories induce conformity has led us to the identification of three continuous variables which are equally pertinent to and operative in both kinds of groups. The first of these variables defers to the *source or basis of the authority exerted.* We have used polar terms to define the continuum of authority source: *personal* at one end and *positional* at the other. Authority which is purely personal in origin is exemplified by the charismatic leader, whose followers voluntarily obey him because of his unique, individual attributes, and because of the emotional bonds between him and his followers. Purely positional authority is exemplified by the army officer who, by virtue of his ability to apply coercive sanctions, can demand conformity. Personal authority ideally is an emotional appeal, presupposing close emotional ties, while positional authority is a rational, emotionally neutral command, presupposing the ability to enforce compliance, without regard for individual preferences.

How do these polar sources of authority operate in the family and factory? In the family, a father may request his son to conform to his wishes to please him, presupposing that his son's affection for him will motivate him to want to do so. Or, he may insist on conformity on the grounds that he is the father, he is older, he knows what's best, and so forth, treating as irrelevant any emotional bonds between him and his son, and implying that his requests can be enforced if necessary. Similarly, the factory foreman may induce compliance with his wishes by appealing to the worker's liking for him, by being a nice guy, or, he may merely indicate that as the superordinate, he has the right to demand compliance. Further, he has coercive sanctions at his disposal in case there is any question about the matter.

Our second variable refers to the intended outcome of the influence being exerted by the authority. What are the authority's *goals* for the individual over whom he has control? Toward what ends does he aspire in his attempts to induce conforming behavior?

Again, our contrast between family and factory is helpful, for we find that both kinds of organizations are oriented toward both these kinds of goals. The father's goals for his son may emphasize the *expressive*, but he must also concern himself with rearing a child who will be able to meet externally originating demands, such as passing his courses in school, and getting and holding a job. The factory foreman of necessity emphasizes *instrumental* goals, since matters such as output and productivity are involved with the explicit rationale of the institution, but he is also concerned with the workers' morale and the quality of the interpersonal relations between himself and the workers in situations that do not directly bear on work goals.

Finally, a variable has been identified which refers to the practices used by the authority figure in attaining his goals for the subordinate. To what extent are the *techniques* used by the authority figure *emotional* and to what extent *rational?* A technique may be described as emotional when it involves the *feelings* of the authority, for example, expressions of anger, affection, approval or disapproval. A rational technique typically involves the bestowal, removal or withholding of goods, services and privileges. Emotional techniques are usually less intentionally or self-consciously applied than are rational, which necessarily involve a minimum of spontaneity and a maximum of premeditation, and incidentally, are often more "appropriate" in the sense of being fair or proportionate.

The father may communicate his desires to his son in a myriad of ways. He may reward or punish him by a great range of emotional techniques, including subtle, nonverbal cues such as smiling, frowning, and touching. Inevitably, he must also deliberately apply sanctions which he considers appropriate and must formally assert his authority by rational techniques such as confinement of the son, restricting his use of family possessions and the like. The factory foreman, in addition to using rational techniques such as docking pay, giving bonuses and time off, influences and motivates the worker by subtle, interpersonal communications indicating his pleasures and displeasures.

These variables may be summarized thus:

1. Authority source: Personal
                                    Positional

2. Goals: Expressive
                    Instrumental

3. Techniques: Emotional
                        Rational

It is apparent that these variables are so closely intertwined as to be aspects of one another; all refer to the primary and formal attributes of interactions. By distinguishing between them, however, it becomes possible to locate any group at any point in time as possessing more or fewer primary and formal attributes on several dimensions rather than one. If this multidimensional view of the family's conformity-inducing function is to be of heuristic value to research, it must be integrated with other conceptualizations in the field. To illustrate the extent to which the viewpoint expressed here can be related to the finding of other writers, two frequently recurring problems of family studies—efficacy of child rearing techniques and effects of a broken home—will be examined using these variables.

Zelditch's (1955) consideration of the expressive and instrumental functions of the family in our society as sex-linked is particularly fruitful and relevant to our conceptualization. He has described the mother as being the expressive leader in the family and the father as the instrumental. This notion may be taken, in our scheme, as implying that the mother's interactions with the child should be consistently in the primary direction of the primary-formal continuum for all three variables. This would mean that it is appropriate for the mother's authority to be *personal,* her goals *expressive* and her techniques *emotional.* Correspondingly the father as instrumental leader should interact with the child in a consistently more formal manner. His authority should be positional, his goals instrumental and his techniques rational. Numerous questions which might be readily operationalized are raised by assuming consistency. To what extent is there such consistency on the part of mothers and fathers, so that mothers are more primary and fathers more formal in their relations with the child? What are the implications of consistency or lack of consistency among these dimensions for the effectiveness of the socialization process? What are the implications for personality development of such consistency or its absence?

Viewed in this light, it can be seen that Parsons' (1949) article on sources and patterns of aggression in the western world and Green's (1960) article on the middle class male child and neurosis refer to just such questions as these. Both authors describe the tendency of middle class mothers to use "personality-absorbing techniques" (highly emotional techniques) to promote instrumental goals in their children. The mother manipulates the child by using her personal authority, and gives or withholds her love on the basis of the child's successes and failures outside the family. Thus the child who fails in school feels he has failed to show he loves his mother, and that she in turn will withhold her love from him. This combination of personal authority, emotional technique and instrumental goal arouses great anxiety and guilt in the child, a situation which is unquestionably a powerful motivation to success. But as both Parsons and Green have suggested, the effectiveness of such a tactic is not the only consideration; the personality damage which may be sustained by the child as a result must also be taken into account. An everyday instance of an inappropriate combination of goals and techniques is found in the father who is in a rage because his son does not show him enough respect. He demands this respect as his paternal prerogative and takes the son's car away to make sure he is respected in the future. Such a juxtaposition of a rational technique and an expressive goal (which is by no means uncommon) is considered ludicrous and ineffectual on face value. The investigation of the most desirable combinations of our three variables in terms of the relative balance of primary and formal characteristics, taking into account psychological consequences as well as efficiency, is an area which could be examined by direct research as well as by recasting extant studies and concepts into these terms.

The heuristic value of using these three variables is exemplified further by considering how they may operate in the much-discussed matter of the broken home, that is, a family in which one parent is missing. One of the most important issues of the broken home situation is the difficulties faced by the remaining parent in socializing the child without the assistance of an opposite sex partner. In our terms, a broken home is an instance of a critical position becoming vacant. One may then ask, what are the strategies open to the remaining parent in dealing with this lacuna? How, if at all, can the parent contrive to make up to the child for the missing incumbent?

To demonstrate the kinds of questions raised by this approach, we may consider an example of the child as an adolescent son and the position unfilled as that of father. The mother has six basic alternatives open to her. (1) She may do nothing, perhaps because she feels the position cannot and should not be filled, since no one else will have the personal attributes of the previous incumbent, and that position and personal parental duties are inextricable. (2) She may re-marry and let the step-father fill the position as he sees fit. Alternatives three through six represent attempts by the remaining family members to cope with the situation through their own efforts, that is, without bringing in a new incumbent. (3) The mother may try to compensate for the missing parent by intensifying her role as expressive leader in relation to her son. This would involve making her techniques more emotional, her authority more personal and her goals more expressive. For example, she might go out of her way to spend time talking with her son about his attitudes and emotions; she might be more demonstrative of affection, reveal her intimate feelings to him, and in various ways strengthen and deepen the personal bonds between them. (4) She may attempt to compensate for the absent father by taking over his functions, that is, becoming the instrumental leader herself; thus she would base her authority on her parental position, use rational techniques in dealing with her son and encourage task-oriented behavioral goals for him. This would mean she would, so to speak, be a father to her son, perhaps by taking him camping and fishing, counseling him on vocational possibilities, tutoring him in his school work, and generally relating to him in terms less personal, more rational and formal, than was previously the case. (5) The mother may attempt to be both expressive and instrumental leader at the same time. She may spend time talking with her son, showing him how to fix the lawnmower, play ball with him, and tell him of her problems, attempting, as the familiar saying goes, "to be both father and mother to him." (6) The mother may manipulate the son himself into the missing position, by urging him to take on the responsibilities which are properly the father's. The son may be expected to bring money into the home for household expenses, help discipline younger children, offer emotional support to his mother, and in many ways, subtle and overt, become the "man of the family."

These six alternatives, incidentally, seem equally applicable to homes in which the father is physically present but is weak, ineffectual, perpetually absent or isolated from the mainstream of family life.

There are obvious hazards in all these alternatives, particularly the last four, which involve the mother's or son's attempt to fill the vacant position. In the first instance, the mother's intensification of expressive leadership may emotionally overwhelm the son. This situation is particularly dangerous at a time in the son's development when, as psychoanalysts have pointed out, oedipal conflicts resurge with great force. Further, the son's failure to be instructed in the achievement of instrumental tasks may damage his chances of success in society. In the second instance, wherein the mother assumes the role of instrumental leader, she may overlook the son's emotional needs and desires for primary interactions with her. In addition, because instrumental and expressive roles are sex-linked, her assumption of the instrumental role may confuse the son regarding what constitutes appropriate feminine and masculine behavior. Should he come to equate instrumental goals with femininity, he might find it necessary to reject both the goals and his mother, in his attempt to establish a masculine identity. As Parsons has pointed out, the boy raised exclusively by his mother may even be driven to antisocial behavior if he associates her urging him to be a "good boy" with feminine goals. The third case, in which the mother tries to fill both parental roles at once, may also interfere with the son's establishment of a satisfactory sexual identification. Further, it may maximize the son's dependence on his mother, thus impeding his desire and ability to move toward adulthood. Finally, when the *son* is thrust into the missing position, his adolescence is prematurely cut short so that instead of gradually discarding the status of a youth he is catapulted into an adult role and must assume responsibilities for which he is unprepared socially, emotionally, and physiologically. Such a situation also results in alienating the boy from his peers, whose adolescence is permitted to run its full course.

It has been the purpose of this paper to present some preliminary thoughts and questions growing out of a serendipitous development of the authors' current research on family organization and the socialization of adolescent boys.

By pointing out the often striking instances of similarities between family and factory, we have tried to call attention to the conceptual limitations imposed on the researcher by the use of such over-polarized terms as primary and formal. We have suggested that there are variables which might underlie these general labels, denoting continua upon which a collectivity might be evaluated, with the result that we have become aware of the existence of both formal and primary attributes in so called formal and primary groups.

Although we have concentrated upon the family for the most part, relating the source of authority, types of goals, and techniques of influence to the family socialization process, it is clear that a similar application of these concepts could be made with equal relevance to the factory or to any formal organization. The same problems which may occur in the family due to inconsistency of goals, techniques, and authority source, may have obvious analogues in the industrial organization. But this we shall leave for further papers, projects, or investigators.

Further research based on the conceptual outline developed here can be directed toward several major foci. Our own research deals with the successful or unsuccessful socialization of the adolescent by the family. We are concerned with the family's utilization of formal or primary procedures as outlined above, and the relative occurrence of each pattern in families whose children appear to be making satisfactory progress in school, peer and community affairs, as contrasted with families whose children are not making satisfactory progress.

Only one focus among many has been treated here; it can and should be followed by examinations of formal and primary behavior in the family over time, for example, to consider the changes which have occurred in the American family in its movement from a patriarchal economically based group to an emotionally based, democratic system. Different subcultures in our society—the Negro family, the suburban family, the immigrant family—all offer situations for analysis according to the balance of primary and formal goals, techniques and authority. In addition, crosscultural studies, utilizing family data covering a range of societies, from the preliterate to the urban industrial, may actually allow us to examine the roots and developmental processes of organizational authority, and its relation to personal influence.

Finally, it is possible that studies of the family emphasizing its structure and organization can bring to the arena of family research the benefits of a greater number of theoretical systems and methodological devices. These are urgently needed, and if an extension of conceptual schemes can be effected such that organizational and family theory can be blended in mutual support, behavioral science in general and our knowledge of human social development in particular is certain to benefit.

Parental interaction is an important factor in adolescent socialization. This study, a survey of 1278 high-school boys, asks questions pertaining both to the boys' perceptions of their parents and to the parent-child interaction. The boys saw their fathers as colder and more distant and their mothers as more friendly. Younger adolescent boys were accepting of parental authority as they grew older. However, they expressed dissatisfaction with parental authority and understanding.

W. W. MEISSNER, S. J.

Parental Interaction of the Adolescent Boy

A. INTRODUCTION

In the last few years, the awareness of the importance of the home environment and the pattern of interaction between the parents and the child has become central in the search for a better understanding of personality development and adjustment. The adolescent years represent a crucial period in the formation "identity" (Erikson, 1959) and in the formation of values, ideals, and attitudes; and the formation of values, ideals, and attitudes is profoundly influenced by the relations that obtain between the adolescent and his parents. Disturbances in the development of identity or the "identity diffusion" that has been thought to underlie the defective adjustment of so many adolescents (and, subsequently, adults) in American culture has been traced to the influence of inconsistencies in intrafamilial relationships and early deprivation (Beres, Gale, and Oppenheimer, 1960). Also, evidence has been provided that seems to link delinquency, which is a major symptom of identity diffusion, with a defect in parental identification and a lack of strong and open affection (Andry, 1960).

While the importance of the parent-child interaction has been widely accepted, no clear understanding has emerged as to what factors are crucial in the parent-child interaction. The importance of the mother's role has been accepted ever since Sullivan's work (Sullivan, 1953), but more recently the father's influence on a child's development has received emphasis. Andry's investigations (1960) seem to imply that a child's failure to identify with his father and inadequate communication with his father are central elements in the etiology of delinquency. Further, current studies in family dynamics have focused on the importance of the father's role (Bowen, Dysinger, and Basamanis, 1959; Lidz et al., 1956, 1957). Undoubtedly, the significant environment within a family is compounded not only of the level of adjustment and functioning of each parent individually or not only of the pattern of the interaction of the parents with each other, but also of the manner in which both parents interact with the growing adolescent. This study is directed to the assessment of the frequency of occurrence of certain typical parent-child interactions in a population of normal adolescent boys.

B. PROCEDURE

The results presented arise from a 217-item questionnaire that was given to 1278 high-school boys attending nine schools. The schools were private, denominational schools under Catholic direction and were located in the states of New York, Pennsylvania, New Jersey, and Maryland. The questionnaires were given with a standard set of instructions read to the subjects by the test administrator. The test forms were sent in a sealed envelope to each administrator, who opened the envelope in the presence of the subjects, and immediately after the questionnaires were completed resealed the forms in an envelope for delivery to the investigator.

The subjects were selected randomly according to classes in their respective schools and they represented the medium range in academic achievement in their schools. Three hundred thirty-one were freshmen; 313, sophomores; 343, juniors; and 291, seniors. Ages ranged from 13 to 18, with average ages as follows: freshmen, 14.3 years; sophomores, 15.2 years; juniors, 16.2 years; and seniors, 17.2 years.

Results from the questionnaire were tabulated, per cents were computed, and chi squares were determined (Hess, 1960).

C. FAMILY CHARACTERISTICS

The families from which the boys came can be described as average middle-class families, and the average family group consists of father, mother, and siblings. Only 13 percent of the subjects reported any persons living in the home other than members of the immediate family group. In 6 percent of the families the father was deceased; in 2 percent of the families the mother was deceased. Eight of the subjects lost a parent before the subject reached the age of 2 years; 13, between the ages of 2 and 6; 28, between the ages of 6 and 10; and

41, after the age of 10. Only 4 percent of the boys reported divorce or separation of parents, not an unexpected figure in a predominantly Catholic population.

The families, for the most part, appear to have been financially stable; but 21 percent of the subjects reported that financial troubles were a source of difficulty at home, and 27 percent of the subjects reported a mother engaged in some form of work outside the home. The parents were predominantly native-born Americans, with only 14 percent of the fathers and 10 percent of the mothers having been born outside the United States. The proportion of Catholics in this population is strong: 91 percent of the fathers and 96 percent of the mothers profess the Catholic faith.

The only significant difference between fathers and mothers is educational level (Anastasi and Foley, 1953). Seventy percent of the fathers and 72 percent of the mothers had progressed beyond the high-school level, but 37 percent of the fathers and 54 percent of the mothers failed to finish college. Thirty-three percent of the fathers and only 17 percent of the mothers had graduated from college or had received some postgraduate training.

Not quite 13 percent of the boys indicated that illness is a source of frequent home difficulty.

D. PERCEPTION OF PARENTS

Whatever may be the attitudes or behavior of parents toward their children, the effect on the children is mediated through the children's perception of them (Ausubel et al., 1954) and there seem to be detectable differences between the perceptions of parents and adolescents. Hess (1960), for example, has shown that (while the descriptions of teenagers of themselves tend to agree with descriptions of them by their parents) teenagers expect their parents to underrate them; and parents expect the teenagers to overestimate the maturity and ability of teenagers. Adolescents rate parents higher than parents rate themselves on every item on which adolescents were questioned. These findings can be explained easily on the basis of the high valuation put on adult status by the adolescent who is struggling to define his own identity; but, at the same time, the explanation raises the question of the relationship between the objective situation and the adolescent's perception of it. In other words, the adolescent's perception of his home and parents is colored to a certain extent by his own needs.

The questionnaire responses suggest that certain differences exist between the perceptions of fathers and mothers and that these differences may be meaningful for understanding the interactions between adolescents and their parents. The differential parental characteristics can be listed as follows:

Father
Colder and more indifferent.
More old-fashioned.
Less understanding.
More unreasonable.

Mother
More friendly and interested.
More nervous.
More understanding.
More reasonable.

Thirty-five percent of the students felt that their fathers were cold or indifferent; only 13 percent thought this of their mothers. Fifty-one percent thought their fathers more or less old-fashioned; 41 percent regarded their mothers that way. Thirty-nine percent thought their fathers understood the subject's difficulties; 54 percent thought their mothers did. Thirteen percent thought their fathers "nervous"; 30 percent perceived their mothers as "nervous."

The typical relationship that emerges is decidedly more positive in regard to the mother than it is in regard to the father. Although the configuration may or may not run counter to the presumptive identification of the male child with the father figure, it raises a question about the influence of typical parental perceptions on the course of child development. Apparently the father figure becomes fixed with the role of mediator of parental authority and restriction; while the mother is perceived as responding more to emotional needs for sympathy, acceptance, and understanding. Moreover, the trends in the data, while not always significant, suggest that the foregoing perceptions become more dominant as one moves from the first year to the senior year of high school.

In general, the attitudes toward parents tapped by our questions were positive. The majority thought their parents not overly careful or concerned about them (62 percent) or overly strict (85 percent). Most felt proud of their parents and liked to have them meet their friends (74 percent).

E. PARENT-CHILD INTERACTION

As the young boy proceeds through the adolescent period, the pattern of his interactions with his parents shifts in both positive and negative dimensions. The dimensions of interaction, in which the shifts are statistically significant ($p < .05$), can be listed as follows:

Positive
1. Increased feeling of adequate social opportunity.
2. Increased feeling of sufficient social freedom.
3. Increased acceptance of parental authority.
4. Increased valuation of father's guidance.

Negative
1. Increased dissatisfaction with home life.
2. Increased unhappiness in the home.
3. Decrease in amount of leisure time spent at home.
4. Increased conflict with parents over religion.
5. Decreased approval of parental guidance.
6. Increase in seeing friends disapproved by parents.
7. Increased feeling of the imposition of parents' ideas.
8. Decreased valuation of father's understanding of personal problems.
9. Increased feeling of being misunderstood by parents; more misunderstood by father than mother:

The overall picture is one of gradual alienation from parental influence and increasing rebelliousness against parental control. The shifts, however, are variable. As might be expected, reports of satisfaction and happiness in the home situation are high (80 percent and 89 percent respectively), and a large majority (84 percent) report that half or more of their leisure time is spent at home. Dissatisfaction and unhappiness, however, increase significantly as the boy grows older.

Religious belief does not provide a singular source of conflict. Only 7 percent report that differences in the religious beliefs of their parents have ever caused them any difficulty, and only 16 percent report that they have ever come into conflict with their parents on the question of religion. There is a trend, however, toward increasing conflict as the boy grows older. This patten coincides with the previously reported finding (Meissner, 1961) that religious belief becomes a primary source of serious doubt for this same group in their junior and senior years. This increasing concern would be likely to express itself in conflict with the parents.

Most of the boys do not feel that their parents' demands are excessive, but 18 percent feel that their parents expect more than they can ordinarily accomplish. The large majority, however, approve of the manner in which their parents guide them (73 percent).

These attitudes undergo a significant shift ($p < .01$) between the freshman year (79 percent) and the junior year (68 percent).

The adolescent period is one of increasing social and heterosexual contacts; consequently it is to be expected that the regulation of these activities provides a common source of friction between the adolescent and his parents. In general, the majority of our subjects report that their parents encourage them to bring their friends into the home (75 percent) and, to a lesser extent, that their parents approve of all their friends (54 percent). Parental approval is reported as increasing steadily until the junior year and dropping off sharply in the senior year ($p < .02$). However, when parents do not approve of particular friends, only 34 percent stop going with those friends.

Most of the parents (75 percent) have the practice of setting a time for their sons to be home at night, but the practice seems to be observed less frequently as the boys grow older (freshmen, 83 percent; sophomores, 82 percent; juniors, 76 percent; and seniors, 60 percent). The difference between seniors and each of the other groups is significant at the .01 level; that between juniors and freshmen is significant at the .05 level. Coincident with a relaxation of parental restriction, there is an increasing feeling that the boys are being treated as maturely as they should be (freshmen, 54 percent; sophomores, 64 percent; juniors, 73 percent; and seniors, 77 percent). A majority of the boys (66 percent) feel that they are given as much social freedom as other boys, and the frequency of that feeling parallels closely their feelings of being maturely treated (freshman, 55 percent; sophomores, 65 percent; juniors, 70 percent; seniors, 74 percent). One-half of the boys (50 percent) claim that they argue for greater liberty when they feel they deserve it.

In a minority of cases, parents are listed as the first source of sex information. Fathers are given as the source of first sex information by 22 percent of the boys; mothers, by 20 percent. For the most part, parents seem to be successful in giving such information. Only 11 percent of the boys report that they lost confidence in their parents because of the way the sex issue was handled. In the majority of cases (73 percent), the parents are acquainted with the girls whom the boys date, and conflict with the parents over girl friends is not frequent (13 percent).

A large majority of the boys (87 percent) recognize that parents exercise legitimate authority over them, but the figure fluctuates significantly between class groups. The shift that occurs between the freshman and senior years may reflect a maturing acceptance of the intellectual awareness of the grounds of parental authority or it may reflect a greater degree of identification with adult figures and adult status. In any case, parents are selected as the persons whom the boys obey more frequently than they do any other authority figure (83 percent). Ninety percent of the boys report that they understand the reason why they should obey their parents.

Parental authority, however, is not accepted without resistance. A small minority of the boys feel that the discipline in the home is too severe (10 percent), and 19 percent express the feeling that they are not treated as young men of their age should be treated. The majority, however, feel that in the exercise of responsibility their parents give them sufficient opportunity (58 percent). At the same time, 28 percent are not satisfied with the opportunities made available to them for responsible activity. Some boys (32 percent) report that they are frequently scolded by their parents, and an even larger number (42 percent) express the feeling that parents tend to impose their own ideas and customs. This latter feeling grows more frequent as the boy matures, possibly because of the increasing influence on him of opinions and attitudes derived from his peer group and because of other influences external to the home. Finally, 14 percent feel that parents exert too much authority over them.

Negative attitudes toward parental authority and discipline are damaging because the internalization of parental norms is an essential step in the development of a responsible person. The formation of a mature identity depends in part on the stable and mature use of authority on the part of the parents; so unless the adolescent maintains positive attitudes the developmental pattern is more likely to be one of rejection and rebellion than one of acceptance. More often than not the question of rebellion does not arise so much as does the question of the adolescent's need and desire to establish his independence. When parental norms are presented in an authoritarian manner there is a tendency to develop negative attitudes toward them, and this tendency becomes more noticeable as the child grows older or shows better verbal intelligence. When parental restrictions are presented with rational motivations there is a tendency for positive attitudes to assert themselves (Pikas, 1961).

Perhaps the most important area of interaction between the adolescent and his parents is that of communication. It is particularly during the period of adolescence that the maturing young man needs the counsel and advice of his elders to enable him to work his way through the conflicts and turmoil characteristic of that period of development. In the present study, 33 percent of the boys claim that they do discuss difficulties and personal problems with their fathers. Almost 39 percent feel that their fathers understand their difficulties, while the rest of the subjects are divided between those who feel their fathers do not understand them (30 percent) and those who are still undecided (31 percent). There a definite trend between the freshmen and the seniors (freshmen, 45 percent; seniors, 33 percent) to call into question the father's understanding. Fifty-three percent of the boys say that they discuss their problems with their mothers, and 54 percent feel that the mother understands the difficulties.

The father's influence regarding guidance seems to become relatively more dominant as the boy grows older. This trend presents a pattern much different from the previously observed pattern of discussing problems and difficulties. Apparently, adolescent boys turn to the father when there is a question of working out the ordinary everyday affairs; but, when immediate problems and difficulties arise, they tend to turn to the mother.

A small percent of the boys (9 percent) report that they fear their fathers rather than love them. In all age groups, there is a consistent tendency to feel more often misunderstood by the father than by the mother. The fixation of the perception of the mother establishes an expectation of continued feminine responsiveness in the future marriage relationship. The more negative fixation of the perception of the father, however, may have the effect of inhibiting the acceptance of the more masculine characteristics that depend on internalization of norms of restrictive discipline. Internalization is essential to the development of a strong sense of masculine identity. At the same time, the positive aspect of the significantly increased valuation of the father's guidance must be kept in mind.

The results of this study imply that there is a pattern of increasing alienation from parental influence and control that can be traced through the critical years of adolescence. There is a growing acceptance of the principle of parental authority and increased respect for parental judgment, especially significant because the strong Catholic influence would have been expected to have reinforced parental authority and to have stressed the value of obedience.

It is not clear, however, that the independent indications justify an identification of the visible pattern as one of rebelliousness. Analysis in terms of "rebelliousness" may reflect a prejudice dictated by a vested interest. From the point of view of the adolescent, the growing indications of decreasing parental authority may represent nothing more than a critical phase of differentiation from parental influence: an essential part of development toward mature and independent functioning.

In conclusion, the author suggests that there is a relationship between identifiable perceptions of parental figures and patterns of interaction between the adolescent and his parents, and that there is a determinable shift in these perceptions reflected in shifting patterns of interaction.

F. SUMMARY

A total of 1278 high-school boys were asked to answer 217 questions on areas of interaction between themselves and their parents. The results indicate that certain typical perceptions of father and mother can be identified, and that these perceptions are significantly different. Also identified were patterns of interaction that reveal significant shifts between the early and the late years of high school. The shifts, generally, are in the direction of parental alienation and increased rebelliousness. An attempt was made to relate the boys' perceptions of parental perceptions to the developing pattern of interaction with the parents.

The Changing Role of Women

What is implied by the term "womanhood"? Erik Erikson believes that at this moment in world history it is necessary to define anew the identity of the sexes. He feels that it is now imperative that woman's creativity be understood and woman's voice be heard in the conduct of human affairs.

ERIK H. ERIKSON

Inner and Outer Space: Reflections on Womanhood

1.

There are a great number of practical reasons for an intensified awareness of woman's position in the modern world: reasons concerning the availability of women for jobs in which *they are needed* and of their employability in jobs which *they need* in view of intensified industrial competition, international and national. But I believe that there are deeper and darker reasons. The ubiquity of nuclear threat, the breakthrough into outer space, and increasing global communication are all bringing about a total change in the

sense of geographic space and of historical time, and thus they neces-
sitate a redefinition of the identity of the sexes within a new image
of man. I cannot go here into the alliances and oppositions of the two
sexes in previous styles of war and peace. This is a history as yet to
be written and, indeed, discovered. But it is clear that the danger of
man-made poison dropping invisibly from outer space into the mar-
row of the unborn in the wombs of women has suddenly brought
one major male preoccupation, namely, the "solution" of conflict by
periodical and bigger and better wars to its own limits. The question
arises whether such a potential for annihilation as now exists in the
world should continue to exist without the representation of the
mothers of the species in the councils of image-making and of decision.

The frantic and diffused preoccupation with the differences between the sexes and the question as to what kind of woman, now that
equality assumes a new and world-wide importance, should be mass
manufactured in the future in place of the types now favored by the
mass media also reflect a widespread sense on the part of both sexes
that a great psychological counterforce has been neglected in what
has purported to be progress toward a technological millennium.
The special dangers of the nuclear age clearly have brought male
leadership close to the limit of its adaptive imagination. The dominant male identity is based on a fondness for "what works" and of
what man can make, whether it helps to build or to destroy. For this
very reason the all too obvious necessity to sacrifice some of the
possible climaxes of technological triumph and of political
hegemony for the sake of the mere preservation of mankind is not
in itself an endeavor enhancing the male sense of identity. True, an
American president felt impelled to say, and said with deep feeling:
"A child is not a statistic"; yet the almost desperate urgency of his
pleas made clear enough the need for a new kind of political and
technological ethics. Maybe if women would only gain the determination to represent as image providers and law givers what they
have always stood for privately in evolution and in history (realism
of householding, responsibility of upbringing, resourcefulness in
peacekeeping, and devotion to healing), they might well be mobi-
lized to add an ethically restraining, because truly supranational,
power to politics in the widest sense.

This, I think, many men and women hope openly and many
more, secretly. But their hope collides with dominant trends in our
technological civilization, and with deep inner resistances as well.
Self-made man, in "granting" a relative emancipation to women,
could offer only his self-made image as a model to be equaled; and

much of the freedom thus won by women now seems to have been spent in gaining access to limited career competition, standardized consumership, and strenuous one-family homemaking. Thus woman, in many ways, has kept her place within the typologies and cosmologies which men have had the exclusive opportunity to cultivate and to idolize. In other words, even where equality is closer to realization it has not led to equivalence, and equal rights have by no means secured equal representation in the sense that the deepest concerns of women find expression in their public influence or, indeed, their actual role in the game of power. In view of the gigantic one-sidedness which is threatening to make man the slave of his triumphant technology, the now fashionable discussion, by women and by men, as to whether woman could and how she might become "fully human" in the traditional sense is really a cosmic parody, and for once one is nostalgic for gods with a sense of humor. The very question as to what it is to be "fully human" and who has the right to grant it to whom indicates that a discussion of the male and female elements in the potentialities of human nature must include rather fundamental issues.

An interdisciplinary symposium, therefore, cannot avoid exploring certain emotional reactions or resistances which hinder concerted discussion. We all have observed the fact that it seems almost impossible to discuss woman's nature or nurture without awaking the slogans (for and against) of the all too recent struggle for emancipation. Moralistic fervor outlives changed conditions, and feminist suspicion watches over any man's attempt to help define the uniqueness of womanhood. Yet it still seems to be amazingly hard for the vast majority of women to say clearly what they feel most deeply, and to find the right words for what to them is most acute and actual, without saying too much or too little, and without saying it with defiance or apology. Some who observe and think vividly and deeply do not seem to have the courage of their native intelligence, as if they were somehow afraid on some final confrontation to be found to have no "real" intelligence. Even successful academic competition has, in many, failed to correct this. Thus women are tempted quickly to go back to "their place" whenever they feel out of place. I would also think that a major problem exists in the relationship of leading women to each other and to their women followers. As far as I can judge, "leading" women are all too often inclined to lead in too volatile, moralistic, or sharp a manner (as if they agreed to the proposition that only exceptional and hard women can think) rather than to inform themselves of and to give voice to what the mass of undecided women are groping to say and are willing to stand by, and thus what use they may wish to make of an equal voice in world affairs. Here, maybe, countries in the stages of rapid development or urgent recovery are more fortunate, for immediate needs are more obvious, and free choices restricted.

On the other hand, the hesitance of many men to respond to the new "feminist" alarm, as well as the agitated response of others, may suggest explanations on many levels. No doubt there exists among men an honest sense of wishing to save at whatever cost a sexual polarity, a vital tension and an essential difference which they fear may be lost in too much sameness, equality, and equivalence, or at any rate in too much self-conscious talk. Beyond this, the defensiveness of men (and here we must include the best educated) has many facets. Where men desire, they want to awake desire, not empathize or ask for empathy. Where they do not desire, they find it hard to empathize, especially where empathy makes it necessary to see the other in yourself and yourself in the other, and where therefore the horror of diffused delineations is apt to kill both joy in otherness and sympathy for sameness. It also stands to reason that where dominant identities depend on being dominant, it is hard to grant real equality to the dominated. And, finally, where one feels exposed, threatened, or cornered, it is difficult to be judicious.

For all of this there are age-old psychological reasons, upon only a very few of which will I be able to throw light with my essay. But even a limited report, in the present climate, calls for an acknowledgment from the onset that ambivalences and ambiguities of ancient standing are apt to be temporarily aggravated rather than alleviated by attempts to share partial insight in these matters.

2.

There is another general consideration which must precede the discussion of a subject which is so incompletely formulated and which always retains an intense actuality. Every discussant will and must begin where he feels his own field has succeeded or failed to do justice to the issue as he sees it, that is, where he feels he is coming from and going within his own advancing discipline. But since the intricacies of his discipline and of his position in it cannot be intimately known to all discussants, he is apt to be confronted with the remark which a Vermont farmer made to a driver who asked him for directions: "Man, if I wanted to go where you want to go, I wouldn't start here."

Here is where I am, and where I intend to go. In my preface to the book which grew out of the Youth issue of *Daedalus*, I pointed out that that extraordinary symposium failed to develop fully—although Bruno Bettelheim made a determined start—the problem of the identity of female youth. This is a severe theoretical handicap. For the student of development and practitioner of psychoanalysis, the stage of life crucial for the understanding of womanhood is the step from youth to maturity, the state when the young woman relinquishes the care received from the parental family and the extended care of institutions of education, in order to commit herself to the love of a stranger and to the care to be given to his and her offspring. In the *Daedalus* issue on Youth, I suggested that the mental and emotional ability to receive and to give *Fidelity* marks the conclusion of adolescence, while adulthood begins with the ability to receive and give *Love* and *Care*. If the terms here capitalized sound shockingly virtuous in a way reminiscent of moralistic values, I offer no apology: to me, they represent human strengths which are not a matter of moral or esthetic choice, but of stark necessity in individual development and social evolution. For the strength of the generations (and by this I mean a basic disposition *underlying* all varieties of human value systems) depends on the process by which the youths of the two sexes find their respective identities, fuse them in love and marriage, revitalize their respective traditions, and together create and "bring up" the next generation. Here whatever sexual differences and dispositions have developed in earlier life become polarized with finality because they must become part of the whole process of production and procreation which marks adulthood. But how, then, does a woman's identity formation differ by dint of the fact that her somatic design harbors an "inner space" destined to bear the offspring of chosen men and, with it, a biological, psychological, and ethical commitment to take care of human infancy? Is not the disposition for this commitment (whether it be realized in actual motherhood or not) the core problem of *female* fidelity?

The psychoanalytic psychology of women, however, does not "start here." In line with its originological orientation, i.e. the endeavor to infer the meaning of an issue from its origins, it begins with the earliest experiences of differentiation, largely reconstructed from women patients necessarily at odds with their womanhood and with the permanent inequality to which it seemed to doom them. However, since the psychoanalytic method could be developed only in work with acutely suffering individuals, whether adults or children, it was necessary to accept clinical observation as the original starting point for investigating what the little girl, when becoming aware of sex-differences, can *know* as observable fact, can *feel* because it causes intense pleasure or unpleasant tension, or may *infer* or *intuit* with the cognitive and imaginative means at her disposal. Here it would be as unfair as it would be easy to extract quotations from psychoanalysts who were much too circumspect not to offer at least on the margins of their discourses extensive modifications of Freud's position. Nevertheless, I think it is fair to say that the psychoanalytic view of womanhood has been strongly influenced by the fact that the first and basic observations were made by clinicians whose task it was to understand suffering and to offer a remedy; and that they by necessity had to understand the female psyche with male means of empathy, and to offer what the ethos of enlightenment dictated, namely, the "acceptance of reality." It is in line with this historical position that they saw, in the reconstructed lives of little girls, primarily an attempt to observe what could be seen and grasped (namely, what was there in boys and hardly there in girls) and to base on this observation "infantile sexual theories" of vast consequence.

From this point of view, the most obvious fact, namely that children of both sexes sooner or later "know" the penis to be missing in one sex, leaving in its place a woundlike aperture, has led to generalizations concerning women's nature and nurture. From an adaptive point of view, however, it does not seem reasonable to assume that observation and empathy, except in moments of acute or transitory disturbance, would so exclusively focus on what is *not* there. The female child under all but extreme urban conditions is disposed to observe evidence in older girls and women and in female animals of the fact that an inner-bodily space—with productive as well as dangerous potentials—does exist. Here one thinks not only of pregnancy and childbirth, but also of lactation, and of all the richly convex parts of the female anatomy which suggest fullness, warmth, and generosity. One wonders, for example, whether girls are quite as upset by observed symptoms of pregnancy or of menstruation as are (certain) boys, or whether they absorb such observation in the rudiments of a female identity—unless, of course, they are "protected" from the opportunity of comprehending the ubiquity and the meaning of these natural phenomena. Now, no doubt, at various stages of childhood observed data will be interpreted with the cognitive means then available, will be perceived in analogy with the organs then most intensely experienced, and will be endowed with the impulses then prevailing. Dreams, myths, and cults attest to the fact that the vagina has and retains (for both sexes) connotations of a devouring mouth as well as an eliminating sphincter, in addition to being a bleeding wound. However, the cumulative experience of being and becoming a man or a woman cannot, I believe, be entirely dependent upon fearful analogies and phantasies. Sensory reality and logical conclusion are given form by kinesthetic experience and by series of memories which "make sense"; and in this total actuality the existence of a *productive inner-bodily space* safely set in the center of female form and carriage has, I think, a reality superior to that of the missing organ.

This whole controversy has, I am sure, little to do with the starting point of most participants in this symposium. If I nevertheless start from here, it is because I believe that a future formulation of sex-differences must at least include post-Freudian insights in order not to succumb to the repressions and denials of pre-Freudian days.

3.

Let me present here an observation which makes my point wordlessly. Since it has already been presented on a number of other occasions, I should admit that I am the kind of clinical worker in whose mind a few observations linger for a long time. Such observations are marked by a combination of being surprised by the unexpected and yet somehow confirmed by something long awaited. For this same reason, I am apt to present such observations to various audiences, hoping each time that understanding may be deepened.

It was in the observation of preadolescent children that I was enabled to observe sex-differences in a nonclinical setting. The children were Californian boys and girls, aged ten, eleven, and twelve years, who twice a year came to be measured, interviewed, and tested in the "Guidance Study" of the University of California. It speaks for the feminine genius of the director of the study, Jean Walker Macfarlane, that for over more than two decades the children (and their parents) not only came with regularity, but confided their thoughts with little reservation and, in fact, with much "zest" —to use Jean Macfarlane's favorite word. That means, they were confident of being appreciated as growing individuals and eager to reveal and to demonstrate what (so they had been convincingly told) was useful to know and might be helpful to others. Since this psychoanalyst, before joining the California study, had made it his business to interpret play-behavior—a nonverbal approach which had helped him to understand better what his small patients were not able to communicate in words—it was decided that he would test his clinical hypotheses by securing a number of play-constructions from each child. Over a span of two years, I saw 150 boys and 150 girls three times and presented them, one at a time, with the task of constructing a "scene" with toys on a table. The toys were rather ordinary: a family; some uniformed figures (policeman, aviator, Indian, monk, etc.); wild and domestic animals; furniture; automobiles. But I also provided a variety of blocks. The children were asked to imagine that the table was a moving picture studio; the toys, actors and props; and they themselves, moving picture directors. They were to arrange on the table "an exciting scene from an imaginary moving picture," and then tell the plot. This was recorded, the scene photographed, and the child complimented. It may be necessary to add that no "interpretation" was given.

The observer then compared the individual constructions with about ten years of data in the files to see whether it provided some key to the major determinants of the child's inner development. On the whole this proved helpful, but that is not the point to be made here. The experiment also made possible a comparison of all play constructions with each other.

A few of the children went about the task with the somewhat contemptuous attitude of one doing something which was not exactly worth the effort of a young person already in his teens, but almost all of these bright and willing youngsters in somber jeans and gay dresses were drawn to the challenge by that eagerness to serve and to please which characterized the whole population of the study. And once they were "involved," certain properties of the task took over and guided them.

It soon became evident that among these properties the spatial one was dominant. Only half of the scenes were "exciting," and only a handful had anything to do with moving pictures. In fact, the stories told at the end were for the most part brief and in no way comparable to the thematic richness evidenced in verbal tests. But the care and (one is tempted to say) esthetic responsibility with which the children selected blocks and toys and then arranged them according to an apparently deeply held sense of spatial propriety was astounding. At the end, it seemed to be a sudden feeling of "now it's right" which made them come to a sense of completion and, as if awakening from a wordless experience, turn to me and say, "I am ready now,"—meaning: to tell you what this is all about.

I, myself, was most interested in defining the tools and developing the art of observing not only imaginative themes but also spatial configurations in relation to stages of the life cycle, and, of course, in checking psychoanalytic assumptions concerning the sources and forms of neurotic tension in prepuberty. Sex-differences thus were not the initial focus of my interest in spatial behavior. I concentrated my attention on how these constructions-in-progress moved forward to the edge of the table or back to the wall behind it; how they rose to shaky heights or remained close to the table surface; how they were spread over the available space or constricted to a portion of the space. That all of this "says" something about the constructor is the open secret of all "projective techniques." This, too, cannot be discussed here. But soon I realized that in evaluating a child's play-construction, I had to take into consideration the fact that girls and boys used space differently, and that certain configurations occurred strikingly often in the constructions of one sex and rarely in those of the other.

The differences themselves were so simple that at first they seemed a matter of course. History in the meantime has offered a slogan for it: the girls emphasized inner and the boys outer space.

This difference I was soon able to state in such simple configurational terms that other observers, when shown photographs of the constructions without knowing the sex of the constructor (nor, indeed, having any idea of my thoughts concerning the possible meaning of the differences), could sort the photographs according to the configurations most dominant in them, and this significantly in the statistical sense. These independent ratings showed that considerably more than two thirds of what I subsequently called male configurations occurred in scenes constructed by boys, and more than two thirds of the "female" configurations in the constructions of girls. I will here omit the finer points which still characterized the atypical scenes as clearly built by a boy or by a girl. This, then, is typical: the girl's scene is an *interior* scene, represented either as a configuration of furniture without any surrounding walls, or by a *simple enclosure* built with blocks. In the girl's scene, people and animals are mostly *within* such an interior or enclosure, and they are primarily people or animals in a *static* (sitting, standing) position. Girls' enclosures consist of *low walls*, i.e. only one block high, except for an occasional elaborate *doorway*. These interiors of houses with or without walls were, for the most part, expressly *peaceful*. Often, a little girl was playing the piano. In a number of cases, however, the *interior was intruded* by animals or dangerous men. Yet the idea of an intruding creature did not necessarily lead to the defensive erection of walls or the closing of doors. Rather the majority of these intrusions have an element of humor and of pleasurable excitement.

Boys' scenes are either houses with *elaborate walls* or *facades with protrusions* such as cones or cylinders representing ornaments or cannons. There are *high towers;* and there are *exterior scenes.* In boys' constructions more people and animals are *outside* enclosures or buildings, and there are more *automotive objects* and *animals moving* along streets and intersections. There are elaborate automotive *accidents,* but also traffic channeled or arrested by the *policeman.* While high structures are prevalent in the configurations of the boys, there is also much play with the danger of collapse or *downfall; ruins* were exclusively boys' constructions.

The male and female spaces, then, were dominated, respectively, by height and downfall and by strong motion and its channelization or arrest; and by static interiors which were open or simply enclosed, and peaceful or intruded upon. It may come as a surprise to some, and seem a matter of course to others, that here sexual differences in the organization of a play space seem to parallel the morphology of genital differentiation itself: in the male, an *external* organ, erectible and *intrusive* in character, serving the channelization of *mobile* sperm cells; *internal* organs in the female, with vestibular *access,* leading to *statically expectant* ova. The question is, what *is* really surprising about this, and what only too obvious, and in either case, what does it tell us about the two sexes?

4.

Since I first presented these data a decade and a half ago to workers in different fields, some standard interpretations have not yielded an iota. There are, of course, derisive reactions which take it for granted that a psychoanalyst would want to read the bad old symbols into this kind of data. And indeed, Freud did note more than half a century ago that "a house is the only regularly occurring symbol of the (whole) human body in dreams." But there is quite a methodological step (not to be specified here) from the occurrence of a symbol in dreams and a configuration created in actual space. Nevertheless, the purely psychoanalytic or somatic explanation has been advanced that the scenes reflect the preadolescent's preoccupation with his own sexual organs.

The purely "social" interpretation, on the other hand, denies the necessity to see anything symbolic or, indeed, somatic in these configurations. It takes it for granted that boys love the outdoors and girls the indoors, or at any rate that they see their respective roles assigned to the indoors of houses and to the great outdoors of adventure, to tranquil feminine love for family and children and to high masculine aspiration.

One cannot help agreeing with both interpretations—up to a point. Of course, whatever social role is associated with one's physique will be expressed thematically in any playful or artistic representation. And, of course, under conditions of special tension or preoccupation with one part of the body, that body part may be recognizable in play-configurations. The spokesmen for the anatomical and for the social interpretations are thus both right if they insist that neither possibility may be ignored. But this does not make either exclusively right.

A pure interpretation in terms of social role leaves many questions unanswered. If the boys thought primarily of their present or anticipated roles, why, for example, is the policeman their favorite toy, traffic stopped dead a frequent scene? If vigorous activity outdoors is a determinant of the boys' scenes, why did they not arrange *any* sports fields on the play table? (One tomboyish girl did.) Why did the girls' love for home life not result in an increase in high walls and closed doors as guarantors of intimacy and security? And could the role of playing the piano in the bosom of their families really be considered representative of what these girls (some of them passionate horseback riders and all future automobilists) wanted to do most or, indeed, thought they should pretend they wanted to do most? Thus the boys' *caution outdoors* and the girls' *goodness indoors* in response to the explicit instruction to construct an *exciting movie scene* suggested dynamic dimensions and acute conflicts not explained by a theory of mere compliance with cultural and conscious roles.

I would suggest an altogether more inclusive interpretation, according to which a profound difference exists between the sexes in the experience of the groundplan of the human body. The spatial phenomenon observed here would then express two principles of arranging space which correspond to the male and female principles in body construction. These may receive special emphasis in pre-puberty, and maybe in some other stages of life as well, but they are relevant throughout life to the elaboration of sex-roles in cultural space-times. Such an interpretation cannot be "proven," of course, by the one observation offered here. The question is whether it is in line with observations of spatial behavior in other media and at other ages; whether it can be made a plausible part of a developmental theory; and whether, indeed, it gives to other sex-differences closely related to male and female structure and function a more convincing order. On the other hand, it would not be contradicted by the fact that other media of observation employed to test male and female performance might reveal few or no sexual differences in areas of the mind which have the function of securing verbal or cognitive agreement on matters dominated by the mathematical nature of the universe and the verbal agreement of cultural traditions. Such agreement, in fact, may have as its very function the *correction* of what differentiates the experience of the sexes, even as it also corrects the idiosyncrasies separating other classes of men.

The play-constructing children in Berkeley, California will lead us into a number of spatial considerations, especially concerning feminine development and outlook. Here I will say little about men; their accomplishments in the conquest of geographic space and of scientific fields and in the dissemination of ideas speak loudly for themselves and confirm traditional values of masculinity. Yet the play-constructing boys in Berkeley may give us pause: on the world scene, do we not see a supremely gifted yet somewhat boyish mankind playing with history and technology, and this following a male pattern as embarrassingly simple (if technologically complex) as the play-constructions of the preadolescent? Do we not see the themes of the toy microcosm dominating an expanding human space: height, penetration, and speed; collision, explosion—and cosmic super-police? In the meantime, women have found their identities in the care suggested in their bodies and in the needs of their issue, and seem to have taken it for granted that the outer world space belongs to the men.

5.

Many of the original conclusions of psychoanalysis concerning womanhood hinge on the so-called genital trauma, i.e. the little girl's sudden comprehension of the fact that she does not and never will have a penis. The assumed prevalence of envy in women; the assumption that the future baby is a substitute for the penis; the interpretation that the girl turns from the mother to the father because she finds that the mother not only cheated her out of a penis but has been cheated herself; and finally the woman's disposition to abandon (male) activity and aggressivity for the sake of a "passive-masochistic" orientation: all of these depend on "the trauma," and all have been built into elaborate explanations of feminity. They all exist; and their psychic truth can be shown by psychoanalysis, although it must always be suspected that a special method bares truths especially true under the circumstances created by the method, here the venting in free association of hidden resentments and repressed traumata. These truths, however, assume the character of very partial truths within a theory of feminine development which would assume the early relevance of the productive interior and would thus allow for a shift of theoretical emphasis from the loss of an external organ to a sense of vital inner potential; from a hateful contempt of the mother to a solidarity with her and other women; from a "passive" renunciation of male activity to the purposeful and competent activity of one endowed with ovaries and a uterus; and from a masochistic pleasure in pain to an ability to stand (and to understand) pain as a meaningful aspect of human experience in general, and of the feminine role in particular. And so it is, in the "fully feminine" woman, as such outstanding writers as Helena Deutsch have recognized even though their nomenclature was tied to the psychopathological term "masochism" (a word which is derived from the name of an Austrian man and novelist who described the perversion of being sexually aroused and satisfied by having pain inflicted on him, even as the tendency to inflict it has been named after the Marquis de Sade).

When this is seen, much now dispersed data will, I believe, fall into line. However, a clinician must ask himself in passing what kind of thinking may have permitted such a nomenclature to arise and to be assented to by outstanding women clinicians. This thinking is, I believe, to be found not only in the psychopathological beginnings of psychoanalysis, but also in the original analytic-atomistic method employed by it. In science, our capacity to think atomistically corresponds to the nature of matter to a high degree and thus leads to the mastery over matter. But when we apply atomistic thinking to man, we break him down into isolated fragments rather than into constituent elements. In fact, when we look at man in a morbid state, he is already fragmented; so that in psychopathology an atomizing mind meets a phenomenon of fragmentation and is apt to mistake fragments for atoms. In psychoanalysis we repeat for our own encouragement (and as an argument against others) that human nature can best be studied in a state of partial breakdown or, at any rate, of marked conflict because—so we say— a conflict delineates borderlines and clarifies the forces which collide on these borderlines. As Freud himself put it, we see a crystal's structure only when it cracks. But a crystal, on the one hand, and an organism or a personality, on the other, differ in the fact that one is inanimate and the other an organic whole which cannot be broken up without a withering of the parts. The ego (in the psychoanalytic sense of a guardian of inner continuity) is in a pathological state more or less inactivated; that is, it loses its capacity to organize personality and experience and to relate itself to other egos in mutual activation. To that extent its irrational defenses are "easier to study" in a state of conflict and isolation than is the ego of a person in vivid interaction with other persons. Yet I do not believe that we can entirely reconstruct the ego's normal functions from an understanding of its dysfunctions, nor that we can understand all vital conflict as neurotic conflict. This, then, would characterize a post-Freudian position: the complexes and conflicts unearthed by psychoanalysis in its first breakthrough to human nature are recognized as existing; they do threaten to dominate the developmental and accidental crises of life. But the freshness and wholeness of experience and the opportunities arising with a resolved crisis can, in an ongoing life, transcend trauma and defense. To illustrate this, let me briefly remark on the often repeated statement that the little girl at a given stage "turns to" her father, whereas in all preceding stages she had been attached to the mother. Actually, Freud insisted only that a theoretical libido was thus turning from one "object" to another, a theory which was, at one time, scientifically pleasing because it corresponded to a simple and (in principle) measurable transfer of energy. Developmentally seen, however, the girl turns to the father at a time when she is quite a different person from the one she was when primarily dependent on her mother. She has normally learned the nature of an "object relationship," once and for all, from the mother. The relationship to the father, then, is of a different kind, in that it happens when the girl has learned to trust (and does not need to retest) basic relationships. She autonomously develops a new form of love for a being who in turn is, or should be, ready to be responsive to the budding (and teasing) woman in her. The total process thus has many more aspects than can be condensed in the statement that the girl turns her libido from the mother to the father. Such transfer can, in fact, be reconstructed only where the ego has been inactivated in some of its capacity to reorganize experience in line with emotional, physical, and cognitive maturation; and only then can it be said that the girl turns to the father *because* she is disappointed in the mother over what the mother has seemingly refused to give her, namely, a penis. Now, no doubt, some unavoidable or excessive disappointment, and the expectation that a new relationship will make up for all the deficiencies of all the old ones, play an eminent role in all changes of attachment from an old to a new person or activity. But in any healthy change the fresh opportunities of the new relationship will outweigh the repetitious insistence on old disappointment. No doubt, also, new attachments prepare new disappointments. The increasing commitment to an inner-productive role will cause in the small woman such phantasies as must succumb to censorship and frustration, for example, in the insight that no daughter may give birth to her father's children. No doubt also the very importance of the promises and the limitations of the inner productive space exposes women to a sense of specific loneliness, to a fear of being left empty or deprived of treasures, of remaining unfulfilled and of drying up. This, no less than the strivings and disappointments of the little "oedipus" are fateful ingredients of the human individual and of the whole race. For this very reason it seems decisive not to misinterpret these feelings as totally due to a resentment of not being a boy or of having been mutilated.

It will now be clear why and in what way the children's play constructions evoked in me a response combining the "unexpected and yet awaited." What was unexpected was the domination of the whole space by the sex-differences—a dominance going far beyond the power of any "symbolism" or a "representation" of the morphology of sex organs. The data was "awaited," above all, as nonclinical and nonverbal support of pervasive clinical and developmental impressions concerning the importance of the "inner space" throughout the feminine life cycle. For, as pointed out, clinical observation suggests that in female experience an "inner space" is at the center of despair even as it is the very center of potential fulfillment. Emptiness is the female form of perdition—known at times to men of the inner life (whom we will discuss later), but standard experience for all women. To be left, for her, means to be left empty, to be drained of the blood of the body, the warmth of the heart, the sap of life. How a woman thus can be hurt in depth is a wonder to many a man, and it can arouse both his empathic horror and his refusal to understand. Such hurt can be re-experienced in each menstruation; it is crying to heaven in the mourning over a child; and it becomes a permanent scar in the menopause. Clinically, this "void" is so obvious that generations of clinicians must have had a special reason for not focusing on it. Maybe, even as primitive men banned it with phobic avoidances and magic rituals of purification, the enlightened men of a civilization pervaded by technological pride could meet it only with the interpretation that suffering woman wanted above all what man had, namely, exterior equipment and traditional access to "outer" space. Again, such envy exists and is aggravated in some cultures; but the explanation of it in male terms or the suggestion that it be borne with fatalism and compensated for by a redoubled enjoyment of the feminine equipment (duly certified and accepted as second rate) has not helped women to find their places in the modern world. For it made of womanhood an ubiquitous compensation neurosis marked by a repetitious insistance on being "restored."[1]

---

1. The question of the innermost extent of the woman's total sexual response cannot be discussed here.

6.

In approaching the place of sexual differentiation in basic social organization, I will also call on a visual and nonverbal impression. Recent motion pictures taken in Africa by Washburn and deVore[2] demonstrate vividly the morphology of basic baboon organization. The whole wandering troop in search of food over a certain territory is so organized as to keep within a safe inner space the females who bear future offspring within their bodies or carry their growing young. They are protectively surrounded by powerful males who, in turn, keep their eyes on the horizon, guiding the troop toward available food and guarding it from potential danger. In peacetime, the strong males also protect the "inner circle" of pregnant and nursing females against the encroachments of the relatively weaker and definitely more importunate males. Once danger is spotted, the whole wandering configuration stops and consolidates into an inner space of safety and an outer space of combat. In the center sit the pregnant females and mothers with their newborns. At the periphery are the males best equipped to fight or scare off predators.

I was impressed with these movies not only for their beauty and ingenuity, but because here I could see in the Bush configurations analogous to those in the Berkeley play structures. The baboon pictures, however, can lead us one step further. Whatever the morphological differences between the female and the male baboons' bony structures, postures, and behaviors, they are adapted to their respective tasks of harboring and defending the concentric circles, from the procreative womb to the limits of the "productive" and defensible territory. Thus morphological trends "fit" given necessities and are therefore elaborated by basic social organization. And it deserves emphasis that, even among the baboons, the greatest warriors display a chivalry which permits the female baboons, for example, to have weaker shoulders and lesser fighting equipment.

Whether, when, and in what respects, then, a female in any setting is "weaker" is a matter to be decided not on the basis of comparative tests of isolated muscles, capacities, or traits but on that of the functional fitness of each item as part of an organism which, in turn, fits into an ecology of divided function.

Human society and technology has, of course, transcended evolutionary arrangement, making room for cultural triumphs and liberties as well as for physical and psychological maladaptation on a large scale. But when we speak of biologically given strengths and

---

2. Three films taken in Kenya, 1959: "Baboon Behavior," "Baboon Social Organization," and "Baboon Ecology."

weaknesses in the human female, we may yet have to accept as one measure of all difference the biological rockbottom of sexual differentiation. In this, the woman's productive inner space may well remain the principal criterion, whether she chooses to build her life partially or wholly around it or not. At any rate, many of the testable items on the long list of "inborn" differences between human males and females can be shown to have a meaningful function within an ecology which is built, as any mammalian ecology must be, around the fact that the human foetus must be carried inside the womb for a given number of months; and that the infant must be suckled or, at any rate, raised within a maternal world best staffed at first by the mother (and this for the sake of her own awakened motherliness as well as for the newborn's needs), with a gradual addition of other women. Here years of specialized woman-hours of work are involved. It makes sense, then, that the little girl, the bearer of ova and of maternal powers, tends to survive her birth more surely and is a tougher creature, to be plagued, to be sure, by many small ailments, but more resistant to some man-killing diseases (for example, of the heart) and with a longer life expectancy. It also makes sense that she is able earlier than boys to concentrate on details immediate in time and space, and has throughout a finer discrimination for things seen, touched, and heard. To these she reacts more vividly, more personally, and with greater compassion. More easily touched and touchable, however, she is said also to recover faster, ready to react again and elsewhere. That all of this is essential to the "biological" task of reacting to the differential needs of others, especially infants, will not appear to be a farfetched interpretation; nor will it, in this context, seem a deplorable inequality that in the employment of larger muscles she shows less vigor, speed, and coordination. The little girl also learns to be more easily content within a limited circle of activities and shows less resistance to control and less impulsivity of the kind that later leads boys and men to "delinquency." All of these and more certified "differences" could be shown to have corollaries in our play constructions.

Now it is clear that much of the basic schema suggested here as female also exists in some form in all men and decisively so in men of special giftedness—or weakness. The inner life which characterizes some artistic and creative men certainly also compensates for their being biologically men by helping them to specialize in that inwardness and sensitive indwelling (the German *Innigkeit*) usually ascribed to women. They are prone to cyclic swings of mood while they carry conceived ideas to fruition and toward the act of disciplined creation. The point is that in women the basic schema exists within a *total optimum configuration* such as cultures have every reason to nurture in the majority of women, and this for the sake of collective survival as well as individual fulfillment. It makes little sense, then, when discussing basic sex-differences to quote the deviations and accomplishments (or both) of exceptional men or women without an inclusive account of their many-sided personalities, their special conflicts and their complex life histories. On the other hand, one should also emphasize (and especially so in a post-Puritan civilization which continues to decree predestination by mercilessly typing individuals) that successive stages of life offer growing and maturing individuals ample leeway for free variation in essential sameness.

Thus only a total configurational approach—somatic, historical, individual—can help us to see the differences of functioning and experiencing in context rather than in isolated and senseless comparison. Woman, then, is not "more passive" than man simply because her central biological function forces her or permits her to be active in a manner tuned to inner-bodily processes, or because she may be gifted with a certain intimacy and contained intensity of feeling, or because she may choose to dwell in the protected inner circle within which maternal care can flourish. Nor is she "more masochistic" because she must accept inner periodicities (Benedek) in addition to the pain of childbirth, which is explained in the Bible as the eternal penalty for Eve's delinquent behavior and interpreted by writers as recent as de Beauvoir as "a hostile element within her own body." Taken together with the phenomena of sexual life and motherhood, it is obvious that woman's knowledge of pain makes her a "dolorosa" in a deeper sense than one who is addicted to small pains. She is, rather, one who "takes pains" to understand and alleviate suffering, and who can train others in the forbearance necessary to stand unavoidable pain. She is a "masochist," then, only when she exploits pain perversely or vindictively, which means that she steps out of, rather than deeper into, her female function. By the same token, a woman is pathologically passive only when she becomes too passive within a sphere of efficacy and personal integration which includes her disposition for female activity.

One argument, however, is hard to counter. Woman, through the ages (at any rate, the patriarchal ones), has lent herself to a variety of roles conducive to an exploitation of masochistic potentials: she has let herself be incarcerated and immobilized, enslaved and infantilized, prostituted and exploited, deriving from it at best what in psychopathology we call "secondary gains" of devious dominance. This fact, however, could be satisfactorily explained only within a new kind of biocultural history which (and this is one of my main points) would first have to overcome the prejudiced opinion that woman must be, or will be, what she is or has been under particular historical conditions.

7.

Am I saying, then, that "anatomy *is* destiny"? Yes, it is destiny, insofar as it determines the potentials of physiological functioning, and its limitations. But anatomy also, to an extent, co-determines personality configurations. The modalities of woman's commitment and involvement, for better *and* for worse, also reflect the groundplan of her body. We may mention only woman's capacity on many levels of existence to (actively) include, to accept, to "have and hold" —but also to hold on, and to hold in. She may be protective with high selectivity, and overprotective without discrimination. That she must protect means that she must rely on protection—and she may demand overprotection. She too has her organ of intrusion, the nipple which nurses; and her wish to succor can, indeed, become intrusive and oppressive. It is, in fact, of such exaggerations and deviations that many men and also women think when the unique potentials of womanhood are discussed.

In all of this, however, the problem is not whether a woman is "more so" than a man, but how much she varies within womanhood, and what she makes of it within the leeway of her stage of life and of her historical and economic opportunities. For man, in addition to having a body, is *some*body; which means he is an indivisible personality *and* a defined member of a group. In this sense Napoleon's dictum that *History is destiny,* which was, I believe, to be counterpointed by Freud's dictum that destiny lies in anatomy (and one often must know what a man tried to counterpoint with his most one-sided dicta) is equally valid. In other words: anatomy, history, and personality are our *combined destiny.*

Men, of course, have shared and taken care of some of the concerns for which women stand: each sex can transcend itself to feel and to represent the concerns of the other. For even as real women harbor a legitimate as well as a compensatory masculinity, so real men can partake of motherliness—if permitted to do so by powerful mores.

In search of an observation which bridges biology and history, an extreme historical example comes to mind in which women elevated their procreative function to a style of life when their men seemed totally defeated.

This story was highlighted for me on two occasions when I participated in conferences in the Caribbean and learned of family patterns prevailing throughout the islands. Churchmen have had reason to deplore, and anthropologists to explore, the pattern of Caribbean family life, obviously an outgrowth of the slavery days of plantation America, which extended from the northeast coast of Brazil through the Caribbean half-circle into the southeast of the present United States. Plantations, of course, were agricultural factories owned and operated by gentlemen whose cultural and economic identity had its roots in a supraregional upper class. They were worked by slaves, that is, by men who, being mere equipment, were put to use when and where necessary, and who often had to relinquish all chance of becoming the masters of their families and communities. Thus the women were left with the offspring of a variety of men who could give neither provision nor protection, nor provide any identity except that of a subordinate species. The family system which ensued is described in the literature in terms of circumscriptions: the rendering of "sexual services" between persons who cannot be called anything more definite than "lovers"; "maximum instability" in the sexual lives of young girls, who often "relinquish" the care of their offspring to their mothers; and mothers and grandmothers who determine the "standardized mode of co-activity" which is the minimum requirement for calling a group of individuals a family. These are, then, called "household groups"—single dwellings occupied by people sharing a common food supply. These households are "matrifocal," a word understating the grandiose role of the all-powerful grandmother-fugure, who will encourage her daughters to leave their infants with her, or at any rate to stay with her as long as they continue to bear children. Motherhood thus became community life; and where churchmen could find little or no morality, and casual observers little or no order at all, the mothers and grandmothers had to become fathers and grandfathers, in the sense that they exerted the only continuous influence resulting in an ever newly improvised set of rules for the economic obligations of the men who had fathered the children. They upheld the rules of incestuous avoidance. Above all, so it seems to me, they provided the only superidentity which was left open after the enslavement of the men, namely, that of the worthwhileness of a human infant irrespective of his parentage. It is well known how many little white gentlemen benefited from the extended fervor of the nurturant Negro woman—southern mammies, creole das, or Brazilian babas. This phenomenal caring is, of course, being played down by the racists as mere servitude, while the predominance of personal warmth in

Caribbean women is decried by moralists as African sensualism or idolized as true feminity by refugees from "Continental" womanhood. One may, however, see at the roots of this maternalism a grandiose gesture of human adaptation which has given the area of the Caribbean (now searching for a political and economic pattern to do justice to its cultural unity) both the promise of a positive maternal identity and the threat of a negative male one: for the fact that identity relied on the mere worth of being born has undoubtedly weakened economic aspiration in many men.

That this has been an important historical issue can be seen in the life of Simon Bolivar. This "liberator of South America" originated in the coastal region of Venezuela, which is one anchorpoint of the great Caribbean half-circle. When in 1827 Bolivar liberated Caracas and entered it in triumph, he recognized the Negress Hipolita, his erstwhile wetnurse, in the crowd. He dismounted and "threw himself in the arms of the Negress who wept with joy." Two years earlier, he had written to his sister: "I enclose a letter to my mother Hipolita so that you give her all she wants and deal with her as if she were my mother; her milk fed my life, and I knew no other father than she" (translation not mine). Whatever personal reason can be found for Bolivar's attitude toward Hipolita (he had lost his mother when he was nine, etc.) is amply matched by the historical significance of the fact that he could play up this relationship as a propaganda item within that often contradictory ideology of race and origin which contributed to his charisma throughout the continent he conquered.

That continent does not concern us here. But as for the Caribbean area, the matrifocal theme explains much of a certain disbalance between extreme trustfulness and weakness of initiative which could be exploited by native dictators as well as by foreign capital and has now become the concern of the erstwhile colonial masters as well as of the emancipated leaders of various island groups. Knowing this, we may understand that the bearded group of men and boys who have taken over one of the islands represents a deliberately new type of man who insists on proving that the Caribbean male can earn his worth in production as well as in procreation without the imposition of "continental" leadership or ownership.

This transformation of a colorful island area into an inner space structured by woman is an almost clinical example to be applied with caution. And yet it is only one story out of that unofficial history which is as yet to be written for all areas and eras: of how women have attempted to balance the official history of territories and domains, markets and empires; the history of women's quiet creativity in preserving and restoring what official history had torn apart. Some stirrings in contemporary historiography, such as attempts to describe closely the everyday atmosphere of a given locality in a given historical era, seem to bespeak a growing awareness of a need for, shall we say, an integrated history.

8.

We speak of anatomical, historical, and psychological facts; and yet, it must be clear that facts reliably ascertained by the methods of these three fields by the same token lose a most vital interconnection. Man is, at one and the same time, part of a somatic order of things, and part of a personal and of a social one. To avoid identifying these orders with established fields, we may call them Soma, Psyche, and Polis, and yet know that each can be hyphenated with the other to designate new fields of inquiry such as psycho-somatic and psycho-social. Each order guards a certain intactness and also offers a leeway of optional or at least workable choices; while man lives in all three and must work out their complementarities and contradictions.

Soma is the principle of the *organism,* living its *life cycle.* But the female Soma is not only comprised of what is within a woman's skin (and clothes). It includes a mediatorship in evolution, genetic as well as socio-genetic, by which she creates in each child the somatic (sensual, and sensory) basis for his physical, cultural, and individual identity. This mission, once a child is conceived, must be completed. It is woman's unique job. But no woman lives or needs to live only in this extended somatic sphere. She must make (or else neglect) decisions as a citizen and worker, and of course, as an individual; and the modern world offers her ever greater leeway in choosing, planning, or renouncing her somatic tasks more knowingly and responsibly.

The sphere of *citizenship* I call Polis because I want to emphasize that it reaches as far as the borderlines of what one has recognized as one's "city," and it is clear that modern communication makes such a communality ever larger if not global. In this sphere women can be shown to share with men a close sameness of intellectual orientation and capacity for work and leadership. "Political" equality, however, can live up to this fact only by encompassing for women a position in the political sphere which goes beyond an occasional voice (whispered or shouted) and a periodic vote for male politicians and for issues exclusively determined by men. It even goes beyond the active participation in politics and government. In this sphere, too, the influence of women will not be fully actualized until it reflects without apology the facts of the "inner space" and the potentialities and needs of the feminine psyche. It is as yet unpredictable what the tasks and roles and opportunities and job specifications will be once women are not merely adapted to male jobs but when they learn to adapt jobs to themselves. Such a revolutionary reappraisal may even lead to the insight that jobs now called masculine force men, too, to inhuman adjustments.

In the sphere of Psyche, psychoanalysis has come to understand an organizing principle called ego.[3] Ego-organization mediates between somatic and personal experience and political actuality in the widest sense. To do so it uses psychological mechanisms common to both sexes—a fact which makes intelligent communication, mutual understanding, and social organization possible. It is in the ego that the equivalence of all truly individualized experience has its organizing center, for the ego is the guardian of the *indivisibility of the person.* No doubt militant individualism has inflated this core of individuality to the point where it seemed altogether free of somatic and social considerations. However, psychoanalysis is making it clear that the active strength of the ego (and especially the identity within the individuality) is inseparable from the power of somatic development and of social organization. Here, then, the fact that a woman, whatever else she may also be, never is not-a-woman, creates unique relations between her individuality, her bodily intimacy, and her productive potentials, and demands that feminine ego-strength be studied and defined in its own right.

It should be clear, then, that I am using my definitions concerning the central importance of woman's procreative task not in a renewed attempt to "doom" every woman to perpetual motherhood and to deny her the equivalence of individuality and the equality of citizenship. But since a woman is never not-a-woman, she can see her long-range goals only in those modes of activity which include and integrate her natural dispositions. An emancipated woman thus does not necessarily accept comparisons with more "active" male proclivities as a measure of her equivalence, even if and after it has become quite clear that she can match man's performance and competence in most spheres of achievement. True equality can only mean the right to be uniquely creative.

---

3. The term ego—in all but narrow professional circles—is fighting a losing battle against its popular and philosophical namesakes, the inflated and the self-centered and self-conscious "egos." Nevertheless, the term must be used as long as the concept represents an important trend in psychoanalytic theory.

We may well hope, therefore, that there is something in woman's specific creativity which has waited only for a clarification of her relationship to masculinity (including her own) in order to assume her share of leadership in those fateful human affairs which so far have been left entirely in the hands of gifted and driven men, and often of men whose genius of leadership eventually has yielded to ruthless self-aggrandizement. Mankind now obviously depends on new kinds of social inventions and on institutions which guard and cultivate that which nurses and nourishes, cares and tolerates, includes and preserves.

Before he left Harvard, Paul Tillich in a conversation expressed uneasiness over the clinical preoccupation with an "adaptive ego" which, he felt, might support (these are my words) further attempts at manufacturing a mankind feeling so "adapted" that it would be unable to face "ultimate concerns." I agreed that psychoanalysis was in danger of becoming part of such vain streamlining of existence; but that in its origin and essence, it intends to *free* man for "ultimate concerns." For such concerns can begin to be ultimate only in those rare moments and places where neurotic resentments end and where mere adaptation is transcended. I think he agreed. One may add that man's Ultimate has too often been visualized as an infinity which begins where the male conquest of outer spaces ends, and a domain where an even more omnipotent and omniscient Being must be submissively acknowledged. The Ultimate, however, may well be found also in the Immediate, which has so largely been the domain of woman and of the inward mind. Such considerations would lead us to the *temporal* aspects (here neglected throughout) of the space-time experience of womanhood.

Data from a survey of college women reveal that a woman's life goals, particularly her educational and occupational aspirations, are guided by the type of sex-role ideology acquired in adolescence. These two sex-role ideologies—traditional and contemporary—have two distinct life patterns, within each of which women are able to find fulfillment and meaning in their life.

JEAN LIPMAN-BLUMEN

How Ideology Shapes Women's Lives

The "women's liberation" movement has brought to the fore the age-old question of what kinds of behavior are socially appropriate for women and men. It is often said that women tend to act on the basis of feelings and emotions rather than on the basis of reason. The motivating force behind female behavior is rarely seen as being ideology. It is becoming increasingly apparent, however, that certain ideologies can predict the values and behavior of women with remarkable accuracy. These powerful systems of beliefs, which shape the destiny of women in ways never imagined by Freud, are transmitted implicitly rather than explicitly; they usually guide the behavior of women silently and without their being consciously aware of it.

Such ideologies are largely based on a woman's concept of what kinds of behavior are appropriate to her role as a female. In the study I shall describe here female-role ideology referred primarily to a woman's system of beliefs regarding the appropriate behavior of women with respect to men. The study, which involved an extensive survey of the life plans of married women, was conducted under the auspices of the Radcliffe Institute in Cambridge, Mass., in 1968 (before the women's liberation movement had had a major impact). A detailed questionnaire was mailed to the wives of graduate students in the Boston area. Out of the 1,868 responses a sub-sample of 1,012 wives who had attended college was selected for analysis. The questionnaire inquired into early childhood experiences, academic achievements and plans, past and present family situations, personal values and life goals.

The age of the women who responded ranged from 18 to 54, with 23.4 years as the median. Forty-two percent of the women had been married one year or less, another 43 percent had been married from two to five years and 15 percent had been married more than five years. The mean number of years married was 3.2. Sixty percent of the women had no children, 21 percent had one child, 12 percent had two children, 5 percent had three children and 2 percent had four or more children. Since the women selected for analysis were all married to graduate students, their socioeconomic status was fairly homogeneous. Their original family backgrounds, however, were quite varied and in their diversity were presumably not unlike the backgrounds of the larger population of women who have attended college.

An index of female-role ideology was developed to encompass two major dimensions of the adult female role: an internal dimension, based on issues of task-sharing between husband and wife, and an external dimension, related to patterns of appropriate female behavior outside the home. Responses to a six-item scale were summed to obtain a female-role-ideology score. Although sex-role ideologies form a continuum, we grouped the respondents into two polar categories, which we labeled "traditional" and "contemporary." An oversimplified version of the traditional ideology is the belief that under ordinary circumstances women belong in the home, caring for children and carrying out domestic duties, whereas men are responsible for the financial support of the family. The contemporary ideology holds that the relationships between men and women are ideally egalitarian and that husbands and wives may share domestic, child-rearing and financial responsibilities. In our study sample 27 percent of the women adhered to the traditional ideology and 73 percent held the contemporary view.

Studies by Ruth E. Hartley and others in the early 1960's have shown that by the age of five, children have developed a sex-role ideology with well-defined notions of appropriate behavior for men and women. Because girls are presumably socialized at an early age to either the traditional or the contemporary sex-role ideology, the belief system is likely to shape much of their life pattern. Here a number of important questions arise. What kind of family do women with the contemporary or traditional ideologies come from? What adolescent relationships did they have with their parents? How is female-role ideology related to a woman's present life-style? How does it affect her life choices, particularly her educational and occupational aspirations? Are the contemporary and traditional ideologies associated with different hierarchies of values? Are married women with the contemporary viewpoint as happy with their life as women with the traditional viewpoint?

In America college education is regarded as a major avenue to career opportunities and a desirable style of life. Therefore it is not surprising that there is a strong relation between the educational aspirations of a college woman and her plans to pursue a professional career. What link is there, if any, between a woman's concept of her sex role and her educational plans?

In our study educational aspiration was measured by the response to the question: "What is the highest level of academic training that you expect to obtain?" As I have noted, all the women in the

EDUCATIONAL ASPIRATION

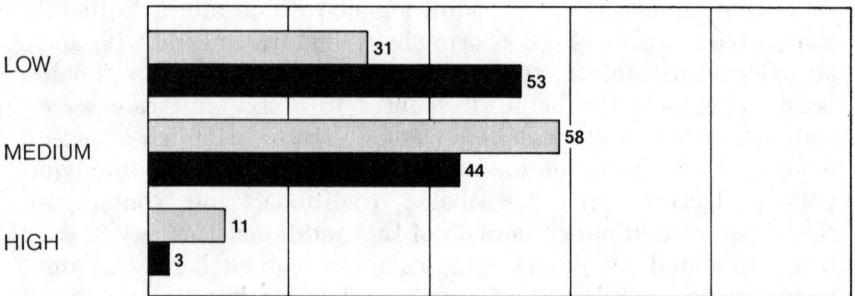

LOW	31 / 53
MEDIUM	58 / 44
HIGH	11 / 3

MODE OF ACHIEVEMENT

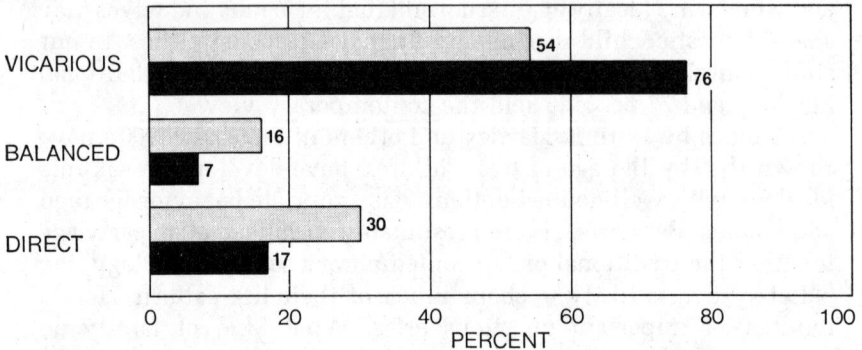

VICARIOUS	54 / 76
BALANCED	16 / 7
DIRECT	30 / 17

0   20   40   60   80   100
PERCENT

SEX-ROLE IDEOLOGY affects a woman's educational aspirations and how she seeks to satisfy her need for achievement outside the home. Women with a contemporary view (*gray bars*) have higher educational goals and are more likely to satisfy their achievement needs through their own efforts than women who hold a traditional view (*black bars*).

study sample had completed at least part of a college program. The responses were grouped into three categories: low aspiration, medium aspiration and high aspiration. Women with low aspiration did not plan to seek a degree beyond the bachelor level; those with medium aspiration planned academic work up to and including a master's degree; those with high aspiration planned doctoral or post-doctoral studies.

Analysis of the data revealed that there was a strong interaction between a woman's concept of the female role and her educational aspiration. More than half of the women who held the traditional view of the female role did not plan to seek a degree beyond the bachelor's level, whereas a majority of the women with the contemporary viewpoint aspired to graduate studies, with 58 percent having medium aspiration and 11 percent having high aspiration. Only 3 percent of the women with the traditional viewpoint had high educational aspiration (see illustration on page 282).

In order to gain a more precise understanding of how sex-role ideology is related to educational aspiration we examined a possible linking factor: mode of achievement. Mode of achievement is a measure of how a woman seeks to satisfy her need for achievement outside the home. There were three categories for mode of achievement: direct, balanced and vicarious. Women who preferred the direct mode felt it necessary to satisfy their achievement needs completely or predominantly through their own efforts; those who chose the balanced mode placed equal weights on their husband's accomplishments and on their own; those who selected the vicarious

MODE OF ACHIEVEMENT

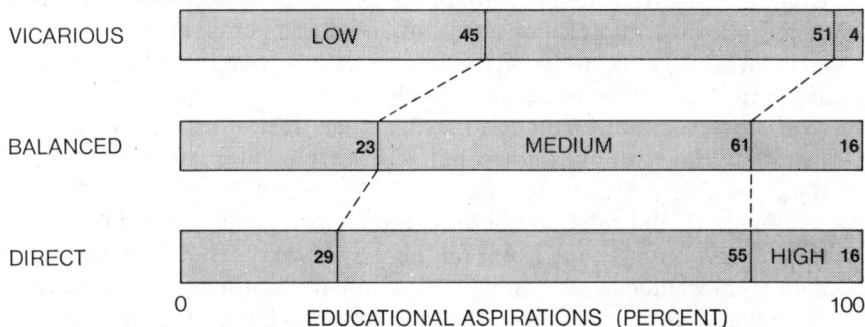

VICARIOUS	LOW 45	51 4
BALANCED	23 MEDIUM 61	16
DIRECT	29 55 HIGH 16	

0   EDUCATIONAL ASPIRATIONS (PERCENT)   100

MODE OF ACHIEVEMENT and educational aspirations were closely linked. Vicarious achievers tended to have lower educational goals than did the balanced or direct achievers.

mode fulfilled their achievement needs either completely or predominantly through the accomplishments of their husband.

Since girls often are socialized in early childhood to satisfy their achievement needs passively by identification with the accomplishments of their father or their brothers, it is not surprising that they transfer this vicarious mode of achievement to their husband when they marry. The survey data show the strength of such socialization: a majority of all the women in the sample, both in the contemporary and in the traditional categories, sought to satisfy their achievement needs vicariously. As might be expected, those with the traditional ideology adhered much more to the vicarious mode, with 76 percent selecting this means of satisfying their achievement needs compared with 54 percent of those with the contemporary viewpoint. Almost a third of the college women with the contemporary ideology, but only a sixth of those with the traditional one, felt that they had to satisfy their achievement needs primarily through their own accomplishments. Relatively few seemed to prefer the balanced mode in which the accomplishments of husband and wife had equal weight.

There was a clear connection between mode of achievement and educational aspiration. Women who were passive, who sought vicarious satisfaction of their achievement needs, were more likely to express low educational aspiration, whereas balanced and direct achievers had higher educational aspirations. The relation between sex-role ideology and educational aspiration changed somewhat for vicarious achievers. Among those who held the contemporary view of female roles and were also vicarious achievers, educational aspiration was reduced so that they could not be distinguished from women in the traditional group in terms of expectations for doctoral or postdoctoral studies. For balanced and direct achievers there was an even stronger relation between sex-role ideology and educational aspiration, with the contemporary-ideology women 19 percent more likely to have plans for doctoral studies than the traditional-ideology women, who strongly tended not to have plans for further education.

In short, the relation between female-role ideology and educational aspiration is contingent on the way a woman has been socialized to meet her achievement needs outside the home. It is quite clear that the vicarious mode and the traditional view are linked and tend to predispose a woman to limit her educational goals. The balanced and direct modes of achievement are linked to the contemporary view of sex roles and tend to encourage high educational aspirations.

Since it appears that women are socialized at an early age to a female-role ideology, let us examine the family background of the respondents. Obvious socioeconomic indexes, such as parents' income, education or occupation, surprisingly had no bearing on the daughter's sex-role ideology. In fact, none of the usual socioeconomic characteristics of the family was related to female-role ideology. Women with the contemporary ideology were just as likely to come from homes with incomes of less than $3,500 as those with the traditional view were. Parents with a college education, including a doctoral degree, were just as likely to produce daughters with the traditional sex-role ideology as daughters with the contemporary one.

Another usually important factor, childhood religion, failed to show a statistically significant influence on sex-role ideology, although a Catholic upbringing tended to produce slightly more women with the traditional viewpoint than a Protestant or a Jewish upbringing did. And in spite of the common opinion that city dwellers are less bound by traditional attitudes than people raised in rural areas, women who came from rural homes were as likely to hold contemporary sex-role attitudes as women from urban and suburban areas were.

It is worth noting that homes disrupted by divorce, separation or death did not differ from intact homes in the proportion of traditional-ideology and contemporary-ideology women they produced. This holds true regardless of the age of the daughter when the home was disrupted. Moreover, having sisters or brothers, either younger or older, had no effect on sex-role ideology. Working mothers have been both praised and damned for the effects of their outside commitment on their children. In our sample whether or not a mother worked had no perceptible impact on her daughter's sex-role ideology. Nonworking mothers were just as likely as employed mothers to have daughters with the contemporary view of the female role.

In the light of these negative demographic findings, do childhood family variables contribute anything to the ideology of college women? If there is such an influence, we must seek the answer in more subtle factors such as the marital relationship between the parents. Women with a contemporary sex-role ideology tended to come from families in which most of the time neither parent was dominant or from families in which the mother was dominant. When the father was more dominant in the marriage, the tendency of the daughter to develop the traditional concept of the female role was enhanced.

CONTEMPORARY   TRADITIONAL

TOTAL SAMPLE   73   27

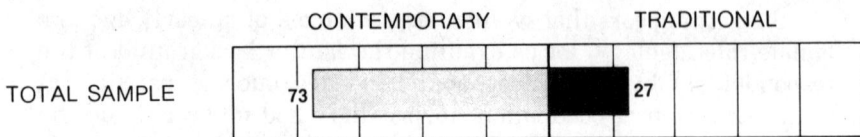

DOMINANT PARTNER IN PARENTS' MARRIAGE

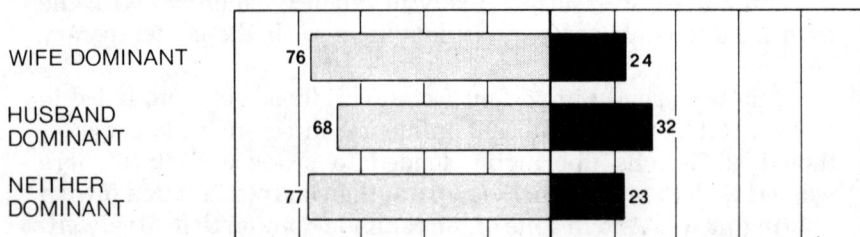

WIFE DOMINANT   76   24

HUSBAND
DOMINANT   68   32

NEITHER
DOMINANT   77   23

MOTHERS' SATISFACTION WITH LIFE

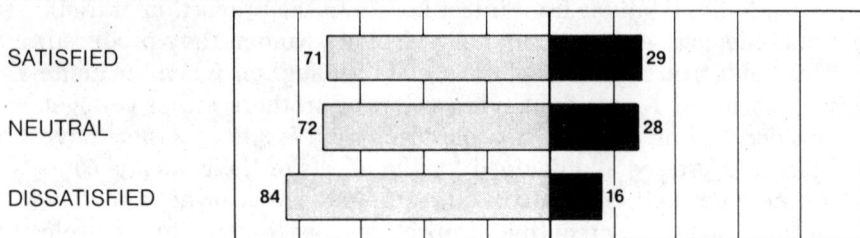

SATISFIED   71   29

NEUTRAL   72   28

DISSATISFIED   84   16

MOTHERS' ATTITUDE TOWARD HOMEMAKER ROLE

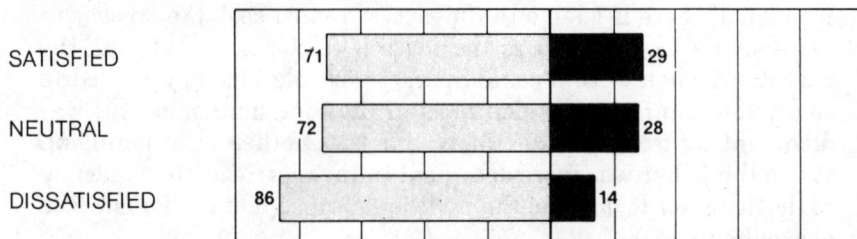

SATISFIED   71   29

NEUTRAL   72   28

DISSATISFIED   86   14

PARENTAL ENCOURAGEMENT FOR DAUGHTER TO ATTEND GRADUATE SCHOOL

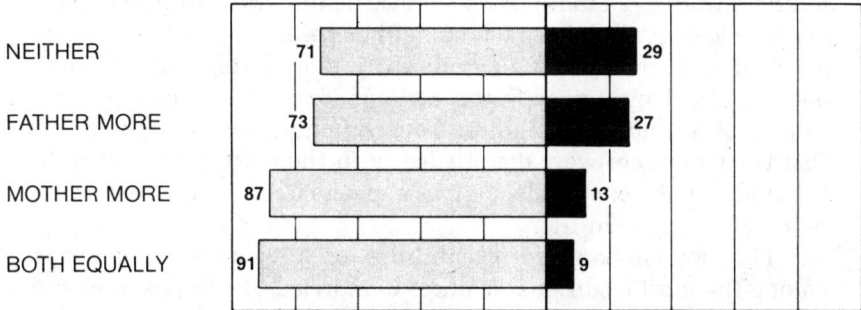

NEITHER	71	29
FATHER MORE	73	27
MOTHER MORE	87	13
BOTH EQUALLY	91	9

PARENT MOST ADMIRED

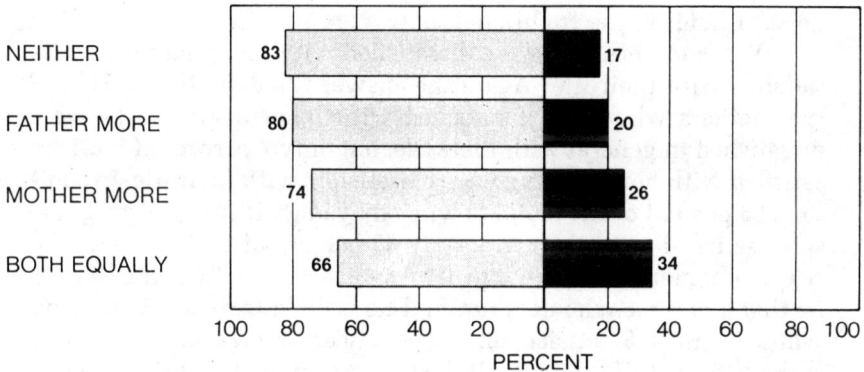

NEITHER	83	17
FATHER MORE	80	20
MOTHER MORE	74	26
BOTH EQUALLY	66	34

100   80   60   40   20   0   20   40   60   80   100

PERCENT

PARENTAL INFLUENCES on daughter's sex-role ideology (*gray and black bars*) were not expected variables such as income, education or religion but rather qualitative factors such as dominant parent, mothers' attitudes, encouraging parent and most admired parent.

An important predictor of a woman's female-role ideology is her perception of her mother's overall satisfaction with life. Dissatisfied mothers were more likely than satisfied ones to rear daughters with the contemporary view of the role of women, and satisfied mothers were more likely to have daughters with the traditional orientation. In traditional homes where the father was dominant, dissatisfied mothers were even more likely to raise daughters with the contemporary ideology. In homes where neither parent was dominant, dissatisfied mothers were not significantly more likely than satisfied ones to raise daughters with the contemporary view of female roles. Interestingly enough, daughters from contemporary homes who felt that their mothers were dissatisfied with their life did not turn to the traditional sex-role ideology as a means of avoiding dissatisfaction with their own life.

The homemaking responsibilities of a woman are perhaps among the most traditional features of married life. Does a mother's attitude toward homemaking influence her daughter's sex-role attitudes? The answer is yes. Mothers who were dissatisfied with homemaking had a greater tendency than satisfied homemakers to raise daughters with the contemporary view (see illustration on pages 286-287). Daughters of mothers who were satisfied with household tasks or had a neutral attitude toward them had the greatest likelihood of holding the traditional view.

Were mothers who were dissatisfied with household work less satisfied with their life? Again the answer is a definite yes. Half of the mothers who were dissatisfied with homemaking tasks were dissatisfied in general with their life, but only 7 percent of mothers satisfied with homemaking were dissatisfied with their life. In addition, 85 percent of the mothers who enjoyed their homemaking role were satisfied with their life. Only 35 percent of the mothers who rejected homemaking found general satisfaction in their life. It may be that a mother who does not find household tasks satisfying and whose overall life satisfaction is low may encourage her daughter to seek a different life pattern. Higher education, particularly graduate school, represents a different way for a woman to allocate her time and energy. Is there, then, a connection between a mother's encouraging her daughter to go to graduate school and the daughter's concept of the female role? Apparently there is. A mother's encouragement enhanced the tendency toward the contemporary viewpoint more than a father's encouragement alone. When both parents equally encouraged their daughter to go to graduate school, however, the daughter was most likely to have the contemporary sex-role ideology.

**MOTHERS' ATTITUDE
TOWARD HOMEMAKER ROLE**

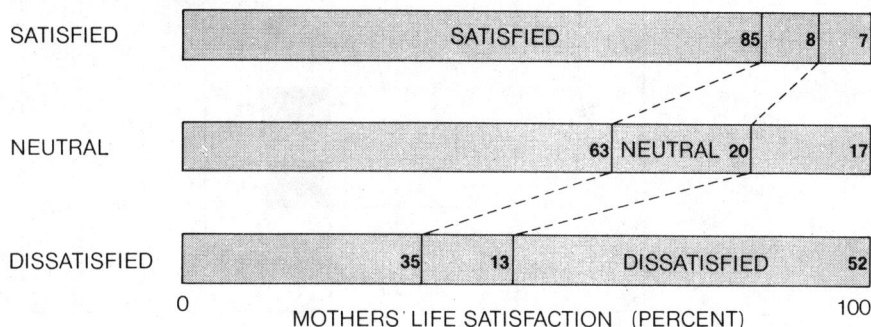

SATISFIED	SATISFIED	85	8	7

NEUTRAL	63	NEUTRAL 20	17

DISSATISFIED	35	13	DISSATISFIED	52

0   MOTHERS' LIFE SATISFACTION (PERCENT)   100

MOTHERS' SATISFACTION with life and homemaking were clearly related. Mothers perceived by daughters as satisfied homemakers were likely to be perceived as satisfied with life. Dissatisfied homemakers tended to be seen as being dissatisfied with life.

Although sex-role ideology may be developed in early childhood, it is usually not until adolescence that a girl begins to apply her system of beliefs to her life pattern. At this stage her interaction with her parents presumably would help her to test and adjust the viability of the attitudes and beliefs that had been guiding her since childhood. Do daughters with the contemporary ideology have a pattern of development in adolescence that is different from the pattern of daughters with the traditional view of the female role? In a general way it appears to be so. Women who emerge with the contemporary ideology tend in adolescence to achieve a certain psychological distance from their family, to evolve a sense of separateness as individuals.

Admiration for a parent may be regarded as an index of willingness to remain an integral part of the family. In describing their relationships with their parents during adolescence, women with the contemporary ideology were the most likely to have rejected both parents as objects of admiration: 83 percent of the women who reported that they admired neither parent adhered to the contemporary female-role ideology. There was also a slight tendency for women who admired their fathers more than their mothers to hold the contemporary view, whereas women who admired their mothers more tended to favor traditional sex-role attitudes.

Efforts to please a parent provide another clue to a daughter's willingness to maintain a close sense of identification with that

**PARENT DAUGHTER
TRIED TO PLEASE**

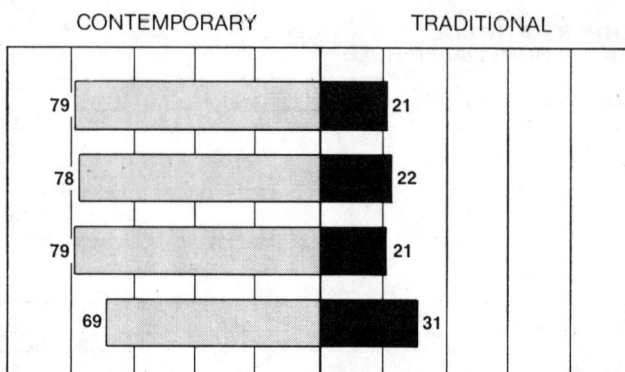

CONTEMPORARY   TRADITIONAL

NEITHER
PARENT

79   21

FATHER MORE
THAN MOTHER

78   22

MOTHER MORE
THAN FATHER

79   21

BOTH EQUALLY

69   31

MOST CRITICAL PARENT

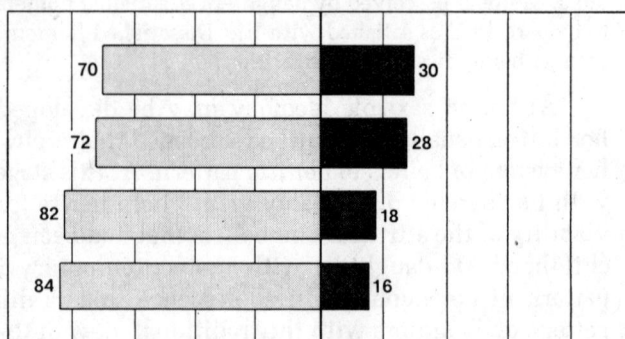

NEITHER
PARENT

70   30

FATHER MORE
THAN MOTHER

72   28

MOTHER MORE
THAN FATHER

82   18

BOTH EQUALLY

84   16

MOST FRUSTRATING PARENT

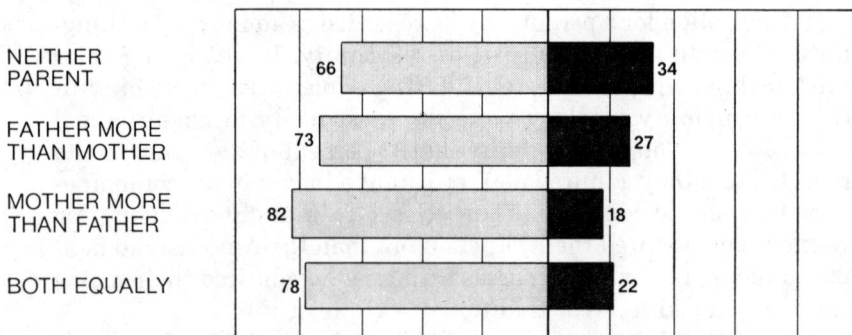

NEITHER
PARENT

66   34

FATHER MORE
THAN MOTHER

73   27

MOTHER MORE
THAN FATHER

82   18

BOTH EQUALLY

78   22

SELF-RATING OF LONELINESS IN ADOLESCENCE

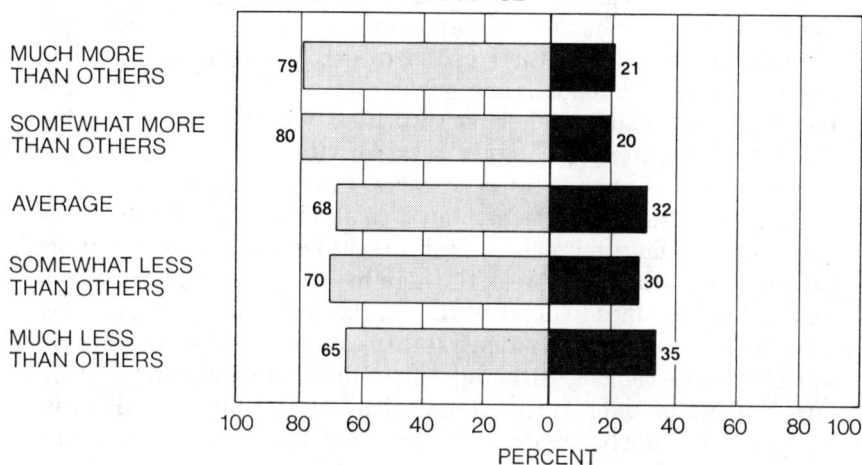

MUCH MORE THAN OTHERS: 79 / 21
SOMEWHAT MORE THAN OTHERS: 80 / 20
AVERAGE: 68 / 32
SOMEWHAT LESS THAN OTHERS: 70 / 30
MUCH LESS THAN OTHERS: 65 / 35

100 80 60 40 20 0 20 40 60 80 100
PERCENT

OTHER PARENTAL FACTORS that influenced the daughter's sex-role ideology were which parent the daughter tried to please most, most critical parent and most frustrating parent. Women with a contemporary view tended to be lonelier than their peers in adolescence.

parent. Women who reported that they did not try to please either parent, who sought to keep their distance, were more likely to hold the contemporary view than women who tried to please both parents (see illustration on pages 290-291). The amount of criticism from a parent is another indicator of the kind of rapport between daughter and parent. Of the women who reported that they were constantly criticized by both parents, 84 percent held the contemporary view. Women with the contemporary viewpoint tended to have a critical mother, whereas women with the traditional viewpoint recalled having a critical father. Women with the contemporary ideology were frustrated most by their mother; those with the traditional viewpoint were more likely to say that neither parent frustrated them.

To feel that one's parent has been successful in life is to recognize and approve of the parent's overall life pattern. Adolescents who regard their parents as being successful are better able to accept their parents as role models and to pattern their own lives in a similar fashion. Rejection of the parental life pattern may force the adolescent to seek new approaches to the conduct of life. This is borne out in the data from the study: women with the contemporary ideology tended to regard both parents as being unsuccessful, and those with the traditional viewpoint tended to see both parents as being successful. The desire of an admiring daughter to please her parents and to tolerate their criticism and her inclination not to regard parental demands as being frustrating are consistent with the daughter's acceptance of her parents' life-style. It is not surprising that such daughters tend to see both parents as being successful.

Approval of parents by an adolescent may be important to family living in traditional terms, but a relatively unquestioning attitude toward familial values and life-styles may make it more difficult for a woman to break through to an alternative life-style as an adult. Reluctance to break with familiar patterns and values may have implications for a woman's ability to adapt to new and perhaps enriching experiences. Although the traditional viewpoint may ensure continuity and security, it may also lead in later life to dissatisfaction, particularly where a changing external environment may require flexibility in adapting to new conditions.

The reluctance to please parents, coupled with a decreased admiration for parents and a tendency to see them as frustrating and critical, are closely associated with the contemporary sex-role ideology. They may be the first steps in a woman's developing a sense of distance from the family in which she grew up. Gaining a sense of oneself as an individual is a necessary step toward enlarging one's sense of self-fulfillment. In a rapidly changing environment self-fulfillment may take on a new meaning that requires a new life-style for women, including new roles such as student and worker as well as the customary ones of wife and mother.

All psychological growth has certain costs, and it is relevant to ask at what price a contemporary ideology has been acquired. A sense of loneliness in adolescence may be considered one kind of short-term psychological price paid for developing new patterns of behavior. Women who held contemporary sex-role beliefs reported that they were lonelier than their peers in adolescence; women with the traditional viewpoint were less likely to be lonely than their peers. If the short-term effects of the contemporary sex-role ideology are painful, what about the long-term consequences? It appears that adult women with the contemporary sex-role ideology are just as happy with their present life as are women with the traditional viewpoint. Furthermore, there does not appear to be any difference in the anxiety levels of the two groups of women.

Differences in sex-role ideology might be expected to produce differences in value systems, and the hierarchy of values of the

CONTEMPORARY   TRADITIONAL

```
                         ─80─
INTELLECTUAL CURIOSITY─────   │

                         ─75─
                                        ───EMOTIONAL MATURITY
                              │         ───MORALS AND ETHICS
                         ─70─

                                        ───INTERPERSONAL SKILL
                                        ───INTELLECTUAL CURIOSITY
                         ─65─
MORALS AND ETHICS──────────
EMOTIONAL MATURITY─────────────        ───HAPPINESS

                         ─60─  ─┬
                               PERCENT
INTERPERSONAL SKILL ───────
                         ─55─

INTELLECTUAL ABILITY───────            ───CONSCIENTIOUSNESS
CREATIVITY ─────
HAPPINESS ──────────────     ─50─

CONSCIENTIOUSNESS──────── ─45─

                                       ───EFFICIENCY
                                       ───INTELLECTUAL ABILITY
                         ─40─
                                       ───CREATIVITY

EFFICIENCY ──────────────── ─35─
```

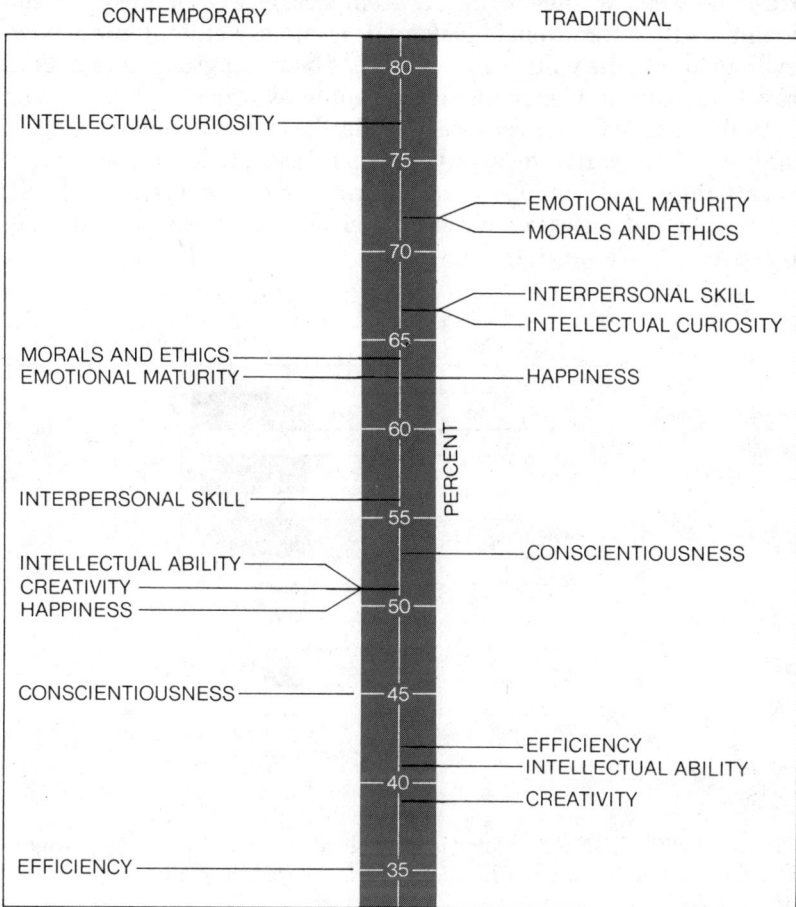

HIERARCHY OF VALUES of women with contemporary sex-role ideology differed from that of women with traditional views. Ranking is based on values rated as most important.

women in the contemporary category indeed differed from that of the women in the traditional group. The contemporary position placed the highest value on intellectual curiosity; the traditional one put emotional maturity, morals and ethics first (see illustration above). Moreover, women with the traditional set of beliefs attached special meaning to interpersonal skills, happiness and conscientiousness.

For analytical purposes I have been stressing the striking contrasts between women with a contemporary sex-role ideology and
women with a traditional ideology. It is equally enlightening, however, to look at the values these usually divergent groups share. Both
rated honesty and understanding people as crucial qualities, and
both depreciated perseverance, the ability to work under pressure,
ambition, competitiveness, physical stamina and realism. Somewhat
surprisingly, both groups gave low ratings to the qualities of self-
confidence, enthusiasm, courage, physical attractiveness and sexuality.

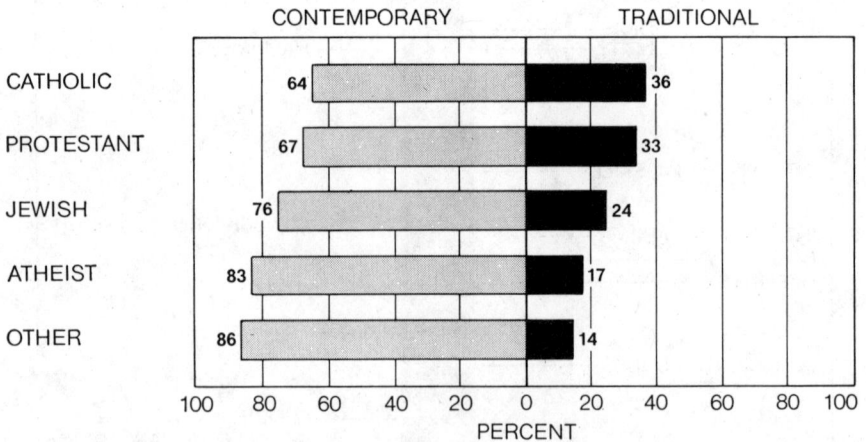

CONTEMPORARY   TRADITIONAL

CATHOLIC   64   36

PROTESTANT   67   33

JEWISH   76   24

ATHEIST   83   17

OTHER   86   14

100   80   60   40   20   0   20   40   60   80   100
PERCENT

PRESENT RELIGION was related to sex-role ideology but childhood religion
was not. Women with non-Christian beliefs favored the contemporary view
of sex roles.

I have noted that childhood religion was unexpectedly found to
be unrelated to present sex-role ideology. In view of this finding it
was surprising to discover that there was a strong association between the present religious affiliation of a woman and her attitude
toward sex roles. Women who espoused atheism, who had no formal
religion or who professed Judaism or Eastern religions clearly
tended to favor the contemporary sex-role ideology. Adult Protes-
tants and Catholics were more likely to hold the traditional viewpoint. This is all the more puzzling because there was also a distinct
association between childhood religion and present religion.
    The key to the puzzle appears to be religious conversion. For
women who had maintained the religion they had had as children

PRESENT RELIGION (NONCONVERTS)

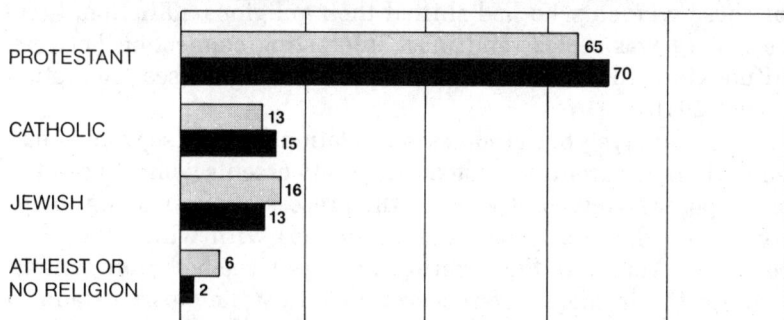

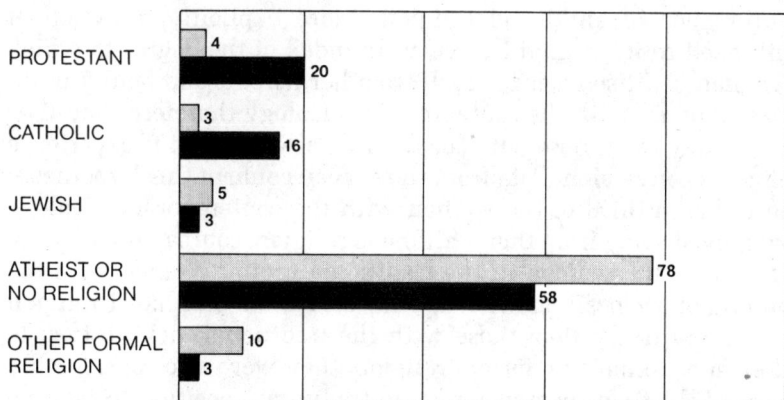

PROTESTANT	65 / 70
CATHOLIC	13 / 15
JEWISH	16 / 13
ATHEIST OR NO RELIGION	6 / 2

PRESENT RELIGION (CONVERTS)

PROTESTANT	4 / 20
CATHOLIC	3 / 16
JEWISH	5 / 3
ATHEIST OR NO RELIGION	78 / 58
OTHER FORMAL RELIGION	10 / 3

RELIGIOUS CONVERSION

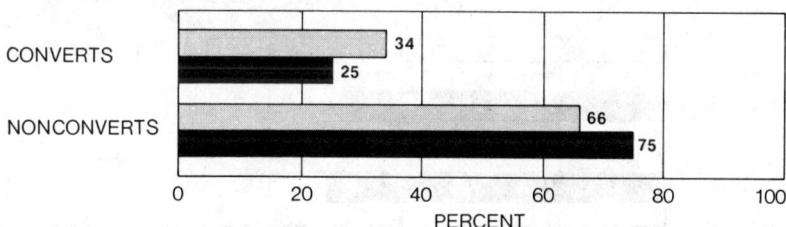

CONVERTS	34 / 25
NONCONVERTS	66 / 75

0   20   40   60   80   100
PERCENT

RELIGIOUS CONVERSION was a linking factor between childhood religion, present religion and sex-role ideology. For women who maintained their childhood religion (*top graph*) there was no statistically significant link between religion and sex-role ideology. For converts (*middle graph*) there was a strong association between religious views and sex-role views: converts with contemporary view (*gray*) moved away from Christianity more than converts with traditional (*black*) view of sex roles. Women who held a contemporary view were more likely to have converted from their childhood religion (*bottom graph*).

296 The Changing Role of Women

there was no link between sex-role ideology and present religion. For those women who had shifted their religious affiliation, however, there was a clear and most interesting connection between attitudes toward the female role and present religion (see illustration on page 295).

In our analysis of the adolescent relationships these women had had with their parents we noted that as adolescents women with the contemporary viewpoint were in the process of disengaging themselves from the family patterns and values with which they had grown up. Women in the traditional category seemed more willing to accept the frame of reference provided by their parents and to continue to live within it. If this interpretation is correct, there should be some indirect confirmation of it in terms of rejection or continuance of childhood religion. More explicitly, rejection of childhood religion might serve as an index of the degree to which a woman has disengaged herself from her parents and family traditions. Women with the contemporary ideology therefore should be more likely than those with the traditional viewpoint to experience religious conversion. Data from the survey confirm this hypothesis: more than a third of the women with the contemporary ideology had moved away from their childhood religion, compared with only a fourth of the women in the traditional group. Women with the contemporary position who had rejected their childhood religion were more likely than those with the traditional view to turn to atheism or to have no formal religion; they were also considerably more likely than women with the traditional position to take up

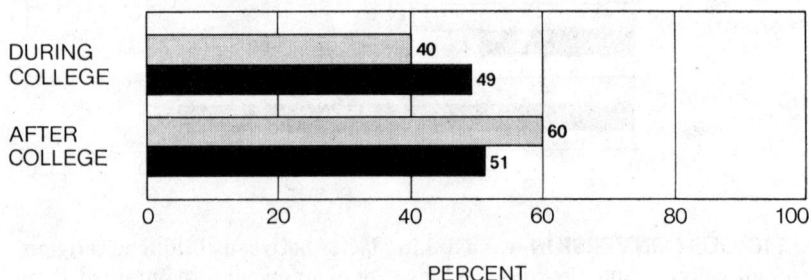

INFLUENCE OF SEX-ROLE IDEOLOGY on time of marriage was significant, with women holding a contemporary view more likely to complete their college studies before marrying.

Eastern religions (in which, we might speculate, they sought for new meaning in their life). Women in the traditional category who had converted were much more likely than women with the contemporary viewpoint to move toward the familiar religions of Protestantism and Catholicism.

It was interesting to examine whether or not women who attached great importance to intellectual qualities tended to act on these values in their daily life. One indicator is to see if women with the contemporary ideology were more likely than those with the traditional viewpoint to postpone marriage until the completion of their college studies, an action that would be consistent with placing a high value on intellectual activity. A look at the educational level of the respondents at the time of their marriage immediately brings out the fact that women with the contemporary ideology were indeed more likely than those with the traditional viewpoint to marry after the completion of their college studies. Women in the traditional group, who did not set such a high value on intellectual qualities, tended to marry while they were still in college.

It would appear that sex-role ideology is an important factor in predicting values. Does it also influence the degree of satisfaction women derive from informal activities with other women? Do women with the contemporary sex-role ideology derive less enjoyment from casual interaction with other women? This turns out to be the case. Women with the contemporary viewpoint said that they enjoyed activities such as chatting and card-playing much less than other women of their age; women in the traditional group tended to rate themselves as being average in this respect.

If these common female activities outside the home are less than exciting to women with the contemporary ideology, what about the three major roles of a married woman within the family: her conjugal role, her maternal role and her homemaker role? Women who saw the relationship between the sexes in contemporary terms were just as likely to express satisfaction with their husband as women who took the more traditional view of marriage. Moreover, among the women in the sample who had children, mothers with the contemporary ideology were just as satisfied with their maternal role as were mothers in the traditional group. When it came to satisfaction with the role of homemaker, a different picture emerged. Women with the contemporary viewpoint were noticeably less enthusiastic about homemaking. Contrary to television advertisements for detergents and other household products, not all women find delight in cleaning house or washing clothes. Women with the contemporary

SATISFACTION WITH WIFE ROLE

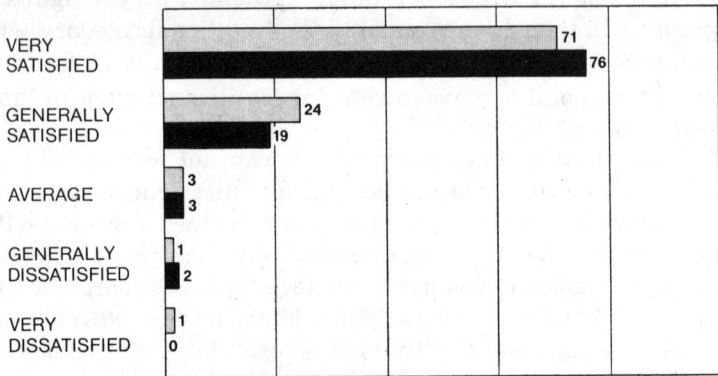

VERY
SATISFIED
71
76

GENERALLY
SATISFIED
24
19

AVERAGE
3
3

GENERALLY
DISSATISFIED
1
2

VERY
DISSATISFIED
1
0

SATISFACTION WITH MATERNAL ROLE

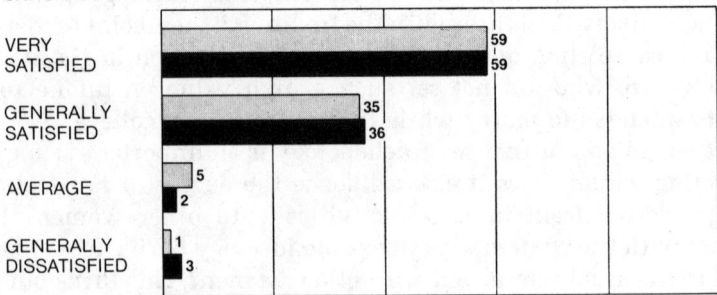

VERY
SATISFIED
59
59

GENERALLY
SATISFIED
35
36

AVERAGE
5
2

GENERALLY
DISSATISFIED
1
3

SATISFACTION WITH HOMEMAKER ROLE

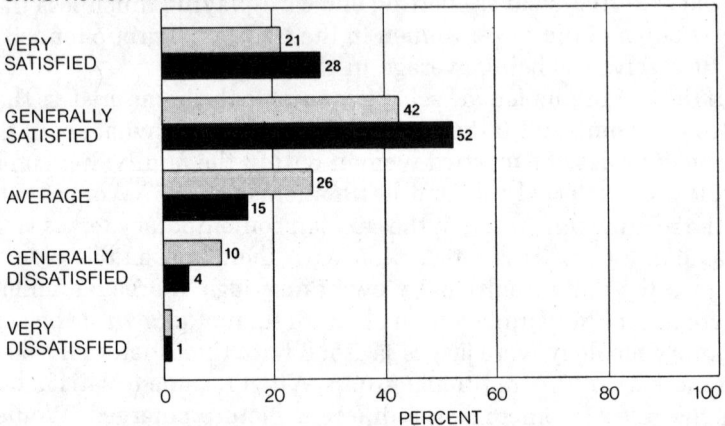

VERY
SATISFIED
21
28

GENERALLY
SATISFIED
42
52

AVERAGE
26
15

GENERALLY
DISSATISFIED
10
4

VERY
DISSATISFIED
1
1

0   20   40   60   80   100
PERCENT

SATISFACTION profiles of women with contemporary and traditional views were found similar regarding wife and mother roles (*top and middle graphs*). Women with contemporary views, however, expressed less satisfaction about homemaking responsibilities.

position were not reluctant to convey their dislike for these household tasks. On the other hand, activities that allow more self-expression or creativity, such as cooking, entertaining, interior decorating, sewing and shopping, were equally acceptable to women in both categories.

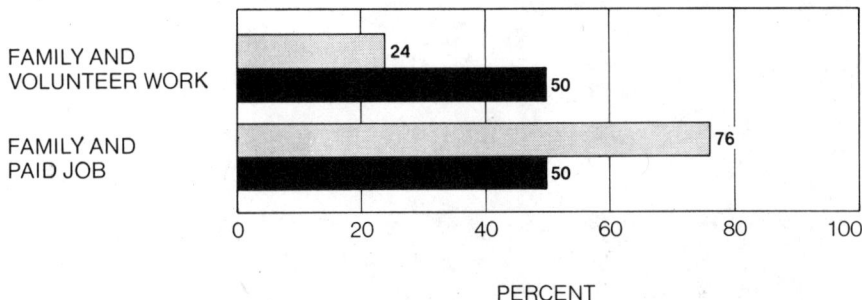

FAMILY AND
VOLUNTEER WORK

FAMILY AND
PAID JOB

```
0        20        40        60        80        100
```

PERCENT

IDEAL LIFE ROLES differed for women with contemporary and traditional sex-role-attitudes. Women with contemporary view (*gray*) favored family and paid employment, whereas women with traditional view (*black*) split equally between family and employment.

The two groups of women have distinctly different concepts of the ideal life. For the woman in the traditional category the ideal life consists in devoting her energies to family and volunteer social activities. Fifty percent of the women in this group reported that their choice for the most satisfying way of life involves family and volunteer projects; only 24 percent of the women in the contemporary group gave this response. More than three-quarters of the women in the contemporary category said that the most satisfactory life-style is a combination of family and full-time or part-time employment.

Although it is clear that ideology affects life goals and choices, does it also produce differences in the self-concepts of women? Self-esteem, the acceptance of oneself as an individual, is an important component of one's self-image. How do the two groups in our survey compare in self-esteem? Curiously, the women in both groups have remarkably similar self-esteem profiles. Women in both categories express equal confidence in their competence as wife and mother. Their sense of competence regarding their ability as student, employee and community participant is also similar. Wives with the traditional viewpoint rate their ability to solve complex problems just as favorably as contemporary wives. The traditional and contemporary sex-role viewpoints lead to two distinct life patterns, but within each ideological position women are able to find fulfillment and meaning in their life.

*Recent national surveys indicate that the United States has become a con-
tracepting society. Ruth B. Dixon states that even this fact does not guarantee the end of undesirable pregnancies. A woman's decision to have a
particular pregnancy is rather related to the options society offers her to
express herself in roles other than continual motherhood—and in her freedom to assume these roles. This emancipation still seems a long way in the
future.*

RUTH B. DIXON

Hallelujah the Pill?

What do women want? Freud's famous question, for which he con-
fessed he had no answer, is scarcely a mystery for many women
today in the liberation movement. What women want, they say, is
at the very least complete control over their own bodies, that is, their
own reproductive behavior, thus ending involuntary pregnancy and
compulsory motherhood. The second thing they want is a full range
of choice among alternative life styles—career and homemaking,
bricklaying and engineering, marriage and motherhood and so on
into various permutations and combinations, all realized through a
variety of true options, the choice among them to be relatively free
of pressure and coercion.

There is little doubt that in this country we are moving rapidly
toward the ideal of "body control," toward the separation of sexual
expression from pregnancy and childbirth. Consider that early in
the century couples were being advised in manuals like *The Science
of Eugenics and Sex Life* (1914) that "women are affectionate, and
when they nestle close to a man, they excite sexual desire on the part
of the man. Married couples will do well to sleep in separate beds.
By this means, intercourse occurs less often, and health is preserved;
for *opportunity* is the cause of much useless and injurious intercourse." Abstinence was the preferred method for avoiding pregnancy and for improving genetic quality. "Unfortunately for the
race," writes one medical expert, "irresponsible sexual intercourse is
so largely the rule among the married, that unwelcome, sickly and

viciously inclined children are thrust into the world with no chance to make their own lives such as will be worth living."

But this is 1970. Gone are the days when women lived in terror of the sexual embrace because it meant still another pregnancy, still another year of sickness, still another child to care for. Gone are the days when separate bedrooms and locked doors were offered as solutions for the desperate. Technology has progressed, and with great rumblings the Mountain has given birth to—the Pill!

THE CONTRACEPTING SOCIETY

Has the pill brought with it the emancipation of women, as so many have claimed? What *are* women doing with this revolutionary knowledge? Are they enjoying sex but declining marriage? Are they marrying their lovers but deciding against a future as merely wife and mother? Are they reluctant to bear children after one or two? Just what effect has the pill had on the timing and the number of marriages and births in recent years?

Recent national surveys indicate that the United States has indeed become a contracepting society. At least 90 percent of all married couples have practiced or intend to practice contraception at some point in their married lives, and when this figure is added to the 5 percent or so who know themselves to be sterile, there are very few who are willing simply to let the babies come willy-nilly. Contrasted with patterns in many less-developed nations where perhaps only 5 to 10 percent ever intentionally practice any form of birth control, and where most women profess to know of no method of preventing pregnancy, the achievement is startling. Contraception in the United States is being adopted earlier in marriage, and class, racial and religious differences are diminishing. The largest gains in birth control practices in the last 15 years or so have occurred among previously reluctant or unknowledgeable women, most notably among Catholics (especially the better educated), among the less educated in general, among younger women and among nonwhites, especially in the South. With the closing of these gaps, contraception is becoming truly universal.

To speak of a contracepting society is one thing; to explore just who does the contracepting and how effectively is another. Class biases in the availability of services—especially those due to physicians they see as aloof or money-hungry, and to the inability of lower-class women to pay for safe abortions (either legal or illegal) —are still strong. Middle- and upper-middle-class women definitely come out ahead in the degree to which they are able to plan their pregnancies. They are more likely to know about a number of different kinds of contraception, to approve of them, to have access to them, to have used them and to have used medically sound and highly effective female methods. In this sense such women are indeed "liberated."

Among the poor, knowledge of contraception—often more folklore than truth in the first place—is rarely integrated into actual practice in an effective way. The knowledge somehow remains "out there," something that other people might find helpful or have some luck with, but not themselves. "I've heard about lots of ways, but I don't know if they're any good," says one man about birth control. A woman who says she douches "sometimes" adds, "I didn't know nothing when I got married. I never talked to no one about it. . . . Now I've talked around a little bit and I learned about the douche and my husband used a rubber once." But the whole effort is seen too quickly as futile when casual and sporadic attempts at birth prevention meet with repeated failure. One estimate for the years 1960 to 1965 is that approximately 40 percent of the children born to poor and near-poor couples were unwanted by one or both parents, compared to 14 percent of births to "non-poor" couples. Yet these unsuccessful users must be placed among the "contraceptors" in our society, those who have practiced birth control at some time in the past or intend to do so in the future.

Keeping in mind that being a user means very different things in different contexts, we can see that trends in the last few decades are nevertheless encouraging. We have witnessed not only a remarkable increase in the use of contraception and in attitudes favorable to its use but an interesting change in the methods most frequently employed. In the 1930's the most popular techniques were withdrawal, the condom and the douche; in the mid-fifties, the condom, diaphragm and rhythm. Then came the pill. First licensed for prescription in June 1960, the pill in five years had become by all odds the favorite method of birth control in the United States. A national sample survey in 1965 indicated that a third of the married women had tried the pill, and for a fourth it was the method they had used most recently (including one-fifth for Catholic wives). The old reliables—the condom, rhythm and especially the diaphragm—had dropped heavily out of favor. The intrauterine device (IUD), available generally only since 1964, is steadily growing in favor.

The implications of changing styles of contraception are important: there has been a definite transition from less effective methods and from those used by the male to highly effective female methods and, in the case of the pill and the IUD, to methods that the woman may use unbeknownst to her partner and without disturbing the spontaneity of the sexual act. This development is crucial. It means that women are for the first time truly able to control their own bodies in a *private* way, whether their mates agree or not.

This brings us to a moral dilemma that we might refer to as another dimension of Kate Millett's "sexual politics": should it be the responsibility, privilege or right of the woman to be in sole charge of marital fertility? Is it fair to leave her with the trump card? After all, not only is she then in a position deliberately to refuse her husband a child without his knowing (since the pill and IUD are invisible to him), she is also in a position to produce a child that he may not want and to blame the event on "contraceptive failure." Obviously neither outcome is desirable. But the husband on his part can do the same, although not so inconspicuously. A lower-class woman with five children who had wanted only two, when asked what method of contraception she was now using, complained, "That's the trouble, we don't use anything. I think my husband is going to put on a rubber and he don't half the time. . . . He is the one that is careless and goes in for too much fooling around. He doesn't have all the work and trouble!" In a secure relationship this dimension of sex normally remains latent or unconscious; the husband and wife mutually agree on what one or the other should do. But in a relationship tinged with resentment or mistrust, the political dimension becomes manifest. In this type of situation it would seem all the more important for a woman to be in charge of reproduction, since the consequences of conception will be primarily hers to bear. "He doesn't take care of the kids; *I* have to all the time," sighs one woman.

It is interesting that mutual agreement tends to be related to class. The lower in the social scale one goes, the more likely it is that couples find their sex life with each other unsatisfying and experience some conflict over the responsibilities of contraception. Too, lower-class wives are more likely than middle-class wives to want *fewer* children than their husbands: one-quarter of nonwhite women reported such a discrepancy of views in 1960. For these women, acquiring the means to resist their husband's empire-building impulses is crucial.

Now that women in every social group are increasingly taking the responsibility of birth control onto themselves and are acquiring knowledge of and access to methods they can use privately, the relevant question to ask is this: Just how emancipated are American women in their new role as charge d'affaires of their own reproduction?

THE PILL IS NOT ENOUGH

The answer is obvious: even though women are increasingly practic-
ing efficient contraception, they are not even beginning to free themselves from their family-centered identities. Male-expressed fear
that women on the pill would toss away their traditional wife-
mother obligations have so far proved groundless. That this is so is
apparent in three simple facts: American women still marry earlier
on the average than in any other industrialized country, and almost
all marry eventually; average family size is still higher than in most
Western countries, with fewer women remaining childless or settling for only one child; and American women want for themselves,
and consider ideal, higher numbers of children than in practically
any other industrialized country. We are still a highly familistic
society. The never-married woman and the childless wife are deviant.

Let us begin with marriage. It is true that marriage rates have
fallen off slightly in recent years and that the average age at first
marriage for females has slowed its long decline and taken a small
turn upward. Earlier in the century women were marrying on the
average in their 21st or 22nd year. Just after the end of World War
II their median age at first marriage was 20.5 years, dropping to 20.1
years in 1956 and rising again to 20.3 in 1960 and up to 20.8 in 1969.
But the single most popular time for getting married is the legal
minimum, 18, and over one-quarter of American females marry at
this age. This puts American brides, at least on the basis of 1960
figures, a full year younger on the average than those in Canada,
Australia and New Zealand and from one to five years younger even
than those in a number of highly traditional societies—Taiwan,
Thailand, Ceylon, Hong Kong and the Philippines, among others—
and certainly younger than those in Japan.

Not only do American women marry earlier but more of them
get married. In this respect they are far more marriage-minded than
in former years, for only 5.0 percent of women aged 35 to 44 in 1969
had never married and an even lower proportion of women aged 30
to 34 in 1967. Thus the slight tendency to postpone marriage at the
younger ages since 1960 has been counteracted by a greater tendency
to marry in the middle or late twenties, with the result that marriage
is becoming more universal, not less. Compare these figures to those
in Western Europe and the other English-speaking nations where
one usually finds about one-eighth of all women passing through
their childbearing years without marrying, and up to one-fifth in
some cases.

The greatest differentiating factor in the timing and quantity of marriage for women is education; race and religion by themselves make little difference. Women with more education marry later, and more remain unmarried throughout their childbearing years (about one-tenth of college girls and one-quarter of those with some graduate education). Whether they remain unmarried voluntarily, however, is a moot point. One study exploring romanticism as a motivation for marriage uncovered these startling figures when American female college students were asked in the early sixties the question "Ideally, if it were up to you, would you like to get married?" only 1.4 percent said no. Compare this to 12.5 percent of female university students among the Singapore Chinese who said no, 18.6 percent in Burma and 28.2 in India!

Women also feel less and less compelled to remain in unsatisfactory marriages (as do men), for divorce rates are continuing to climb. In 1962 the United States surpassed Egypt to win the honor of having the highest divorce rate of any country in the world for which reliable statistics are available, but a sudden liberalization of Russian divorce laws in 1966 has put the United States in second place since then, with Egypt and several Eastern European nations next in line. Nevertheless, the high divorce rate apparently does not reflect a growing disenchantment with marriage in this country, for rates of *remarriage* among the divorced are also on the increase. Instead of deciding that marriage is not the inevitable solution to our personal problems we are simply jumping in and out of marriages at a faster rate.

PUTTING ONE'S MIND TO IT

Then come the babies. It is unfair to compare reproductive behavior now to that in the depression when family size was necessarily small and when one-fifth of the women who had ever been married passed through their reproductive years without bearing children at all and another fifth bore only one. But we can take the depression years as an example of what American couples can do about their fertility when they really put their minds to it, and in this case they managed to keep their completed family size down to 2.4 children on the average. All this before the pill. In 1969, by contrast, the average family size of ever-married women in their early forties was 3.1 children, and even women in their early thirties had already produced an average of 2.9 babies each. Only among the younger cohorts in the last five years are there signs that the baby boom of the fifties and early sixties is finally easing slightly. Analysis of this decline at younger years has shown that it is *not* due to the pill per se but to a greater determination among young couples to use *some* form of effective contraception, whatever it may be. However the total *numbers* of babies born will of course leap upward as 20 million baby boom daughters themselves enter their reproductive years, as they are now beginning to do.

The downward trend in the crude birthrate from its postwar peak in 1957 is easy to misinterpret. A couple of years ago when the birthrate had dropped to its lowest point since the depression, newspapers were full of expert "analyses" of the alleged growing reluctance of the American woman to have children. Many saw the two-child family coming back as a popular ideal. But the decline of the crude birthrate, which refers to the number of births per year per thousand persons, is largely an artifact of changes in the age composition of the population in which women of childbearing years make up a smaller proportion of the total population, and of changes in the timing of births and marriages. The drop in the birthrate since 1957 does not necessarily mean that married couples are having fewer children or that they are beginning to desire smaller families. As we pointed out, women in their early thirties in 1969 had already borne 2.9 children on the average, compared to 2.6 for women the same age in 1960 and 2.2 in 1954. Women under 30 have been reproducing slower, but whether they will continue their reduced fertility at older ages or make up the lost births at a future time remains an open question.

FAMILY SIZE DESIRES

The actual reproductive behavior of the American woman tells only part of the story; perhaps more important to her future emancipation is the evidence on her *desired* and *ideal* fertility. This is where her consistently family-centered orientation truly reveals itself.

The ideal family size of American couples has not changed radically in the last several decades. Gallup polls from 1936 to 1966 show a low of 2.7 in 1943 and a high of 3.6 in 1966 when couples were asked the rather vague question, "What do you think is the ideal number of children for the average American family?" But the most frequently mentioned ideal has progressed from two children in 1940 to three children in 1945 to four children in 1960 and 1965, with both small and large families becoming less popular. In a large 1965 national survey *90 percent* of married women mentioned from two to four children as the ideal family size, 75 percent saying three or four. The homogeneity of family size ideals is amazing.

Personal desires (people don't necessarily consider the general norm ideal for themselves) are slightly less homogeneous, but even here 80 percent of the women questioned wanted from two to four children for themselves, and 70 percent expected to have this many. Only 4 percent wanted either no children or just one. However, women expect on the average to have *fewer* children than they would really like to have, or than they consider ideal for the average American family. In other words, if conditions were better, women would be having even more babies. In 1960 a national sample of women considered 3.4 children ideal but at the time of the interview wanted 3.3 children for themselves (or 3.7 if their life "could be relived") and expected to have 3.1. In 1965 the comparative figures were 3.3, 3.3 and 3.2.

Although actual fertility is an inverse function of occupation, education and income, desired fertility is quite another matter. One study showed virtually no variation by husband's income with a mean desired family size centering on 3.3 children; others show much less of a variation in desired family size than in actual fertility. This means that actual fertility tends to be lower than desired fertility the higher one goes in the social scale; women with some college education desired 3.2 children in 1965 but expected to have 2.9. The reverse is the case among the poor. Nonwhite women who had less than a high school education wanted 3.5 children but expected 4.2.

Ideal, desired and expected family size are consistently higher for Catholic women than for non-Catholics, and it is the college-educated Catholic women who have the most "expansionist" desires of any group: 3.9 children in 1965 and 4.8 in 1960! Lowest fertility desires are found among college-educated black women who wanted 2.7 children in 1965.

Even women who work, who have worked for a number of years since their marriage and who work primarily because they enjoy it and not for financial reasons want on the average 3.0 children! They are just as fertility-minded as the next person, but their active participation in non-familial roles opens up options not available to other women, and their creativity apparently goes in several directions. Although these career women want on the average three children, they expect to have only two. Thus the stereotype that it is primarily unfeminine women who go into careers is obviously false; married women who are enthusiastic about working *do* have family interests and *do* want children, but they want other, often competing, things as well. Women in higher status occupations—the professions, managerial and advanced clerical work and crafts—are more likely to remain childless (about 20 percent do so) and to have smaller families when they become mothers than are women employed in sales, farm or service work (from 10 to 15 percent childless). Employed women are twice as likely to be childless as women not in the labor force. Among all occupational groups specified in the census it is the female social scientists who are the least fertile! In 1960 over one-third of ever-married white women aged 35 to 44 in this category were childless, and the whole group averaged only 1.35 children each.

There are two kinds of emancipation—or shall we say the lack of it—implicit in the figures we have been discussing. The first is the problem of excess fertility, of having more children than one wants to have either through ignorance about contraception or through its inefficient practice. This is an important factor in the high fertility of the poor. Although we have been talking of the fertility of the married, the problem also holds for the unmarried. Women can become emancipated only when the threat of unwanted pregnancy ending either in adoption or forced marriage or illegitimate motherhood is gone, and this is possible only when a young girl or woman does not have to depend on the casual interest of her partner for contraceptive care.

Yet there is another kind of emancipation—a kind that we apparently have not even begun to approach. This is the emancipation from family life, from the primary identity of a woman in her role as wife and mother. Childless marriages are such a statistical rarity that one must assume that *voluntary* childlessness is almost nil. The one-child family is fast disappearing. Practically every married woman now has at least two children, and although she compensates for her increasing propensity to have this many by stopping after three or four, she is establishing herself in the service of a family as firmly as she knows how. According to the information we have on her desires and ideals she would do so even more freely if it were not for certain constraints on her reproductive behavior, primarily the cost of educating her children. At the same time, even with the increase in contraceptive knowledge and practice among the young, illegitimacy is on the increase, and one can only assume that many of these pregnancies are wanted and intended. A recent report from the National Center for Health Statistics estimated that one-third of all firstborn children in the United States are premaritally conceived, although most of course are legitimized by a hasty marriage before they are born. If these births are involuntary, women are victimized by their lack of control over their own bodies. If they are voluntary, women are in many cases "victimized" by their desire to rush into marriage and childbearing in order to gain an identity for themselves, in order to be adults and participate in a narrowly defined adult world. The pressures in our society to marry and to have children are almost impossible to resist.

What the statistics show us and what common sense supports is that the pill, which we have used here as a symbol of what contraception can do, is nothing but an instrument of the will of the user. It doesn't act by itself to reduce the birthrate. It doesn't free women who have no real desire to be, in this sense, free. What it does is to permit them to have their children when they want them, to stop having them when they want to stop and to settle down in their three- or four-child households in the secure and happy knowledge that things worked out exactly as they had planned. The pill brings one form of emancipation, but it does not bring the other. And that is where the real work needs to be done.

THE CASE FOR DEMOGRAPHIC DIVERSITY

Trends in marriage and motherhood since the 1930s tell a story that is both hopeful and discouraging. The discouraging part is that women are marrying earlier and more are getting married than in any other Western industrialized nation or previously in this country. Too, marriages are taking place in a more concentrated span of years in the life of each cohort. Transformed into real-life experience, this means that when women reach the age of 19 or 20 they discover that their female friends all seem to be getting married at once, and, anxious to avoid being the odd-one-out in a rapidly dwindling minority, they latch onto the first reasonably acceptable partner in order to retreat into a safe, recognized slot in the community structure. The same thing is happening to motherhood. Along with the larger desired family size—four is now most popular—one finds a telescoping of desires into the two-to-four child range and a telescoping of the timing of childbearing. When marriage rates and family size desires are as high and as uniform as they are in the United States, can they reflect real freedom of choice? As it stands now, conformity to social norms encouraging and glorifying family life appears to be the order of the day.

Although conformity is a difficult phenomenon to measure, there is general agreement that it plays an important role in shaping decisions about whether to have children and about how many are appropriate. The widely accepted norm is that one should have as many children as one can afford—no more, no less. One study found that most wives wanted to have about the same number of children as they said they thought their married friends of the same age would have. Married couples who want no children are considered highly deviant. As one woman seeking treatment for sterility put it, "I openly say now that we want children because I can remember in the very beginning I used to act like it didn't matter and I remember overhearing one girl saying something about our not wanting any children and it hurt very much to think they thought we were just being real selfish and didn't want any family." Even those who want only one or two are considered selfish or else too poor to have more. Parents of many children are said to be loving, generous and prosperous. One should *want* many children, but one should not have more than are financially feasible.

There is an encouraging underside to the story of the last few decades that may provide some real hope for the future, however. First, the low marriage rates and small families of the depression years were more a function of hardship than of real desire. When times were better couples went back to fulfilling their "natural" inclinations to marry earlier and to have more babies. Our reproductive behavior is now less constrained by financial worries than it was, and the potential for fulfilling our individual wants is greater. There is after all, nothing admirable about a society with high proportions of single and childless married women when this condition arises solely from the fact that many want to marry and have children but few can afford to do so. The low birthrates of Eastern European countries may make it appear as though women are more emancipated from traditional roles than they are here, but closer inspection reveals that their reduced fertility is necessary because wives *must* work if they wish to live in reasonable comfort, and they simply cannot manage a household with more than one or two children.

Second, we may also find hope in the growing homogeneity of marital and fertility behavior and desires in the United States because it means that class, racial, religious and other group differences are breaking down and that marriage and motherhood are not the privileged prerogative or the unwished destiny of one group more than another. We noted that desired family size varies little by social class although actual fertility varies inversely. As poor and less-educated women are increasingly able to bring their fertility in line with their desires, they come closer to the goal of achieving maximum control over their own bodies—a goal that upper-middle-class women have already achieved. Surely this is a good thing.

Now, having reached the point where marriage and motherhood are financially feasible for most groups, unlike the depression years, and having reached the point where women are almost universally able—if they wish—to decide on the timing and the number of their children for themselves, we are ready to move on to the next stage—a stage of demographic diversity of a new sort.

Obviously this new freedom cannot come without first providing women with alternative sources of financial support, recognition, companionship, security, sexual fulfillment and a sense of belonging, or without providing alternative outlets for creativity, ambition and love. New forms of work, new forms of communal living are needed if we are to break away from our dependence on the isolated nuclear family for emotional sustenance. Minor alterations of the present structure will not do the trick because we will still be left with our pervasive need for *closeness*—a need that in the present system can be satisfied only in the private nests of our miniature and separate worlds. Thus we cannot expect that the high value now attached to family life and to children among all social classes will simply vanish as soon as other opportunities for women are available. The data on the family size desires of working women and highly educated women make this quite clear. Marriage and children satisfy special needs and provide special pleasures that are not offered in any other sphere, the way our society is now constituted.

But with meaningful work and meaningful communal life the compulsion to seek private solutions to loneliness and alienation would be reduced. We could visualize a new era in which demographic patterns become an accurate reflection of *individual* needs, talents and predispositions instead of a reflection of strongly conformist social and economic group pressures induced by the lack of alternatives. Instead of living in a society where three out of four women get married between the ages of 18 and 23 and in which 19 in 20 have married by the time they reach 40, we could look forward to a society in which some marry young, others marry in their thirties or forties or choose not to marry at all. Instead of concentrating our childbearing in the mid-twenties and producing the socially appropriate three or four children, more women could remain childless, more could have just one, and the rest could spread out according to individual temperament. We could even begin to share each other's children. Instead of *having* to search out our own small burrows each with its mother and father and babies, some could choose such a private world freely and others choose larger and more fluid "families" of men and women and children, or of single friends or whatever.

As choices expand it is doubtful that more women would marry and have children since this is the universal pattern now, although some might well decide to have more children than they do. But certainly many would choose the opposite if the rewards of remaining single and childless were increased, or at least if the severe penalties that women in these positions now experience were lifted. Values can change. Only then, only when control over reproduction can be used to choose freely a life style uniquely suited to individual qualities, will women be able to say fully and truthfully, "Hallelujah the Pill!"

Three

School

America's public schools are here characterized as highly successful melting pots, from which students from a variety of distinctive environments emerge as standardized products. Adducing data from a study which compared creativity with high intelligence as each is encouraged by the schools, Professor Friedenberg contends that originality is suppressed in the school's attempt to hand down prevailing middle class values and styles. He suggests that non-public schools are valuable as they provide alternative educational experiences.

EDGAR Z. FRIEDENBERG

The School as a Social Environment

Our free public high school has from the beginning discharged two paramount social functions, neither of which has burdened secondary education elsewhere to anything like the same extent. The first of these is to build a common pattern of values and responses among adolescents from a diversity of class and ethnic backgrounds; the high school is a very important unit in our traditional system of melting pots. The second has been to help youngsters, as we say, to better themselves. In most industrial countries this second function

314

has by now assumed about as much importance as it has in the United States; but this is recent.

Until World War II secondary education of university preparatory quality in the rest of the world was essentially education for adolescents who had a reasonably high level of ascribed status. They came, as we used to say, from good homes; and, good or not, what they learned in school was culturally continuous with what they were used to at home. The same symbols had roughly the same meanings in both *ambiances.* In the United States, however, this was not true.

The public high school, being locally run, has generally deferred in various ways to the claims of status, devoting a preponderance of its resources and granting a preponderance of its rewards to solidly middle-class boys and girls to the relative neglect of lower-status youngsters, whom it often treats with great hostility. But its *own* folkways and traditions are not solidly middle-class; and if the higher-status youngsters are more favorably treated than their lower-status classmates, it must be recognized that the high school also extracts from them extra service as laboratory specimens for aspiring lower-status youth, and that the favor they receive is to some extent vitiated by the experience of immersion in a shabby-genteel and often envious environment for a period of years.

The melting pot and mobility functions of the high school are complementary. In combination, they are peculiarly potent. The atmosphere of the high school is permeated by the values they generate when combined. The combination is synergistic, and it really works. Taken as the high school directs, public education efficiently produces the kind of individual who can, and does, operate to sustain and augment his own position in a limitless variety of situations; and who does so with a characteristic American style regardless of his antecedents. This is just as true of rich antecedents as poor, and probably truer. The American ideal of equality is nowhere stronger than in public education; and if its administrators tend to be "realistic" about status, they nevertheless keep a school in which an upper-class vocabulary or accent is informally corrected as surely as that of the slum; and the *insouciance* and spontaneity of rich and poor alike is reduced to the guarded good humor of the executive. In metropolitan areas, at least, the high school dropout rates for upper- and lower-status students appear to be roughly comparable. Figures on this are not available to my knowledge, because schools do not directly record the social class of their students, and upper-status youngsters who leave public school for private school are not considered dropouts. But leave they do, in large proportions;

and they are not always fleeing from the Negro. Even from the suburbs that have so far excluded Negroes, upper-class white parents manage to send their children to Chaminade or Country Day, and the Negroes they meet there may ask them home to dinner, if they like them.

Upper-class rejection of the public school of course reflects a variety of motives, including sheer snobbery and an often erroneous presumption that the private school selected can get its students into Ivy colleges. But it also reflects a search for what parents call higher standards. On examination these standards often turn out to be no higher than those of the public school, but decidedly different from them. No more and no better work may be demanded of students, but it is slightly different work, and it is demanded for different reasons. This is true, of course, only of those private schools that do, in fact, have a social function different from the public schools. To the extent that the school depends for patronage on the anxiety of ambitious and socially insecure parents, it will compound the defects of the public school and add a few of its own. All private schools in America, no doubt, receive many helpless adolescents from such sources; but there are still some schools in which these students do not set the tone and they may therefore find refuge and real help in working out the meaning of their own lives under the illumination of disciplined study. This is harder for the public school to provide under its twin mandate to serve as a melting pot and a rocket to the moon.

There is something to be learned from etymology. The original meaning of education as a "drawing-out" makes an important point about the process—the same point that John Dewey and the progressive education people, at their best, also made. Education, if it is to have any depth, must start with and be derived from the life-experience of the student, which is in some measure unique for every boy or girl. It must cultivate this experience with a disciplined and demanding use of the best resources offered by the humanities and the sciences—to help the individual understand the meaning of his own experience. The consequence of such education, though it clearly leads the student to share in a universal cultural heritage, is more fundamentally to *sharpen* his individuality, to clarify and emphasize to *him* the ways in which he is unique.

A school that serves as a melting pot must inhibit this process, not facilitate it. Its purpose is to establish a common response to certain key stimuli, regardless of how different the respondents started out to be. Not only the content becomes stereotyped; so do the values underlying it, for the function of the school is to make it unnecessary to take account of the differences that might have resulted from the heterogeneity of life. If often fails, of course, and the student's folder receives a notation that his personality is defective; that he underachieves or is immature or emotionally disturbed—perfectly true, too; regression and ritualized internal conflict are classical responses to unbearably painful pressure on the emerging self.

When, however, the mandate to contribute to social mobility is joined to the melting pot process, the result is far more inhibitory to education. The student now learns that it is no longer sufficient to give the same answer; he must learn to distinguish the *right* answer. And he must learn to do this reliably and, as nearly as possible, automatically while his inner voice continues to shriek that the answer is wrong. Of course, his inner voice gradually gets a lot softer and more plaintive, and may finally show up as nothing more than a symptom. At this juncture, however, it would be a little unfair to say that the student's values are stereotyped; a real value has emerged. It has become important to him to learn to give the right answer quicker and more often than the next boy, who now is seen as a competitor rather than a person. And the inner voice is no longer irrelevant. It becomes, instead, the voice of the betrayer.

Professors Jacob W. Getzels and Philip W. Jackson in their recent work on *Creativity and Intelligence*[1] illustrate this process statistically. They drew their sample from a private, university-affiliated high school which afforded them, I should judge, an unusually abundant supply of the kind of "far-out" youngster that their methodology defines as creative. Their independent variables—that is, the criteria by which they assigned individual youngsters to their "high-creative" group—are essentially measures of "divergent thinking," as Professor J. P. Guilford of the University of Southern California defines this kind of mental activity in contrast to the "convergent thinking" of conventional high IQ students. Getzels and Jackson, in other words, started out by setting up a procedure in which the kind of adolescent who is especially prone to find a wealth of unconventional meanings in familiar material, and to use these meanings to arrive at perfectly workable but sometimes shockingly original solutions to problems, was contrasted with the kind of adolescent who is adept at setting such meanings aside as distractions and marching with power and determination along the path of conventional wisdom.

---

1. Jacob W. Getzels and Philip W. Jackson, *Creativity and Intelligence* (New York: John Wiley & Sons, Inc., 1962).

From a sample of 449 private high school students with a mean IQ of 129, Getzels and Jackson selected 26 students who were in the top 20 per cent on their Guilford-type measures of creativity, but not in IQ; and 28 who were in the top 20 per cent in IQ, but not in creativity. The two groups were then compared with each other and with the total group of 449 on school performance as measured by standard achievement tests; teachers' preferences for having them, when identified by name, in class; and the quality and manner of their response to a series of pictures like those used in the Thematic Apperception Test.

Both groups did equally well on the subject-matter tests of school achievement, and better than the total group of 449. The teachers, however, preferred the high IQ students to both the "high creatives" and those who had not been included in either group; and though they did prefer the high creatives to the average student, the difference was too small to be statistically significant. It should be borne in mind that this was a private secondary school with an exceptionally intelligent student body, and teachers who, to some extent, had chosen to teach gifted students and were accustomed to them. But they nevertheless preferred school achievement to be expressed in conventional terms, which the creatives were unlikely to do.

Getzels and Jackson quote illustratively the following sample responses to one of their story-pictures.

> One picture stimulus was perceived most often as a man in an airplane reclining seat returning from a business trip or conference. A high IQ student gave the following story: "Mr. Smith is on his way home from a successful business trip. He is very happy and he is thinking about his wonderful family and how glad he will be to see them again. He can picture it, about an hour from now, his plane landing at the airport and Mrs. Smith and their three children all there welcoming him home again." A high-creative subject wrote this story: "This man is flying back from Reno, where he has just won a divorce from his wife. He couldn't stand to live with her any more, he told the judge, because she wore so much cold cream on her face at night that her head would skid across the pillow and hit him in the head. He is now contemplating a new skid-proof face cream."

This is perhaps sufficient to illustrate the contrasting cognitive styles of Getzels' and Jackson's high creatives and high IQ's; and also to suggest what it is that teachers dislike about the former. The youngsters in their high-creative sample *do* disrupt the social environment. You can lead them to the pot; but they just don't melt, they burn. Intelligent and perceptive critics of Getzels' and Jackson's work have pointed out that the actual power of the creative students to create anything worthwhile remains, at their age, unestablished; but their prickliness, hostility, and aggression show up on nearly every instrument of the study. Getzels and Jackson included among their procedures one of having each subject draw whatever he liked on a sheet of paper captioned "Playing Tag in the School Yard." The drawings of the high IQ subjects are literal and humorless, "stimulus-bound"; the high creatives' drawings are fantastic and comical, with something of the quality of Till Eulenspiegel about them; but they are also gory. Combining Getzels' and Jackson's Tables 10 and 11,[2] we get the following statistics on these drawings as they rate them:

| | TYPE OF STUDENT | |
	High IQ	*High Creative*
Number of students in sample	28	26
Humor present	5	14
Humor absent	23	12
Violence present	1	9
Violence absent	27	17

We do not, of course, know how this spiral of reciprocal hostility starts; whether the youngsters become hostile and sarcastic because they are punished for their originality, even though at first they express it openly, innocently, and warmly; or whether a youngster will only think and feel divergently if he starts with a certain detachment from and distrust of conventional, established attitudes and procedures. Most likely—say, on the basis of such a cogent analysis as that in Ernest G. Schachtel's brilliant and classic paper, "On Memory and Childhood Amnesia,"[3] the beginnings of creativity in the exploratory sensuality of childhood are quite free from hostility; they are innocent, though hardly chaste. But exploratory sensuality is punished long before the child gets to school, and certainly before he gets to high school. Among the initially gifted, the high creatives are perhaps those who have received enough affection through the total process that they can afford to respond to insult by getting angry and verbally swatting back. The high IQ's have been

---

2. *Ibid.,* p. 49. The tables indicate that the statistical probability of a chance difference between high IQ's and high creatives, as great as that shown here, is .02 or less.
3. Ernest G. Schachtel, "On Memory and Childhood Amnesia," *Metamorphosis* (New York: Basic Books, Inc., 1959), pp. 279–322.

treated wholly as instruments of parental aspirations, even at home, and become anxious at any sign that they are getting off the track; anger and hostility are beyond their emotional means. The findings of Getzels and Jackson on the home background of their contrasting subjects bear this out.

But their most poignant data were obtained from an instrument that they called the Outstanding Traits Test. This consisted of 13 thumbnail descriptions of such traits as social skill, goal-directedness and good marks, using phrases like "Here is the student who is best at getting along with other people"; "Here is the student who is best able to look at things in a new way and to discover new ideas"; "Here is the outstanding athlete in the school," and so forth. The students in their sample were asked to rank these 13 descriptions in three different ways: as "preferred for oneself," as "favored by teachers," and as "believed predictive of adult success." The rank-order correlations obtained between the high IQ and high creative students as to how these traits contributed to later success was *unity;* as to what teachers preferred, it was 0.98. The high creative and high IQ students, in short, were in absolute agreement as to what traits would make a person succeed in adult life; they were virtually agreed as to what teachers liked in students—though the two ratings were not identical. Nevertheless, the correlation between the two groups' ratings of these traits as "preferred for oneself" was only 0.41. This can only be interpreted to mean that one or both of these groups believed that pleasing teachers and becoming successful was just not worth what it cost, even though they agreed completely as to what that cost would be.

Which group rejected the image of success that both shared? The data clearly permits me to resolve this question and end your suspense. Here, instead of correlations *between* the high IQ's and the high creatives, we need, of course, correlations *within* each group for the three possible bases of sorting. Here they are:

	STUDENTS	
Components of Correlation	*High IQ*	*High Creative*
Personal traits believed "predictive of success" and "favored by teachers"	0.62	0.59
Personal traits "preferred for oneself" and "believed predictive of adult success"	0.81	0.10
Personal traits "preferred for oneself" and "believed favored by teachers"	0.67	−0.25

I would interpret these statistics to mean that the high creatives cannot bring themselves to be what they believe success requires, and are even more strongly repelled by what the teacher demands. The correlation coefficients on the two "favored by teachers" categories are really very curious and interesting across the board. I find a .6 correlation here astonishingly low for *both* groups—with these N's of 26 and 28 such a correlation has little statistical significance. While, for the high IQ's, the correlation between "preferred for one-self" and "predictive of success" is high, for the high creatives, it is negligible.

BOTH HIGH IQ's AND HIGH CREATIVES SHOW A NEED TO ACHIEVE

All these data could be explained very satisfactorily by the hypothesis that the high creatives, spontaneous and joyful as the happy-go-lucky Negro slave of song and story, just don't give a damn; that this is their way of singing "Hallelujah, I'm a bum." But it won't do. Using two standard measures of the need to achieve, David McClelland's *need: achievement* and Fred L. Strodtbeck's V-score, Getzels and Jackson were unable to find any significant differences between the two groups, or between either group and the total population of 449; the figures given for the high creatives are actually slightly higher on both measures. So we must turn for our interpretation to the relationship between the students and the school itself.

Both groups, I infer, see the teacher as on the side of success, but being too naive and square to be a very reliable guide as to how to go after it. Since the high IQ's are determined to *be* the kind of person who succeeds, this reduces the relevance of the teacher to him, but not the relevance of the school. Or to put it another way, the importance of the school as the monitor of his progress is quite enough to bring the high IQ to terms with it; and the terms are generous enough not to demand that he listen to what it actually says. To the high creative, the whole experience is rather frustrating and annoying, and relevant only because there is no viable alternative to high school for a middle-class adolescent. Lower-class adolescents who are not interested in economic success or who feel the school too suffocating can just drop out, go off on a kick, and let the authorities conceal their relief while they pretend to search for them. But this kind of direct action would cost the middle-class youngster his role, and cause him too much anxiety to be a satisfactory alternative. Generally he stays, and looks for ancillary satisfactions in specialized relationships with his peers, in sports or hobbies or sometimes sex and even love, building up a credential while inwardly rejecting the qualities the credential symbolizes.

For both groups, however, the function of the school becomes essentially liturgical, not epistemological. It isn't supposed to make sense. It is not appropriate to believe, disbelieve, or test what one is taught in school. Instead, one *relates* to it; one tries to figure out why this line has been taken rather than another, to figure out what response is expected, and give it.

The result is a peculiar kind of moral vacuity; a limitation of responsible *perception,* and therefore, of moral behavior, to situations that are wholly concrete and immediate. The public school is not primarily an educational institution. I have forgotten who first said that most Christians would feel equal consternation at hearing Christianity denounced and at seeing it practiced; it ought, presumably, to have been Mary. But I am quite sure that this could justly be said of most Americans with respect to public education. In many ways, the relationship of the school to the community is like that of a TV station that carries mostly network programs but that is largely dependent on local advertising for support. Like the TV station, the school has its own technical staff, and such autonomy as it possesses is derived from their custody of the mysteries and the records, rather than from any considerable measure of popular deference to their authority. The entertainment provided is frequently of high quality and shrewdly geared to the public taste. Concessions to the intellect and culture, provided as a public service, tend to be more ponderous, conventional, and unconvincing. Though the staff likes to boast about how much of this sort of thing they program, they are self-conscious about it, and rather fearful. The commercials for the local way of life are interminable, boring, and egregiously dishonest, and the audience knows it. But they are hard to change for they are the real basis for the support the school receives. And they are effective, as good commercials are, not so much in stimulating an active desire for the product as in convincing the audience that only a social misfit would be without it.

STUDENTS PREPARE FOR NEXT STEP

What the students learn best in high school is how to function in and utilize a limited power network to achieve limited personal and social objectives. They learn how to get along and make ready for the next onward state. By the time they reach college, they are likely to be thoroughly impatient of anything else; and in our culture, college seldom tries their patience much; the process continues. To me, the most interesting finding in a recent study of medical students[4] is the righteous resentment with which the young medics respond to instruction in medical—to say nothing of social—theory. What they want from medical school is conventional knowledge and practical hints (what they call pearls) and a clear road to the practitioner's license. To get this they are willing to work like dogs; but they resist any suggestion that they work like a higher primate.

Doctors, of course, have notoriously high IQ's, and it is not astonishing that medical students should resemble Getzels' and Jackson's high IQ's in their characteristic cognitive style. But they are also quite creative, when they feel that circumstances and the American Medical Association permit; as are many high IQ's. Creativity and intelligence, like height and weight, are undoubtedly highly correlated. Getzels and Jackson adopted a classic design for their study to permit them to examine contrasts; just as biologists studying human metabolism might deliberately set out to study the differences between short, fat people and tall, thin ones. But both are exceptional, which is why the sample fell from 449 to 28 in one quadrant and 26 in the other. Had they chosen to study youngsters who were in the top 20 per cent in both creativity and IQ, they would probably have found 60 or so in the sample. How would *they* have fared in school?

Getzels and Jackson tell us nothing about this. My own understanding and observation of public education suggests that they would probably be very successful, indeed, and would be well received by the school and acquire a substantial proportion of positions of leadership. We would accept them as our best young Americans —executive material. And the school would teach them to be discreet: not to let their creativity get the upper hand, not to jeopardize their chances by antagonizing persons more stupid than themselves who might nevertheless turn up later on some committee that was passing on them. The pitch would be made on a high moral plane —usually in terms of keeping their availability so as not to impair their usefulness—but the net effect would be to convince the youngster that he ought not to get out of line or speak out of turn, if he hoped ultimately to put his creativity to use in the service of, say, General Electric or the United States Food and Drug Administration.

A statistic frequently cited in the United States is that we spend a little more on hard liquor than we do on public education. I have just finished reading a book which seems to me more striking in its educational implications than any work directly *about* education

---

4. Howard S. Becker, Blanche Geer, Everett S. Hughes, and Anselm L. Strauss, *Boys in White* (Chicago: University of Chicago Press, 1962).

since Martin Mayer's *The Schools.*[5] This book is Theodore H. White's *The Making of the President 1960;*[6] and after reading it I find that datum shocking. We ought to be spending a *lot* more on hard liquor. We are going to need it, and besides, it works. But I have introduced Mr. White's book into this discussion, not primarily as a vivid portrait of the failure of public education to instruct a trust-worthy electorate—though that, according to James Madison, was its essential function—but to allude to one particular passage as a spe-cific illustration of creativity and what happens to it. Mr. White gives a circumstantial account of Richard Nixon's suspiciousness of the press and ineptness in communicating with it, which made the job of the reporters assigned to cover his campaign—for papers pri-marily committed to his support—almost impossible. The reporters themselves came to dislike and distrust Mr. Nixon and his program. In their dispatches, no hint of their actual feelings or personal ap-praisal appeared.

But Mr. White reports:

Then having done their duty, they began frivolously to write imagi-nary dispatches of what they felt would be a more accurate transcrip-tion of their private understanding. I reproduce here a few leads of such dispatches as illustrations of what happens when the press feels itself abused.

Guthrie Center, Iowa [read one]—Vice-President Nixon said today farmers should eat their way out of the surplus problem. . . .

Guthrie Center, Iowa [another]—Vice-President Nixon admitted today that the farm problem was too big for the Republican Party to handle. He said that if elected President, he would appoint Senator Hubert H. Humphrey as Secretary of Agriculture and let him wrestle with the problem. . . .

Guthrie Center, Iowa [another]—Vice-President Nixon today called on Pope John XXIII for guidance in finding a solution to the troublesome farm problems which have plagued Catholic, Jew and Protestant alike. . . .[7]

My point is that Mr. White also illustrates what doesn't happen even when the press feels itself abused. These "imaginary dis-patches" may well afford "a more accurate transcription of their private understanding" than what the reporters actually transmit-ted. Their responsibility as reporters, I should say, included that of

5. Martin Mayer, *The Schools* (New York: Harper & Brothers, 1960).
6. Theodore H. White, *The Making of the President 1960* (New York: Atheneum, 1961).
7. *Ibid.,* pp. 274–275.

letting the public know not only what Mr. Nixon had said but what they thought he was actually like, properly labeled, of course, as a subjective judgment. This they were too canny to release until too late for it to do any good.

It is self-evident, I believe, that the quality of these imaginary dispatches is identical with the quality of the picture stories produced by the high creatives in Getzels' and Jackson's study, but the factually correct dispatches are the kind of response the high IQ's produce. The reporters, then, must have been both; but they had learned better than to be both when the chips were down and people were watching. They were not deliberately taught this in school, but school is a very good place in which to learn it.

Mr. White further writes:

> One had to see Nixon entering a small Iowa village, the streets lined with schoolchildren, all waving American flags until it seemed as if the cavalcade were entering a defile lined by fluttering, peppermint-striped little banners ... to see him at his best ... These people were his natural constituency, his idiom their idiom ...[8]
>
> ... He woke in Marietta, Ohio, on Monday, October 25th, to begin his last 'peak' effort and it was clear from his first speech of the day that he was at one with his audience as he had not been since he had passed through the corn fields of Iowa in the first week of the campaign. A sign outside the courthouse of Marietta, Ohio, read: High School Debaters Greet World Debater—the sign was apropos, and of the essence of his last trip as he revived. For he *was* a high-school debater, the boy who had, some thirty years before, won a Los Angeles *Times* prize for his high-school oration on the Constitution. He was seeking not so much to score home a message as to win the hearts of his little audiences. ...[9]

It *is* a little like entering a defile. Some of us would prefer to enter a demurrer. On the basis of cognitive style I would infer that this would include a disproportionate number of high creatives. But how, in the present public high school, does one go about it?

One of the traditional forms of demurrer in our society is to get up and slowly walk away. We have always counted on pluralism as our most effective weapon against conformity and, in de Tocqueville's phrase, "the tyranny of the majority"; and I think it is one of the best social instruments that could be devised and inherent in the nature of democracy. For that reason, I am very much in favor of private and parochial schools. As a matter of social policy, I think

8. *Ibid.*, p. 277.
9. *Ibid.*, p. 300.

they should receive some tax support. I am not a constitutional lawyer, and I cannot judge the legal merits of the argument that aid to church schools, granted at their request, would constitute the Congress making a law respecting an establishment of religion. Personally, I think this is a ridiculous interpretation of the First Amendment; but, then, the First Amendment has always been my favorite passage of the Constitution, and I am naturally reluctant to believe that it is against anything that I favor.

I am convinced that private schools—and in this country many of these are church-supported—contribute more to the general welfare even than they do to their own constituency. We so desperately need alternative life-styles and *ethical models that are related to a particular community and to the experience of life within it,* rather than recipes for tearing away from one's roots and learning to function smoothly among successively more affluent groups of strangers. As to the risk of encountering God, well, it is true that He can be very tricky. But I doubt if the encounter can be altogether avoided. It would certainly not harm any youngster—rather in the spirit of the New England gentlewoman who took up the study of Hebrew at the age of eighty-five—to learn how to confront Him and thrash out those issues on which they were in disagreement. Adolescents generally get along very well with God, anyhow. The Creation is exactly the kind of thing they can imagine having done themselves, and they can sympathize with the kind of trouble He got himself into by acting out His creative impulse. It is only in later life, the image having become somewhat tarnished, that the meeting tends to be rather embarrassing to both.

It is difficult to suggest practical ways in which the public school might represent and support a greater diversity of values and a less purely instrumental conception of learning. At present, the public high school lacks dignity. It is often incoherent. Whatever is learned of graciousness and leisure in English or art class—and it isn't likely to be much—is undercut by the food and the noise and standing in line in the cafeteria. The social studies class may discuss civil liberty, but the students still need a pass to walk through the hall and school disciplinary procedures are notably lacking in due process. The students are encouraged to get together in groups to discuss important issues, as long as there is somebody to represent all sides and the criticism doesn't go too deep. But there isn't any place to do it that is out of reach of the public address system announcing when you have to go to get your yearbook picture taken or directing Tom Brown to report to the principal's office *at once;* the efficiency of the p.a. system depends on the fact that you can't get away from it.

All these are trivial; what is not trivial is the continuous experience, day after day and year after year, of triviality itself; of being treated like a tiny unit in an administrative problem. So, really, it does add up; this is *how* you are taught not to take yourself too seriously. This is where you learn that whatever may be officially said, actual official decisions are made with the short-run purpose of getting the job done and keeping out of trouble. This is where you learn to keep your conversation brief, friendly, and to the point, instead of getting all hung up on ideas like an egghead or an Oxbridge don.

Of course, these things and worse occur in many private schools which can also be barren and stultifying. But when they are, there is at least the theoretical possibility of appealing to an explicit educational tradition that transcends American middle-class practice to try and change them. These *are* basic American middle-class values, however; so there is not much use appealing there, though a smart public school administrator may develop considerable skill in identifying subgroups in his community that take education and youngsters more seriously. But it is a laborious and dangerous process. Public school administrators who try to give their communities better education than they are used to have a very short life expectancy. If you wish to see a case study of such a situation in detail, *Small Town in Mass Society,*[10] contains a superb one. But you know it already.

There is nothing wrong with the school as a social environment, except what is wrong with America. One of the sailors in my company when I was in the Navy during World War II had a stock proposal that he used to make with reference to any of our mates who was seriously annoying him. "Let's ostracize him," he said. "You hold him, and I'll do it." Technically, what Coleman proposes is the exact contrary. But I am afraid it comes to the same thing in the end.

It seems to me, then, that I have no choice but to conclude on a note of satisfaction. As a social environment the public high school, by and large, functions very effectively. It is expected to socialize adolescents into the American middle-class, and that is just what it does. You can actually see it doing it. If that isn't what you want, go fight Livingston Street.*

10. Arthur J. Vidich and Joseph Bensman, *Small Town in Mass Society* (Princeton, New Jersey: Princeton University Press, 1958).
* [The offices of the New York City Board of Education are at 110 Livingston Street.]

Stepping back from the school system to examine its products as they interact with the culture at large, Paul Goodman finds youth isolated in a restrictive subculture. In this article he focuses on the speech of that subculture—its vocabulary, its content and its roots in the speech of adult society—and concludes that the hip, semi-articulate speech of adolescents is at the bottom a substitute for other, more meaningful questions they cannot ask.

PAUL GOODMAN

The Universe of Discourse in Which They Grow Up

Let us now consider the interaction of school and the general culture as a climate of communication and ask:

What happens to the language and thought of young Americans as they grow up toward and through adolescence?

In the institutional speech, a child hears only one world-view. In the nature of the case, every mass-medium caters to a big common-denominator of opinion and taste, but even more influential is that the mass-media interlock. "News," for instance, is what is selected as newsworthy by two or three news services; three almost identical broadcasting networks abstract from the same; and the same is again abridged for the *Junior Scholastic.* Even for this news, only 60 towns in America now have competing newspapers (in 1900 there were 600). Similarly, the "standard of living," the way to live respectably and decently, is what is shown in the ads in a few mass-circulation magazines and identically in the TV commercials. Movie-sets of respectable life come from the same kind of engineers. Similarly, "political thought" is the platforms of two major parties that agree on all crucial issues, like the Cold War and the Expanding Economy, and that get practically all of the coverage by the same newspapers and broadcasters.

Much of this public speech is quite meaningless. The ads compete with high rhetoric but the commodities are nearly the same, and a child can see that our lives are not *quite* so vastly occupied by soap, cigarettes, and beer. Politicians are very polemical, but they avoid any concrete issues that might differentiate the candidates and lose votes. The real meaning of the speeches, the goal of profits and power, is never stated. By age 11 or 12, bright children, perhaps readers of *Mad* magazine, recognize that most of the speech is mere words.

The interlocking of the schools into the system is more serious, for here the children have to work at it and cooperate. The story is the same. The galloping increase of national tests guarantees that the class-work will become nothing but preparation for these same tests. Corporation talent-scouts hover in the high schools, and even the primary schools are flooded with corporation brochures. Excellent scientists in Washington who chart courses in science and mathematics understand that there must be leeway for individuality and guesswork; but in the hands of incompetent teachers, the national standard naturally becomes an inflexible ruler. And TV and machine-teaching are formal statements that *everybody apperceives in the same way, with no need for dialogue.*

Apart from family, children have little speech with any adults except schoolteachers. But the crowding and scheduling in school allow little chance or time for personal contact. Also, increasingly in grade schools as well as in colleges, the teachers have abdicated their personal role to specialist counselors and administrators, so that confiding and guidance tend to occur only in extreme situations. One must be "deviant" to be attended to as a human being.

This public speech cannot easily be tested against direct observation or experience. Urban and suburban children do not see crafts and industries. Playthings are prefabricated toys; there is little practical carpentry, plumbing, or mechanics; but there are do-it-yourself kits. The contrast of city and country vanishes in endless conurbation. Few children know animals. Even basic foods are packaged and distributed, and increasingly precooked, in the offical style.

And a child hears less of any rival style or thought. The rival world-view of (even hypocritical) religion is no longer influential. Children do not know the Bible. Eccentric classical children's literature is discouraged by librarians because it does not fit educators' word-lists and is probably unhygienic. The approved books are concocted according to the official world-view. Other more exciting reading, like comic books, does not contrast to life but withdraws from it, is without reality or feeling. The movies are the same more insidiously, because they are apparently adult and real. Finally, the ideal models of careers with their characters and philosophies— scientist, explorer, nurse, writer—have been normalized to TV sterotypes: they are all the same Organization Man, though they wear various costumes.

Nevertheless, this one system of meaning, although homogeneous and bland, is by no means sparse or quiet. On the contrary, the quantity of public speech, plays, information, cartoons is swamping. The tone is jumpy and distracting. In the schools, exposure occurs with intense pressure of tests for retention and punishment for failure to retain.

No one can critically appreciate so many images and ideas; and there is very little solitude or moratorium to figure them out. A child is confused. And he is also anxious, because if the information is not correctly parroted, he will fall off the school ladder and be a drop-out; or he will not be hep among his little friends.

At a childish level, all this adds up to brainwashing. The components are (a) a uniform world-view, (b) the absence of any viable alternative, (c) confusion about the relevance of one's own experience and feelings, and (d) a chronic anxiety, so that one clings to the one world-view as the only security. This *is* brainwashing.

Of course, in all societies and periods of history small children are subject to brainwashing, for they are weak, ignorant, economically dependent, and subject to bullying. In some ways in our society the brainwashing of children is not so pernicious as it has been at other times, for there is less corporal punishment, less extreme poverty, less fear of death, and less brutal toilet-training and sexual disciplining. On the other hand, the ideological exposure is unusually swamping, systematic, and thorough. Profit societies, like garrison states, invade every detail of life. But worst of all is that parents are as baffled as the children; since the areas of choice and initiative are so severely limited, they too lose touch with personal and practical information.

Thus, despite our technology of surplus, our civil peace (?), and so much educational and cultural opportunity, it is hard for an American child to grow toward independence, to find his identity, to retain his curiosity and initiative, and to acquire a scientific attitude, scholarly habits, productive enterprise, poetic speech.

Unfortunately, the pervasive philosophy to which children are habituated as they grow up is the orthodoxy of a social machine not interested in persons, except to man and aggrandize itself. Especially not young persons.

Then what happens when, with this background of impersonal and stereotyped language, the child becomes adolescent: awkward and self-conscious, sexually hungry and falling in love, searching for identity, metaphysical, shaken in religious faith or undergoing religious conversion, his Oedipus-complex reviving, making a bid for freedom from home, grandiosely ambitious, looking for a vocation, eager to be serviceable as a human being? At best, in organic communities, rational communication breaks down and the community has recourse to rites of passage.

The American world-view is worse than inadequate; it is irrelevant and uninterested, and adolescents are spiritually abandoned. They are insulated by not being taken seriously. The social machine does not require or desire its youth to find identity or vocation; it is interested only in aptitude. It does not want new initiative, but conformity. Our orthodoxy does not bear metaphysics. Religious troubles are likely to be treated as psychotic; they are certainly disruptive of urban order and scholastic scheduling. Many, maybe most, of the careers that are open are not services to humanity; that is not why businesses are run, nor why bombs are stockpiled. Idealism is astonishingly without prestige.

The adolescent sexual situation is peculiarly ambiguous. We are in a transitional phase of the sexual revolution and there is a breakdown of repression (keeping out of mind) and also less inhibition of sexual behavior. Yet neither in the economy, the housing, nor the family pattern is there any provision for the changed mores. Quite the contrary, the years of tutelage even tend to lengthen, especially for middle-class youth in colleges whose administrations regard themselves as *in loco parentis.* The offical mental-hygienic ideology bears little relation to the stormy images and imperative demands of adolescent love. In the elementary and junior high schools, sexual facts do not officially exist. But an adolescent is supposed to be sexual or there is alarm.

Embarrassment—the inability to express or reveal one's needs and feelings to the others—is universal among adolescents. But in our society it is especially problematic. The embarrassment contains or will contain hostility to those who will not pay attention or will put one down; and also despair at the futility of trying to make oneself clear. For there is not even a common language relevant to one's burning private facts—how pathetic it is to hear adolescents using the language of TV marriage-counselors, or of movies! Inevitably, silent hostility is retroflected as self-denigration. An adolescent ceases to believe in the rightness of his own wants, and soon he even doubts their existence. His rebellious claims seem even to himself to be groundless, immature, ridiculous.

Broadly speaking, the difficulties of adolescent communication, both in speaking and listening, are kinds of embarrassment. Let us here discuss adolescent speechlessness, in-group language and subculture, and how adolescents finally give up their own meaning and swallow the official adult philosophy hook, line, and sinker.

Embarrassment may be grounded in too strong desire and confusion, or in hostility and fear.

Paling and blushing embarrassment in expressing lust or aspiration is largely due to confusion caused by powerful feelings that have been untried, or vague new ideas that seem presumptuous. It is akin to ingenuous shame, which is exhibition suddenly inhibited because it is (or might be) unacceptable. With courage and encouragement, such speechless embarrassment can falter into sweet or ringing poetic speech, by which the youth explains himself, also to himself. More common with use, however, is for the youth to inhibit his stammering and to brazen out the situation with a line imitated from the mass-media or salesmanship. For example, the strategy is to "snow" the girl rather than talk to her. Thereby he proves that he is grownup, has an erection etc., but he sacrifices feeling, originality, the possibility of growth, and the possibility of love.

The speechless embarrassment of hostility is fear of retaliation if one reveals oneself. Suppose a youth is reprimanded, advised, or perhaps merely accosted by an authoritative adult, e.g. a guidance counselor; he will maintain a sullen silence and not give the adult the time of day. His presumption is that the adult is setting a trap, could not understand, does not care anyway. The youth cannot adopt a breezy line, as with a peer, for the adult has more words. He will be taken as fresh, hostile, or in bad taste. Therefore it is best to say nothing, expressing (perhaps unconsciously) a blazing contempt. In this situation, the youth's interpretation is not too erroneous, except that the authority is usually not malevolent but busy and perhaps insensitive.

Suppose, however, the adult is a good teacher who does care for the young persons and would like to reach them in meaningful terms, not the orthodoxy. Then, as Frank Pinner has pointed out, it is likely that the teacher's dissenting ideas will be met by a wall of silence that makes communication impossible. The young are so unsure, and their distrust is such, that in the crisis of possible contact they prefer to cling to safe conformity, even though among themselves they may bitterly attack these same conformist ideas.

Even worse, there is an hermetic silence about anything deeply felt or threatening; such things are unspeakable even to one's peers, no less to adults. One may boast to a friend about a sexual conquest or fret about poor grades, but one may not reveal that one is in love or has a lofty aspiration. Or to give a tragic example: Puerto Rican boys will chatter endless small talk and one-up one another, but nobody will mention that one of their number has just been sent to jail or that one has just died of an overdose of heroin. If the forbidden subject is mentioned, they do not hear it. They cannot psychologically afford to relate themselves, their verbal personalities, to the terrible realities of life. (Incidentally, I have heard from teachers in the New York schools that there is a similar cleavage in many young Puerto Rican's knowledge of the English language. They seem to talk English fluently as long as the subject is superficial and "grown-up"; but they are blank in many elementary words and phrases, and are quite unable to say, in English, anything that they really want or need.)

To diminish embarrassment, since communication with the adults is cut off, there is developed an increasingly exaggerated adolescent "sub-culture," with its jargon, models, authors, and ideology. Let us first distinguish between a "sub-culture" and a "sub-society."

An intense youth sub-society is common in most cultures. In our culture, the interest in sexual exploration, dancing, simple exciting music, athletics, cars and races, clubs and jackets, one-upping conversation, seems to be natural to youth—just as many adult interests are naturally irrelevant and boring to them. Also, the sharing of secrets, often mysterious even to themselves, is everywhere a powerful bond of union among adolescents; and certainly their business is nobody else's business. The Youth Houses of some primitive communities institutionalize all this rather better than our own boarding-schools and colleges, which are too ridden with *in loco parentis* regulations.

The development of such a sub-society into a full-blown sub-culture, however, is not normal, but reactive. It signifies that the adult culture is hostile to adolescent interests, or is not to be trusted; that parents are not people and do not regard their children as people; that the young are excluded from adult activities that might be interesting and, on the other hand, that most adult activities are *not* worth growing up into as one becomes ready for them. Rather, on the contrary, the adults are about to exploit the young, to pressure them into intrinsically boring careers, regardless of proper time or individual choice.

Normally there is not a "youth culture" and an "adult culture," but youth is the period of growing up in the one culture. With us, however, youth feels itself to be almost out-caste, or at least manipulated. It therefore has secrets, jargon, and a lore of sabotage and defense *against* the adult culture.

But then, since the intellectual life of callow boys and girls in isolation from the grown-up economy and culture is thin gruel, youth interests are vastly puffed up into fads, disk-jockeys, politically organized gangs and wars, coterie literature, drugs and liquor, all frantically energized by youthful animal spirits—and cleverly managed by adult promoters. The teenage market is more than $10 billions a year, in jackets, portable radios, sporting goods, hair-dos, bikes, and additional family cars. Needless to say, this secondary development is simply a drag on the youthful spirit. It is largely frivolous and arbitrary, yet it is desperately conservative and exerts a tremendous pressure of blackmail against nonconformers or those ignorant of the latest, who will be unpopular. It makes it hard to talk sense to them, or for them to talk sense, whether adolescent or adult. And of course there is no chance for intelligent dissent from the official philosophy and standard of life. Naturally, too, especially in the middle class, the regressed adults play at and sponsor every teenage idiocy.

Inevitably, the high school—with its teenage majority and adult regime—becomes a prime area for sabotage and other fun and games. I have heard James Coleman, who has most studied these phenomena, express the opinion that the average adolescent is really *in* school, academically, for about ten minutes a day! Not a very efficient enterprise.

A certain number of the young gang up and commit defiant delinquencies. These are partly the revolt of nature—for there is much in our society that is insulting and intolerably frustrating. They are partly reactive against *whatever* happens to constitute "correct" behavior. And they are partly a pathetic bid for attention, as it is said, "We're so bad they give us a Youth Worker."

A pathetic characteristic of recent middle-class adolescent subculture is taking on the language and culture of marginal groups, Negroes and Latin Americans, addicts, Beat dropouts from the colleges and the Organized System. This is appropriate, for these others too are abused and disregarded; they are in the same case as the adolescents. But such a culture is hardly articulate. Also, there is something exploiting about imitation authentic out-caste people, who live as they do not by choice but by necessity.

Nevertheless, for many of the woefully embarrassed, this semi-articulate speech—saying "man" and "cat" and "like, man"—makes conversation possible. The adolescent culture is something to talk about and this is a style to talk in. The words of one syllable of jive, the thoughts of one syllable of Beat, the content of kicks, movies, and high school dances, are not a wide discourse, but they foster being together, and everybody can democratically participate.

Unfortunately, the small talk drives out real talk. It is incredibly snobbish and exclusive of sincerity and originality. Embattled against the adult world that must inexorably triumph, adolescent society jealously protects itself against meaning.

To adolescents of sixteen, the adult world must seem like a prison door slamming shut. Some must get jobs which are sure not to fit them and in which they will exercise no initiative whatever. Others must engage in the factitious competition for college-entrance. Either process is formidable with forms and tests. The kids are ignorant of the ropes and ignorant of what they want. Disregarded by the adults, they have in turn excluded adult guidance or ideas looking toward the future. But their adolescent bravado is now seen to be unrealistic and even ridiculous. Having learned nothing, nor fought any battles, they are without morale.

Their weakness can be observed vividly on college campuses. Students gripe about the moral rules by which they are still absurdly harassed at 18 and 19 years of age. It's ironical; if they had quit school and were assembly-line workers, they would be considered responsible enough to come and go, have sex, and drink.—Yet it comes to nothing but griping; they do not feel justified to enforce their demands, for they have never had this issue, or any issue, out with their parents. Similarly, they are unhappy about the overcrowded classes, the credits, the grading; they know they are disappointed in the education they are getting; yet they are so confused about what they do want that they are speechless.

And just in the colleges, which are supposed to be communities of scholars, face-to-face communication is diminished. The adolescent sub-culture that persists is irrelevant to the business going on, except to sabotage it, but the adolescent community is *not* replaced by close acquaintance with learned adults. The teachers hold the students off and, as I argued in *The Community of Scholars,* it is a chief function of orderly administration to keep the students out of contact with the teachers and the teachers out of contact with one another. Naturally, as long as the students are isolated with one another, they can be treated as immature, which they are.

The dialogue with the subject-matter, with Nature and History, is as skimpy as with the teacher. Colleges are not interested in such things any more—it has little Ph.D. value. The student is told the current doctrine and is trained to give it back accurately. And still proving his masculinity and doing a snow-job, the student thinks that the purpose of a course is to "master the subject." Necessarily, in the conflict with the adult world, the young suffer a crushing defeat. There are various ways of surviving it. Some give up on themselves and conform completely—a few indeed become more royalist than the king (but these are often psychopathic, middle-class

delinquents). Others make rationalizations: they will return to the
fray later when they are "better prepared." Or, "The most important
thing is to get married and raise a normal family," they will hold
onto feeling and meaning for their family life, or perhaps for their
"personal" behavior. A surprising number tell you that the goal of
life is $50,000 a year.

The psychology of the introjection is evident: defeated, they
identify with what has conquered them, in order to fill the gap with
some meaning or other. Once they have made the new identification,
they feel strong in it, they defend it by every rationalization.

An alternative philosophy that has recommended itself to some
older adolescents is hipsterism. A hipster cushions the crushing
defeat by society by *deliberately* assuming convenient roles in the
dominant system, including its underworld, to manipulate it for his
own power or at least safety. The bother with this idea—it is the
argument of Thrasymachus in Plato's *Republic*—is that the hipster
cannot afford to lose himself, or even to become unselfconscious. He
must be ahead of every game. Then he cannot grow by loving or
believing anything worthwhile, and he exhausts himself in business with what he holds in contempt, deepening his own cynicism
and self-contempt. But hipsterism does provide a satisfaction of mastery and victory which ward off his panic of powerlessness, passivity, and emasculation. It is a philosophy for chronic emergency,
during which communication consists inevitably of camouflage and
secrecy, "playing it cool," or of gambits of attack to get the upper
hand.

The conditions that I have been describing, and the youthful
responses to them, sadly limit human communication and even the
concept of it. "Communication" comes to be interpreted as the transfer of a processed meaning from one head to another which will
privately put it in a niche in its own system of meanings. This
system is presumably shared with the others—one can never know.
And in this presumptive consensus, the exchanged information adds
a detail or a specification, but it does not disturb personality or alter
characteristic behavior, for the self has not been touched. At most,
the information serves as a signal for action from the usual reper-
tory.

Among Americans, this sentiment of consensus, "understanding," is so important that much speech and reading does not
even give new information, but is a ritual touching of familiar bases.
(This is evident in much newspaper reading, in after-dinner
speeches, and so forth.) But the case is not much different with active

speech that is supposed to affect choice, e.g. in politics, for no disturbing issues are broached, nor anything that one would have to think
new thoughts about. The underlying consensus is assumed—is sig-
nalled by the usual words—and no important alternative is offered.
The consensus is *presumably* shared, but any dialectic to test
this assumption is in bad form, just as it is impolite to question a
loose generalization made in small talk, and say "Prove it." In ideal
cybernetic theory, the exchange of information is supposed to alter
the organisms conversing, since they must make internal readjust-
ments to it; but my observation is that no such alteration occurs. The
chief meaning of conversation is its own smooth going on.

By contrast, the active speech of salesmanship is more lively,
because it is meant importantly to change behavior, toward buying
something; it is not meant merely to soothe. Thus, strikingly, TV
commercials are the only part of TV that makes novel use of the
medium itself, employing montage and inventive music, playing
with the words, images and ideas. The pitch of a salesman is likely
to be *ad hominem,* in bad form, both flattering and threatening.
(Needless to say, there is no dialogue; the hearer is passive or dumbly
resistant.) But of course, in salesmanship, apart from the one pre-
thought transaction, the consensus is powerfully protected; the TV
ad and the program that it sponsors avoids anything that might
surprise, provoke, or offend any single person in an audience of
millions.

Consider what is lost by this narrow concept of communication
as the exchange of processed information with which each com-
municant copes internally. (a) The function of speech as the shaping
expression of pre-verbal needs and experiences, by which a speaker
first discovers *what* he is thinking. Such speech cannot be entirely
pre-thought and controlled; it is spontaneous. (b) The function of
speech as personally initiating something by launching into an environment that is *unlike* oneself. Initiating, one presumes there is no
consensus; otherwise why bother speaking? (c) Most important of
all, the function of speech as dialogue between persons *committed
to the conversation*—or between a person and a subject-matter in
which he is absorbed. This result in change of the persons because
of the very act of speaking; they are not fixed roles playing a game
with rules.

Speaking is a way of making one's identity, of losing oneself
with others in order to grow. It depends not on prior consensus with
the others, but on trust of them. But, in my opinion, the speech
defined in most contemporary communication theory is very like

the speech of the defeated adolescents I have been describing. It is not pragmatic, communal, poetic, or heuristic. Its function is largely to report in a processed *lingua franca.*

Speech cannot be personal and poetic when there is embarrassment of self-revelation, including revelation to oneself, nor when there is animal diffidence and communal suspicion, shame of exhibition and eccentricity, clinging to social norms. Speech cannot be initiating when the chief social institutions are bureaucratized and pre-determine all procedures and decisions, so that in fact individuals have no power anyway that is useful to express. Speech cannot be exploratory and heuristic when pervasive chronic anxiety keeps people from risking losing themselves in temporary confusion and from relying for help precisely *on* communicating, even if the communication is Babel.

As it is, people have to "think" before they speak, rather than risking speaking and finding out what they mean by trying to make sense to others and themselves. In fact, they finally speak English as though they were in school.

The articles printed here were selected from a number of the underground high-school newspapers that flourished between 1967 and 1970. The students whose writings appear come from typical American homes in suburbs, cities, and rural America. The particular statements that are included deal with subjects that students know well. These include the routines that make daily school life a prison, the adult reaction to long hair, and how television portrays the teenager.

DIANE DIVOKY (EDITOR)

How Old Will You Be in 1984?

SUCCESS

Congratulations. You've finally made it. You've gotten into the best school in the city. You enter the hallowed halls, overawed at the Greek statues (evidences of the high cultural level) and proceed to the assembly hall where the headmistress welcomes you and reminds you of the high standards of the school. You work hard for six years, memorizing—it doesn't matter whether you understand it or not, just as long as you can shoot back the answers. You then apply to the college of your choice (Ivy League—of course) and are readily accepted. Enlightened by a Liberal Arts course, you graduate with honors and marry a nice professional man. You move to a nice suburb, bring up nice kids, and send them to that nice school which has undoubtedly improved with age.

What more could you want?

—SURGITE
Girls' Latin School
Boston, Massachusetts

NOTES FROM LIFE

High school is really and truly a drag. Standing on line for a goddam hour to see some crotchety old man and you can't even smoke a cigarette so you settle for picking your nose and when you finally get into his office you're so up-tight that you forgot what you came down for and you couldn't care less and it's only second period on the first day and you *know* you ain't gonna make it for a whole year. And you realize, now that you're a senior, that the only things you learned in the last three years were how to roll a joint and how to rap your way out of suspension. For that you spend 8 hours a day of completely insane torture. Now you're a senior and you know how to sit in your assigned seat and raise your hand when you have to go. So why don't you drop out? Well, there's that thing they call the Selective Service System, right?

Did you ever notice that it's only the kids who're hip to the whole thing that they send to shrinks? Blessed be the ignorant.

—SANSCULOTTES
New York City

HAIR

I was watching a rock band on TV and my father caught sight of the lead singer who had hair past his shoulders. After gazing at the performance a few minutes, my father spoke. He said that in 1945 that man would have been considered a very disturbed homosexual.

This set me to thinking. My considered reaction was this: Such suspicions were nurtured on very good grounds, because if he had worn his hair that way in 1945, he probably would have been a homosexual.

But it is different today. Now it is irrational to use the length, and perhaps ornate styling, of a male's hair to cast aspersions on his manhood.

It appears to me that there is a clear and understandable reason why a boy wearing weird clothes and long hair bothers many straight people, particularly older ones. When today's parents were brought up, their parents were quite unable to cope with the changes in their relationship, as man to wife, that the development of our society had brought about. A young woman was no longer dependent on a husband to live. This meant the husband's traditional role of importance was diminished. Such a loss cut down his ego and necessitated the finding of a new basis on which to rest his practical importance to his wife. As a result our grandparents based their relationship on sex. This required that the sexual role of each mate be clearly defined—by superficialities. To our grandparents these traits were virtual differentia between femininity and virility.

The reason we, their grandchildren, have cast off these values is that, in coping with the same problem—the diminishing of the husband's vital role—we have been lucky enough to find a better solution. We base our marriages on friendship, warmth and closeness as well as sex, which we do not in fact emphasize nearly as much as did our predecessors. The first three criteria do not require clear separation of the sexes. So there is no need for men to suppress the supposedly "feminine" instincts they are not, culturally speaking, supposed to have. Nor need they exaggerate their acceptably "masculine" qualities. Thus, the young man today can freely display adornment and indulge his vanity, just as the female in our culture has always been allowed to do.

To me, long-haired boys epitomize masculinity because they are so sure of their own. With this confidence they feel free to ignore the traditional inhibitions placed on boys. Maybe, hopefully, they are becoming aware of the absurdity of a society that demands distinguishing trappings to mark man from woman.

> —Susan Scibetta
> GAUDIO, Dulaney High School
> Towson, Maryland

WHO?

The question is: who, exactly, does all the pot smoking at school? The obvious users are the long haired, radical members of our student body, who, if not arguing some point, walk around with a dreamy look on their faces, seeming to be lost in their own little worlds, with the same answer for everything—"wow."

This seems to be a fairly good generalization, and everyone seems to take their smoking for granted.

But, you might ask, is this the only element of the student body who participate in such underhanded, illegal "activities"? The answer is no. Who would guess that many of the off-season jocks (and even some of those that are in-training) like to splurge on the weekends with a stimulant more satisfying than alcohol? And how could the establishment even imagine that quite a few of those innocent-looking, school-spirited, collegiate, social-climbing "young ladies" have been secretly turning on, and will, in most probability, do it again?

And what of our civic minded SGA reps and officials? You cannot feasibly leave them out nor can you exclude those greasy looking potential dropouts who pass around joints during lunch.

All in all, one must agree that you just cannot rely on what a person is on the inside by his outward appearance. You must search deep into the inner mind.

Now, why do our administrators have locks on their doors ...
—Barbara Goldfarb
THE FIRST AMENDMENT, Northwood High School
Silver Spring, Maryland

MOD SQUAD or HOW TO WASTE AN HOUR ON TUESDAY

The Tee Vee industry has got to be the most retarded industry in the United States. Its pitiful attempts to gauge the mood of the country stop being funny after Monday and get downright sickening by Tuesday. Typical of this mass media mess is *The Mod Squad* (Tues., 6:30, ABC). It appears that those responsible for this slop thought they could make modern day Eliot Nesses out of three turncoat narcos. So they have created a monster-show about three ex hip-biker types who go around doing their best for Law'n Order and engaging in such heroic activities as beating the crap out of flower children.

But it just don't come off! *Mod Squad* is the kind of show during which a person forgets the first half hour before the second half is over. The plot is the same cops & robbers stuff that's been blasting at us since we were born (right in front of the Tee Vee). And the characters, they're right out of "beach-surfer" movies and Coca Cola commercials. Add to this some 40-year-old grade Z script writer's idea of how young "mods" talk and you've got a long-haired version of the Hardy boys (or Spin & Marty if you remember the Mickey Mouse Club) and their Lady Clairol girlfriend, suntanned Nancy Drew. *Mod Squad* is nothing but a phony, tinseled, Madison Avenue version of modern America.
—Frank B. James
THE AMERICAN REVELATION, Elgin High School
Elgin, Illinois

ADMINISTRATION DIRGE

Please excuse our waves of fear and jealousy.
Try to realize, and understand:
Realize that we love you.
Understand how.

We know it's hard for you to believe our words when we oppress
you.
When we question and mock your dress, your thoughts, your
standards.

Our world is a world of fear.
We have been programmed, modified, and stamped
By those before us.
A generation long since passed from our world
Of hypocrisy and hate.

We fear a unified student body
For our job is to divide you.
That way you are more easily conquered
And neatly fitted into a mold.
A mold that when you emerge from it, will cause you to remain
insignificant blobs.
In a complex computerized society
That has nothing to offer,
And one hell of a lot to take.
Of course, you must remember we're only trying to protect your
rights and freedom.

We have taken the very spirit of individuality from you;
Stabbing and tearing down your very existence,
One so real, one that so few possess.
Then rejoice writing you up in our (growing) up-tight files;
Only to remove you from them and pass you on when you
graduate,
With hopes that you will be the sterilized, plastic product
That we have contributed so much to the making of.

Whether you be lying abed a battle field some day,
Or taking our jobs,
We will be filled with perverted artificial happiness.
But remember the system we've dedicated our lives to is
vulnerable
It fears many things,
Most of all: questions, unity, and resistance!

—TRADITIONS
Eau Claire, Wisconsin

JEDGARHOOVY

'Twas midnight and the F.B.I.
  Did grope and giggle in the trees.
In wait for a dissenter they did lie,
  For justice needs t' be appeased.

Beware the draft-dodger, my son!
  The hair so long, the tight-clad loin—
When he appears I want you to run,
  And kick him in the groin!

Then we'll drag him off to jail, my friend,
  He said with maxome mirth,
For burning a piece of paper he'll spend
  Five years in Leavenworth.

We've got all the evidence that we need,
  He spoke in a furtive tone,
For all his letters we did read,
  And we also tapped his phone.

The Commie appeared—flying high
  With a flower in his lapel.
The agent knee'd, and with a sign
  Of pain the hippie fell.

And hast thou ruptured the rebel man?
  O valiant prince come to me!
True justice still lives in our land,
  And brotherhood from sea to sea.

'Tis twelve-thirty, but the F.B.I.
  No longer sits in the tree,
For the sinner is slain. Oh me, oh my,
  America, the land of the free!

—James Ryan
  RAZIR, Needham High School
  Needham, Massachusetts

Peter Marin's view of education for the young runs counter to today's re-
vival of vocationalism in the schools. What we need most from each other
are simple human decencies. Educators may devise new models, new pro-
grams, innovate and reinnovate, but something has always been left out.
What do students need? The private assumption of responsibility for others.
The few real teachers are trying to live their lives in the company of stu-
dents as fully and humanly as possible—all else is rhetoric and nonsense.

PETER MARIN

Children of the Apocalypse

> *To oppose Fascism, we need neither*
> *heavy armaments nor bureaucratic*
> *apparatuses. What we need above all*
> *is a different way of looking at life and*
> *human beings. My dear friends, with-*
> *out this different way of looking at life*
> *and human beings, we shall ourselves*
> *become Fascists.*   —SILONE.

I am not really interested in "education" as a subject. What moves
me more are the problems of the young. At best, questions about
education should be treated topically: as a way of living with the
present, of *making do.* But there is something beyond that too, a way
of looking at men and women, a visionary expectation, that keeps us
seeking the most human ways of making do. But the most human
ways of making do these days have little to do with our rhetoric
about the public schools, and we forget in the midst of it what we
really owe the young.

But knowing what we owe them means knowing what is going
on, and it is hard to get a fix on that. Whatever happens is shrouded
in folds of propaganda and rhetoric, abstraction and fantasy. *Revolu-*
tion, Repression, The Age of Aquarius, The Counter-Culture, Law
and Order, The Great Society, The Death of Reason, The Psychedelic
Revolution. . . . It goes on and on—a vast illusion comprised of ban-
ners and winking neon meanings that fog the frantic soup in which

we swim: the mixture of innocent yearning and savagery, despair and exhilaration, the grasping for paradise lost, paradise *now,* the reaching for a sanity that becomes, in frustration, a new kind of madness.

If this is not the kingdom of apocalypse, it is at least an apocalyptic condition of the soul. We want the most simple human decencies, but in our anguish we are driven to extremes to find them. We reach blindly for whatever offers solace. We yearn more than ever for some kind of human touch and seem steadily less able to provide it. We drift in our own confusion, chattering about the "future": at once more free and more corrupt, more liberated and bound, than any others on the face of the earth.

In the midst of it, adrift, the young more than ever seem beautiful but maimed, trying against all odds to salvage something from the mess. With daring and luck many seem to survive, and some few thrive, but too many others—more than we imagine—already seem destined to spend their lives wrestling with something very close to psychosis. Despite all our talk we have not adequately gauged their suffering. Theirs is a condition of the soul that marks the dead end of the beginnings of America—a dreadful anomy in which one loses all access to others and the self: a liberation that is simultaneously the most voluptuous kind of freedom and an awful form of terror.

Merely to touch in that condition, or to see one another, or to speak honestly is to reach across an immense distance. One struggles with the remnants of a world-view so pervasive, so perverse, that everyone must doubt whether it is possible to see anything clearly, say it honestly, or enter it innocently. The tag ends of two dozen different transplanted foreign cultures have begun to die within us, have already died, and the young have been released into what is perhaps the first true "American" reality—one marked, above all, by the absence of any coherent culture.

The problem is not merely that the "system" is brutal and corrupt, nor that the war has revealed how savage and cynical a people we are. It is, put simply, that "social reality" seems to have vanished altogether. One finds among the young a profound and befuddled sense of loss—as if they had been traumatized and betrayed by an entire world. What is release and space for some is for the others a constant sense of separation and vertigo—a void in which the self can float or soar but in which one can also drift unmoored and fall; and when one falls, it is forever, for there is nothing underneath, no culture, no net of meaning, nobody else.

That is, of course, what we have talked about for a century: the empty existential universe of self-creation. It is a condition of the soul, an absolute loss and yearning for the world. One can become anything—but nothing makes much sense. Adults have managed to evade it, have hesitated on its edges, have clung to one another and to institutions, to beliefs in "the system," to law and order. But now none of that coheres, and the young seem unprotected by it all, and what we have evaded and even celebrated in *metaphor* has become, for a whole generation, a kind of daily emotional life.

The paradox, of course, is that the dissolution of culture has set us free to create almost anything—but it also deprived us of the abilities to do it. Strength, wholeness, and sanity seem to be functions of *relation,* and relation, I think, is a function of culture, part of its intricate web of approved connection and experience, a network of persons and moments that simultaneously offer us release and bind us to the lives of others. One "belongs" to and in culture in a way that goes beyond mere politics or participation, for belonging is both simpler and more complex than that: an immersion in the substance of community and tradition, which is itself a net beneath us, a kind of element in which men seem to float, protected.

That is, I suppose, what the young have lost. Every personal truth or experience puts them at odds with the "official" version of things. There is no connection at all between inner truth and what they are expected to be; every gesture demanded and rewarded is a kind of absolute lie, a denial of their confusion and need. The "drifting free" is the sense of distance; it is distance—not a "generation" gap, but the huge gulf between the truth of one's own pain and possibilities and the world's empty forms. Nothing supports or acknowledges them, and they are trapped in that gulf, making the best of things, making everything up as they go along. But that is the most basic and awful task of all, for it is so lonely, so dangerous, so easily distracted and subverted, so easily swayed. The further along one gets the more alone one is, the more fragile and worried, the deeper into the dark. It is there, of course, that one may need help from adults, but adults have no talent for that at all; we do not admit to being in the dark—how, then, can we be of any use?

If all this is so, what sense can one make of the public schools? They are stiff, unyielding, microcosmic versions of a world that has already disappeared. They are, after all, the state's schools, they do the state's work, and their purpose is the preservation of things as they were. Their means are the isolation of ego and deflection of energy. Their main structural function is to produce in the young a self-delusive "independence"—a system of false consciousness and need that actually renders them dependent on institutions and the state. Their corrosive role-playing and demand systems are so extensive, so profound, that nothing really human shows through—and when it does, it appears only as frustration, exhaustion, and anger.

That, of course, is the real outrage of the schools: their systematic corruption of the relations among persons. Where they should be comrades, allies, equals, and even lovers, the public schools make them "teacher" and "student"—replaceable units in a mechanical ritual that passes on, in the name of education, an "emotional plague"; a kind of ego and personality that has been so weakened, so often denied the experience of community or solitude, that we no longer understand quite what these things are or how to achieve them.

Whatever one's hopes or loves, each teacher is engaged daily in that same conspiracy to maim the young. But I am talking here about more than the surface stupidities of attendance requirements, grades, or curriculum. Those can be changed and updated. But what seems truly untouchable is what lies behind and beneath them: the basic irredeemable assumptions about what is necessary, human, or good; the treatment of the person, time, choice, energy, work, community, and pleasure. It is a world-view so monolithic and murderous that it becomes a part of us even while we protest against it.

I remember returning one fall to a state college in California after a summer in the Mexican mountains. I had been with my friends, writing, walking, making love—all with a sense of freedom and quietude. That first day back I felt as I always did on campus, like a sly, still undiscovered spy. After all, what was it all to me? I walked into my first class and began my usual pitch: They would grade themselves, read what they wanted or not at all, come to class or stay home. It was all theirs to choose—their learning, their time, their space. But they were perplexed by that. Was it some kind of trick? They began to question me, and finally one of them asked, exasperated: "But what can we do if we don't know what you *want?*"

It was a minimal satori. I could not speak. What ran through my mind was not only the absolute absurdity of the question but the lunacy of our whole charade: the roles we played, the place we met, the state's mazelike building, the state's gigantesque campus, and, beyond all that, what we mean by "schooling," how we had been possessed by it. I knew that whatever I answered would be senseless and oppressive, for no matter how I disclaimed my role, whatever I said would restore it. So I stood there instead in silence, aware that what I had taken lightly to be mad was indeed mad, and that one could never, while there, break through those roles into anything real.

Well, almost never. The most human acts I have ever found in our colleges and high schools are the ones most discouraged, the surreptitious sexuality between teachers and students. Although they were almost always cramped and totally exploitive, they were at least some kind of private touch. I used to imagine that one fine afternoon the doors of all the offices would open wide with a trumpet blast, and teachers and students would emerge to dance hand in hand in total golden nakedness on the campus lawns in a paroxysm of truth. In a sense, what I imagined then is close to what sometimes happens more realistically in the student strikes and demonstrations. One finds in the participants a sense of exhilaration and release, a regained potency and a genuine transformation of feeling: the erotic camaraderie of liberation. There is an immense and immediate relief at the cessation of pretense. It is one's role, as well as the rules, which is transgressed, and one somehow becomes stronger, more real—and suddenly at home.

But that doesn't happen often, and usually only in the colleges, and the young are left elsewhere and almost always to suffer in silence the most destructive effect of the schools—not their external rules and structure, but the ways in which we internalize them and falsify ourselves in order to live with them. The state creeps in and gradually occupies us; we act and think within its forms; we see through its eyes and its speaks through our mouths—and how, in that situation, can the young learn to be alive or free?

We try. We open the classroom a bit and loosen the bonds. Students use a teacher's first name, or roam the small room, or go ungraded, or choose their own texts. It is all very nice; better, of course, than nothing at all. But what has it got to do with the needs of the young? We try again. We devise new models, new programs, new plans. We innovate and renovate, and beneath it all our schemes always contain the same vacancies, the same smells of death, as the schools. One speaks to planners, designers, teachers, and administrators; one hears about schedules and modules and curricular innovation—new systems. It is always "materials" and "technique," the chronic American technological vice, the cure that murders as it saves. It is all so smug, so progressively right—and yet so useless, so far off the track. One knows there is something else altogether: a way of feeling, access to the soul, a way of speaking and embracing, that lies at the heart of all yearning or wisdom or real revolution. It is that, precisely, that has been left out. It is something the planners cannot remember: the living tissue of community. Without it, of course, we shrivel and die, but who can speak convincingly about that to those who have never felt it?

I remember talking to one planner about what one wants from others.

"Respect," he said. "And their utmost effort."

"But all I want," I said, "is love and a sense of humor."

His eyes lit up. "I see," he said. "You mean positive feedback."

Positive feedback. So we debauch our own sweet nature. I don't want positive feedback, nor do the young. What they need is so much more important and profound—not "skills" but qualities of the soul; daring, warmth, wit, imagination, honesty, loyalty, grace, and resilience. But one cannot be taught those things; they cannot be programed into a machine. They seem to be learned, instead, in activity and communion—in the *adventurous presence of other real persons.*

But there is no room in the schools for that. There is no real hope of making room there. Those who want to aid the young must find some other way to do it. Yes, I know, that is where most of the young still are. I can hear the murmurs protesting that only the demented, delinquent, or rich can go elsewhere. But that is just the point. This is the monolithic system of control that must be broken. We have wasted too much time and energy on the state's schools, and we have failed to consider or create alternatives. Now it is time to cut loose from the myth. We must realize once and for all that, given the real inner condition of the young, the state's schools are no place to try to help them.

But if that is the case, my friends ask, what *do* you do? I have no easy answers. There are cultural conditions for which there are no solutions, turnings of the soul so profound and complex that no system can absorb or contain them. How would one have "solved" the Reformation? Or first-century Rome? One makes accommodations and adjustments, one dreams about the future and makes plans to save us all, but in spite of all that, because of it, what seems more important are the private independent acts that become more necessary every day: the ways we find as *private persons* to restore to one another the strengths we should have now—whether to make the kind of revolution we need or to survive the repression that seems likely.

What I am talking about here is a kind of psychic survival: our ability to live decently beyond institutional limits and provide for our comrades enough help to sustain them. What saves us as men and women is always a kind of witness: the quality of our own acts and lives. This is the knowledge, of course, that institutions bribe us to forget, the need and talent for what Kropotkin called "mutual aid" —the private assumption of responsibility for others.

I remember talking one evening with a student who was arguing the need for burning things down. Her face was a stiff, resisting mask of anger and grief.

"But what else," she said, "can I do?"

I wasn't sure. "Try to get to the bottom of things. Try to see clearly what we need."

"But when I see clearly," she said, "I freak out."

"That's why we need friends," I said.

"But I have no friends."

And she began to cry. That is it precisely. How does one really survive it? There is nothing for such pain save to embrace it, to heal it with warmth, with one's own two hands. One comes to believe that what each of us needs is an absolute kind of lover—not for the raw sex, but for what is sometimes beneath and intrinsic to it: a devoted open presence to perceive, acknowledge, and embrace what we are.

That is the legitimacy which comes neither from the ballot nor the gun, a potency, resilience, and courage that one can learn only by feeling at home in the world. But how can the young feel that? There are few such lovers, and the other old ways are gone. Once upon a time one had a lived relation to culture, or place, or the absolute. But God has vanished and the culture is tattered and savage and "place" has become the raw, empty suburb or the ghetto.

What else is left? Not much. Only others: those adrift in the same dark, one's brothers and sisters, comrades and lovers—the broken isolate bits of a movable kingdom, an invisible "community" that shares, inside, a particular fate. It is only in their eyes and arms, in their presence and affection, that one becomes real, is given back, and discovers the extent of one's being.

What we are talking about here are really acts of love, the gestures by which one shares with others the true dimension and depth of the world. Those gestures are a form of revelation, for they restore to others a sense of what is shared. But one can only make them when one feels free, when the space we inhabit is our own, an open environment, a "field" in which we can begin to see clearly, act freely—and be real.

I know that this is shaky ground. How can one explain what one means by real? It is experiential and subjective: a quality and condition of some kind of deeply inhabited moment. We talk about ecstasy and ego-death and peak experience, but those seem equally imperfect ways of describing the experience of *being in the world.* One *is.* That is all. Our chronic sense of isolation dissolves; there is a correspondence, an identity, between inner and outer, world and world. It is a making whole; it knits together the self at the same time that the self is felt to be a part, the heart, of what surrounds it.

What it is, always, is a reclamation of our proper place in the world—and those who want to help the young must realize that it cannot happen in the schools. Perhaps, after all, it doesn't really matter whether we transgress their limits by leaving them or while staying within them, so long as we learn to ignore them wherever we are. Can one do that while still in the state's schools? I don't think so. But perhaps some teachers want to try—and why not? Perhaps it *is* worth the effort and anguish—as long as one always remembers that one's primary obligation is not to the system, not the state, but to the young—and not as a teacher, but as an equal and ally. That obligation—like a doctor's or lawyer's—is absolute, more important than our own comfort or job, and it can be satisfied only when one is willing to refuse, point-blank, to do anything that really damages the young—no matter who programs or asks for it. One must be willing to suspend the rules, refuse one's role, reject the system— and live instead with the young—wherever you find them—as the persons we really are. If that is impossible in the schools, then one must be willing to leave the schools and take the young, too—into the street, into one's own home—wherever we can live sensibly together.

Perhaps what schools need are "escape committees" of resistance devoted, like the draft resistance, to discovering alternatives for the young. We have plenty of working models, places such as the First Street School in New York or Berkeley's Other Ways; the "free schools" scattered on either coast; community day-care centers and ghetto storefront schools; female liberation groups; communes of all kinds; free clinics; therapeutic centers like Synanon; experimental colleges; the hard-edged courage of the Panthers and Young Lords. All of these function in different ways as an education in liberation: the attempts of people to move past institutions and do for themselves what the state does not.

Not everyone can do it, of course. It is a scary idea. Our heads are heavy with a fear of "dropping out." The institutional propaganda convinces too many of us that there is one world here and another there, and that there is some kind of illegitimate limbo where our actions dissolve in the air. But *there* is simple private life, the life of the street, the free relations between persons, and it is only there, these days, that one can be free or real enough to serve the young. But if it is dangerous out there, it is also incredibly lovely at times, full of learning, full of freedom, and only those who have lived or traveled with the young in those open fields know just how exhilarating, if exhausting, it is.

But what about the future? When I talk with my friends these days the sugarplum visions dance in their heads, and they tell me about their systems and salvations, or the dawning age of Aquarius and the new consciousness. Well, I want to believe it. But these days there is also the cop at the door with his gun, and the new mechanical men, and also something in me, the old Adam, the old father, whispering *not yet, not yet.* I remember a man I knew in New York who ate nothing but bologna and cheese sandwiches, and when he broke his jaw and had to sip through a straw he dumped bologna and cheese and bread in his blender, added milk, and had his usual sandwich.

Which is to say, the future changes, but we may not. Whatever there is on the other side of this confusion will be, at best, not so different from what we already have now, on occasion, in our best moments. No new senses, no third sexes, no cosmic orgasms, no karmic rebirths. No, if we are daring and lucky, what will be "revolutionary" will simply be that more of us, all of us, will have more of a chance for a decent human life—good comrades and lovers, a few touches of ecstasy, some solitude and space, a sense of self-determination.

I once asked a student what she would do if she awoke in paradise.

"Walk around," she said. "Get something to eat."

I don't have any other answer. We will do what we do now—but we will do it better. We will sit talking with friends around a table, do some decent work, hold one another guiltlessly in our arms, touch a bit more softly, more knowingly. We will understand a bit more and dance a bit more and breathe a bit more and even think a little more—and all, perhaps, a bit more intelligently, more bravely.

That isn't much, but it is also almost everything, and what we are forced to do now is learn how to do all that for ourselves. There is no one to show us how—no program, no system. One can only have such lives by trying to live them, and that is what the young are trying to do these days, all on their own, whether we help them or not. The few real teachers I know, those really serving the young, are simply those who try to live such lives in their company, as freely and humanly as they can. The rest of "education" is almost always rhetoric and nonsense.

Four

Work and Life Style

The discontinuity between adolescence and the assumption of adult roles is
stated by Paul Goodman in an adolescent's terms: "during my productive
years I will spend eight hours a day doing what is no good." Stressing man's
need to do something worthwhile, the author analyzes career models offered
by modern technological America. He concludes that adolescents shun work
when they see its outcome as, for example, brilliantly-produced rigged quiz
shows.

PAUL GOODMAN

Jobs

It's hard to grow up when there isn't enough man's work. There is
"nearly full employment" (with highly significant exceptions), but
there get to be fewer jobs that are necessary or unquestionably useful; that require energy and draw on some of one's best capacities;
and that can be done keeping one's honor and dignity. In explaining
the widespread troubles of adolescents and young men, this simple
objective factor is not much mentioned. Let us here insist on it.

By "man's work" I mean a very simple idea, so simple that it is
clearer to ingenuous boys than to most adults. To produce necessary

food and shelter is man's work. During most of economic history most men have done this drudging work, secure that it was justified and worthy of a man to do it, though often feeling that the social conditions under which they did it were *not* worthy of a man, thinking, "It's better to die than to live so hard"—but they worked on. When the environment is forbidding, as in the Swiss Alps or the Aran Islands, we regard such work with poetic awe. In emergencies it is heroic, as when the bakers of Paris maintained the supply of bread during the French Revolution, or the milkman did not miss a day's delivery when the bombs recently tore up London.

At present there is little such subsistence work. In *Communitas* my brother and I guess that one-tenth of our economy is devoted to it; it is more likely one-twentieth. Production of food is actively discouraged. Farmers are not wanted and the young men go elsewhere. (The farm population is now less than 15 per cent of the total population.) Building, on the contrary, is immensely needed. New York City needs 65,000 new units a year, and is getting net, 16,000. One would think that ambitious boys would flock to this work. But here we find that building, too, is discouraged. In a great city, for the last twenty years hundreds of thousands have been ill housed, yet we do not see science, industry, and labor enthusiastically enlisted in finding the quick solution to a definite problem. The promoters are interested in long-term investments, the real estate men in speculation, the city planners in votes and graft. The building craftsmen cannily see to it that their own numbers remain few, their methods antiquated, and their rewards high. None of these people is much interested in providing shelter, and nobody is at all interested in providing new manly jobs.

Once we turn away from the absolutely necessary subsistence jobs, however, we find that an enormous proportion of our production is not even unquestionably useful. Everybody knows and also feels this, and there has recently been a flood of books about our surfeit of honey, our insolent chariots, the follies of exurban ranch houses, our hucksters, and our synthetic demand. Many acute things are said about this useless production and advertising, but not much about the workmen producing it and their frame of mind; and nothing at all, so far as I have noticed, about the plight of a young fellow looking for a manly occupation. The eloquent critics of the American way of life have themselves been so seduced by it that they think only in terms of selling commodities and point out that the goods are valueless; but they fail to see that people are being wasted and their skills insulted. (To give an analogy, in the many gleeful onslaughts on the Popular Culture that have appeared in recent years, there has been little thought of the plight of the honest artist cut off from his audience and sometimes, in public arts such as theater and architecture, from his medium.)

What is strange about it? American society has tried so hard and so ably to defend the practice and theory of production for profit and not primarily for use that now it has succeeded in making its jobs and products profitable and useless.

Consider a likely useful job. A youth who is alert and willing but not "verbally intelligent"—perhaps he has quit high school at the eleventh grade (the median), as soon as he legally could—chooses for auto mechanic. That's a good job, familiar to him, he often watched them as a kid. It's careful and dirty at the same time. In a small gargage it's sociable; one can talk to the customers (girls). You please people in trouble by fixing their cars, and a man is proud to see rolling out on its own the car that limped in behind the tow truck. The pay is as good as the next fellow's, who is respected.

So our young man takes this first-rate job. But what when he then learns that the cars have a built-in obsolescence, that the manufacturers do not want them to be repaired or repairable? They have lobbied a law that requires them to provide spare parts for only five years (it used to be ten). Repairing the new cars is often a matter of cosmetics, not mechanics; and the repairs are pointlessly expensive —a tail fin might cost $150. The insurance rates therefore double and treble on old and new cars both. Gone are the days of keeping the jalopies in good shape, the artist-work of a proud mechanic. But everybody is paying for foolishness, for in fact the new models are only trivially superior; the whole thing is a sell.

It is hard for the young man now to maintain his feelings of justification, sociability, serviceability. It is not surprising if he quickly becomes cynical and time-serving, interested in a fast buck. And so, on the notorious *Reader's Digest* test, the investigators (coming in with a disconnected coil wire) found that 63 percent of mechanics charged for repairs they didn't make, and lucky if they didn't also take out the new fuel pump and replace it with a used one (65 per cent of radio repair shops, but *only* 49 per cent of watch repairmen "lied, overcharged, or gave false diagnoses").

There is an hypothesis that an important predisposition to juvenile delinquency is the combination of low verbal intelligence with high manual intelligence, delinquency giving a way of self-expression where other avenues are blocked by lack of schooling. A lad so endowed might well apply himself to the useful trade of mechanic.

Most manual jobs do not lend themselves so readily to knowing the facts and fraudulently taking advantage oneself. In factory jobs the workman is likely to be ignorant of what goes on, since he performs a small operation on a big machine that he does not understand. Even so, there is evidence that he has the same disbelief in the enterprise as a whole, with a resulting attitude of profound indifference.

Semiskilled factory operatives are the largest category of workmen. (I am leafing through the U.S. Department of Labor's *Occupational Outlook Handbook*, 1957.) Big companies have tried the devices of applied anthropology to enhance the loyalty of these men to the firm, but apparently the effort is hopeless, for it is found that a thumping majority of the men don't care about the job or the firm; they couldn't care less and you can't make them care more. But this is *not* because of wages, hours, or working conditions, or management. On the contrary, tests that show the men's indifference to the company show also their (unaware) admiration for the way the company has designed and manages the plant; it is their very model of style, efficiency, and correct behavior. (Robert Dubin, for the U.S. Public Health Service.) Maybe if the men understood more, they would admire less. The union and the grievance committee take care of wages, hours, and conditions; these are the things the workmen themselves fought for and won. (Something was missing in that victory, and we have inherited the failure as well as the success.) The conclusion must be that workmen are indifferent to the job because of its intrinsic nature: it does not enlist worthwhile capacities, it is not "interesting"; it is not his, he is not "in" on it; the product is not really useful. And indeed, research directly on the subject, by Frederick Herzberg on Motivation to Work, shows that it is defects in the intrinsic aspects of the job that make workmen "unhappy." A survey of the literature (in Herzberg's *Job Attitudes*) shows that Interest is second in importance only to Security, whereas Wages, Conditions, Socializing, Hours, Ease, and Benefits are far less important. But foremen, significantly enough, think that the most important thing to the workman is his wages. (The investigators do not seem to inquire about the usefulness of the job—as if a primary purpose of *working* at a job were not that it is good *for* something! My guess is that a large factor in "Security" is the resigned reaction to not being able to take into account whether the work of one's hands is useful for anything; for in a normal life situation, if what we do is useful, we feel secure about being needed. The other largest factor in "Security" is, I think, the sense of being needed for one's unique contribution, and this is measured in these tests by the primary importance the workers assign to being "in" on things and to "work done being appreciated."

Limited as they are, what a remarkable insight such studies give us, that men want to do valuable work and work that is somehow theirs! But they are thwarted.

Is not this the "waste of our human resources"?

The case is that by the "sole-prerogative" clause in union contracts the employer has the sole right to determine what is to be produced, how it is to be produced, what plants are to be built and where, what kinds of machinery are to be installed, when workers are to be hired and laid off, and how production operations are to be rationalized. (Frank Marquart.) There is *none* of this that is inevitable in running a machine economy; but *if* these are the circumstances, it is not surprising that the factory operatives' actual code has absolutely nothing to do with useful service or increasing production, but is notoriously devoted to "interpersonal relations": (1) don't turn out too much work; (2) don't turn out too little work; (3) don't squeal on a fellow worker; (4) don't act like a big-shot. This is how to belong.

Let us go on to the Occupational Outlook of those who are verbally bright. Among this group, simply because they cannot help asking more general questions—e.g., about utility—the problem of finding man's work is harder, and their disillusion is more poignant.

He explained to her why it was hard to find a satisfactory job of work to do. He had liked working with the power drill, testing the rocky envelope of the shore, but then the employers asked him to take a great oath of loyalty.

"What!" cried Rosalind. "Do you have scruples about telling a convenient fib?"

"No, I don't. But I felt uneasy about the sanity of the director asking me to swear to opinions on such complicated questions when my job was digging with a power drill. I can't work with a man who might suddenly have a wild fit."

... "Why don't you get a job driving one of the big trucks along here?"

"I don't like what's in the boxes," said Horatio sadly. "It could just as well drop in the river—and I'd make mistakes and drop it there."

"Is it bad stuff?"

"No, just useless. It takes the heart out of me to work at something useless and I begin to make mistakes. I don't mind putting profits in somebody's pocket—but the job also has to be useful for something."

... "Why don't you go to the woods and be a lumberjack?"

"No! They chop down the trees just to print off the *New York Times!*"

(Goodman *The Empire City,* III, i, 3.)

The more intelligent worker's "indifference" is likely to appear more nakedly as profound resignation, and his cynicism may sharpen to outright racketeering.

"Teaching," says the *Handbook*, "is the largest of the professions." So suppose our now verbally bright young man chooses for teacher, in the high school system or, by exception, in the elementary schools if he understands that the elementary grades are the vitally important ones and require the most ability to teach well (and of course they have less prestige). Teaching is necessary and useful work; it is real and creative, for it directly confronts an important subject matter, the children themselves; it is obviously self-justifying; and it is ennobled by the arts and sciences. Those who practice teaching do not for the most part succumb to cynicism or indifference—the children are too immediate and real for the teachers to become callous—but, most of the school systems being what they are, can teachers fail to come to suffer first despair and then deep resignation? Resignation occurs psychologically as follows: frustrated in essential action, they nevertheless cannot quit in anger, because the task is necessary; so the anger turns inward and is felt as resignation. (Naturally, the resigned teacher may then put on a happy face and keep very busy.)

For the job is carried on under impossible conditions of overcrowding and saving public money. *Not* that there is not enough social wealth, but first things are not put first. Also, the school system has spurious aims. It soon becomes clear that the underlying aims are to relieve the home and keep the kids quiet; or, suddenly, the aim is to produce physicists. Timid supervisors, bigoted clerks, and ignorant school boards forbid real teaching. The emotional release and sexual expression of the children are taboo. A commercially debauched popular culture makes learning disesteemed. The academic curriculum is mangled by the demands of reactionaries, liberals, and demented warriors. Progressive methods are emasculated. Attention to each case is out of the question, and all the children—the bright, the average, and the dull—are systematically retarded one way or another, while the teacher's hands are tied. Naturally the pay is low—for the work is hard, useful, and of public concern, all three of which qualities tend to bring lower pay. It is alleged that the low pay is why there is a shortage of teachers and why the best do not choose the profession. My guess is that the best avoid it because of the certainty of miseducating. Nor are the best *wanted* by the system, for they are not safe. Bertrand Russell was rejected by New York's City College and would not have been accepted in a New York grade school.

Next, what happens to the verbally bright who have no zeal for a serviceable profession and who have no particular scientific or artistic bent? For the most part they make up the tribes of salesmanship, entertainment, business management, promotion, and advertising. Here of course there is no question of utility or honor to begin with, so an ingenuous boy will not look here for a manly career. Nevertheless, though we can pass by the sufferings of these well-paid callings, much publicized by their own writers, they are important to our theme because of the model they present to the growing boy.

Consider the men and women in TV advertisements, demonstrating the product and singing the jingle. They are clowns and mannequins, in grimace, speech, and action. And again, what I want to call attention to in this advertising is not the economic problem of synthetic demand, and not the cultural problem of Popular Culture, but the human problem that these are human beings working as clowns; that the writers and designers of it are human beings thinking like idiots; and the broadcasters and underwriters know and abet what goes on—

> Juicily glubbily
> Blubber is bubbily
> delicious and nutritious
> —eat it, Kitty, it's good.

Alternately, they are liars, confidence men, smooth talkers, obsequious, insolent, etc., etc.

The popular-cultural content of the advertisements is somewhat neutralized by *Mad* magazine, the bible of the twelve-year-olds who can read. But far more influential and hard to counteract is the *fact* that the workmen and the patrons of this enterprise are human beings. (Highly approved, too.) They are not good models for a boy looking for a manly job that is useful and necessary, requiring human energy and capacity, and that can be done with honor and dignity. They are a good sign that not many such jobs will be available.

The popular estimation is rather different. Consider the following: "As one possible aid, I suggested to the Senate subcommittee that they alert celebrities and leaders in the fields of sports, movies, theater and television to the help they can offer by getting close to these (delinquent) kids. By giving them positive 'heroes' they know and can talk to, instead of the misguided image of troublemaking buddies, they could aid greatly in building these normal aspirations

for fame and status into wholesome progressive channels." (Jackie
Robinson, who was formerly on the Connecticut Parole Board.) Or
again: when a mass cross-section of Oklahoma high school juniors
and seniors was asked which living person they would like to be, the
boys named Pat Boone, Ricky Nelson, and President Eisenhower; the
girls chose Debbie Reynolds, Elizabeth Taylor, and Natalie Wood.

The rigged Quiz shows, which created a scandal in 1959, were
a remarkably pure distillate of our American cookery. We start with
the brute facts that (a) in our abundant expanding economy it is
necessary to give money away to increase spending, production, and
profits; and (b) that this money must not be used for useful public
goods in taxes, but must be plowed back as "business expenses," even
though there is a shameful shortage of schools, housing, etc. Yet
when the TV people at first tried simply to give the money away for
nothing (for having heard of George Washington), there was a great
Calvinistic outcry that this was demoralizing (we may gamble on
the horses only to improve the breed). So they hit on the notion of
a real contest with prizes. But then, of course, they could not resist
making the show itself profitable, and competitive in the (also
rigged) ratings with other shows, so the experts in the entertain-
ment-commodity manufactured phony contests. And to cap the cli-
max of fraudulence, the hero of the phony contests proceeded to
persuade himself, so he says, that his behavior was educational!

The behavior of the networks was correspondingly typical.
These business organizations claim the loyalty of their employees,
but at the first breath of trouble they were ruthless and disloyal to
their employees. (Even McCarthy was loyal to his gang.) They want
to maximize profits and yet be absolutely safe from any risk. Consider their claim that they knew nothing about the fraud. But if they
watched the shows they were broadcasting, they could not *possibly,*
as professionals, not have known the facts, for there were obvious
type-casting, acting, plot, etc. If they are not professionals, they are
incompetent. But if they don't watch what they broadcast, then they
are utterly irresponsible and on what grounds do they have the
franchises to the channels? We may offer them the choice: that they
are liars or incompetent or irresponsible.

The later direction of the investigation seems to me more important, the inquiry into the bribed disk-jockeying; for this deals directly with our crucial economic problem of synthesized demand,
made taste, debauching the public and preventing the emergence
and formation of natural taste. In such circumstances there cannot
possibly be an American culture; we are doomed to nausea and
barbarism. And *then* these baboons have the effrontery to declare

that they give the people what the people demand and that they are not responsible for the level of the movies, the music, the plays, the books!

Finally, in leafing through the *Occupational Outlook Handbook,* we notice that the armed forces employ a large number. Here our young men can become involved in a world-wide demented enterprise, with personnel and activities corresponding.

Thus, on the simple criteria of unquestioned utility, employing human capacities, and honor, there are not enough worthy jobs in our economy for average boys and adolescents to grow up toward. There are of course thousands of jobs that are worthy and self-justifying, and thousands that can be made so by stubborn integrity, especially if one can work as an independent. Extraordinary intelligence or special talent, also, can often carve out a place for itself—conversely, their usual corruption and waste are all the more sickening. But by and large our economic society is *not* geared for the cultivation of its young or the attainment of important goals that they can work toward.

This is evident from the usual kind of vocational guidance, which consists of measuring the boy and finding some place in the economy where he can be fitted; chopping him down to make him fit; or neglecting him if they can't find his slot. Personnel directors do not much try to scrutinize the economy in order to find some activity that is a real opportunity for the boy, and then to create an opportunity if they can't find one. To do this would be an horrendous task; I am not sure it could be done if we wanted to do it. But the question is whether anything less makes sense if we mean to speak seriously about the troubles of the young men.

Surely by now, however, many readers are objecting that this entire argument is pointless because people in *fact* don't think of their jobs in this way at all. *Nobody* asks if a job is useful or honorable (within the limits of business ethics). A man gets a job that pays well, or well enough, that has prestige, and good conditions, or at least tolerable conditions. I agree with these objections as to the fact. (I hope we are wrong.) But *the question is what it means to grow up into such a fact as: "During my productive years I will spend eight hours a day doing what is no good."*

Yet, economically and vocationally, a very large population of the young people are in a plight more drastic than anything so far mentioned. In our society as it is, there are not enough worthy jobs. But if our society, being as it is, were run more efficiently and soberly, for a majority there would soon not be any jobs at all. There is at present nearly full employment and there may be for some

years, yet a vast number of young people are rationally unemployable, useless. This paradox is essential to explain their present tem-
per.

Our society, which is not geared to the cultivation of its young,
is geared to a profitable expanding production, a so-called high standard of living of mediocre value, and the maintenance of nearly full
employment. Politically, the chief of these is full employment. In a
crisis, when profitable production is temporarily curtailed, government spending increases and jobs are manufactured. In "normalcy"
—a condition of slow boom—the easy credit, installment buying,
and artificially induced demand for useless goods create jobs for all
and good profits for some.

Now, back in the Thirties, when the New Deal attempted by
hook or crook to put people back to work and give them money to
revive the shattered economy, there was an outcry of moral indignation from the conservatives that many of the jobs were "boondoggling," useless made-work. It was insisted, and rightly, that such
work was demoralizing to the workers themselves. It is a question
of a word, but a candid critic might certainly say that many of the
jobs in our present "normal" production are useless made-work. The
tail fins and built-in obsolescence might be called boondoggling. The
$64,000 Question and the busy hum of Madison Avenue might cer-
tainly be called boondoggling. Certain tax-dodge Foundations are
boondoggling. What of business lunches and expense accounts?
fringe benefits? the comic categories of occupation in the building
trades? the extra stagehands and musicians of the theater crafts?
These jolly devices to put money back to work no doubt have a
demoralizing effect on somebody or other (certainly on me, they
make me green with envy), but where is the moral indignation from
Top Management?

Suppose we would cut out the boondoggling and gear our society to a more sensible abundance, with efficient production of quality goods, distribution in a natural market, counterinflation and
sober credit. At once the work week would be cut to, say, twenty
hours instead of forty. (Important People have already mentioned
the figure thirty.) Or alternately, half the labor force would be unemployed. Suppose too—and how can we not suppose it?—that the
automatic machines are used generally, rather than just to get rid of
badly organized unskilled labor. The unemployment will be still
more drastic.

(To give the most striking example: in steel, the annual increase
in productivity is 4 per cent, the plants work at 50 per cent of capacity, and the companies can break even and stop producing at *less*

than 30 per cent of capacity. These are the conditions that forced the steel strike, as desperate self-protection. (Estes Kefauver, quoting Gardiner Means and Fred Gardner.)

Everybody knows this, nobody wants to talk about it much, for we don't know how to cope with it. The effect is that we are living a kind of lie. Long ago, labor leaders used to fight for the shorter work week, but now they don't, because they're pretty sure they don't want it. Indeed, when hours are reduced, the tendency is to get a second, part-time job and raise the standard of living, *because* the job is meaningless and one must have something; but the standard of living is pretty meaningless, too. Nor is this strange atmosphere a new thing. For at least a generation the maximum sensible use of our productivity could have thrown a vast population out of work, or relieved everybody of a lot of useless work, depending on how you take it. (Consider with how little cutback of useful civilian production the economy produced the war goods and maintained an Army, economically unemployed.) The plain truth is that at present very many of us are useless, not needed, rationally unemployable. It is in this paradoxical atmosphere that young persons grow up. It looks busy and expansive, but it is rationally at a stalemate.

These considerations apply to all ages and classes; but it is of course among poor youth (and the aged) that they show up first and worst. They are the most unemployable. For a long time our society has not been geared to the cultivation of the young. In our country 42 per cent have graduated from high school (predicted census, 1960); less than 8 per cent have graduated from college. The high school trend for at least the near future is not much different: there will be a high proportion of drop-outs before the twelfth grade; but *markedly* more of the rest will go on to college; that is, the stratification will harden. Now the schooling in neither the high schools nor the colleges is much good—if it were better more kids would stick to it; yet at present, if we made a list we should find that a large proportion of the dwindling number of unquestionably useful or self-justifying jobs, in the humane professions and the arts and sciences, require education; and in the future, there is no doubt that the more educated will have the jobs, in running an efficient, highly technical economy and an administrative society placing a premium on verbal skills.

(Between 1947 and 1957, professional and technical workers increased 61 per cent, clerical workers 23 per cent, but factory operatives only 4½ per cent and laborers 4 per cent.—Census.)

For the uneducated there will be no jobs at all. This is humanly most unfortunate, for presumably those who have learned something in schools, and have the knack of surviving the boredom of those schools, could also make something of idleness; whereas the uneducated are useless at leisure too. It takes application, a fine sense of value, and a powerful community-spirit for a people to have serious leisure, and this has not been the genius of the Americans.

From this point of view we can sympathetically understand the pathos of our American school policy, which otherwise seems so inexplicable; at great expense compelling kids to go to school who do not want to and who will not profit by it. There are of course unpedagogic motives, like relieving the home, controlling delinquency, and keeping kids from competing for jobs. But there is also this desperately earnest pedagogic motive, of preparing the kids to take *some* part in a democratic society that does not need them. Otherwise, what will become of them, if they don't know anything?

Compulsory public education spread universally during the nineteenth century to provide the reading, writing, and arithmetic necessary to build a modern industrial economy. With the overmaturity of the economy, the teachers are struggling to preserve the elementary system when the economy no longer requires it and is stingy about paying for it. The demand is for scientists and technicians, the 15 per cent of the "academically talented." "For a vast majority (in the high school)," says Dr. Conant in *The Child, the Parent, and the State,* "the vocational courses are the vital core of the program. They represent something related directly to the ambitions of the boys and girls." But somehow, far more than half of these quit. How is that?

Let us sum up again. The majority of young people are faced with the following alternative: Either society is a benevolently frivolous racket in which they'll manage to boondoggle, though less profitably than the more privileged; or society is serious (and they hope still benevolent enough to support them), but they are useless and hopelessly out. Such thoughts do not encourage productive life. Naturally young people are more sanguine and look for man's work, but few find it. Some settle for a "good job"; most settle for a lousy job; a few, but an increasing number, don't settle.

I often ask, "What do you want to work at? If you have the chance. When you get out of school, college, the service, etc."

Some answer right off and tell their definite plans and projects, highly approved by Papa. I'm pleased for them, but it's a bit boring, because they are such squares.

Quite a few will, with prompting, come out with astounding stereotyped, conceited fantasies, such as becoming a movie actor when they are "discovered"—"like Marlon Brando, but in my own way."

Very rarely somebody will, maybe defiantly and defensively,

maybe diffidently but proudly, make you know that he knows very well what he is going to do; it is something great; and he is indeed already doing it, which is the real test.

The usual answer, perhaps the normal answer, is "I don't know," meaning, "I'm looking; I haven't found the right thing; it's discouraging but not hopeless."

But the terrible answer is, "Nothing." The young man doesn't want to do anything.

—I remember talking to half a dozen young fellows at Van Wagner's Beach outside of Hamilton, Ontario; and all of them had this one thing to say: "Nothing." They didn't believe that what to work at was the kind of thing one *wanted.* They rather expected that two or three of them would work for the electric company in town, but they couldn't care less. I turned away from the conversation abruptly because of the uncontrollable burning tears in my eyes and constriction in my chest. Not feeling sorry for them, but tears of frank dismay for the waste of our humanity (they were nice kids). And it is out of that incident that many years later I am writing this book.

Consumerism is out. This is the basic message of the counter-culture of youth. Technological progress, cleanliness, and newness no longer need be worshipped. Know your necessities and provide for them only. The credo of the counter-culture is to stop being a consumer and become a producer —a producer of a more humane and decent society.

ERNEST CALLENBACH

The Counter-Culture Thrust: Living Poor With Style

POOR IS "IN"

An unexpected crisis has come upon America. We have finally realized that the rosy picture of life given us in the fifties and sixties by magazines and newspapers and politicians is false. . . .

This failure of the old American way is naturally generating a new life-style, arising to challenge the old. Millions of young people who grew up in the rank atmosphere of warfare-state "affluence" have seen the consequences of that way—and found it wanting.

They are not sure what they want instead, but they know what they don't want.

They don't want to be the unwilling backers of troops in costly and immoral foreign wars. They don't want to be obedient consumers, salivating like Pavlov's dogs before an advertisement. They don't want to work at meaningless jobs—producing junk or shuffling a corporation's bureaucratic papers—in order to buy more stuff from which neither they nor their families nor their friends get any real joy. They want to be free men and women. And to be that, they are willing to be poor: to drop out of the corporations and universities and official culture and instead try building up a life-style that will suit them. This can mean scrounging, scavenging, welfare, do-it-yourself, subsistence farming, communes, odd jobs, part-time jobs. It's not an easy life. But it can be a real and personal and satisfying life—fit for a man to live. . . .

THE COVETOUS SOCIETY

The Ten Commandments tell us that we are not to covet our neighbor's wife, or his goods. If we took this seriously, modern business would collapse in a day. The very foundation of contemporary society is covetousness. We are trained to covet practically from the day of birth.

If we get into situations where there is nothing around to covet, we get nervous—like first-time campers, or tourists in East European countries who wonder why there aren't more downtown shop windows. We are, in fact, conditioned exactly like trained rats in a maze. Galvanized into action by a paycheck, we nose around, hunting for the ultimate purchase which will satisfy our hunger. Since most of us never have enough money for more than a few of the available toys, we are spared the dreadful realization that comes to the rich: there really isn't that much worth coveting. We go on busily and endlessly sniffing after the bait, and finally we drop dead in the maze, without ever stopping to consider whose game we have been playing.

In order to stop coveting, it may be necessary to be able to enjoy a lot of goods for a while. At any rate, this seems to be why the majority of hippies are from middle-class backgrounds: they've seen all their parents' toys and had a lot of their own, and they know by experience (which is how we learn almost everything we ever learn) that coveting is a bum trip. To people who all their lives have been deprived of the goodies enjoyed by the middle classes and the rich, the suggestion of doing without sounds like the old recommendation from rich people that the poor should enjoy being poor and honest.

But if coveting is your trip, you should at least try to get through it as quickly as possible. Work your ass off, put your money into all the goodies you can manage, spend your time in stores, read *Consumer Reports,* talk to experts: really sink yourself into it for a while.

Then kick it, and get back to figuring out what you really want to do with your life.

Every culture, like every person's life, has both a material and a spiritual side. In the development of an American counter-culture, much of the ground clearing has already been done: we have rejected the decadent national values of militarism, unbridled polluting technology, and the obnoxious pursuit of individual profit at the expense of the people at large.

We are not yet so critical about how we *do* wish to live. However, many new philosophical and political ideas are busily threading their way through our society. Some people who reject the anti-sex and anti-nature bias of Western "civilization" turn to Zen or other kinds of Buddhism which emphasize man's existence as part of nature, and encourage simplicity and directness in living. Some people who reject the authoritarian relationships inherent in modern business and even in electoral democracy turn to anarchism—which is not a doctrine of chaos, but an elaborate political theory based on the assumption that man is just as capable of living in relative peace without a coercive social structure as other animals are. People who are disgusted at the rape of the landscape caused by industrial society sometimes turn back to the American Indians for inspiration about how to live on the land without wrecking it—gathering wild foods, living in portable houses. Some people study other so-called "primitive" cultures for ideas about how man can achieve a better ecological balance with his environment. And some people, by experimenting with drugs that affect perception or produce visions, attempt to get in touch with the underlying realities of their own minds—or at least to escape the dead routines of the conventional thinking they have been taught.

Living has to do with how you eat and sleep and where you live and with whom; with how you relate to jobs and money; with machinery, furniture, and other objects; with how you dress; with how you deal with the law, the government, the police, the army. To every habit and convention of the old American culture, we are developing counter-patterns and counter-habits—anti-habits, sometimes, or the rejection of any habits at all, in favor of a fluidity from which new things may come.

So far the new ways have only begun to challenge the old. But already they have aroused the fears and resistances commonly stirred up by revolutionary thinking. The new ways have a powerful attraction, and they are spreading out from our tumultuous cities throughout the land. Their outward signs have begun to appear even in small cities and towns: brighter clothes, longer hair, funky old cars, rock music, drugs, organic and unsprayed foods, freer sexual relationships. Like a vast tribe of wandering Gypsies, people freed from the old conventions are spreading out.

Some preach the gospel to willing (and sometimes unwilling) ears. Some prefer to live quietly, letting the force of their example serve. Some are political, ready to argue how the miserable, desperate psychological condition of middle-class life is the result of the needs of the giant corporations and the military-industrial elite which controls them—and how American foreign policy is an extension abroad of these oppressive policies. Some are mystical, believing that only by putting your own soul in order, through meditation or drugs or religion, can you hope to live a contented life. But through all these variations of emphasis there runs a common disdain for the traditional American way—the life of work-work-work, buy-buy-buy.

And slowly, even among the squarest of citizens, the suspicion is growing that it is the very nature of our vastly developed industrial system to produce an environment which is poisonous to our bodies and toxic to our minds. Perhaps the making and buying of goods is *not* the main goal of a sane society. Perhaps a bigger Gross National Product is not a god worth sacrificing our lives to. Perhaps we must question the whole orientation of American values. The early labor-union leader Sam Gompers once summed up the aims of the labor movement as "More!" But maybe now we need less—and better?

Paradoxically, this question is being asked just when millions of black Americans are making a stong push to get what has been denied them since slavery. Black revolutionaries see this trend toward acquisitiveness as evil because it obscures the fact that the black population as a whole is still getting poorer relative to the white population. It seems clear, at any rate, that poor people of all races must stand together and organize politically to bring about a new life of real freedom and equality. . . .

What is different about the present moment is that modern education and mass communications have made practically everybody realize that we now have the resources and the technology to provide a decent living for all. And for the first time in history, sizable masses of people are deciding that a decent modest living is all they want: they are leaving the middle-class money chase and *deciding* to be poor—not miserably poor, of course, but poorer in money so they can be richer in time, in enjoyments, in living a life that makes sense to human beings instead of to machines and accountants.

DANGEROUS DOUBTS

Changing your life in this way means questioning many of the old ideals Americans have thought they had to live by.

Take *labor saving*, for example. Saving the labor of walking or bicycling by riding around in cars all the time has put Americans into probably the worst physical shape of any nation on earth. Saving labor by buying precooked or prefabricated foods not only makes your diet less interesting, but it may actually make you work *harder:* you have to work about ten extra minutes at your job to earn the difference between a cake made from a mix and a scratch cake. And the scratch cake will contain no preservatives or other suspect chemicals; besides, it will taste better, and will give you the pleasure of having done something satisfying for yourself, in just the way you want it.

Take *technological progress.* For years we have been told about the wonders of modern science. But it is now clear that much of our proud progress is illusory—and that many of our supposed advances do at least as much harm as good. Thus, for instance, chemical insecticides like DDT were welcomed as miracles of chemistry that would save crops from every kind of bug. It has taken us twenty years to realize that DDT kills some bugs but gives free rein to others, so that an orchard may be saved from peach borers but is then overrun with tiny mites. Worse still, DDT accumulates in water, in vegetables, in animals and fish. In 1969 it was discovered that Lake Michigan salmon were so full of DDT they were dangerous to eat. Human breast milk contains so much DDT that if it were bottled it would be illegal to ship it across state lines. (It is still better than cow's milk, however.) DDT has even led to the virtual extermination of several bird species whose eggshells are becoming too fragile to hatch.

Much of the new technology, then, seems to be bad for the human race, and we should subject all innovations to careful, personal, human, and ecological checks. If a new device contributes to the ugliness, impersonality, dirt, heat, noise, garbage, and air pollution of the world, we ought to reject it. Certainly we should keep it out of our houses. . . .

Take *cleanliness.* Americans have a fetish for washing. They buy staggering quantities of soaps and detergents and are constantly washing themselves, their children, their cars, their clothes. They tend to feel that unless a thing shines there must be something wicked about it. But biologically, man does not take well to all this shininess. Soaps and detergents wreck his skin and hair and give him rashes. Shiny cars hurt his eyes on the highways; his cities are so glaring he has to wear sunglasses. Having varnished or lacquered or polished everything, he is deprived of the variations in texture and pattern which occur in the natural world for which evolution prepared him.

Even natural smells are suppressed. Does anyone really want to smell another person who is "soapy-clean"? Our sense of smell happens to be a highly personal and immensely powerful emotional force; whether we like it or not, we are extremely sensitive to the smells of our families, our lovers, our households, our own bodies. Americans are willing to admit that babies smell nice, but that's about all. Basically, the American tradition is anti-biological. . . .

Take the idea of *"new."* The American mania for newness is drummed into us to convince us that our old things can't be any good, and we'd better hurry up and earn some money to replace them. But the new ones probably won't be as much fun to use as the old. They'll break down quicker, they are almost sure to be uglier, and they cost a hell of a lot more. A handy rule for a saner life is this: If you are lucky enough to possess something you like that's lasted for more than a couple of years, hang onto it. You'll probably never find a new one half as good.

Take the concept of the *nuclear family.* Earlier Americans lived in "extended-family" groups—a dwelling contained not only a father, mother, and children, but probably an aunt or uncle or so, probably a grandfather or grandmother, and possibly nephews, cousins, or other relatives. Houses were, on the whole, larger in those days, though many city people lived in slum tenements as they do now.

Today a family is supposed to consist of only two parents and their children. Grandparents are shoved off into rest homes or left to live by themselves. Everybody who is single is expected to provide for himself or herself. The present way has its advantages, as anybody with a senile parent will quickly point out. But it is on the whole a colder, more impersonal way. Like many other aspects of the American traditional pattern, it puts people into closer touch with machines, but removes them from human contact.

Modern young people are less and less convinced that the nu-

372 Work and Life Style

clear pattern is habitable, and they are therefore experimenting with communal living, both in the cities and countryside. These experiments are usually attempted by people who are not related to each other except through common experience: drugs, disillusionment with the university, political or religious consciousness. Some communes share vegetarian food practices. Some who have rejected the whole idea of city living turn to American Indian ways. There are many disagreements in and between communes, for once you cast off the old ideas, many new ones spring up, and it takes time to test them. Like the two-person family or any other human arrangement where people are in extended contact and intimacy with each other, communes are not havens of peace and tranquility. (As is well known, the best way to be perfectly tranquil is to be dead.)

The old extended-family pattern was based on two things: blood relationship and economic necessity. The big family enabled the individual to spend less money, have more pleasures, and be better protected against the dangers of life. Today, we like to ignore the dangers and imagine that science or the police have conquered them. However, as Americans become more realistic, they are becoming aware of their own vulnerability: they know that they will need help against disease, accident, crime, poverty, death, and their own families are often far away—at the other end of the country, or off at war. Commune dwellers, thus, are trying to see whether the bonds of common ideas and common needs are strong enough to sustain new kinds of groupings, where say ten to thirty people, often including permanent or married couples and children, live together and share housing, food, child raising, and so on.

The economic advantages are impressive. Let's take a group of only ten persons—three couples, two children, and two single persons. (This is roughly the minimum size of another stable social grouping—the wolf pack.) Under the conventional way of life they would have to rent five separate apartments or houses; as a commune they rent one large house or very large apartment. Each day, under the old system, fifteen separate meals would have to be prepared— and at a far greater cost than if all the cooking were done in one place. Costs for laundry, heating, lights, and so on will be far less per person than if separate dwellings are maintained. Even if each couple or person has individual radio/TVs, typewriters, irons, and other small items of personal property, it is possible on the average to live in a commune for less than half of what the old way requires. For many people existing on welfare, unemployment, disability, or retirement incomes, this can mean the difference between pleasant survival and utter poverty. . . .

Many communes, especially in rural areas, have been started on ambitious scales. Often rural groups plan to be self-sufficient concerning food, shelter, and clothing—though the land to live on generally comes from a family inheritance, a gift, or some other outside source. Some communes are positively puritanical, with rigid work duties, obligatory ceremonies, and careful planning of every aspect of life—totally opposite from the middle-class view of communes as permanent round-the-clock orgies. However, a former country dweller like myself knows that subsistence farming is extremely difficult to survive on in this country no matter how hard-working the communards may be. City kids who don't know a ewe from a moo will obviously have a very hard time, but so will handy, skilled, and reasonably lucky people who take advantage of every agricultural advance and work doggedly. The fact is that to produce all your food and even part of your clothing through individual farming takes such large amounts of energy that very few Americans are up to it. Every commune that hopes to endure, therefore, needs some steady, though perhaps not very large source of outside income—occasional or part-time jobs, welfare, or whatever. This will make it possible to divert some energies to the production of things which are unavailable commercially in the desired quality, or things which are overpriced commercially, things which can be produced with little money risked.

RESOURCES FOR THE NEW WAYS

There is as yet no solid, effective, comfortable style of living poor in this country. Instead of working out ways of living that are suitable for human beings who are free, we tend to straggle along in the foul exhausts of the advertisers. ...

CONSUMERISM, SCRIMPING, AND OTHER BUM TRIPS

Newspapers and magazines abound with advice about how to "save" money by spending it wisely—how to be a smarter consumer. Some advice of this kind can be useful, and there is some of it in this book. But the real point is to *stop being a consumer*—that is to say, a creature whose social role is to buy stuff. A "consumer" is a kind of servant of the industrial society. It produces tons of lettuce, he eats lettuce, perhaps selecting one type over another. It produces hair dryers; he buys hair dryers, studiously comparing brand names. In short, he is playing the corporations' game.

You only really save money, and time, and your freedom, by *not* buying—ultimately, by "paying" attention not to what they are trying to get you to pay attention to, but to things that personally matter to you.

It is not easy to discover what personally matters to you. By the time a kid is six or eight, he has been exposed to thousands of hours of television commercials. And by the time he has finished high school, he has been thoroughly brainwashed into thinking about (and wanting) all the stuff that has been presented on TV, in magazines, and in the households of fellow brainwashed citizens.

We must stop being consumers and become *producers:* producers of ideas, of friendships, of beautiful objects, of better relationships among all people, of a more humane and decent society.

One of the chief secrets of learning to live well without much money is that it is bad to scrimp. Penny-pinching is bad for the spirit. Few of the ideas in this book involve the mean and depressing kind of trim-here and squeeze-there budgeting often recommended to people without enough money. Instead, the wise and free person recognizes that buying things (with all the cost consciousness and calculation it involves) is not the central question. The central question is *how to organize your life.* If you decide to organize it by your own standards and desires and needs, you will find that buying takes on an entirely different aspect.

For one thing, you will come to know what your necessities really are. Obviously these will include food and shelter and clothes —possibly on a more modest scale than you tended to think. But they may also include music, or flowers or a southern-exposure window; privacy or an open-door policy; lots of heat or lots of fresh air; bright lights or dim.

Furthermore, you will discover that buying is not the only and often not a desirable way to obtain things. St. Francis is said to have remarked that to beg is best, to steal is next, and to buy is worst of all. This doctrine tends to appeal most to those who crave the excitement of stealing. But I would think that the saintly bird lover did not sufficently study his birds: to a bird, begging, stealing, and buying are all irrelevant terms; and in this and other respects we can learn by watching our fellow animals who have not been corrupted by speech or ideas.

American Indians too once lived upon the land like birds— taking what they needed, but without destroying the fabric of plant and animal life which produced it. The "taking" was hard—as anyone knows who has tried to subsist even a short time by hunting and gathering food, or who has tried to construct a shelter and implements without machine-made tools. And it is an aristocratic illusion, usually held by people with unearned income from parents or inheritances, that men can live in any numbers without a good deal of hard work. Occasional saints (or sinners) bring it off, but they are isolated persons for whom the essentials of life—some bread, a roof at night, some wine—can indeed be begged, or borrowed, or shoplifted. The real problem in modern industrial society, capitalist or socialist, is that we must work *for others,* not for ourselves. When we seek money by offering our time and energy in the labor market we are putting ourselves at the disposal of others, and the purposes of the work we are assigned are often so remote they have no meaning.

We do need money to buy food and shelter. Still, by redirecting our energies, we may find that we need to *buy* far less and can *make* far more.

This also saves money: instead of paying $75 for a bed in a furniture store, you can make one for $25. But that is only a fringe benefit. What counts most is that instead of working for someone else over the hours needed to produce that extra $50, you were working for yourself, in your own place, with your own companions, at your own pace, with your own ideas and designs and materials and tools. The resulting bed is *your* bed—in a way no Simmons bed could ever be.

Calling themselves consumers, modern Americans are literally consumed by the industrial system—and on two fronts: they must sacrifice to it their alienated labor, to get money; and to get food, shelter, and other needs they are confined in the maw of the marketplace, which offers many choices but only with the exchange of money. Thus money becomes the measure of all things, including your life: all goods and all people become cost-rated commodities. While the US government rates a Vietnamese civilian killed "by accident" at a few thousand dollars (if anything), a good wage-earner run down by a truck at home may be worth a hundred thousand— as defined by his potential earning power, or perhaps his insurance policies. When such standards become widespread, the value of human life *in itself* is forgotten. All life is consumed by "the cash nexus," as Marx called it—the bargaining act by which every thing and person is weighed at somebody's cash register.

We can escape the cash nexus only to the extent we escape dealing with cash.

Thus in this [chapter] many ideas are put forward not as ways to "save money" but to avoid dealing with it altogether. What I hope to do is to show that a whole system of attitudes and practices exists, in embryonic form, which can help us combat our fatal dependence on the cash nexus—and thus give us the courage and strength to use our own powers, our own imaginations, directly on our own behalf. We need to live with our own hands, to control our own beings. In a world where everything from a steam shovel to a coffin can be rented and cost-accounted and deducted from income taxes, we must defend our own life spaces, lest we find ourselves rented too.

In the full-blown industrial state such as we inhabit, the "duties" of the citizen are to work steadily and obediently, pay taxes and union dues, vote when called upon, consume enough goods to keep the economy going, and occasionally trot off to the other side of the world to fight for some dictatorial regime and save the national face. We must struggle politically to defend ourselves from such a well-organized fate—let them build robots! But in order to struggle we must also and at the same time develop a different way of living: of eating and sleeping, of loving, of traveling about, of educating ourselves and our children, of amusing ourselves, of securing medical care and political redress. The old-style American way of life securing been gobbled up in the industrial age, and spat out upon the ruined landscape. What we must do now is build a counter-culture, a new Way.

The problems we face, in trying to make modern America habitable for human beings again, are not to any serious degree technical. They are problems of *holiness:* we are searching for ways of restoring dignity and importance to daily events. It is, in a sense, a religious quest. We have to relearn how to pay true attention to what we are doing, because there is little solid pleasure in things done thoughtlessly or mechanically. We must learn to eat holy, dress holy, smoke holy, wash holy, and so on.

Since organized religion has abandoned the people, people must create their own religion. The beginning seems to lie in something rather like the American Indian's concept of "medicine." The things we use and wear, if we make them with care and use them with respect, take on "good medicine"; they become holy because of the sincerity of our regard for them and the extent of our commitment to them. It is hard for disposable goods to be holy. When we buy manufactured goods, even of honest quality (which is hard to find), it is always doubtful whether our spirit can enter into them. Best of all are those things which are old, have been well loved, and have become holy through association with people we love and respect: ancestors, old friends, great men or women.

It is very hard to find the right way, and no person should lightly despise another's way. Out of the welter of present industrial society, it will probably take us several generations to sort out those few things which are essential to mankind—and to reject the others, of which no truly human or holy use can be made. We should be patient with each other's experiments, but cleave to our task, now that we know what it is; it leaves little room for cant or credulity.

Five

Religious Faith

Adolescence is a period of questioning, flux, and tension between extremes.
The belief in God does not escape this kind of questioning. The rejection of
religion and religious conversion are each characteristic of adolescence and
both these extremes may occur in the same individual. Many young people
emerge from this time of life less bound to traditional religious institutions
but with a workable and sustaining faith.

JAMES A. KNIGHT, MD

Religious-Psychological Conflicts of the Adolescent

The dynamics of the adolescent's interest in or rejection of religion
show great diversity. Often, religion is a source of distress or conflict
to the adolescent. No general inference can be made except that the
religious area appeals to certain adolescents as a medium for orient-
ing themselves, and often reflects their attempt to establish themselves as individuals with their own identity and personal set of
values. Overtly expressed disbelief in God is oftener encountered in
adolescence than at any other age, yet it is typical of the paradox of
adolescence that it is also characterized as the most religious period
in life. These extremes may be met at different times in the same
young person. In their efforts to examine their religious beliefs and

arrive at a faith that is their own, adolescents may deliberately expose themselves to a variety of religious experiences.

Freud's great biographer Ernest Jones was involved in just such a self-examination during his adolescence. He recalls:

> Those years, from sixteen to eighteen, were indubitably the most stirring and formative of my life. The starting point was the problem of religion, which covered more personal sexual ones. Since the age of ten I had never been able to give my adherence to any particular creed, but my conscience troubled me badly and impelled me to seek in every direction for enlightenment. I prayed earnestly, frequented the diverse religious services available, and read widely on both sides. From that time dates my lasting interest in religious phenomena and the meaning of their importance to the human soul.[1]

An introductory statement seems indicated here about religious development and the meaning of religious faith. Sigmund Freud made an extensive study of infantile sexuality and showed how various strands of emotional experience in the child came together in the course of development to issue in the mature experience of genital union with the opposite sex.[2] He also showed that certain individuals stopped short of the mature sexual experience and remained unable to express their sexuality except in immature forms. Some sought help in their distress, and many of these could be aided through psychotherapy. Others, constitutionally incapable of reaching mature development, had to rest content with whatever degree of maturity they had managed to achieve.

The religious development of the individual may be analogous to his psychosexual development. One may then recognize immature forms of religious development in childhood and adolescence. The various strands of immature experience unite and issue in something that may be called religious maturity. If one accepts this line of thought, one would expect to find that certain individuals had stopped short of a mature experience. Part of this group would contain persons who were incapable of progressing further because of some inadequacy in their constitution. Others would be those who wished or needed to progress, but were unable to do so because of conflicts within their own personality or with their environment.

Although the psychiatrist is hesitant to give an opinion of what constitutes religious maturity or faith, because of the theological

---

1. Ernest Jones, *Free Associations: Memories of a Psycho-Analyst* (New York: Basic Books, 1959), p. 57.
2. Sigmund Freud, "Three Essays on Sexuality," *Complete Works* (New York: Macmillan, 1963), VII.

nature of the question, he can attempt a partial definition in psychological terms. A mature religious faith includes the sense that there is a power in the universe that is greater than the individual; that the experience of this power is of supreme value to the individual concerned; and that through this experience life acquires a new meaning, although the experience cannot be arrived at through the operation of reason. Such a statement, although only a skeleton, one can clothe in the creeds and practices of his established church. In simplest terms, one may give his definition of faith as a capacity to trust in a divine being, the commitment to a system of values, and the participation in a way of life that makes all significant aspects of life sacred.

The adolescent's religion can be described as his relationship to whatever he holds ultimate; as well as the shared ritualistic and ethical response that ensues from that relationship.[3] This ultimate is symbolized in the words, myths, rites, and rituals of the tradiion in which he was reared. The tradition remains secondhand, however, until the youth examines it and claims it for his own. Through conflict and struggle, he may manage to see his own life experience within the drama of the religious reality and make some commitment to these realities. "Religion provides both the parental symbols for alienation and reconciliation and the solution beyond the parent images."[4]

The adolescent phase is generally reputed to contain many religious conflicts related to normal psychological growth and development. These conflicts are the central concern of this chapter.

AREAS OF CONFLICT

REBELLION AND REBUILDING

Recently, a psychiatrist mentioned that at breakfast on a Sunday morning, his adolescent son announced his atheism. Prior to that he had considered the ministry as a vocation. About the same time, another physician's son, who had also considered the ministry as a vocation, announced his atheism. It was later discovered that these two newly avowed atheists were friends and had been in dialogue with one another on religious matters. Both sets of parents were deeply troubled and wondered what was happening in the thinking of their sons.

---

3. Charles W. Stewart, "The Religious Experience of Two Adolescent Girls," *Pastoral Psychology*, 77 (1966): 50–51.
4. Ibid.

It is not uncommon for an adolescent to enter a stage of atheism, or probably better, agnosticism. The meaning of this fairly common experience in adolescence probably has something to do with the individual's previous relationship to both his father and to God.

In the small child, the being called God is probably conceived as being human and not spiritual, for the supreme value is found in the parents. Freud attempted to show in *The Future of an Illusion*[5] that the idea of God was no more than an infantile picture of the father. Many take issue with Freud for seeming to forget that the father might also be for the child the carrier of the projection of the God image. Thus it is probably natural that the child's religious experience should be bound up with the parents. If development proceeds normally, his projections onto them are gradually withdrawn, with the result that they become to him more human and less divine.

Many a young person during adolescence is not yet mature enough in his religion to distinguish between God and father. During adolescence, one of his tasks is to separate God from father. To accomplish this, he involves himself in struggles with authority for freedom and independence. In order to clarify his confusion and begin his movement toward independence, he may reject God or father, or possibly both. After that, he may begin working through his rebellion and arrive at a new understanding of and relationship to God and father. Religion then is used in an appropriate and not conflictive manner.

The adolescent, as a part of his movement toward independence, feels constrained to examine and reconstruct the religious beliefs given him by his family. He may discard certain of the religious beliefs of childhood as he struggles in his search for his own set of values and his own identity. In order to become fully emancipated from his parents, the adolescent usually must doubt the religious attitudes, standards, and value system of his parents. Involvement with and support from his peers involve the adolescent in a comparison of his religious beliefs with those of others. Such a comparison usually results in some change, ranging from abandonment to renewed intensity.

In actuality, the adolescent's rebellion against religion is often against what he thought was taught him. He is rejecting chiefly his own childhood conceptions, for which he may illogically blame his culture, parents and church. Many years may pass before he realized

---

5. Sigmund Freud, "The Future of an Illusion," *Complete Works,* trans. Strachey (London: Hogarth Press, 1961), XXI.

that his rebellion was not so much against parents, church or culture as against his own immaturity. Not many things can be as upsetting to parents as an adolescent struggling with emancipation, attacking their treasured value system.

Some adolescents raise doubts about God through an examination of the problem of evil. They state that their greatest conflicts and deepest questioning focus on the problem of evil viewed in the context of the avowed goodness of God. Their arguments deal not only with evil in man but, more searchingly, evil in the natural world. Dostoevsky dealt with the same issue in a magnificent passage in *The Brothers Karamazov* in which Ivan speaks to Alyosha.[6]

The adolescents speak of the brutalities and unjust sufferings of this world, of disease, of the violence of nature in storm and earthquake, of innocent children as victims of man and nature's inhumanity. They go on to say that such evil is incompatible with the picture of the loving Father-God. Therefore, they may conclude that there is no God, or if there were, and he permitted such, they want nothing to do with him. Adolescents, after such a declaration, may betray deeper and more revealing feelings in their dreams. If they are asked about their dreams, they not infrequently report dreams that betray a hungry, longing search for a powerful, loving and good God. Thus, their questioning can be used to sustain their rebellion.

A young person whom I saw sometime ago illustrates well the issues raised here regarding good and evil, God and father. She was an attractive and intelligent 20-year-old girl and the wife of a graduate student. She had made two recent suicide attempts. Her depression, which had lasted two years, was growing worse. Before it, she had gone through a period of self-doubt, and thrown away all her previous religious beliefs and training; and when she could believe no longer, she lost the love that she once felt for mankind. Depression was her constant companion, and the conclusion that life was not worth living began to plague her. She spoke as movingly as Ivan about the evil in the world and the dark side of God. She spoke of the closeness she had always felt for her father, a clergyman. In the last few years she had come to the conclusion that he was a human being with many weaknesses and not the god she thought he was. About the time she lost faith in him, she lost faith also in God. Her world had been held together, she stated, through her closeness to her father and her church. Faith became doubt and, with the doubting, her world fell apart. Her guilt, lack of identity, and feelings of

---

6. Feodor Dostoevsky, *The Brothers Karamazov* (New York: Grosset, 1956), pp. 276–288.

unworthiness precipitated a chronic depression of suicidal proportions.

Her nuclear conflict related to her father. Strong oedipal ties,
which continued into adolescence, began to frighten her, and she felt
compelled to create some distance between herself and him. It
seemed reasonably clear also that her concept of God was confused
with her concept of her father, and her religious faith centered in
father instead of God. The task confronting her was to separate God
from father in order to clarify her relationship with each one. This
was the goal in psychotherapy.

HYPERRELIGIOSITY

Rebellion against parental authority may take the form of hyperreligiosity, indulged in as a device for harassing his parents. The
young person may compare his parents to religious leaders in the
community, and painfully point out parental deficiencies. He may
require that his parents remain almost constantly in church with
him. Parents do not know how to deal with such a display of piety
and are afraid to discourage what ought to be a good thing. Sometimes the hyperreligiosity is coupled with obsessional blasphemous
thoughts or other distorted manifestations of religion. Such an
adolescent is usually in militant opposition to himself as well as to
the outside world. Progress in the emotional development of the
adolescent is usually accompanied by a corresponding change in his
religious attitudes, wherein the distortions are replaced by more
mature religious expressions.

There is a moderately high incidence of scrupulosity among
certain groups of adolescents. A recent study revealed that one of
four sophomores in a Catholic high school and one of seven Catholic
college students admitted to current scrupulosity.[7] Scrupulosity has
been noted in adolescents with other religious affiliations, or none
at all. And it must be stressed that much of it is transitory and not
necessarily indicative of severe pathology.

Although the obsessive compulsive behavior is of a religious
and spiritual nature, the problem is basically not a moral but an
emotional one. The core problem is in the handling of both sexual
and aggressive impulses. The competitive theme is strong with the
need to excel. Sibling rivalry is usually intense. Such adolescents are
frequently manipulative, passively resistive and provocative. Their
sexual conflicts have strong oedipal overtones. They use the com-

---

7. P. A. Riffel, "The Detection of Scrupulosity and Its Relation to Age and Sex"
(Unpublished Dissertation, Fordham University, 1958).

mon defenses seen in the obsessive compulsive syndrome: reaction formation, denial, undoing, and isolation. Excessive guilt is usually seen, frequently accompanied by a depressive element.[8]

It is characteristic of the adolescent for intuitions to arise in the psyche of the existence of a strength and a wisdom that are infinitely above those of any human being. If he has been kept in touch with the beliefs and practices of his faith, the adolescent now begins to consider what he has been taught. Intuitively he realizes that a mighty, unseen and spiritual being exists somewhere and must be shown due regard. If the adolescent becomes deeply caught up in the religious life, he may become so split between the instinctual and the spiritual that he rejects his humanity, particularly in its sensual and feeling aspects. He believes that he can live as a saint only if he does not have these feelings. This split, it is generally felt, has its roots in faulty adult treatment of the person's sexual impulses during the earlier years. A pitfall of the split is that often the adolescent succeeds only for a time in being religious and virtuous. The expelled humanity then returns with devastating power and may shatter to bits the religious superstructure. The environment should afford the young person a constant opportunity to evolve a natural pattern of religious experience, or else such an experience will wither away before the assault of instinctual forces that attack every adolescent from the unconscious.

Some adolescents, around the age of 18 or 19, identify strongly with God. Such an identification, by its very nature, is immature behavior and grows out of the adolescent's sense of weakness more often than feelings of omnipotence. It is easy for dogmatism and even fanaticism to be incorporated in the character structure of such an individual. Psychotherapists rarely see the religiously fanatic adolescent, for usually the rebellious and atheistic are referred for therapy. The fanatically religious adolescent may be deeply involved in church activity and his conduct completely approved by both church leaders and parents.

As long as these individuals can talk about their relationship with God as a private matter, whether during adolescence or in later years, they can avoid confrontation with self. They may even enter a religious vocation to avoid any commitment to God or to people. They become immune to being touched or questioned by anybody. Later, disappointments develop, and some of them find themselves

---

8. Otto Fenichel, *The Psychoanalytic Theory of Neurosis* (New York: Norton, 1945). See also W. W. Weisner and P. A. Riffel, "Scrupulosity: Religion and Obsessive Compulsive Behavior in Children," *American Journal of Psychiatry*, 117 (1960): 314–318.

in a psychiatrist's office. The most revealing question that can be asked such a person is: "When did God begin to disappoint you?"

RELIGIOUS CONVERSION

Mental conflict is the seedbed of religious conversion. Conversions occur commonly during adolescence, for adolescence is a time of major emotional turbulence, great ideological receptivity, and maximum experiential intensity. William James associated religious conversion with the "ordinary moulting-time of adolescence," and held the conviction that conversion is in its essence a normal adolescent phenomenon, incidental to the passage from the child's small universe to the wider intellectual and spiritual life of maturity.[9]

When conversion occurs, it seems to come like a flash. Actually, the fury has been churning and finally bursts forth like a volcanic eruption. Intense soul-searching usually precedes the climactic event, in which cherished ideals are in battle with unacceptable wishes. When the way out of the struggle takes the form of a religious conversion, the adolescent truly has a peak experience as well as feelings of ecstatic fulfillment and boundless energy. For him it is genuinely a rebirth. The effect of the experience may be to preserve the sanity of the individual—or render him ill.

"Why does one individual have a normal reaction to his religious experience and another a pathological reaction?" The difference is probably in ego strength. After the conversion experience, the adolescent feels overcome by the presence of God within him, and he feels he is becoming God or Godlike. He begins to think that possibly he is losing his mind, but then decides that this is too wonderful a thing to fall in the category of insanity, and he begins to evaluate himself and search the Scriptures for an understanding of his conversion experience. He goes on to integrate and fit the experience into his life. His head and his heart are strong enough to contain this transforming experience. On the other hand, the adolescent with a somewhat weak ego feels the impact of such a conversion experience and may immediately declare that he *is* God or Christ. He is overwhelmed by the experience, for his head and heart are too small to contain the experience. He may become either a babbling idiot, declaring himself God, or a frozen catatonic with an expression of ecstasy on his face. Of course, there are pathological reactions less extreme than these two.

The impact of a genuinely deep religious experience is almost always overwhelming. The whole history of man's encounter with

---

9. William James, *The Varieties of Religious Experience* (New York: Modern Library, 1929), p. 196.

God points this out. Time and again the prophets avoided hearing
the voice of God, seeing him, or letting him get hold of them in any
way, because they were afraid they could not contain themselves
after such an encounter. This is illustrated beautifully in the biblical
books of Isaiah and Jeremiah.

SEX

A major area of religious conflict concerns sex. The adolescent's
sexual drive is so powerful that it is rarely possible for him wholly
to sublimate it in nonsexual activities. Usually, he resorts to masturbation, for he has practically no other recourse for the direct release
of his sexual tensions. Masturbation is almost always followed by
feelings of guilt. Since most churches and religious leaders have
moral injunctions against masturbation, it is usually felt that these
injunctions are responsible for these feelings. Reassurances about
masturbation from physician, priest, or parent rarely succeed in
assuaging the guilt of the adolescent.

 Why is it so difficult for the adolescent to find relief from his
guilt over masturbation? Psychoanalytic research has revealed that
masturbation is almost invariably associated with fantasies that
have their origin in early childhood. Usually it is the fantasies associated with masturbation, not the mechanical act, that generate
guilt. Highly disguised and generally not accessible to the conscious
mind of the adolescent, the fantasies relate to his incestuous attachments of early childhood.[10]

 Anyway, masturbation is regarded as an immature expression
of the sexual impulse. After the adolescent liberates himself from
earlier incestuous attachments, hopefully he will find sexual satisfaction within the framework of marriage and family life.

 The adolescent also has some serious religious or moral conflicts
over premarital sexual relations. His conflicts in this area have often
called for his serious examination of the religious code by which he
was reared. Thus, he feels squeezed between a strong need for expression of his sexuality and the controls and demands of his religious upbringing. He then may challenge, attack or rebel against the
religious controls. Not infrequently he may turn strongly to religion
to help him control his sexuality.

 Inability to resolve the conflict between maintaining his moralistic, religious orientation to life and giving vent to his sexual feelings may cause an adolescent to be fearful of his impulses and to
become somewhat depressed. He may feel that God has failed him

10. Louis Linn and Leo W. Schwarz, *Psychiatry and Religious Experience* (New York:
 Random House, 1958), p. 67.

in not helping him control his sexual thoughts. If such a person has sexual thoughts in church, he finds such an experience exceedingly painful, to the point of having to stay away from church services. Such a person discovers in his horror that not even in church is he safe from sensual thoughts or erotic sensations. Because of this, he develops a fear of the place that he feels has failed to save him. On the other hand, because of the omniscience of God, he feels he is desecrating the church, knowing himself to be the subject of erotic processes while in it. Such awarenesses may then be repressed in symptom formation.[11]

Religious leaders often make a statement such as "religion and sex are on the same party line." They are implying that some of the emotional experiences associated with religious worship render the individual more acutely aware of his sexual feelings and possibly more open to some kind of sexual expression. A psychiatrist, teaching in one of the South American medical schools, did a study of the adolescents in his city. He found, to his astonishment, a fairly fixed pattern to behavior of the adolescents on certain religious feast days. The adolescent boys participated all day in the religious programs at the church. Then at night they went to a house of prostitution and had sexual relations. They referred to these prostitutes with the nickname "Mother."

Other adolescents are in such moral conflict over their sexuality that any kind of arousal or expression may be producer of psychobiologic disturbances, frequently of a gastrointestinal nature. One of the severest cases of anorexia nervosa I have seen was that of a teenage girl whose illness developed almost immediately after having sexual relations for the first time. A college student reported visiting a house of prostitution with his friends and how sexually excited he was by being there; then a prostitute came up to him and asked very sweetly and seductively, "Have you dated yet?" Immediately he was filled with disgust, became nauseated and vomited. An adolescent girl came for psychotherapy because of her conflicts over her sexuality, which was causing her great embarrassment. She was not sure whether she should let any boy touch her physically in any manner. At times she permitted some physical contact; then when she was kissed and felt sexual arousal, she almost invariably became nauseated. All three of these adolescents wanted help with understanding and handling their sexuality in the context of their moral convictions and religious beliefs.

11. James A. Knight, *A Psychiatrist Looks at Religion and Health* (New York: Abingdon, 1964), pp. 148–149.

FINITENESS AND THE LIMITATION OF TIME

The adult world is likely to believe that death is rarely a concern of the adolescent. Yet the enigma of aberrant behavior as well as the source of the idealism of youth may be related to, or even centered in, the adolescent's concept of death.[12] The problems often labeled *identity* or *purpose* may be related to the need to find a satisfactory sublimation for anxiety about death either in religion or other altruistic choices.

The Psalmist has prayed, "So teach us to number our days that we may apply our hearts unto wisdom." Such words point up for the individual an awareness that time is limited. What is it that brings the allocation of time into sharp focus? When does this acute awareness come? For some, it is that point when they cease to measure their age by the distance from their birth and start to measure it by the distance to their estimated death. For others, it is when they begin wondering for the first time whether they are wasting the time left to them. Some are constrained to number their days when a death occurs in their family, when they lose a friend or great leader, or when sickness befalls them and the sick bed furnishes a setting for contemplation and meditation.

Rarely is the adolescent aware that time does not last forever. However, he can experience a heightened consciousness of time and of his personal finiteness and deal successfully with this traumatic crisis. Soren Kierkegaard has said, "There comes a midnight hour when all men must unmask." The awareness of the finiteness of time is the unmasking moment for the individual. He experiences both anxiety and guilt as he contemplates what the future will bring, the predicament of his existence, and the issue of fulfilling his potentialities. So in his solitude, the discovery takes place of his aloneness, his exile, his anxiety, and his guilt.

It is healthy, although difficult, for the adolescent to recognize that his future is limited and that time passes whether one is busy or bored. After acquiring such insight, the adolescent can be helped to focus on the contents of the future: hopes, aspirations, goals, obligations, ambitions, and intentions. Through achievement, he can find a sense of identity and continuity, and he can be challenged to use his time remaining in the search for his ideal.

It must be stressed that it is most difficult for an adolescent to comprehend or accept his finiteness. This may be related in part to his appraisal of himself as able to do anything in the world or solve

---

12. Armand Maurer, "Adolescent Attitudes Toward Death," *Journal of Genetic Psychology*, 105 (1964): 75–90.

any problem if given the opportunity. This particular aspect of youthful development is designated by Pumpian-Mindlin as "omnipotentiality."[13] There is no occupation that is inaccessible or vocation that he cannot attain. He can indulge in wild flights of the imagination, for he knows no limits to fantasy and accepts only grudgingly any limits to reality. Pumpian-Mindlin emphasizes that, at the same time, the adolescent finds it difficult to do one thing and follow it through to completion. To do so would mean to commit himself to a single task primarily, and this he is not yet prepared to do. When he moves into young adulthood, he must forgo his omnipotentiality for the sake of the acquisition of a particular skill or accomplishment. The step from omnipotentiality to commitment channels the diffuse omnipotential energy into a specific direction. The suddenness with which young people shift their vocational goals is related to this quality of omnipotentiality and to their inability to accept the commitment necessary for their passage from youth to adulthood. This feeling of omnipotentiality permits the adolescent to roam and search in many fields and climes before responding to the social and maturational necessity of commitment.

I have seen adolescents who postpone making a vocational commitment because of unconscious fears of death and the feeling that growing up means growing toward death. Maybe such individuals are represented in our society by the "perennial adolescent," the dilettante, the "jack of all trades and master of none." Others with the same fear retreat into fantasy, often regressing to the level of infantile omnipotence and magical thinking, to which youthful omnipotentiality is genetically related.

One ought also to examine academic failure of some college students in this context. An occasional student has a trait of not being able to finish tasks, and this characteristic has usually been with him for years. Although intelligent and able to succeed in college studies, such a student may fail to graduate in his major by only a few months. One such student spoke of the emptiness of time and the fear of death. The need not to finish things, including college, became a way for him to deny the passage of time. Time did not hold a promise of future fulfillment, but a rapid journey toward inevitable death. In his acute awareness of time's passage, he attempted vainly to control it by filling it with activities, avoiding quiet periods or even moments of meditation, and by being constantly "on the go." Even periods of study he had to avoid, for self-confrontation

---

13. Pumpian-Mindlin, "Omnipotentiality, Youth, and Commitment," *Journal of the American Academy of Child Psychiatry,* 4 (1965): 1–18.

seemed to occur during these periods. Compulsive activity, in the form of unfinished and endlessly repeated tasks, isolates and attempts to order and control time through repetition that leads nowhere and, therefore, not to death. Fortunately or unfortunately, one's efforts to kill time or drag oneself backward are seldom successful in curbing one's thoughts of the future.

On the other hand, an awareness of death leads the consciousness of the individual straight to essentials. Adolescents are often deeply disturbed over what occupation or career to choose. If the adolescent is confronted by the thought of death, he is forced to view life as a whole and to think seriously and immediately about how he is going to spend that life. He is coerced into asking, "What is the meaning of life and what is the purpose of my human existence?" He goes on to ask, "What do I want out of life and what will yield the highest fulfillment in it?" He must then begin decision-making regarding courses of study and activities. Daily he must confirm or revise his initial decision. Obviously he can change his mind even after he surrenders his omnipotentiality. Not only does such an adolescent explore vocational counseling but investigates literary, philosophic and religious ideas. Only rarely does the thought of death become morbid or depressing for him; on the contrary, it is revitalizing. If he acquires this important insight into the inevitable condition of man, to some extent he can take his life into his own hands, recognize that death is inevitable, and make the most of what he has.

Death anxiety manifests itself physically in individuals prone to psychobiologic disturbances, one of which may be insomnia. Some insomniacs are afraid that death may catch them asleep, although this awareness is not usually on a conscious level. Sleep is a state in which the sleeper is not "in control" or "not at the controls," and anything can happen during this defenseless state without one's own volition. Frequently, people with sleep difficulties have suffered severe feelings of intellectual inferiority since childhood. They believe that in order to maintain what is at best a precarious control, they must remain awake. The adolescent is not immune to insomnia or other psychobiologic disturbances, and a careful exploration of these may reveal some psychological problems with important religious dimensions.

THE REGRESSIVE WORSHIPPER

Another type of adolescent in religious conflict is the one who has "lost faith in God" in the face of hardship or of unanswered prayer.

Such a one is almost always the child of possessive and overindulgent parents, who have denied him nothing, except his right to separate from them. Of the two parents, the mother is the possessive one who denied her maternal drive to help the child grow up and away from his dependence on her. In primitive religiosocial cultures where the Earth Mother was the goddess venerated, the greatest withdrawal of her favor was from the regressive worshipper.[14] The intuition of early man was aware that the individual who is not allowed or not able to sacrifice his dependence on comfort and security will not, when older, have the capacity to make those psychic sacrifices that alone can help him to mature in his relationship with God and man.

PHYSICAL ILLNESS

Religion may become a focus of great concern during the physical illness of an adolescent. A person in the grip of an illness feels some threat to his own identity. John Donne said: "In poverty I lack but other things; in banishment I lack but other men; but in sickness, I lack myself." The availability of support through religion may exercise a critical influence in helping prevent the fragmenting of the sick person's world and self. John Gunther's *Death Be Not Proud* contains a moving account of how religion fortified the shaken psychological defenses of a youth suffering from a fatal physical illness.[15] Although religious instruction was not included in his up-bringing, the youth showed a deep religious involvement during his illness. He displayed an inspired courage throughout his suffering. At his insistence, his mother spent many hours reading to him from the Bible, particularly the Book of Job. He returned repeatedly to this book. Throughout this time, however, he made a great display of agnosticism, and one of his poems was entitled "An Unbeliever's Prayer." It is obvious that his religious needs were being met in spite of his questing and questioning and that actually his display of agnosticism was a form of testing, a way of balancing certainty with uncertainty, an effort to see if faith could encompass doubt.

SEARCH FOR PEACE AND UNITY

In the inner struggles that erupt at puberty, social concerns appear a major part of the young person's religion. The reasons for human existence are heatedly debated. The desire to do something to im-

---

14. I. D. Suttie, *The Origins of Love and Hate* (London: Routledge, 1935), p. 128.
15. John Gunther, *Death Be Not Proud* (New York: Harper, 1949).

prove the world is conspicuous and often expresses itself in a concern for world peace. The religious man who fights for social justice becomes the ideal. As one would suspect, the psychological origins of the adolescent's religiosocial idealism lie in part in his yearning for peace within himself. Through the mental mechanism of projecting his inner turmoil onto the outer world, his yearning for peace within himself may take the form of a wish for world peace and social accord. Upheaval in the outer world intensifies his inner conflict, for he needs the steadying influence of moral strength and unity in the world around him. A stable environment helps immensely in meeting the emotional needs of the conflict-ridden youth. Thus religious observances with festive ceremonies and meaningful symbols introduce a stable rhythm into the adolescent's family and community life.

THE HAZARD OF NO STRUCTURE

Adolescents have a need to be exposed to some structure or order of religious beliefs that they can interiorize or reject. In many adolescents, there is such confusion and ignorance about religion that they are unable to deal with the specific traditions in their background. In other words, permissiveness and obscurity in religion give the adolescent nothing to rebel against or to be dependent on. The young person needs to be introduced to the higher value system of the group in which he is living. Where instruction is not given, or where the family and society have become uncertain of basic values and consequently have developed a collective instability and uncertainty about values, one sees a developmental defect in the spiritual and moral dimension of the individual.

Our predicament today seems to have been summarized well by Kenneth P. Landon of American University: "I grew up in an era when it was still respectable to say 'Lord, I believe. Help thou my unbelief.' Now it is more in style to say, 'Lord, I don't believe much. Help thou my use of cybernetics in determining my probabilities and options.' "[16] In such a society, the adolescent's religious conflicts do not find resolution so readily as in a society with a more structured value orientation.

THE ADOLESCENT SPEAKS

Recently, I interviewed 100 adolescents regarding their ideas of the religious conflicts or problems experienced by the average adoles-

16. Kenneth P. Landon, "The Eternal Verities," *Family Forum*, October, 1966, p. 1.

cent. There was no selection of this group except that they were 100 consecutive premedical students who visited Tulane University for interviews as a part of their admissions to Medical School. They ranged from 18 to 21 and came from many sections of our country and variety of universities. They represented the major faiths and a wide spectrum of family commitment to religion, from strong to minimal. Such a sample is biased, however, and one could not claim that it is representative of the typical adolescent of today. At the same time, on the basis of empirical data, its religious concerns and conflicts seem quite similar to those of the average adolescent.

The discussion was opened by asking them to comment on a statement, often made, that adolescents have some special religious problems and conflicts that other age groups may not have.

Essentially all of the group recognized the stage of adolescence as one of questioning, flux, searching for identity and tension between extremes. One student said: "The human situation is one of being up in the air, and my age group spends more time in the air than probably any other age group. Just think, when you are in the air your situation is changing fast."

Such an introductory comment usually preceded the student's discussion of his need to examine the faith given him by parents, to tear it apart, to move in and out of belief, and hopefully to arrive at a new synthesis that was his own and that would be useful to him in crises as well as stable times. All encouraged a searching examination of whatever faith had been given them, and implied that through questioning the basic dogmas taught them they could have their faith strengthened and revitalized. They were quick to emphasize that they were left with many unanswered questions, but had decided that finding the faith, to a great extent, meant seeking the faith. The seeker often finds a new clue each day, and the seeking helps him remain open and broadminded. Some reported walking around in a fog for about three years before they began finding any acceptable answers to the questions they raised. Several interviewees mentioned Bishop Pike as one individual who was asking relevant questions about the religious issues with which they were dealing.

Most of the students minimized the problem of atheism in the average adolescent. They felt that a period of atheism was not uncommon in a young person's life, especially if he were reared in a rigidly religious home. They preferred the term agnosticism, however, to atheism. Such a person would need to rebel and attack in order to free himself enough to arrive at a position where he could examine the issues of faith. The consensus was that usually such a person arrived at a healthier and more stable belief in God than he had before. The adolescents gave the impression that it was essential to rework one's faith, but probably bad to throw it away permanently. They implied, at least, that a disbelief in God could well leave one rudderless. One student told of a college friend who became an atheist and went home and converted his father to atheism. Now his father does nothing but drink. When asked why this happened to the father, he replied: "He became frightened about the future. His world became chaotic. He didn't see any point in going on, I suppose. So he drank to deaden his pain and anxiety."

Some emphasized specifically that rebellion against parental values and subsequent atheism or agnosticism represented primarily a search for identity; and even fads and nonconformity are part of the same search. Essentially all of the students stressed that the rebellion was not idle but purposeful behavior. One student, sobered by the ever-present thought of nuclear warfare and urgently struggling for a religious identity of his own, asked his father: "Why should I follow your pattern when it has gotten me in such a hell of a mess?" Another student, 19, following the same trend of thought, felt that evil in the world was the greatest obstacle to believing in God. "There is so much evil here, where is God?" This student declared herself an agnostic while remaining open to new clues and never quite sure that God did not exist.

Several of the interviewees stated that some of their peers handled religion quite forthrightly. They had put religion out of their minds and probably would not deal with it again for years. A few reported that they themselves were so free of it that the subject never crossed their minds. Although they did not deny conflict in the past, they denied it presently. The total group's estimate of the number of adolescents in the general population who had freed themselves from religion was less than 25%.

A few were quite specific in indicating that for years they looked on their parents as "God figures." Then, slowly and painfully, the awareness dawned upon them that their parents were human and had many problems. Questioning and doubting followed, especially regarding religious matters. They looked everywhere for certainty and when they found any sign of it, they examined it with enthusiasm. One Jewish student stated that after seeing the movie, *The Cardinal,* he had this feeling: "One who believed so deeply must be right. Then I realized that others who believed differently felt just as strongly. I then felt comfortable enough to remain open for new religious insights."

Hypocrisy of religious parents and other religious people in regard to social issues caused pain, confusion and conflict. What was most disturbing was the effort of the "faithful" to bend the biblical teachings to fit their hates, prejudices, or bigotry. The adolescents stated that they would have been less shaken in their struggles if the adult world had acknowledged religious precepts as ideal, and at the same time acknowledged their inability to attain the ideal in their actions. But twisting or distorting the structure of religious morality and idealism, the adolescents felt, left them with no fixed point on which to orient their values or conduct. At the same time, they often found that it was easy for them to profess one thing and act in another way. In such circumstances, when their consciences ached, they found a little comfort in meditating on the hypocrisies of religious people, including their parents.

When asked to comment on their feelings about death as a possible area of conflict, most of them reported that the thought rarely entered their minds. The years ahead were so many that they did not look upon their life as even having any limitation in time. Death, when it occurred, was something that always happened to other persons, not to them. Those who dealt with it and tried to work through their feelings about death were usually those who had lost a relative or had a friend die or killed. One student, whose uncle had been killed recently, had a question addressed to him by his sister that confronted him with death like no experience he had ever had. His four-year-old sister simply asked: "Will he go to sleep in the coffin forever?" It was the word "forever" that he found so sobering, since he could not comprehend why or how one so young could even use the word, to say nothing of understanding it. A few others reported a period in their adolescence when they were afraid of the atom bomb or nuclear war. The usual reaction was: "Why? I am too young to die or be mutilated. I am innocent. Oh God, Why! Oh God, where are you?" In general, however, about 25% of the group interviewed had had some kind of confrontation with death that stimulated them to deal personally with the fact that death was inevitable for them also. In other words, they now realized that their years were numbered and their life span limited.

Almost every adolescent commented on some degree of religious conflict in the handling of his sexuality. The intensity of the sexual feelings was overwhelming at times. It seemed bad to them to have such intense feelings, and above all, the ever-present issue: "How do I handle these feelings?" Most of the students felt that premarital sexual relations were more discussed than indulged in. Some had searched unsuccessfully for the free-love parties that the popular magazines write about. A majority felt, however, that sexual permissiveness with affection may become the prevailing pattern soon. This new pattern will not be free of guilt for many, they reported. Several students mentioned that fraternity life carried with it some expectation of stud performance or opportunities for training as a sexual athlete. A few of these students felt that certain aspects of fraternity life had been the source of their major religious and moral conflicts over sex.

It was obvious from the group interviewed that there seemed no easy way to deal with their sexuality, and whatever activities or thoughts they indulged in frequently brought them guilt and anxiety. One student summarized the ambivalence of this age-group by saying: "You may permit yourself to indulge in some sex relations, but you ought to feel a little guilty afterwards in order to save your self-respect and your moral standards." A few other students made this type of comment: "I wish adults would stop confusing their sexual problems with ours."

The general feeling was that many factors fed the religious ferment and conflict in college. Many professors, as well as the curriculum content itself, raised searching questions. One's classmates and friends shared freely whatever ideas they were struggling with. Then the atmosphere of the college campus is permeated by a superscience approach: only that which can be substantiated in the laboratory is to be accepted. In such an atmosphere, it is often not the "in" thing to go to church or to be religious. The students went on to say that environmental and peer pressures push the average student away from concerns about faith or religious commitment. This freedom to question and challenge, while out of reach of the sheltering and restraining influence of home, furnishes the ingredients for both conflict and change. In such a setting, something as personal and subjective as religious faith has to be refashioned and reexperienced in order to survive and serve them in their new world.

Most of these students testified that although less bound to religious traditions after their period of religious upheaval, they were now more sincere in their belief in God, had a more workable and sustaining faith, and were better qualified to work effectively for a better world. Most felt that they had built their belief-system around a single pillar—belief in God. Not many expressed any great need for the institutional church as an important or essential part of their religion. They went so far as to raise the question of whether the symbols and rituals of the church are even meaningful today. Also a few emphasized that the institutional church has had a part to play in some of the bigotry and hatred among people presently as well as in the past. Thus the church, while proclaiming the brotherhood of man and the fatherhood of God, has at times played a part in fragmenting the family of man.

CONCLUSION

The areas of religious conflict in the adolescent can be identified about as easily by the adolescent as by the specialist in adolescent psychology. Such a creative awareness on his part should be reassuring to the anxious adult world, which feels itself threatened by the tumult and vitality of adolescence. Probably the adolescent is right that it is difficult for him to see and to know God today in our technicologic world, which "worships computers that predict our future, machines that control our present, and bulldozers that destroy our past."

In this critical study of the Jesus movement, Adams and Fox find that most of the members are teenage youth, the "Jesus-boppers." Their motivation springs from a desire to maintain peer-group approval while trying to resolve the identity crisis. However, members deny the future by turning their backs on the temporal world. The movement has, to some extent, been replaced by the cult of Eastern religions, headed by a "Perfect Master." This critical study seems applicable to both types of "trip."

ROBERT LYNN ADAMS & ROBERT JON FOX
Mainlining Jesus: The New Trip

"It's the greatest rush I've ever had," commented one hip young man describing his experience in turning on to Jesus. Similar drug culture metaphors are used by other former drug users who have joined the spreading movement of evangelical religion among the young—a movement that originated largely in Southern California. The ranks of the "Jesus people" or "Jesus freaks," as some call them, have grown considerably during 1970. Thousands have been baptized off the beaches of Southern California, and the movement has spread across the country trailing colorful publicity in its wake.

"We made *Time!*" exulted a young prophet of the movement recently. Bumper stickers substitute "Have a Nice Forever" for the familiar California expression, "Have a Nice Day"; the Jesus-oriented *Free Paper* is sent to 50 states and 11 foreign countries—a biweekly, it claims a circulation of 260,000. In new recordings featuring "Jesus rock" the composers search for spiritual guidance and direction. Musical groups such as The J.C. Power Outlet and The Love Song proliferate. A new social system blends the hip style of dress, music and speech into the "Jesus culture"—something new, yet something old indeed! The Jesus trip is The Great Awakening of 1740 (Jonathan Edwards) revisited; it is American frontier religion revisited with Volkswagens and amplifiers supplanting the horses, wagons and saddlebacks of Cane Ridge, Kentucky, 1801.

The young whites of middle-class background turning toward revivalist religion come from two rather distinct groups. From observations of crowds at religious services, one of these groups consists largely of teenagers whom we call "Jesus-boppers." In them, rock groups turned on to Jesus have a ready-made audience from the large ranks of rock music fans. Free concerts followed by an invitation to accept Jesus Christ attract large youth audiences.

The other element in the Jesus movement is a smaller and more intense group of young adults (usually in their twenties) who have opted out of the drug culture. Many are former peace movement activists who have dropped out of society over the past four or five years. For them, the Jesus movement constitutes a ritual of re-entry into the system.

In our investigation of the Jesus movement we used both observations and interviews. We attended many religious services, interviewing the ministers of the church in Orange County, where the movement is largely centered, visited religious communes, using a formal questionnaire to interview 89 young people. Although the sample is small, it served to add validity to the observations and unstructured interviews, the latter being taped for analysis. We encountered great resistance in the communes to the questionnaire; some attributed their reluctance to an unwillingless to mull over the past. One respondent mentioned that talking about one's past was actually forbidden in the San Francisco commune where he had formerly lived.

A TRIP TO THE CHAPEL

As an institution, Gethsemane Chapel is three years old. It is an independent, nondenominational congregation whose basically conservative Baptist theology is a blend of holiness and pentecostalism. Its ministry is anti-establishment in its rejection of the theology and social positions of the major Protestant denominations. The main minister is a hawk on the Vietnam war, decrying the no-win policy which has been pursued by the government.

Sunday morning and evening as well as several week nights are Bible study sessions, attended mainly by older persons. Some week-night meetings find Gethsemane Chapel jammed with youth, but the big youth night is Wednesday, when a number of musical groups are featured. The church is packed two hours prior to the service—crowd estimates range from 1,300 to 1,400 persons; about one-third are outside listening on loudspeakers and participating visually through the chapel's glass walls. Approximately 80 percent of the audience is female; and less than 5 percent are what could be called hippies. Yet the style of dress is informal—jeans and hip garb and long hair abounds. Over half the crowd consists of early teens and less than 15 percent are over twenty.

A 22-year-old lay minister—a former drug user, with flowing robe, long hair and beard—leads this service. Later, in an "afterglow" he leads a smaller group in receiving the baptism of the Holy Spirit —speaking in tongues. The interaction style in the worship and in the entire movement is intensely personal, a kind of "Gospel Anonymous," with pastors and members first-naming each other.

Gethsemane's services are more holiness than pentecostal in that they follow a definite order, eschewing the freewheeling "do your thing" style of the latter. The young minister mentioned above, whom we shall call Rennie, has been known to silence persons who interrupt to speak in tongues during the service. Informal songs are sung by the congregation, mostly centering around the person of Jesus and his imminent return to earth. Prayers for the sick are offered and testimonies are heard. The ubiquitous "one way" sign (extended index finger with clenched fist) shows the congregation's approval of various elements of the services. Rennie affirms that God desires to heal anything from "warts to cancer." The "flashes" from previous LSD trips can also be cured. One woman (older than most present) testifies that she has been cured of dandruff. "Praise the Lord!" says Rennie. An examination of her head reveals no trace of dandruff.

Following the singing, testimonies and music groups, Rennie reads from the Bible and gives a sermon—often a defense of speaking in tongues. At the close, an invitation is given to accept Jesus. On an average Wednesday night, about 100 young persons come forward, affirm their faith in unison, and are then led to another part of the church to be presented with a Bible. When there are fewer converts, individual counseling was also conducted. Many of the converts are later baptized in the ocean, although apparently no set plan is announced for doing so immediately.

In the afterglow, another Bible study is conducted, after which

Rennie invites those who want the baptism of the Spirit to come forward. A flute player provides an eerie background (he "plays by the Spirit") while Rennie assists those who wish to receive the Spirit, with such blandishments as, "you may kneel, if you wish," or "you may extend your arms toward heaven, if you wish."

Rennie moves in and out among those standing on the platform, touching and speaking to them. Eventually a cadence of people speaking in a babble and singing in tongues intertwines with the mystic tones of the flute. (Many Jesus-boppers report receiving this baptism.) For this part of the service the church is full, but the aisles and the grounds are empty of people; some teenage girls attempt to sit in the aisle to get close to the platform where Rennie is leading the service. Following the afterglow, which is terminated at Rennie's command, certain individuals remain fixed in apparent hysterical stupor. "Counselors" help them to "give in" to the Spirit, some of whom are unable to pull out of their babbling and hysteria.

On Friday nights there are no music groups, although the service is supposedly programmed for youth. Another young lay minister—more square than Rennie—leads this service. The attendance is about one-third of the Wednesday night assemblage, with fewer teenagers present. This difference is likely due to the drawing power of the professional gospel rock groups on Wednesday plus the charisma of Rennie.

THE JESUS COMMUNE

The leaders of Gethsemane Chapel, being interested in reaching young people in the drug culture for Jesus, developed the idea of adopting the commune as a service-oriented institution. And the movement appears to be very successful. Scores of Jesus-oriented houses have sprung up along the entire West Coast under the sponsorship of Gethsemane Chapel.

Visits to these communes reveal a rigid separation of male and female living quarters, with a strict affirmation of asceticism. Many of the occupants have been members of drug-oriented communes, where sexual relations were available. The same individuals appear to move toward early marriage after being saved. Their frequently idealistic conception of marriage is exemplified by the response of one young man, who when asked if he thought sex could be misused in marriage, said, "Certainly not." (He believed that he had misused it out of marriage.)

The communes visited had approximately 20 to 30 permanent residents, although their turnover appears high. When one commune becomes fairly large, another is established; when one is over-populated, members move to another which has space. The commune also serves as a type of crash pad where anyone is welcome to eat and/or sleep.

Money earned by members is given to a central treasury, although one's worldly wealth is not demanded (as was the case in the traditional monastery movement). Yard and gardening work is done for local residents to earn money to support the house as well as to learn to work and live together. Several deacons are in charge of finances plus the physical and spiritual nurture of the house. The leaders deny that there are rules, saying everyone is to follow God's will. Emphasis on cooperation rather than rules appears to be effective in accomplishing the day's tasks. There is a minimum of scheduling, although a list of those preparing breakfast is posted. The diet, which has a heavy starch content, is augmented by fruit and vegetable discards donated by local grocery stores. The direction of the Spirit is sought in all matters, including remodeling and obtaining materials for a new roof, for example.

Persons visiting a commune receive an open and friendly welcome. Such was the case at Mansion Messiah. A tour of the premises may reveal a young man speaking in tongues in the garden, a modest "prayer house" in the back yard, with another young man just leaving it to return to the main building. Just recently the "family" had added the eating room. There were no contractors hired to build the addition, and the plywood and materials for the roof were all donated. "The Lord just showed us where to lay the beams," and the members built the roof. The garage was converted into a bedroom by the members also and holes in the walls were left for the windows. "The Lord provided us with windows to fit the holes." In this bedroom at least nine men sleep, in three bunk-beds, three high, that the men had made themselves.

The girls (about ten in number) do all the cooking, mending, serving, washing, and other housework and hold no outside jobs. The men do the yard work, gardening, repairs around the house, building of furniture and some hold outside jobs. It costs about $2,000 per month to run the house. Donations and contributions help to pay the expenses that are not covered by the men's pay.

Many individuals in the commune appear for the first time in their lives to be learning how to work and live with others. The leaders do not deny that conflicts arise in the house; such conflicts, they emphasize, are a creative opportunity for individuals to learn to live together. The nightly Bible study time is used to deal with such problems; leaders of the evening frequently pick a New Testament passage dealing with mutual sharing and responsibility.

Life in the Jesus movement is ruled by two norms: the Bible and the direct guidance of the Holy Spirit. As their former lives have been physically sensate in relation to drugs and sex, so their "born-again" lives tend to be spiritually sensate. Thus it is difficult to gather information on such mundane topics as finances either at Gethsemane Chapel or in the communes. "The Lord provides" and "right on!" are the expressions one elicits upon bringing up the problem of money. Since all problems are dealt with by the direct guidance of the Spirit (unless explicit Biblical instructions can be found), it is not surprising to find commune members and ministers of the church extremely spiritually sensate in regard to budgets.

During the study of the communes, it became evident that the wide publicity given the movement in the press and on television was affecting the communes' image. These problems and others were observed by a student researcher during her visit to what we term Christus House:

I went to the Christus House on a Friday night. Everyone was sitting around talking and drinking either coffee or tea, waiting for the meeting to start. At about 7:00 p.m. every night the house has a meeting with people who live outside. These are carefully screened by the leader, a deacon named John. The meeting lasts between two and three hours.

While I was waiting for the meeting to begin I talked with several people who were very open to introduce themselves, but very hesitant to carry on a conversation. The first question they asked was "Have you been saved?" I overheard a conversation between two members of the house, one male and one female. The female, Jane, was expressing her previous concern (before being saved) and anxiety about getting married. She said she was glad she didn't have to worry about that any more because it was now in God's hands. The meeting began with guitar music and singing by everyone present. John led the meeting, but everyone was given a chance to talk. This they referred to as "sharing."

At first they shared different encounters they had had during the day. The main topic of discussion was a program on television that afternoon in which John, a girl named June, and several people from another commune participated. They had spent the time talking about God and Christ. John had cut his hair for the program and has suffered "trials" throughout the week because he was afraid the devil was making him do it. They both expressed how upset they had been because they might misrepresent the Lord. However, they were both at ease when they discovered, while on the air, that they didn't really even speak but "it was the Lord speaking through them." They expressed concern with changing their image from that of long-haired, former drug users to conservative, clean-cut citizens. In fact, they showed hostility at the image they thought the public had of them. Others mentioned having individual problems and the Lord leading them to a specific chapter in the Bible that solved the problem. They discussed what the phrase "I love someone but I don't like them" means, as John had just found out from a minister at Gethsemane that afternoon. One member expressed how thrilled he was because it was his first day working for Jesus.

Experience in the communes is dichotomous: one is led either by the Lord or the devil. It was thus very difficult to get very detailed answers to questions. The public (i.e., the "world") is likewise viewed in authoritarian, either-or terms: as in "darkness" and "searching for the light." After the meeting, members left for a theater to witness to people waiting in line. John tends to use scare tactics in a gentle way, illustrated by the fact that he very calmly asked me if I died on the way home, which I might, would I go to heaven? He had also mentioned in the meeting that in the studio that day he had asked someone the same question.

THE JESUS-BOPPERS

Most of the members of the Jesus movement in Orange County seem to be teenage youth—the "Jesus-boppers." Their motivation for being in the movement is apparently twofold, stemming both from a desire for peer-group approval and a need for resolving the identity crisis. According to Erik Erikson's analysis of the teenage years as a period of identity vs. role confusion, puberty marks the beginning of the developmental stage crisis. The physiological revolution within and the tangible adult tasks ahead of them cause youth to be primarily concerned with how they appear to others rather than with what they feel they are. Erikson writes:

> The adolescent mind is essentially a mind of *moratorium,* a psychosexual stage between childhood and adulthood, and between the morality learned by the child, and the ethics to be developed by the adult. It is an ideological mind—and, indeed, it is the ideological outlook of a society that speaks most clearly to the adolescent who is eager to be affirmed by his peers and is ready to be confirmed by rituals, creeds and programs which at the same time define what is evil, uncanny, and inimical.

The Jesus trip seems tailor-made for adolescents. Not only does commitment to Jesus preserve childhood morality with its absolutistic definitions of right and wrong, but it also provides an ideology based on personal, internal and, for the most part, unexplainable experience rather than on critical, rational or realistic analysis. Indeed, the ideology is unchallengeable and thereby not available for analysis by the uninitiated.

The Jesus trip also provides adolescents with the necessary peers, rituals, creeds and programs—brothers, baptisms, speaking in tongues and a source for the ideology, the Bible. Approval and affirmation by peers are guaranteed within the movement. To the droves of young teens who fill Gethsemane Chapel on the nights that the professional music groups perform, Rennie issues the invitation in these words, "Accept Jesus Christ. Don't get left out. Come right now."

The Jesus trip can be seen as an attempt to resolve the crisis of the onset of sexuality by denying sexual feelings. Previous to puberty, the individual has developed to some degree an identity based upon his or her experiences and needs. With the onset of the physiological revolution within and with the growing awareness of adult roles, this identity is threatened; suddenly he must accept a new aspect of identity—sexuality. Successful growth depends on the individual's ability to meet his new needs and expand his identity without threatening the self. Rather than risk the trauma of his adjustment, the individual may resolve the crisis in neurotic fashion: by establishing an ideal by which to deny his feelings. Adolescent idealism represents one such attempt to keep oneself separate from one's real feelings. An example of such denial is this statement by a 16-year-old who had been on drugs and sexually active prior to his conversion:

> I am free, free from the garbage of the world—the kind of stuff that you're a slave to. Jesus said, "Whoever commits sin is a servant of sin." I've quit taking drugs, I've quit getting it on the girls—I've changed, man! Don't you understand? I'm free, free, free—all the time and not just for six to eight hours—all the time. I still have problems, but I don't hassle with them, because I'm free!

We believe that religion as represented in this movement is a step backwards. The Jesus trip, like drugs, appears to be used in such a way as to avoid coming to terms with the anxieties related to the identity crisis. In normal development the new dimensions of identity are added to the previously established identity, modifying it to some degree; some parts of one's previous identity will be discarded, submerged or eradicated by new behavior. Instead of progressing toward adult ethics, the Jesus person clutches tenaciously to childhood morality, with its simplistic black-and-white, right-and-wrong judgments. Rather than developing behavior oriented towards reality, he flies into ideational, ideological abstractions to numb his awareness of his newly arisen needs. Spurning a reality that begins with individual feelings, he subordinates himself to peer approval. For these reasons we term the Jesus trip a pseudo-solution to the identity vs. role confusion crisis.

COMPARING DRUG AND JESUS CULTURES

Members of the Jesus movement have a high incidence of past drug use, with 62 percent of those over 18 and 44 percent of those under 18 having used dope. Only a few individuals were extremely light users, usually of marijuana.

Continuities between the drug and Jesus experiences are as follows: 1) both are outside the modal American life style, in fact, both are anti-establishment in their attempts to create alternatives to the American middle-class life style. Middle-class denominational religion, in the words of one pastor, "is as phony as it can be." 2) Both are subjective and experientially oriented, as opposed to the dominant cultural style, which is objective, scientific and rationally oriented. 3) The nature of the religious experience at Gethsemane Chapel and other holiness-type congregations is wholly consonant with previously experienced drug highs. A common description of the conversion experienced is: "It's a rush like speed."

We found a number of discontinuities between the dope and Jesus trips. As compared with the drug culture, the Jesus trip offers an extremely limited repertoire for action. For the Jesus person, life revolves entirely around Jesus, his acceptance and mission. All events are either of the Lord or of the devil. Brothers and sisters of the faith meet each other with religiously-infused greetings, and "God bless" substitutes for "goodbye." The drug culture as a whole exhibits a much greater variety. Certainly there are drug users whose lives center solely around dope, its procurement and use, but drug use has become quite generalized among a wide variety of people many of whom have a broader range of action alternatives in dealing with reality than the Jesus people.

The Jesus trip represents an almost violent ideological swing from far left to far right, a type of "reaction formation." A shift toward a conservative position in solving world problems is reported by 76 percent of those interviewed. Only two persons have changed toward the left. Of those who reported no change in position, none were "drop-outs" in the usual sense of the word. They represent a more consistent ideological history—no rebellion against parents, a continuity between their childhood religious faith and the adult Jesus movement. Their feelings toward American society, for example, are that it is "pagan like the Roman Empire at the time of Christ" or it is "too complex" for an opinion to have been formed. A slightly more liberal outlook was articulated by one respondent who observed that "the system is great, but people pervert justice." The focus here is still typically on the individual rather than on system change.

Four out of five of those reporting a shift in outlook state that the change coincided with their religious conversion. World problems, they now believe, "can only be solved through finding Christ"; "We can't have peace on the outside if we don't on the inside", "If everyone was a Christian there wouldn't be any world problems."

However, certain Jesus publications in the area encourage a more wordly approach to political and social problems, indeed a very conservative one. For example, the *Hollywood Free Paper* routinely attacks the peace movement. *For Real* made the following comments in the May 1971 edition in an article entitled "The Real Lesson of the Calley Trial":

> The fact is, too many people are bad. Because people are bad, they must be restrained by force. Because they must be restrained by force, police are necessary. Armies, navies and air forces are necessary. Wars are inevitable. Killing is necessary. That's the real lesson of the William Calley trial.

For Jesus people, sexual behavior also undergoes profound alteration when they leave the drug culture. Although 62 percent of the Jesus people in the sample report premarital sex prior to conversion, in most cases asceticism has become the dominant rule since being saved. A few slips are reported "once after conversion," but these can hardly be classified as libertine. Less than 5 percent openly differ with the sexual ethics of the movement and continue to practice premarital sex after their conversion. Another divergency is that the Jesus culture entails re-entering the system, returning to a middle-class work ethic and closing the generation gap. After coming from middle-class backgrounds (72 percent of those reporting father's occupation are from white-collar homes and over two-thirds of these are clearly upper-middle-class occupations), dropping out represents downward mobility; these youth are now re-entering the system, preparing to participate in the work force.

The movement's strong anti-intellectualism, however, is prompting some young people to drop out of college at a time when their re-entry into the system requires additional training. Many Jesus people, however, are still involved in routine educational programs while at the same time they hold anti-intellectual views. Of the 89 young people who answered the questionnaire, 17 had completed high school, 19 were still in college, three had some college, two were college graduates, and many were young high school students.

Several in the sample, who had dropped out of college, cite their religious experience as the motivating force in this decision. A songwriter-itinerant singer for gospel causes asserts that "The more education one has, the less likely one is to join (the) Jesus movement . . . (the) less one becomes childlike . . . becomes hardened." He elaborates that school teaches that science is God, that truth is relative, and that there can be good and evil at the same time, but this is not true.

College graduates are included among the ranks of commune dwellers who tend gardens as a livelihood. Generally, though, the older persons in the movement had dropped out during or after high school and now represent a most interesting sociological phenomenon: downward mobility and movement from church to sect (many come from church-affiliated families). Thus in closing the gap between themselves and their parents by rejoining the system, they have created fresh conflict over their education and religion. However, many parents are so pleased with their return to the system that they are financing their offspring's stay in the commune. One youth mentioned the possibility of going to Europe to an evangelical convention, explaining that his father would pay his expenses.

Preachers at Gethsemane Chapel admonish the audience to "honor thy father and thy mother." Many youth noted their conscious attempts to help them rebuild relationships with their families. Prayers in communes often concern members of the family who have problems and "need to be saved."

Whereas the drug trip represents a quest, the Jesus trip is a panacea. Despite its attendant problems, the drug culture is admirable in its affirmation of the individual's quest for experience and discovery of truth; in this it is not unlike the basis of modern liberal education. The Jesus trip, however, is a cure-all. No problem is too great to be answered easily; the believer desists from solving problems, "leaves it up to the Lord."

Another difference between the two cultures relates to authoritarianism. The free-lance drug culture is by definition nonauthoritarian. The Jesus culture, on the other hand, sees the world in either-or terms. No experience is free from being of God or of the devil. This unequivocal embracing of authoritarianism may be a by-product of the scanty education of many young believers combined with a background of family conflict.

The Jesus culture escapes the leadership problem posed by the individualism of the drug culture. Lewis Yablonski observes how the individualism of the drug scene often leads to a lack of leadership —a vacuum which sometimes allows "deviants" from the scene to wreak havoc on the peace and tranquility desired by the majority. Although leadership in the Jesus movement is attributed to God, there is no want of self-anointed human leaders around to make suggestions: the hierarchy ranges from the deacons in the commune (often young Christians with less than one year's experience of being saved) to the ministers of Gethsemane Church. The ministers are consulted on Biblical and other problems which the deacons in the commune cannot solve.

Before undertaking this study, the writers had theorized that Jesus people who are ex-dopers had participated in a succession of social movements: they began in the peace movement, had dropped out into the drug scene and finally joined the religious revival. The data, however, refute this assumption about the sequence of membership in the various movements, for the use of drugs almost always had preceded participation in the peace movement. We find the mean age of 25 former drug-and-peace people to be 20.3, while the mean age of nondrug-nonpeace participants (Jesus-boppers) is 17.4. Another segment in the sample consists of ex-dopers who were not in the peace movement (16 individuals with a mean age of 20.2, similar to the drug-and-peace group). Only four persons participated in the peace movement, but not in drugs; their mean age is 18.2.

Since the mean ages of the two ex-dope groups is similar, a contrast between them is fruitful. The drug-peace contingent is more likely to report (79 percent) dropping out of society than the nonpeace group (55 percent). However, contrary to popular opinion, their dropping out did not mean total absorption in the quest for individual experience; it did not interfere with New Left political participation by 32 Jesus people in the survey.

If the movements are so dissimilar, why the switch from dope to Jesus? One possibility is the faddishness of the Jesus trip; the same quest for novelty had motivated some to join the drug scene. The hippie faddist finds that drugs and sex are not "where it's at." Those of middle-class background may be torn between their former values and those of the drug scene; they may welcome the Jesus trip as an expedient means of returning to middle-class values, while retaining peer approval. The religious fervor of the Jesus movement provides a more socially acceptable way for them to resolve their conflict; its life style is as much a drop in as a drop out. One can gradually become reoriented to the larger segments of the population without really going too straight. In fact, few changes in life style are required in the move from dope to Jesus.

CRITICISMS OF THE MOVEMENT

The Jesus culture bears watching in the future because of several ironic twists: It is a victim of area right-wing politics, and we foresee its steadily increasing exploitation by reactionary political forces. Pamphlets distributed by the Jesus people are beginning to contain familiar attacks on one-world government, the ecumenical movement among liberal denominations, and other favorite targets of local conservative politicians. Disaffection of the movement's adherents (who generally interpret the teachings of Jesus as condemning all wars) may be expected when they discover that their leaders are militarists. The "true believer" psyche in the Jesus people, however, may well make it possible to rationalize their loyalty to their leaders.

The movement is insular—a cop-out from the realities of social change which face America. A basically white movement, it has no program for reaching the members of another race or less affluent economic groups than those in its area. The attempt to equate denominational religion with the establishment is presently successful; however, when the youth see that the denominational church has stood against racism, war and poverty, the Jesus movement may well fade. As one liberal, establishment, campus minister put it:

> I think the kind of world in which we live leads to some kind of escape. And some of the same kids who were escaping through heroin are now mainlining Jesus, and confusing Jesus with a way of withdrawing from the world and its problems. I can sympathize with them. There are times when I would like to withdraw too.
> Jesus to them is a kind of spirit that they have a union with. Whereas Jesus, for the early Christians, was a man of flesh and blood who took history seriously, and whose concern [was] about the whole man, not just his spirit, not just his soul. Jesus will push someone back into those problems, back into the world, only if they stay with him.

The movement denies the complexity of human nature. It abrogates the psycho-socio-sexual nature of man by dividing the self into physical and spiritual entities; the individual is indoctrinated to anticipate "rapture" when the soul is delivered from the body. Many Judeo-Christian theologians would label this as heresy, citing that the Bible teaches the unity of man's nature.

The movement's faithful show a rapid turnover. This may be related to their return to middle-class society. Some young teens who were in the movement have lessened in religious fervor considerably as they approach the middle-teen years.

The movement denies the future by turning its back on the temporal world. The apocalyptic feature of the movement dissuades young people from rejoining society because they are led to believe that the second coming of Christ is imminent. They need not concern themselves with improving our decaying cities, solving the problems of poverty, war and disease—all can be left up to God. A new pamphlet says the ecology movement is irrelevant because Jesus is coming soon anyway. Similarly the individual has no need for long-range plans; his exclusive concern is with the immediacy of his personal needs. Such myopia will certainly obstruct attempts to bridge the generation gap. (The movement's dropouts will undoubtedly become more oriented toward the future.)

Among the potential trouble spots uncovered in our data is the gap between the ministers' beliefs and those of their followers. For example, the ministers interviewed saw nothing contradictory in being both Christian and economically successful; the young people, particularly the commune members, take the antimaterialism of Jesus seriously. The main minister, as already mentioned, supports the presence of the U.S. fighting forces in Vietnam (his associate—not Rennie—did not dispute his view); but the young people, although no longer participating in the peace movement, nevertheless do not support the war as a just cause. Only two of 89 persons thought the war just, while eight felt it definitely unjust; 23 had no opinion or did not answer; 33 percent of the sample gave a generalized answer that it is wrong to kill; others saw providence of prophecy working in the war; one felt "he would go to Vietnam and try to change the people spiritually," and two persons said Jesus would not be involved—either as hawk or dove.

The communes are the most impressive part of the Jesus movement. The contribution made by their members lies in the simplicity of their life style, their easy acceptance of themselves, their genuine attempts at learning to get along with others and participate in communal tasks. Although they have kicked the drug habit, their abstinence has been too brief to predict how successful they will be giving up drugs permanently. We may wonder what will happen if and when they are no longer high on Jesus. The potential psychological difficulties could be enormous, for in large measure they have channeled their anxieties about their problems into displays of religious fervor rather than coming to terms with the realities of the identity crisis.

This contemporary sermon addresses itself to modern man's spiritual emptiness. Dr. Mead examines some historical shifts in religious thinking beginning with the weakening of traditional religious concepts and extending through a subsequent belief in progress and man's ability to control nature. He concludes with a suggestion of the primacy of man in a social context.

SIDNEY E. MEAD

The Lost Dimension and the Age of Longing

It is good now and then to try to take our bearings as we sail through or drift with the oceanic currents of the universe. For, as Abraham Lincoln said, "If we could first know where we are and whither we are tending, we could better judge what to do and how to do it."

But to know where we are and whither tending religiously is not easy. Even a modicum of confidence that we are following a charted course to some destination other than dusty death, rests upon an unstable foundation of knowledge, faith, and desire. Therefore, in speaking of where I think many of us are today, all I can hope to do is sketch an impressionistic mood-picture concocted of some sound history, of hunches, and sheer feeling.

In sketching such a picture I am quite aware that we today as unique individuals and heirs of all the diversity provided by the attics of the ages, live mentally and spiritually in different worlds. My impression of our present religious state may not be yours. So be it. I have no desire to make converts—and trust you have none either.

But where are we? Max Weber once characterized the movement of history during the past several centuries as "the progressive disenchantment of the world." More recently a historian characterized the history of the past two centuries as the story "of ultimate solutions gone sour." Both leave the impression that there has been a linear movement along a chronological line from "faith" to "doubt."

The impression is wrong. History is not that simple, except to the simple-minded.

I have a friend—a professor and historian who has published many volumes on the history of Christianity from his point of view. To me he appears to live in a stable belief-world, in which the Scriptures provide a source of certain knowledge about man's past, present, and future, and a definite set of standards for judging the meaning of events and the values to be sought. He lives in a world different from the one I inhabit. But, he lives, and he is productive, and he seems to be as contented as the lot of man permits. He "believes" in the traditional sense.

On the other end of the spectrum I know, and you know (perhaps from personal experience), people who live in what has been called "the existential vacuum." Such people, being human, are not guided by instincts. And their drift with the intellectual gulf stream of western civilization has carried them far away from traditional religious beliefs. Of such a person an eminent psychiatrist has said, "No instinct tells him what he has to do, and no tradition tells him what he ought to do; soon he will not know what he wants to do. More and more he will be governed by what others want (and tell) him to do." This describes the "lonely crowd" of David Riesman's "other-directed people." These extremes of belief and unbelief are contemporary. The two poles do not represent a chronological movement as is often supposed.

But by and large we intellectuals are toward the "belief-vacuum" end of the continuum. Perhaps most vocal are those for whom an exhibitionist lack of belief is the hallmark of sophistication. So they pluck the strings of their rebellion against the "faith of our fathers" and chant their cleverness in ferreting out the absurdities of religion. It is better than they should be thus than apathetic.

But for others the kill has been made—the enemy slain. For them the old religious orthodoxy is dead, and to them it seems silly to continue to beat a corpse. As the lust of the hunt and the battle has cooled, reflectively they examine the dead face of religious belief and it "seems no longer that of an enemy." Perhaps their mood is close to that of Archy—Don Marquis' famous cockroach—as he saw the moth fly into the flame and became "a small unsightly cinder": "i wish/there was something i wanted/as badly as he wanted to fry himself."

It is the mood of those who would like to believe, but have discovered that they cannot believe—at least on the terms commonly offered them. They realize now that "believing" is not something one can by taking thought turn on or off. It is not a matter of simple choice but something that flows to one through subtle channels that Christians knew as "grace."

"So I won't believe" some say. But it is not as simple as that either. For apparently if one is to live at all it is not optional whether he will believe in something or not. "Where there is no vision the people perish," wrote the ancient author of Proverbs. And two psychiatrists who watched their fellow prisoners live and die in the concentration camps have said about the same thing respecting individuals. Wrote one, "the vast majority of the thousands of prisoners who died at Buchenwald each year died soon. They simply died of exhaustion, both physical and psychological, due to a loss of desire to live." To this the other adds, "The prisoner who had lost faith in the future—his future—was doomed. With his loss of belief in the future, he also lost his spiritual hold; he let himself decline and became subject to mental and physical decay."

But—believe what? The difficulty many people have with much of orthodoxy is the seeming insistence of its representatives that "you must believe *this,* and you must believe it *this way."* It is for this reason that people in churches are often afraid to express their doubts, and sometimes feel guilty for having them. It was encouraging to note in recent news that there was a conference of Protestant, Roman Catholic, and Jewish laymen who began their discussion of "The Relevance of Faith in Modern Man" with a frank recognition that doubt of the beliefs and practices of his church often betokens the dawn of the member's real faith in God.

I am speaking to those people for whom traditional orthodoxy, as they have known it, is dead, and who know that for them it is dead. At most, with Matthew Arnold on *Dover Beach,* they hear "Its melancholy, long, withdrawing roar." They poignantly stare at the dead face of the old religious belief and sense within themselves a lost dimension—a vacuum to be filled, a longing.

A longing for what? Perhaps few would say it as I say it—they are longing for a "church" almost, not quite, in the traditional sense.

We Americans are the heirs of all the ages, of every land, of every people. But most of the basic motifs of our culture were launched on that "sea of faith" that "was once, too, at the full. ..." It has been said that a culture is the tangible form of religious belief —and the religion of our culture is—or was—the Christian religion.

For centuries—say from the fourth to the eighteenth—the great majority of our Western ancestors lived and moved and had their being in the context of the Christian drama. It was a wonderful myth of the life of Everyman, and of Mankind.

The story of creation, redemption, and judgment enabled the average man to understand universal experience— "and it consoled him . . . to realize that his own life, however barren and limited . . . was but a concrete exemplification of the experience which God had decreed for all the generations of men." He was, like Emerson, held down to his place by the weight of the universe. He knew that at the end there would be a day of reckoning when infallible judgment, cutting through the moral and spiritual ambiguities known to man, would separate the evil from the good and allot to each its just reward. Then the great judge would stoop from above and wipe the tears from the tired eyes of the humblest person when he put earth's burdens down. He knew what human life was, for He was once born of a woman— "O little town of Bethlehem"—lived as a man among men— "was crucified, dead, and buried." But "the third day he rose from the dead"—and that is why the great hallelujah chorus reverberates down through the ages.

Sadly it must be said that somewhere along the line, for many people, the curtain went down on that drama—and neither curtain nor God have risen again. Friedrich Nietzsche's madman still rushes about in our marketplaces crying, "I seek God! . . . Where is God gone? I mean to tell you! We have killed him,—you and I! . . . God is dead!"

"God is dead!"—the line has become so common that even timid clergymen now use it in an attempt to be "honest to God." Meanwhile an increasing number of people who believe well enough that *that* God is dead, say it with the sad observation expressed by one of Arthur Koestler's characters— "Each time a god dies there is trouble in history. . . ."

But why did our God die? Did we kill him? If we did I think it was unintentional deicide committed while we thought we were but obeying His command to go forth and gain dominion over all other created things.

So we may point to that vast, vague area in our history that we call "the rise of science." Concurrently men of faith began to realize that as they marched to fulfill this promise their universe was changing into an immense machine that ran with inexorable precision and without concern for man. The subtle alchemy of human experience was changing God the father of the Lord Jesus Christ with whom we were fellow heirs into an engineer-mechanic who had designed and built the machine, but now was about as remote as those semimythical monsters who in the flat Olympus of Detroit design our automobiles.

A chill settled over the Christian world as God seemed to be fading away like Alice's Cheshire cat, leaving among a residue of the intellectually invincible a disembodied and sentimental grin. "It was," as Carl Becker put it, "as if a rumor had at least become too insistent to be longer disregarded—the rumor that God, having departed secretly in the night, was about to cross the frontiers of the known world and leave mankind in the lurch."

For many this meant what Bertrand Russell suggested: "that man is the product of causes which had no prevision of the end they were achieving; that his origin, his growth, his hopes and fears, his loves and his beliefs, are but the outcome of accidental collocations of atoms; . . . that the whole temple of man's achievement must inevitably be buried beneath the debris of a universe in ruins. . . ."

For the first time in Christendom people were confronted with the question: "Were they living in a world ruled by a beneficent mind, or in a world ruled by an indifferent force?" But what really shocked them was that when they finally became self-consciously aware of the question, they had already accepted the latter answer. One of their spokesmen toward the end of the nineteenth century exclaimed that "he could not agree . . . that the 'new faith' constituted a desirable substitute for 'the waning splendour of the old.'" There is, he continued, an "appalling contrast between the hallowed glory of that creed which once was mine, and the lonely mystery of existence as now I find it. . . ." Such men *felt* "the lost dimension."

What was the "new faith" of which this scientist spoke? It was faith in man. But this is no simple matter.

It has been persuasively argued that as the eighteenth century philosophers dismantled the celestial heaven they rebuilt it on earth of earthly materials. Rejecting salvation mediated through the one who was "truly man and truly God" they postulated salvation through the efforts of successive generations of men. Living on in posterity took the place of an immortality in heaven as a sustaining belief. Robespierre, one of the leaders of the French revolution, addressed a prayer to the new-model god: "O posterity, sweet and tender hope of humanity, thou are not a stranger to us; it is for thee that we brave all the blows of tyranny; it is thy happiness which is the price of our painful struggles; often discouraged by the obstacles that surround us, we feel the need of thy consolations; it is to thee that we confide the task of completing our labors, and the destiny of all unborn generations! . . . Make haste, O posterity, to bring to pass the hour of equality, of justice, of happiness." Thereafter down through the nineteenth century—indeed, down to the present for many people—the hope for one's future and hence the significance of one's life was found in identification with a movement that was likely to endure in history. So Abraham Lincoln at Gettysburg said, "the world will little note nor long remember what we say here, *but it can never forget what they did here."*

Men holding this belief could be as naively rapturous about the bright future of man on earth as ever the writer of the book of Revelation was about the New Jerusalem where death would have no dominion and where there would be no night. Listen to Winwood Reade, writing in 1872: "The beautiful legend will come true; . . . Earth, which is now a purgatory, will be made a paradise, . . . by the efforts of man himself. . . . Hunger and starvation will then be unknown. . . . Governments will be conducted with the quietude and regularity of club committees. The interest which is now felt in politics will be transferred to science. . . . Poetry and the fine arts will take that place in the heart which religion now holds. . . . Not only will Man subdue the forces of evil that are without; he will also subdue those that are within. . . . A time will come when Science will transform (men's bodies). . . . Disease will be extirpated; the causes of decay will be removed; immortality will be invented . . . (and) Man then will be perfect; . . . he will therefore be what the vulgar worship as a god."

That, also, was a beautiful faith—a faith by which thousands of enlightened people lived and did great deeds, creating an era when even "wise men hoped" and believed in progress. But it must sadly be said that god—incarnate in mankind and consequently immortal only as posterity is immortal—that god also died in 1945 when a pigmy bomb left a mushroom-shaped cloud over a Japanese city. What men like Winwood Reade hailed as the god who would transform men's lives and institutions and invent immortality for all, had shown another face. The potential producer of all good was now seen as the potential producer of universal death—by flame and radiation, or slow starvation because of overpopulation, or sheer pollution of the earth's surface.

Slowly it seems to be dawning upon those people who placed their faith and found meaning for their lives in progress through posterity that there may be no "everafter" for mankind to live happily in. There may be no future. Posterity, worshiped as a god, may be even more vulnerable than the old Christian God because we can kill him as easily as we can "overkill" mankind.

There are, then, two aspects of the "lost dimension"—the loss of the ability to believe in the traditional Christian sense, and the loss of ability to assure ourselves that a posterity is a sure thing. For many people god the latter is just as dead as god the former.

It is because the faith in man's future which the eighteenth century taught us to substitute for faith in the Christian God has also collapsed that this becomes *The Age of Longing*— the title of Arthur Koestler's novel in 1951.

Longing for what? Longing for faith, for belief, for a meaning to one's life, and the work one does, for the ability to see something more than a "tale told by an idiot, signifying nothing" in the daily chores one has to do in order to live.

Of course this does not strike everyone at the same time or in the same way. Remember my friend who lives, and lives well, in the old Christian world. And I, as you, know technical intellectuals who still live, apparently quite happily, in the world of Winwood Reade. Others seem to be gifted with the capacity to earn enough in our affluent society to keep up with all the Joneses, all without any apparent concern about the family gods. Of course sometimes we eventually learn that as they gravitated toward the couch, or into an expensive slumber room, they had been living lives of "quiet desperation"—as Henry David Throeau thought was the fate of most of his friends in staid old Concord.

The people of Koestler's novel are these "dispossessed of faith; the physically or spiritually homeless." The burden of their anguish is, "LET ME BELIEVE IN SOMETHING."

What I have given is the description of a mood—not universal of course, but widely prevalent among sensitive people. These people cannot give themselves either to faith in the traditional sense, or to the rich spontaneous faith in man and progress. Therefore it is not to be supposed, as some preachers seem to suppose today, that ridiculing and undermining the belief in man will restore the old kind of faith in God. But, on the other hand, neither can it be supposed —as other preachers appear to do—that undermining faith in the Christian God where it still exists, and ridiculing traditional Christian beliefs and practices will restore the lost faith in man's future. A plague on both these houses!

The people I have in mind seek religious faith—whether they would call it that or not does not matter. Their mood, to repeat, is akin to that of Emerson's soldier after the battle who realizes that the life he had to take cannot ever be recalled—that an enemy once dead is no longer an enemy—that the space he, or it, occupied may now be a fearful vacuum. It is to these people that a church ought to speak —must speak if it is to be more than a congenial company of irrelevant people. What is to be said?

At this point, having tied the religious situation into a desperately complex and hard knot, I wish that like some hardy true-believers I could pronounce it "Gordian" and cut it apart with one deft stroke of the "Sword of the Spirit," the Word of God. But already, it seems to me, too many preachers who do not even understand the question these people of the age of longing are asking, are blithely telling them that "Jesus is the answer."

I cannot be that definite. I can only make a suggestion through the use of figures. There is the figure of "the god behind the gods." The tribes of men forget that human life is a pilgrimage and make comfortable camps beside lakes and pools of truth from which they drink the water of life that sustains them in their particularity. But, Thoreau once said, when a tribe's lake or pool or truth dries up—as all lakes and pools must do—then they must "gird up their lions once more, and continue their pilgrimage toward its fountainhead." Some, of course, will resist moving on and prefer to become fossilized in the drying mud of the old pool. But those who do move toward the living stream might well take as their slogan, "God is dead—God alone is immortal!"

Then there is the figure of the church. And if the church be these people on their pilgrimage toward the fountainhead of life, then the essence of that church is to be found in the congenial relationship between these good companions. For God, 'tis said, is love. And to find other people who are congenial company on the pilgrimage, is to know the presence of that elemental love that is the creative ground of all human *being.*

So I can summarize what I have tried to say in words taken from J. Robert Oppenheimer: ". . . this, as I see it, is the condition of man; and in this condition we can help, because we can love one another."

I hope you can see what he meant, and I mean.

THE CONTRIBUTORS

Robert Lynn Adams is a faculty member in the Department of Sociology at Chapman College, Orange, California.

David Bakan is a Professor of Psychology at York University, Toronto, Canada. Mr. Bakan is the author of *Sigmund Freud and the Jewish Mystical Tradition; The Duality of Human Existence: an Essay on Religion and Psychology; Disease, Pain and Sacrifice: Toward A Psychology of Suffering;* and *Slaughter of the Innocents: A Study of the Battered Child Phenomenon.*

Ernest Callenbach is the author of the book *Living Poor With Style.*

Diane Divoky, a frequent writer of articles on education for numerous magazines, has taught English in public, private and parochial high schools. She was formerly education editor for the *Boston Herald.*

Ruth B. Dixon is Assistant Professor of Sociology at the University of California, Davis. She is interested in population problems in less developed and industrial countries.

Erik H. Erikson, Professor Emeritus in Human Development at Harvard University, has studied the personal-social development of the individual at several stages from childhood to old age. His publications include *Childhood and Society, Young Man Luther, Insight and Responsibility,* and *Gandhi's Truth.*

Dana L. Farnsworth, M.D., is Professor of Hygiene and Director of University Health Services at Harvard University. A former Dean of Students at M.I.T., Dr. Farnsworth has had a lifelong concern for the problems of college students. His major publications in this field include *Mental Health in College and University* and *Psychiatry, Education, and the Young.*

Robert Jon Fox is a faculty member of the Department of Sociology at Chapman College, Orange, California.

Edgar Z. Friedenberg, who is Professor of Education at Dalhousie University, Nova Scotia, Canada, has been called one of education's "romantic critics." Interested primarily in the secondary schools and their students, he has written *The Vanishing Adolescent* and *The Dignity of Youth and Other Atavisms.*

Paul Goodman, recently deceased, was a social critic and author, who taught at The University of Chicago, New York University, and Black Mountain College. His 1956 social critique, *Growing Up Absurd,* is considered to have provided an ideological rationale for the student unrest that broke out on the campuses of many American colleges in the late nineteen sixties.

Kenneth Keniston, author of *The Young Radicals* and *The Uncommitted,* teaches in the Department of Psychiatry, Yale University School of Medicine.

James A. Knight, M.D., a psychiatrist with a major interest in adolescent behavior, is Associate Dean and Professor of Psychiatry at Tulane University, New Orleans, Louisiana.

Phyllis La Farge is a writer whose publications include *Keeping Going,* three juvenile books, and numerous magazine articles including several on women's education.

William R. Larson is Professor of Sociology at California Polytechnic College, Pomona, California.

Robert J. Lifton, M.D., is a professor and psychiatrist at the Yale School of Medicine and author of *Death in Life,* an analysis of the survivors of Hiroshima.

Jean Lipman-Blumen is a postdoctoral fellow in the Department of Sociology, Stanford University. She was formerly project director of the Life Plans Study at the Radcliffe Institute.

Peter Marin has been a fellow at the Center for the Study of Democratic Institutions and Director of Pacific High School. He is co-author with Dr. Allen Cohen of *Understanding Drug Use.*

Craig McGregor is a journalist who has written a critical anthology, *Bob Dylan: A Retrospective.*

Sidney E. Mead, emeritus Professor of Religion at the State University of Iowa, is presently Visiting Professor in the Department of Religion at The University of North Carolina at Chapel Hill. He is ordained in the Unitarian Church. His publications include *The Church in the Modern World* (with A.H. Nichols) and *The Lively Experiment.*

W. W. Meissner, S.J., is a psychologist presently in residence at St. Andrew Babola House, Boston, Massachusetts.

Frank Musgrove is a British sociological and cultural anthropologist currently teaching at Leeds University. He brings a cross-cultural outlook to the question of the effects of historical and sociological processes upon the youth of a culture.

Barbara G. Myerhoff is a Professor in the Department of Sociology and Anthropology at The University of Southern California in Los Angeles.

Robert A. Rosenstone is Associate Professor of History at The California Institute of Technology. He has written articles on both the radical right and radical left and has edited a volume entitled *Protest From the Right.*

Alvin E. Strack is employed with the Smith, Kline and French Pharmaceutical Laboratories in Philadelphia, Pennsylvania.

J. M. Tanner is a Professor of Child Health and Growth at The Institute of Child Health, The University of London. He is the author of *Education and Physical Growth, Growth at Adolescence, 2nd ed.,* and *The Physique of the Olympic Athlete.*

Charles Winick has been Director of Research of the New York State Joint Legislative Commission on Narcotics of the Anti-Defamation League. He is Professor of Sociology at the City University of New York.

THE EDITOR

Alvin E. Winder, editor and author of an article in this collection, is a Professor of The School of Health Sciences and Department of Psychology at the University of Massachusetts, Amherst. A clinical psychologist, he is the co-author of *T-Groups and Therapy Groups in a Changing Society.*

Index

Castration—Loss of the male genital organs. *Castration anxiety* is the mental state associated with the fear of castration. *Castration complex* is a reaction to intimidation stemming from the fear of castration or the restraint of early infantile sexual activity, 68–69

Child labor, 11–14

Childs, G. M., 58

Cognitive—pertaining to the processes involved in learning by means of the intellect, 323

Colson, Elizabeth, 47, 64

Communication: in adolescence, 334–335; in college, 335; in culture, 329; in public speech, 328; in underground papers, 339–344

Compulsory education, 9–11

Conant, James, 365

Convergent thinking—according to Getzels and Jackson, a process representing intellectual acquisitiveness and conformity; contrasted with divergent thinking, a process of intellectual inventiveness and innovation, 317

Correlation coefficient—a number indicating the strength of the tendency of two or more variables to vary concomitantly. Perfect correspondence between the two is expressed by +1.00, perfect inverse correspondence by –1.00, and complete lack of correspondence by 0.00, 320

Counter-culture: 140–143, 366, 376; consumerism, 373–376; extended family, 372; nuclear family, 371; technology, 370

D

Daniell, F. H. B., 63

Defense mechanism—an unconscious device or adjustment by which ideas become divested of their affects or emotional components, 73

Delinquency: girls, 18; Negroes, 18

Demographic—relating to the dynamic balance of a population, especially with regard to density and capacity for expansion or decline, 310

Demos, John, 6

Demos, Virginia, 6

Dostoevsky, Feodor, 381

Divoky, Diane, 339–344

Dixon, Ruth, 301–313

Drugs: 126–159; treatment, 156–159

Dylan, Bob, 124, 205–209, 221

E

Edwards, A. C., 58

Edwards, Newton, 9

Ego—In Sigmund Freud's theory, one of the three divisions of the personality; that conscious part of the personality which mediates both the inner instinctive impulses of the id and the externally learned conscience directives of the super ego (*see also* id, superego), 67, 278

Ego identity, 91

Eisenstadt, S. N., 45, 52, 54, 58

Elkin, Frederick, 18

Elson, Alex, 10

Employment, 11–14, 19

Erikson, Erik H., 19, 63–64, 81–102

Erikson, Kai T., 98

Evans-Pritchard, E. E., 51–52

Existentialism, 142, 181–182

F

Family, 238–246; adolescent boys, 247–255; broken home, 243; parent-child interaction, 247–255

Farber, Jerry, 20

Faris, E., 238

Farnsworth, Dana L., 198–204

Feigelson, Naomi, 20

Fenichel, Otto, 383

Fidelity—seeking something and someone to be true to, 81–102, 260

First Amendment, 341

Firth, R., 56

Fisher, H. A. L., 62

Folger, J., 19

Forster, C. T., 63

Fortes, Meyer, 46, 57, 65

Fox, Robert Jon, 396–409

Frenkle-Brunswick, E., 197

Freud, Anna, 89